Yesterday, Today and Forever

The Continuing Relevance of the Old Testament, Second Edition

Larry R. Helyer
Taylor University

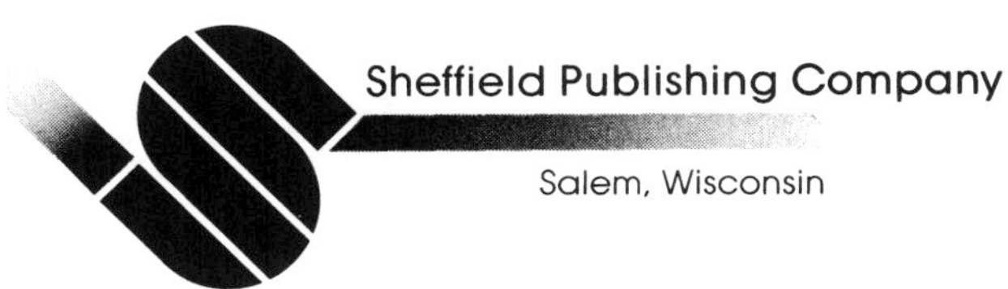

For information about this book, write or call:
Sheffield Publishing Company
P.O. Box 359
Salem, Wisconsin 53168
Telephone: (262) 843-2281
Fax: (262) 843-3683
E-mail: info@spcbooks.com

Cover art by Phillip Ratner, *Moses* from the *Heroes and Heroines* series. Used with permission. For more information, contact:
The Dennis & Phillip Ratner Museum
10001 Old Georgetown Road
Bethesda, MD 20814
(301) 897-1518
www.ratnermuseum.com

ISBN 10: 1-879215-47-0
ISBN 13: 978-1-879215-47-4

Printed in the United States of America

14 13 12 11

Table of Contents

To the memory of my mentor,
Dr. David Allan Hubbard (1928-1996),
who inspired the idea for this book;
and to my students in Biblical Literature 1:
fellow travelers on the way to Zion.

Foreword

What is more relevant in the age of modernity now passing into the age of post-modernity than the revelation God has given in the Scriptures? And with over three-fourths of that word being embodied in the Old Testament, it would seem more than reasonable that that portion of the canon of Holy Scripture should be given some sort of pride of place for those who aspire to know God, his will, and his truth. Alas, for most readers of the Bible, the Old Testament is the last place to which they would turn for a word from God! What an enormous treat is being missed by such a decision!

But despite many hesitancies, the Old Testament turns out to be one of the most pleasing, surprising, and foundational studies for understanding both the New Testament and many current problems in the post-modern age. Dr. Larry R. Helyer has been able to chart one of the most interesting courses for threading one's way through detail that usually bogs most readers down. Without oversimplifying the difficult or jettisoning the complex, he has singled out eight theological themes that allow us to be introduced to the heart of the message of the Bible. Like a guided tour of a city or site in another country, Helyer's text will help you get the "big picture" of the whole of God's revelation by taking you on a tour of eight of the most essential sites.

But why should you even be interested in such a visit to these eight highlights of the essential message of the Old Testament? Simply because the Old Testament is the master issue that affects all of Christian theology! There is hardly one issue that we currently face in the Church or in our modern world where the Old Testament does not possess some foundational pieces of truth that must go into the decision-making process.

This becomes all the more apparent in Helyer's four core concepts that provide the centerpiece around which the permanent value of the Old Testament is described. Foremost among these four core concepts is the unity of God's plan of salvation. Too much emphasis is usually given to the details and particulars of most disciplines, including the study of the Old Testament, with little or no emphasis being placed on any discussion of overarching themes. But here you will see a wonderful balance between a study of the parts and the whole.

The other three core concepts are nonetheless valuable, while also being unusual for textbooks of this sort: faith and politics, faith and the future, and faith and ethics. Helyer rightly resists all of modernity's easy bifurcations between faith and its involvement in the real world. Not everyone will agree with every detail—especially in the area of politics—but no one can afford to think that the faith taught in the Old Testament has nothing to do with one's politics. And what one places one's hope for the future in must be shaped by the God who will be there in the future shaping and governing all that happens. Likewise, how we behave must be directly connected with what we believe, or the people of our generation may turn out to be the biggest phonies around.

So if you are somewhat tentative about starting out on a journey in studying this book that you are not sure will be of much use, do I have news for you: this will literally turn your life upside down. You are in for one of the biggest treats and surprises you have ever had in your academic career! Some of the sections will shape your thinking for this life and for eternity. Here are the sections that I think will have a profound impact on your life: creation, the kingdom of God, worship, the restoration of Israel, and the promise God made to Abraham.

If you give yourself to the study of the Old Testament, you too will become, as I am, a real fan of the older testament from God. Where once the Old Testament may have been thought to be remote and irrelevant, it will be just the opposite: essential for balanced Christian thinking and acting.

Walter C. Kaiser, Jr.
Colman M. Mockler Distinguished Professor of Old Testament
Gordon-Conwell Theological Seminary
South Hamilton, Massachusetts

Preface

> "Therefore every teacher of the law who has been instructed about the kingdom of heaven is like the owner of a house who brings out of his storeroom new treasures *as well as old*" (Mt 13:52).

The Old Testament is the most neglected treasure the church possesses. This is puzzling, especially in a time of widely available, modern translations, study Bibles, study guides and commentaries. Why are there, for example, still so few sermons expounding its message? Why so few Christian young people who truly know and love its contents? Why has its significance not dawned upon our generation with power and conviction? These questions deserve a book-length response. My purpose in this book, however, is to address the problem from a different perspective. I want to stimulate my readers' spiritual taste buds. In so doing, I hope to whet the appetite for more. I invite the reader to enjoy a fest of "rich food for all peoples" (Isa 25:6) and to relive the experience of the psalmist who said, "How sweet are your words to my taste, sweeter than honey to my mouth!" (Ps 119:103)

More than a decade of interaction with college students, primarily freshmen, has enhanced my own taste for the OT (abbreviation for Old Testament). From the outset, I sought to supplement standard OT survey texts by focusing on selected theological themes. My aim was to demonstrate the *significance* and *application* of these themes. Feedback from students indicates that this is what they most valued in their OT course. Accordingly, I have singled out eight theological themes, which, in my opinion, constitute the essential message of the OT.

This approach springs from several convictions. The first is an awareness that the basic theological issues of the OT are as relevant now, at the end of the 20th century, as they were when originally penned. The reason lies in the unchanging nature of what it means to be human. The fundamental questions of human existence are theological questions—

questions which are the same at all times and in all cultures. Questions like: Who am I? How did the world begin? Is there a God? What is God like? How can I know and please God? What will happen to the world and me? The essential message of the OT speaks to these enduring questions, so the passage of centuries has not rendered it out-of-date.

A second conviction is that the OT authoritatively answers these questions. This is so because it alone, among the holy books of various religions, is truly a divine revelation. This is a pre-supposition not argued here except indirectly—indirectly, in that the various themes provide answers having the ring of truth. In short, they give satisfying answers to the basic questions raised. The other sacred writings of the world may contain truth, but cannot stand as the final authority in matters of faith and practice. Of Scripture alone may it be said, ". . . your law is true. . . . Your statutes are forever right . . . your commands are true. . . . All your words are true; all your righteous laws are eternal" (Ps 119:142, 144, 151, 160; see Jn 17:17).

A third conviction relates to student perceptions of the OT. For whatever reasons, many Christian students come to the academic study of the OT viewing it as remote and irrelevant. For many, compared to the New Testament (hereafter NT), it has little to offer. The thrust of this book is the very opposite—the OT is *essential* for a balanced Christian life. We shall explore together how the OT still functions as God's Word, "profitable for teaching, for reproof, for correction, and for training in righteousness" (2Ti 3:16 RSV).

The plan of the book reflects my view of the educational process. I believe students learn best when they are exposed to "core truths" around which new information can be organized. Accordingly, this book isolates four core truths or concepts that provide cohesion for the entire study. The core concepts operate in a spiral fashion so that as the various themes unfold, there is repetition and enlargement.

The first of these core truths is *the unity of God's plan of salvation.* This means that in both the Old and New Testaments God saves humans in essentially the same way. My observations suggest that a sizable number of students begin their study of the Bible at the collegiate level supposing that God saved people in a different manner in the OT than he did in the NT or now. The problem is that, if such a view is maintained, the OT lacks relevance and tends to be ignored. This book argues that the consistency of God's redemptive activity assures us of the dependability and trustworthiness of God. His plan centers on Jesus who is "the same yesterday and today and forever" (Heb 13:8; Ps 102:27). In the words of the hymn, "They who trust him wholly, find him wholly true."

The second core concept deals with *faith and politics.* Students tend to be turned off to politics. Many fail to see any real connection between the message of the OT and the rough-and-tumble world of politics. Besides, politics lacks the immediacy of dating, finding a life partner and deciding on a major! This book tries to raise the consciousness of Christian young people to the indispensability of politics and necessity of engaging our faith commitments (what we believe) with political policy and programs. The tension between our religious convictions and tough political choices is one of the most difficult the Christian experiences. In the OT we read about a remarkable political experiment, which provides a splendid case study for political issues. Amazingly, when issues are reduced to their essentials, they constitute some of the same problems we have faced in United States history and continue to face today. The OT vitally contributes to the political dimension of modern life by providing concrete examples of the struggle between faith and politics. Examples, both negative and positive, shed light on political dilemmas. Even more importantly, the OT raises constantly the underlying problem of faith and politics—the problem of the abuse of power. The repeated warnings concerning this problem and the insights leading to a solution are major contributions of the OT.

A third core concept confronts us, appropriately enough, at the frontier of a new century. *Faith and the future* takes up eschatology—that is, the study of last things. How will human history end and what does God plan for humans and the cosmos in the afterlife? These intriguing questions form the focus of this core concept. Of primary importance is the attitude of hope. Hope is essential for the establishment of a stable, satisfying life. At a time when teenage suicide rates continue to rise and famines, wars and poverty spread across the planet, we need a fresh infusion of hope. The OT radiates with a hope (often in settings where the present seems extremely bleak) that takes hold of God's promises for the future. Our study of this core concept will enable us to grasp how the diverse strands of OT teaching on last things point toward the NT fulfillment in Jesus Christ. It speaks powerfully to us about our own personal encounter with the last enemy, death.

The fourth core concept relates to *faith and ethics.* Ethics pertains to moral values and behavior. Ethics deals with the "oughtness" of life. Some of the crucial questions examined are: How should one conduct his or her life? What, according to the OT, is the basis for determining ethics? What relationship exists between faith (here viewed as the content of what one believes) and ethics (how one behaves)? Of major importance will be the question whether one can separate faith from ethics. This issue has immediate relevance to the Christian college student. Increasingly, students are admitting that their behavior does not always coincide with their expressed and written commitments when they sought admission. We will explore, in the light of the OT, the consequences of compartmentalizing faith and ethics.

These four core concepts, then, serve as organizers around which the selected themes cluster. They provide contact with our modern world.

The seedbed for this book has many ingredients. None, however, has been so enriching as that imparted by Dr. David Allan Hubbard. In the spring of 1974, I participated in his class "Themes in Old Testament Theology" at Fuller Theological Seminary. That class clarified in a fresh way the OT Scriptures. No longer was this collection of writings simply a historical unfolding of the national history of the people of Israel, providing the necessary background for understanding the coming of Jesus of Nazareth. Rather, the OT was also a theological work of first importance, addressing the questions of moderns as well as ancients. Dr. Hubbard's ability to pinpoint the continuing significance of these 39 books inspired, edified and challenged me. I determined that I would attempt to do the same for my future students. Regrettably, Dr. Hubbard did not live long enough to see my fledgling effort; he went to be with the Lord in June of 1996. Although I have not been able to achieve the standards of my mentor, I hope this book causes other students to catch the vision of the abiding message of the OT. If so, my efforts will be amply rewarded.

Larry R. Helyer

Preface to Second Edition

Seven years have passed since the first edition of *Yesterday, Today and Forever* appeared. The responses of my students and other teachers of the Old Testament who have used it as a text have been gratifying. This second edition updates bibliographies, eliminates dated references to popular culture, and attempts to interact a bit more with mainline scholars. The most significant rewriting is the section dealing with the restoration of Israel.

I'd like to take this opportunity to say thanks to the editorial team of Stephen and Cindy Nelson and Jodi Jacobsen for their willingness to undertake a second edition. A more congenial and encouraging editorial team could hardly be found.

Once again, my prayer is that this book will enlighten the path of fellow pilgrims on the way to Zion.

Larry R. Helyer

List of Abbreviations

AB	*Anchor Bible* (Commentary series)
ABD	*Anchor Bible Dictionary*
ANET	*Ancient Near Eastern Texts*
BA	*Biblical Archaeologist*
BAR	*Biblical Archaeology Review*
BASOR	*Bulletin of the American School of Oriental Research*
BDB	Brown, Driver and Briggs, *Hebrew and English Lexicon of the Old Testament*
BibRev	*Bible Review*
BSac	*Bibliotheca Sacra*
ca.	*circa* (Latin), about, approximately
cf.	*confer* (Latin), compare
ch.	chapter (*pl.* chs.)
DOTT	*Documents from Old Testament Times*
EBC	*Expositor's Bible Commentary*
e.g.	*exempli gratia* (Latin), for example
et al.	*et alii* (Latin), and others; used to refer to other verses similar to the one(s) just cited
f.	and following (*pl.* ff.); used after a page, verse, or paragraph number to mean "also the next"
ibid.	*ibidem* (Latin), in the same place; used in an endnote to mean "the same work as the one just cited"
id. (idem)	*idem* (Latin), the same; used in an endnote to mean "the same person as the one just cited"
IDB	*Interpreter's Dictionary of the Bible*
IDBS	*Interpreter's Dictionary of the Bible Supplement*
ISBE	*International Standard Bible Encyclopedia*, 3rd ed.
JBL	*Journal of Biblical Literature*
JETS	*Journal of the Evangelical Theological Society*
JSOT	*Journal for the Study of the Old Testament*
LXX	The Septuagint (Greek translation of the Hebrew Bible)

n.	footnote or endnote
NASB	New American Standard Bible (ET of the Bible)
NBD	*New Bible Dictionary*
NICOT	*New International Commentary on the Old Testament*
NIV	New International Version (ET of the Bible)
NIVSB	*New International Version Study Bible*
NRSV	New Revised Standard Version (ET of the Bible)
NT	New Testament
OT	Old Testament
Sir	Ecclesiasticus, or The Wisdom of Jesus Son of Sirach
TWOT	*Theological Wordbook of the Old Testament*
TynBul	*Tyndale Bulletin*
v.	verse (*pl.* vv.); in the chapter being commented on
WTJ	*Westminster Theological Journal*
ZPEB	*Zondervan Pictorial Encyclopedia of the Bible*

The abbreviations for the books of the Bible follow that of the *NIVSB.*

chapter **1**

An Overview of the Old Testament

Leading Questions

What evidence points to the Old Testament as a divine book?
What evidence displays the humanity of the Old Testament?
What do the Bible and Jesus Christ have in common?
What are the components of redemptive history?
What are the characteristics of redemptive history?

Introduction

> "Lift up your eyes from where you are and look north and south, east and west. All the land that you see I will give you. . . . Go, walk through the length and breadth of the land . . ." (Ge 13:14- 15, 17).

Before looking at the individual themes of the OT, we need to gain an overall appreciation of the collection of documents we are reading. We propose a map identifying the main avenues that will engage our attention. In addition, the claims of the OT need to be considered in any assessment of its contents. In other words, what do the writings say either explicitly or implicitly about their origin and intention? Our initial task in chapter one is to provide a perspective from which the entire contents may be approached.[1]

Characteristics of the Book

A Divine Book

God speaks. The OT testifies to the reality of divine revelation (Ps 147:19). In the pages of this book (the OT viewed as a unitary whole) the living God speaks. One of the characteristic phrases recurring throughout is the expression "This is what the Lord says." To be sure, this expression is found most often in the prophetic books, but its equivalent is clearly present in the historical and narrative portions. For example, in the books of Exodus, Leviticus, and Numbers, we have the repeated expression "The LORD said to Moses" (Ex 4:21). What about a narrative work such as Genesis? Or the books Joshua–2 Kings? These works are infused with the authority of the great Law Book of Sinai (see Jos 1:7-8; Jdg 2:17, 20). They assume the moral, ethical, and spiritual standard of the Ten Commandments. Throughout these works we have instances in which God reveals himself to selected individuals. Furthermore, this revelation can be expressed in words (cf. Ge 12:7). Needless to say, this was the view of Christ and his apostles (Mk 7:9-13; Ro 3:2; 2Ti 3:14-16), as well as the historic position of the Christian Church.

God acts. In literature we pay special attention to the principal character of a narrative. We label such an individual the hero or heroine of the story. Who, it may be asked, is the hero of the OT? Several figures tower above the many who appear on its pages. Individuals like Noah, Abraham, Moses, David, Elijah, Elisha, Isaiah, Jeremiah, and Daniel come readily to mind. But in the final analysis, they occupy only a small portion of the total story. They come and go in succession. There is, however, one all-dominating figure who orchestrates the appearance of all these lesser figures carrying out his plan. This figure is behind the scenes, sets the scenes, directs the scenes, and occasionally, even appears in the scenes himself! He is, without doubt, the hero of the story that unfolds: the true and living God.

A survey of the OT abundantly verifies this observation. *God's attributes, deeds, plans and purpose dominate and control the unfolding story.* A bit of trivia underscores this assertion. The OT consists of some 23,000 verses. Within this mass of text, no fewer than 10,000 times a name of God appears—on the average every 2½ verses! This becomes even more impressive if we add to this the many descriptions and attributes of God. Think of the vivid imagery by which God is described in the Old Testament. He is likened to a shepherd, a rock, a refuge, a warrior, a lion, a mother eagle, to name but a few. We can summarize by saying that the OT centers on God; indeed, it is a book about God.

Because the OT is a book about God, it should come as no surprise that it is also a book *characterized by the supernatural.* That is, it describes events and happenings that transcend what is observed in the natural order. The Red

Sea does not normally part to allow passage for refugees (unless, of course, you are at Burbank Studios in southern California where the "Red Sea" dutifully parts for tourist groups daily!). The Jordan River, likewise, does not stop its flowing on command; the sun does not halt in its daily progression; an ax head does not float; and people are not brought back from the dead. These are illustrations of events contrary to the established laws of nature and belonging to the category of the miraculous or the supernatural.

The problem of the supernatural. This raises a major problem. How are we, who live in the 21st century, to view the supernatural events recorded in Scripture? Did they really happen as described, or were they the result of embellishment (the adding of fanciful or fictitious details) by the Hebrew authors? Were those events capable of being explained in wholly natural terms? I believe that in order to enter into the worldview of the OT, one must be prepared to allow for the presence and interaction of the supernatural. The God who created the universe can, if he so chooses, alter or suspend his normal ways of working. As we proceed through the various themes, an important presupposition will be that the supernatural should be allowed to stand on its own and not be explained away or denied.

Clearly, then, the OT is a book that focuses upon God. God's words and works are center stage. For this reason alone, it ought to command our utmost attention.

A Human Book

There is, however, another important dimension that should not be neglected. *The OT is a book that displays its humanity*. Let's examine several evidences of this.

Human nature portrayed. The OT is a masterpiece in describing human nature. If one wants to understand "what makes us tick," no better source could be consulted than its pages. Here we look into a mirror revealing the unvarnished truth—the warts, blemishes, and flaws of our personalities. We confront our misdeeds, failings, and faults. Like a powerful searchlight, the Scriptures illuminate our secret sins. How does it generally do this? It tells stories of individuals who, like us, struggle with their common humanity. In their failures and weaknesses we see ourselves. One of the noteworthy characteristics of the historians of Israel is their commitment to "telling it like it is." Abraham, Moses, and David, luminaries and heroes, are nonetheless depicted with feet of clay. Abraham can be called "father of all who believe" (Ro 4:11), but he could also lie about his marital relationship to Sarah—not once, but twice (Ge 12:14-20; 20:1-13). David was a man after God's own heart (1Sa 13:14; Ac 13:22), but he could also be an adulterous, deceptive, and murderous man (2Sa 11).[2]

The other side of the coin is that it also informs us about our amazing position in the created order. According to Genesis 1:26-27, we alone, of all created beings, are image-bearers. We can relate to God on a personal level. We can experience an I-Thou relationship with the Creator. He in turn has placed the earth under our supervision and care (see Ge 1–2). The Psalmist celebrates the fact that we are but a little lower than God (Ps 8:5, NASV).

We can summarize this dual perspective by saying that *both the dignity and depravity (moral corruption) of human beings are eloquently and shockingly presented.* Clearly, a primary intention of Scripture is to inform human beings about themselves. In this regard it is worth calling attention to the observations of Dr. Robert Coles of Harvard University. Coles, a psychiatrist and Pulitzer Prize winner in literature, pays this compliment to the Bible:

> Nothing I have discovered about the makeup of human beings contradicts in any way what I learn from the Hebrew prophets such as Isaiah, Jeremiah and Amos and from the Book of Ecclesiastes, and from Jesus and the lives of those he touched. Anything that I can say as a result of my research into human behavior is a mere footnote to those lives in the Old and New Testaments. . . .
>
> The Bible shows us both hope and doom, the possibility and the betrayal. . . . I believe these stories are a part of each one of us. . . .
>
> Some reviewers criticize me for saying the same old things about the nature of human beings: That we are a mixture of good and evil, of light and darkness, of potentiality toward destruction or redemption. They want some new theory, I suppose. But my research merely verifies what the Bible has said all along about human beings. . . . The biblical tradition belongs in our universities, and it's a privilege to call upon it as a teacher.[3]

Human literary activity manifested. Another evidence of the OT's humanity relates to the manner in which the material is written. Here we take up what is called literary genre. Genre refers to type, class, or variety. Applied to the OT, it specifies the different classes or categories of literary compositions occurring within its pages. The OT is not uniform in genre; furthermore, the observable genres parallel those in other ancient Near Eastern literature. In fact, archaeologists have recovered texts much older than the Hebrew Scriptures that display similar literary genres.[4] Clearly the human authors and editors of Scripture made use of the existing literary traditions of their time. The following chart lists some of the literary genres in the OT.

One of these, narrative, is most familiar to us and is a universally shared genre in the various cultures, ancient and modern. The narrative genre simply tells a story. The book of Genesis contains narratives that have no equal in terms of power and appeal. Other splendid examples of narrative are found in Exodus, Numbers, and Joshua–2 Kings. Especially skillful are the narratives found in 1 and 2 Samuel, the stories of Samuel, Saul, and David. Later we will examine some of these literary genres in more depth. The point is that *the Bible contains the features characterizing all great literature*. Humanity has left an indelible mark on the pages of sacred writ.

Human personality and style evidenced. Perhaps the most significant indication of the humanity of Scripture emerges from the distinctive personalities and styles detectible in the writings. When one compares the diction (choice and use of words) and style of the Pentateuch, traditionally ascribed to Moses, with that of Isaiah or Amos, one is aware of the difference. The sensitivity and "martyr complex" of Jeremiah come through as we read this book. In contrast, Ezekiel's passive and rather bizarre personality is quite different from Jeremiah. This is what one would expect if human beings really had a hand in its composition.

A Divine-Human Book

Thus the Bible possesses a dual nature; it is both a divine and a human book. This characteristic places Scripture in a unique category of literature. Its divine origin gives it authority, while its humanity ensures that it communicates on our wavelength. (2Pe 1:21; Ro 15:4; 1Co 10:6, 11) In this regard, the Bible, as the written Word of God, shares a similar status with Jesus Christ, the living Word of God. Both Christ and Scripture possess a duality of nature that is essential to their function in God's plan of redemption (Jo 1:14; 2Ti 3:16).

For the most part, the focus of our attention in this textbook will be upon the humanity of Scripture; however, underlying all the observable traits of Scripture's humanness lies the unshakable foundation of its divine origin. One should not feel threatened by the stress placed upon a careful analysis of the

Scripture as a work of literature. We are not demeaning its importance or authority; we are simply respecting the manner in which God revealed himself for the salvation of humankind. As Jesus was wrapped in swaddling clothes, so Scripture has come to us in the garb of humanity.[5]

Examples of different literary "forms" in the Old Testament

1. **Narrative:**
"Now there was a famine in the land, and Abram went down to Egypt to live there for a while because the famine was severe" (Ge 12:10).

2. **Law:**
A. Apodictic "You shall not steal" (Ex 20:15).
B. Case Law "If a thief is caught breaking in and is struck so that he dies, the defender is not guilty of bloodshed: but if it happens after sunrise, he is guilty of bloodshed" (Ex 22:2).

3. **Blessing and Curse:**
A. Blessing "If you follow my decrees and are careful to obey my commands, I will send you rain in its season, and the ground will yield its crops and the trees of the field their fruit" (Lev 26:3-4).
B. Curse "But if you will not listen to me . . . I will do this to you . . ." (Lev 26:14-16).

4. **Invective and Threat:**
"Woe to you who long for the day of the LORD! Why do you long for the day of the LORD? That day will be darkness, not light" (Am 5:18).

5. **Exhortation:**
"Hear now, O Israel, the decrees and laws I am about to teach you. Follow them so that you may live and go in and take possession of the land that the LORD, the God of your fathers, is giving you" (Dt 4:1).

6. **Wisdom:**
"A wise son brings joy to his father, but a foolish son grief to his mother" (Pr 10:1).

7. **Liturgy:**
"O LORD, who shall sojourn in thy tent? Who shall dwell on thy holy hill? He who walks blamelessly, and does what is right . . ." (Ps 15:1-2).

8. **Confession:**
"Have mercy on me, O God, according to thy steadfast love . . . wash me thoroughly from my iniquity and cleanse me from my sin" (Ps 51:1-2).

The Inspiration and Unity of Scripture

We consider one more issue related to the claims of Scripture for itself. Jesus of Nazareth affirmed the truthfulness of Scripture, which, at that time, consisted only of the OT. The temptation story (Mt 4:1-11; Mk 1:12-13; Lk 4:1-13) makes clear his firm reliance upon Scripture as God's Word. Debates and controversies with the religious leaders likewise demonstrate his attitude toward it. John 10:35 epitomizes his view in these words: "Scripture cannot be broken." In other words, Scripture possesses complete authority and reliability.[6]

The historic Christian church has always confessed that "all Scripture is God-breathed" (2Ti 3:16). Evangelical Christians (in continuity with historic orthodoxy) have understood this confession to involve a superintending ministry of the Holy Spirit. The result is that, without destroying the freedom, individuality, and personality of the authors and/or editors involved, the Spirit of God spoke through human spokespersons. We call this gracious, guiding influence of the Holy Spirit in the process of writing scripture, *inspiration*. While there is much mystery surrounding this work of the Spirit, we can be confident that, when "men spoke from God," they "were carried along by the Holy Spirit" (2Pe 1:21). The end result of this process is a collection of documents that are the rule for faith and practice. That is, Scripture is the final authority for *what* is to be believed and for *how* we are to behave.[7]

Perhaps we can illustrate the process of inspiration by two analogies. The first is the symphony orchestra. Let us imagine that we have arrived early for a performance. We hear the individual musicians warming up. What do we hear during the warm-up period? Noise! Each musician is playing a segment of the score or practicing a scale, without regard to his or her fellow musician. The result is cacophony (harsh, discordant sound) for which we would hardly pay to listen. But then the concertmaster stands and the oboist plays the note of A. At least we now hear all the instruments on the same note! Finally, the conductor comes on stage and holds up the baton. All is quiet, in readiness for the downbeat. When the conductor begins, we hear not cacophony but euphony—pleasing sound. We hear a symphony—a coming together of sound, harmony. Even though the different kinds of instruments are diverse in construction and timbre (tonal quality), together they produce a composition of great power and beauty. The diversity of the several instruments, guided by the composer and conductor, results in a harmonious unity. The following figure visually represents a symphony orchestra and how it is analogous to the work of the Holy Spirit in the production of Scripture.

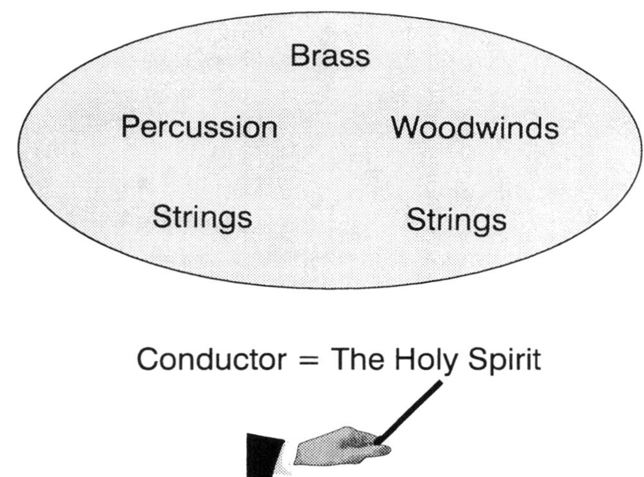

Conductor = The Holy Spirit

Another illustration is the prism. A prism is a crystalline, transparent solid having three sides and the ability to refract or bend light rays. The pleasing effect of the prism is the creation of a rainbow, which really is the color spectrum of ordinary light. Note in the following figure the analogy to Scripture.

As God's revelation comes to us, it is mediated through humans who function as prisms. We see a rainbow consisting of the different wavelengths from red to violet. Similarly, we do not have monochromatic (consisting of one color) uniformity in Scripture. Each author has left his distinctive personality and style on the finished product. Yet, in all of this diversity, there is a marvelous unity—there is a unified phenomenon, answering to the rainbow. The rainbow of Scripture is salvation history.

The unity of Scripture is one of the most powerful arguments for its divine origin. No other diverse collection of literary works, coming from so many different authors and spanning such a wide period of time, can claim such a remarkable unity. There is a connected story that unfolds about God who is establishing his kingdom on earth. Try to find a comparable unity in any collection of literature known and you will realize how amazing the Bible is.[8]

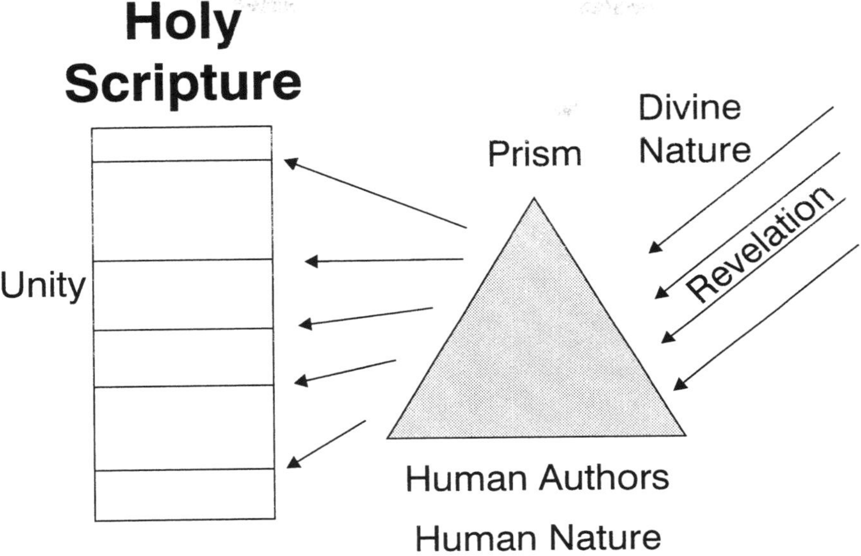

Contents of the Book: Redemptive History

Components of Redemptive History

We have suggested that the unity of Scripture centers upon God and his redemptive plan for the universe. We can thus speak about the OT containing a special kind of history—redemptive history. It will be useful to spend a few moments surveying why a redemptive strategy is necessary and what its components are.

Sin and judgment. The first component is not the most attractive or upbeat. It is, however, profoundly important for understanding who we are and why there had to be a redemptive plan. The component is sin and judgment.

Sin is any lack of conformity to and transgression of God's moral law. It is both an act and attitude as well as a state or condition. The OT consistently witnesses to the fact that all human beings have sinned; it also testifies that they were born with a tendency toward sin—a sin nature. "There is not a righteous man on earth who does what is right and never sins" (Ecc 7:20; see also 1Ki 8:46; Ps 143:2; Pr 20:9; Ro 3:10-12). "Surely I have been a sinner from birth, sinful from the time my mother conceived me" (Ps 51:5; see also Ps 58:3; Job 15:14).

This indictment must not be compromised. Much of modern culture promotes the view that humanity is inherently good. The blame for any misdeeds is placed on the environment or heredity. The false idea survives (though it is constantly denied by sober examination) that education and opportunity can mold humanity into decent, caring, upright individuals. The Scripture portrays quite a different perspective.

The vocabulary of the Hebrew Bible is especially rich in words conveying the idea of sin.[9] This, in itself, points to the importance of the notion among the ancient Hebrews. For example, among the Eskimos, a large vocabulary clusters around the idea of snow. In the United States, one word—snow—serves us for most purposes. In the Eskimo culture, however, where snow is such a pervasive part of their life, an impressive number of different words exist for snow. These varied words indicate the subtle changes that can occur in snow, changes which are so important for the livelihood of the Eskimos. In a similar way, the large number of words for sin in the Old Testament demonstrates the important role this idea occupies in the life and religion of the Hebrews.

Sin documents its presence from its inception among human beings in the persons of Adam and Eve (Ge 3) to the end of the OT witness (Mal 4). (In chapter three we will examine in more depth the profound story of the temptation and fall.) The overall portrayal of sin, emerging from the pages of the OT, is not a pleasant sight. The fact of our fallenness and rebellion constantly confronts us.

The OT teaches that human beings are characterized by *total depravity*. This does not mean that we are all as bad as we could be (thankfully!), but rather, that *all* of our being is affected by sin. Thoughts, emotions, and choices are never insulated from the malign influence of the sin nature. No aspect or activity connected to human existence is immune from the corrupting power of sin. Selfishness and pride masquerade behind the mask of concern for others and humility. To put it another way, the inevitable tendency of the human heart is downward—it is contrary to the high road of God's moral standard. We must not allow the modern voices of humanistic optimism to mute this portrayal. The biblical portrait depicts reality! If we deny it, we are only deceiving ourselves. Jeremiah 17:9 punctures any balloon of self-respect we may harbor about our essential goodness: "The heart is deceitful above all things and beyond cure. Who can understand it?"[10]

A series of apostasies punctuate redemptive history. Apostasy means a falling away from faith and trust in God. Of course the most devastating was the first one in Eden. This event resulted in the fall of the human race—the loss of innocence for all Adam's descendants (see Ro 5:12-21). Following on this disaster, we encounter the stories of Cain, Lamech, the flood, the wilderness wanderings, the failure of Saul, the sin of David, the failure of the northern and southern kingdoms, and so forth. What we have is a dreary rehearsal of a series of apostasies. Certainly Scripture impresses upon us the fearful consequences of sin and apostasy. Paul's point in his letter to the Corinthians is apropos: "Now these things occurred as examples to keep us from setting our hearts on evil things as they did. . . . These things happened to them as examples and were written down as warnings for us . . ." (1Co 10:6, 11).

Following hard on the heels of the series of apostasies come an unnerving series of judgments—judgments consisting of the wrath of God against sin. Here, too, much modern thought has turned a deaf ear to the warnings sounded, or has pictured God as a benign grandfather who merely dotes on his misbehaving offspring. On the contrary, the Bible relates with utmost seriousness a series of catastrophic divine visitations. One thinks of the expulsion of Adam and Eve from the Garden of Eden; the lifelong sentence of wandering for Cain; the horrifying dimensions of the flood; the loss of an entire generation in the "vast and dreadful desert" of Sinai; the stoning of Achan and his family; the monotonous cycle of apostasy, judgment, and repentance in the book of Judges; the incredible family turmoil of David's later reign; and the tragic account of the destruction and deportation of Israel and Judah.

These judgments underscore the gravity of sin and the holiness of God. God's character is such that he cannot sit by passively as the crowning achievement of his created order defiantly thumbs a nose at him and seeks to usurp his place in the scheme of things. God's holiness is repelled by sin just as two similarly charged magnets repel each other. If he did not react against sin, he would be the devil!

We must remember, however, that God's judgment is never without adequate warning. For example, God pleads with Cain (Ge 4:6-7), preaches repentance through Noah (Ge 6:3; see 2Pe 2:5), and sends a steady succession of prophets to warn Israel and Judah of approaching disaster (Am 3:7-8). Scripture makes it abundantly clear that God "wants all men to be saved and to come to a knowledge of the truth" (2Ti 2:4) and is "not wanting anyone to perish, but everyone to come to repentance" (2Pe 3:9). As Amos puts it: "Seek the LORD and live" (Am 5:4).

Redemption and promise. Turning from the dark side of reality, we welcome the ideas of redemption and promise. The OT is a book of hope. Though sin and judgment may appear to predominate, we are never allowed to lose sight of the gracious provision of God to rescue fallen human beings from their prison house of sin. God's grace triumphs over judgment (Ro 5:15, 20). Shortly after the first couple disobeys, the Lord seeks out the hiding, trembling rebels. The rest of Scripture discloses a way back to the now forbidden Garden of Eden (Ge 3:24). The way back is the story of Genesis 3:8–Revelation 22. The theme of redemption involves related ideas such as rescue, recovery, restoration, and reunion. This reclamation project involves not only rebellious humans, but an adversely affected planet as well.

The key actor in this great redemptive effort is the Creator God who is also a Savior God (Ps 25:5; Hab 3:18). God's promise of deliverance, repeated many times over in the pages of the OT, is a scarlet thread that weaves itself throughout the unfolding drama. It is scarlet because, from the very first promise, the shedding of blood is implicit. Adam and Eve are clothed with animal skins, which implies the sacrifice of the animals. *The shedding of blood plays a crucial role in the drama of redemption* (see Ge 3:15, 21). We will examine this idea later in chapter five when we study the sacrificial system of Israel. The Savior God, however, reveals the promise of a deliverer whose portrait becomes more complete as we proceed through the OT. The finished portrait finally appears in the pages of the NT. This promised deliverer is a uniquely anointed person, the Messiah. The development of the Messianic idea will occupy our attention in chapters six through nine.

Covenant and election. Within the overall plan of redemption, a very important concept describes the method by which individuals are rescued from the effects of sin. Two terms stand in close relationship to each other and illuminate the mechanism of deliverance. The terms are covenant and election.

A covenant is *a compact or agreement between two parties binding them mutually to undertakings on each other's behalf.*[11] In the context of the OT, these agreements or covenants are initiated and authorized by the Lord—he is the one who chooses an individual or nation. Sometimes the covenants are unilateral, that is, the Lord pledges himself to an undertaking, which only he can accomplish, on behalf of another party. These are unconditional covenants. Still, the other party is always required to exercise trust in the covenant-making God if its benefits are to be enjoyed. Several covenants divide redemptive history into key phases or stages. These are the Noahic (Ge 9:8-17), Abrahamic (Ge 15:9-21; 17), Sinaitic or Mosaic (Ex 19-24), Levitic (Nu 25:10-31), Davidic (2Sa 7:5-16), and New Covenants (Jer 31:31-34). *The covenant relationship is an essential aspect of redemptive history.*[12]

Obviously a covenant relationship is a desirable situation; but how does one merit such a relationship? The answer is that one does *not* merit or achieve it; the Lord selects or chooses the recipients. This is the doctrine of election—a bone of contention in the history of Christian theology!

It is important that we have clearly in mind two principles that characterize God's election. On the one hand, we need to preserve the freedom of God, his sovereignty, to choose whomever he pleases. Scripture teaches that no one has God in his or her debt; we all deserve punishment, not blessing (Ro 3:23). God, in his grace and mercy, freely chooses to bestow special privilege upon those whom he desires. "It does not, therefore, depend on man's desire or effort, but on God's mercy" (Ro 9:16). The other principle declares that the purpose of this choice is *not exclusive* in intention, but rather, *inclusive*. God chooses *some* in order that they might invite *all* to share the benefits of a covenant relationship. Election is part of missions and evangelism. We are not called to an exclusive club or clique; we are privileged to announce that membership is open to all who will come. "Come, all you who are thirsty, come to the waters; and you who have no money, come, buy wine and milk without money and without cost. . . . Surely you will summon nations you know not, and nations that do not know you will hasten to you . . ." (Isa 55:1, 5). We will examine more closely in chapters five and six this whole process whereby God selects his people, enters into covenant with them, and encourages them to bring others within this circle of blessing.

The Kingdom of God. A final component, which, in my opinion, best expresses what redemptive history is all about, is the Kingdom of God.[13] This expression requires explanation. In our culture the term "kingdom" is usually understood in the sense of realm or territory. While this is involved in the biblical meaning of kingdom, it is hardly the principal idea. Rather, *the Kingdom of God conveys the notion of the active, dynamic rule of God over the created order.* The stress lies on the on-going exercise of God's governance, rather than on the static idea of sphere and location. Exodus 15:18 first announces the essential concept of God's rule, which is reiterated many times in the OT, most notably in the Psalms: "The LORD will reign forever and ever" (see Ps 9:7).

Viewed as a unitary story, the Bible is a dramatic story of a power struggle centered on planet earth. The creation narrative underscores the role of human beings as vice-regents over earth. God entrusts them, as image-bearers, with rule over the planet. Alas, a usurper subverts this rule. By his evil subtlety, Satan engineers a fall from grace for the first human couple. A new reign appears—the reign of sin and death (Ro 5:21), headed up by the "god of this age" (2Co 4:4) and the "prince of this world" (Jn 12:31). Ultimate sovereignty still resides with the Lord, however, and he launches a remarkable counter-offensive for the total liberation of planet earth from the clutches of the evil one. Essentially Genesis 3–Revelation 22 recounts the long campaign involved in subduing a rebellious planet. The key moment—the decisive move on the cosmic chessboard—is the invasion of earth by God himself in the person of Jesus Christ (Lk 2:10-11; Gal 4:4-5). The incarnation unleashes a dynamic movement energized by the Holy Spirit and designed to transform human beings. This transformation, likened to a new birth (Jn 3), involves a change of allegiance. Those who respond to the gospel, the message of liberation, confess that Jesus is Lord (Ro 10:9). This confession, sincerely affirmed, places one in the Kingdom of God (Col 1:13). The new community, created by the Spirit, is the church, the body of Christ (Eph 2:11–3:13).

The OT portrays the opening moves of the conflict to reclaim earth, and prepares the way for the advent of the liberator, Jesus Christ. We will follow the development of this incredible operation from the call of Abraham to the close of the exilic era. The community of faith in the OT period is called Israel. *The checkered career of this people is the focus of redemptive history in the OT*. Glimpses of the outcome of this titanic struggle already appear; indeed, the glorious visions of God's final kingdom on earth sustain the faithful through periods of trial and adversity (Da 2:44; 7:26-27).[14] Chapter seven surveys this all-encompassing theme and discusses its implications.

One further observation: the tremendous popularity of box office hits like *Star Wars*, *Superman*, *Batman*, *Dick Tracy*, and *Spiderman* is not accidental. These films are Hollywood versions of the "greatest story ever told"—the old, old story of the gospel. Notice how the above named movies have a plot based upon the biblical story of redemption: invasion or threat by a sinister, evil person or force, rescue by a hero bigger than life, and final resolution by the victorious hero, though not without severe tests and setbacks. These movies appeal to many because they speak to the actual plight of humanity, overwhelmed by the presence of evil, both personally and corporately. I call this to your attention so that you may be more aware of the power of redemptive motifs, even in the popular culture. Though many may label the gospel "foolishness" (1Co 1:18), they nonetheless display a yearning for deliverance from the tyranny of our common humanity and the forces beyond our control that constantly threaten us. Paul was right: we should never be "ashamed of the gospel, because it is the power of God for the salvation of everyone who believes . . ." (Ro 1:16).

Characteristics of Redemptive History

Finally, we comment on the characteristics of redemptive history. We summarize by using two pairs of descriptive terms.

Separation and distinctiveness. In the first place, redemptive history is marked by the qualities of separation and distinctiveness. Notice how God calls both an individual, such as Abraham (Ge 12:1), and an entire nation, such as Israel (Ex 19:5; Am 3:2; Ezr 10:11), to be separate from the surrounding culture. For Abraham, this even involved his family. Indeed, the book of Genesis unfolds along the lines of a constantly narrowing process. A process of divine selection determines the line of promise from Seth to the family of Jacob and the nation of Israel. The resulting separation is emphasized by a distinctive life-style, which in the case of Israel even displays itself in the choice of diet (Lev 11). The particulars of this separated and distinctive life-style are discussed in chapter five. For now we simply call attention to the fact that this distinctiveness was designed, not only to keep Israel from the moral corruption of pagan culture and society, but also to preserve in Israel those true forms of faith and worship that were revealed by God (Ex 34:27-28).

God's treatment of Israel might be viewed as a form of favoritism, or, even worse, racism. Such is not the case. The Lord called Israel (who was completely unworthy of the honor, Dt 9:1-6) to be a separate people in order that she might be a living witness to the blessedness and joy of obeying God's will. The distinctive life-style reminded Israel of her responsibility to live by and witness to the truth of God in a foreboding and fearful world. As in the case with our discussion of election, we see a missionary thrust in the distinctive life-style enjoined upon Israel. It was not intended to drive others away or to create a barrier through which no contact could occur. It was conceived, rather, to be a light to the Gentiles, beckoning them to experience the relationship Israel was privileged to enjoy with her covenant God, as evidenced in the stories of Rahab, Ruth, and Naaman (Jos 2; 6; Ru; 2Ki 5).

This characteristic of redemptive history is still in effect. The NT writings reinforce the principle. The new covenant people of God are commanded to "come out from them and be separate . . ." (2Co 6:17), which is, by the way, a quotation from Isaiah 52:11! The teachings of Jesus and the NT epistles outline a distinctive way of life. To be sure, many of the OT particulars are dropped or transformed (Mk 7:18-19), but the keynote of obedience remains the same, and the witness factor is undiminished (Mt 5:14-20; 7:24-27; Php 2:12-16).

Selective and episodal. A second characteristic of redemptive history is that it is selective and episodal. By this we mean that out of the many events and happenings that could have been narrated, only a relatively small number are. The biblical writers are highly selective. (The student assigned to read the OT in a semester may be forgiven if he/she thinks that the selection is still rather extensive!)

To illustrate the point, consider the story of Abraham in Genesis 11:27–25:11. In about 13 chapters of text, we have compressed the life of a man who lived 175 years. But even this is not the full story, because the text discloses virtually nothing about Abraham before his 75th year, except who his father was, whom he married, and where he lived. Furthermore, the narrative of Genesis reveals very little about what happened after his 100th year—other than he married again and had six more sons, which is remarkable to say the least! The point is that the narrator focused upon 25 critical years and, within this span, selected several special *moments* in the life of this great patriarch.

Thus the episodes (the incidents and related events) so chosen are vitally important to the overall development of redemptive history. This does not mean that we milk each episode for hidden meanings, but *we constantly ask how the individual episode fits into the total picture*. This method of viewing the individual passages from the standpoint of the entire canon of Scripture is a consciously adopted procedure and constitutes a fundamental principle for the careful study of Scripture.[15] We conclude with this observation: redemptive history may be likened to a time line with knots tied into it. These knots represent revelatory moments in God's redemptive plan. *These moments and their interpretation by inspired biblical writers form the essence of redemptive history*. We will refer back to this concept in chapter seven—it is fundamental to a basic understanding of the nature of Scripture. The following diagram outlines some of the key revelatory moments in redemptive history.

REDEMPTIVE HISTORY
"Key Moments"

Progressive Revelation: Deed/Word Complexes

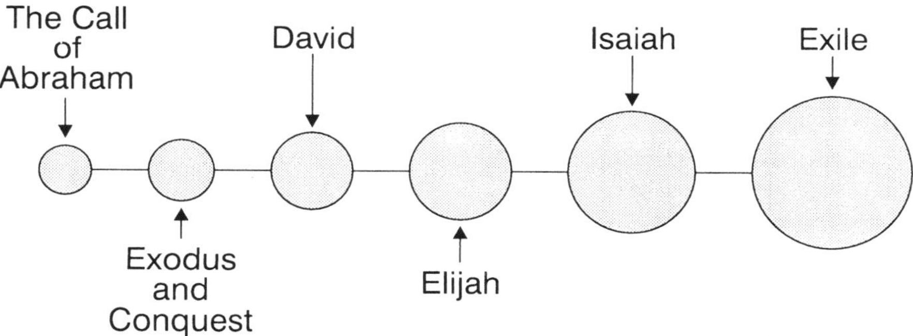

Divine Event Accompanied by Divinely Inspired Interpretation

For Further Discussion:

To what other evidences of the divine origin of Scripture might we appeal?

Why is it important to recognize fully the humanity of Scripture?

How should Christians respond to the charge that the Bible is full of errors?

How would you respond to someone who claimed that the Old Testament was not really necessary for Christian living today?

Why is the unity of the Bible an important witness to its inspiration?

Are there other characteristics of redemptive history?

For Further Reading:

Books and articles supplementing the discussion in this chapter:

Dillard, Raymond B., and Tremper Longman, III. *An Introduction to the Old Testament*, pages 17-36. Grand Rapids: Eerdmans, 1994. Good overview of the nature of the Old Testament and issues involved in reading it.

Doriani, Daniel M. *Getting the Message: A Plan for Interpreting and Applying the Bible*. Phillipsburg, NJ: P & R Publishing, 1996. Very helpful introductory textbook outlining a sound method for interpreting Scripture.

Ewert, David. *From Ancient Tablets to Modern Translations: A General Introduction to the Bible*, pp. 13-34. Grand Rapids: Zondervan, 1983. Brief but helpful discussion of the characteristics of the Bible as a whole and the arrangement of the OT canon.

Fee, Gordon D., and Douglas Stuart. *How to Read the Bible for All Its Worth*. 2d ed. Grand Rapids: Zondervan, 1993. An excellent handbook on how to interpret and apply Scripture. Highly recommended for all Bible study.

Fuller, Daniel P. *The Unity of the Bible: Unfolding God's Plan for Humanity*, pp. 21-96. Grand Rapids: Zondervan, 1992. Fine discussion of the unity and inspiration of the Scriptures by the professor of Biblical Interpretation at Fuller Theological Seminary.

House, Paul R. *Old Testament Survey*, pp. 19-24. Nashville: Broadman, 1992. Emphasizes an appreciation for the literary aspects of Scripture.

Packer, James I. "The Necessity of the Revealed Word." In *The Bible: The Living Word of Revelation*, edited by Merrill C. Tenney, pp. 31-49. Grand Rapids: Zondervan, 1968. Helpful discussion of the doctrine of inspiration.

Ryken, Leland. *How to Read the Bible as Literature*. Grand Rapids: Zondervan, 1984. Especially helpful in explaining the literary nature of the Bible and discussing in some depth the various literary genres found in Scripture.

Sailhammer, John. *Old Testament History*. Grand Rapids: Zondervan, 1998. Helpful overview of redemptive history.

Woudstra, Marten H. "The Inspiration of the Old Testament." In *The Bible: The Living Word of Revelation*, edited by Merrill C. Tenney, pp. 123-140. Grand Rapids: Zondervan, 1968. Defense of the inspiration and authority of the OT.

All of the following books set out the various themes of the OT or demonstrate an over-arching unity:

Bright, John. *The Kingdom of God.* Nashville/New York: Abingdon, 1953. Though dated, this work is a fine exposition of this central theme in the Bible.

Dyrness, William. *Themes in Old Testament Theology.* Downers Grove: InterVarsity, 1979. Helpful treatment reflecting a systematic theology approach.

McComiskey, Thomas Edward. *The Covenants of Promise.* Grand Rapids: Baker, 1985. Argues for a unity in God's plan of salvation under the rubric of promise.

Motyer, Alec, and John Stott. *Story of the Old Testament.* Grand Rapids: Baker, 2001. Overview of the Old Testament written for lay readers.

Robertson, O. Palmer. *The Christ of the Covenants.* Grand Rapids: Baker, 1980. Another study of redemptive history from a covenant theology perspective.

Sauer, Erich. *From Eternity to Eternity.* Grand Rapids: Eerdmans, 1954. Valuable treatment that surveys the entire sweep of redemptive history and shows its unity. Written from a moderately dispensational point of view.

Wright, Christopher J. H. *Knowing Jesus Through the Old Testament.* Downers Grove: InterVarsity, 1995. Shows how the Old Testament points toward the coming of Christ in redemptive history.

Youngblood, Ronald. *The Heart of the Old Testament.* Grand Rapids: Baker, 1971. Brief discussion of leading themes and ideas in the Old Testament by a leading evangelical Old Testament scholar.

Endnotes

1. For the following I am greatly indebted to Oswald T. Allis, *The Old Testament: Its Claims and Its Critics* (n.p.: Presbyterian and Reformed, 1972), pp. 7-19.

2. See Baruch Halpern, *David's Secret Demons: Messiah, Murderer, Traitor, King.* (Grand Rapids: Eerdmans, 2001).

3. "The Crayon Man," *Christianity Today*, 6 February 1987, p. 20.

4. See John H. Walton, *Ancient Israelite Literature in its Cultural Context: A Survey of Parallels Between Biblical and Ancient Near Eastern Literature* (Grand Rapids: Zondervan, 1989). This is a judicious discussion of the parallels between biblical literature and its ANE counterparts.

5. See G. C. Berkouwer's helpful discussion in *Holy Scripture*, trans. Jack B. Rogers (Grand Rapids: Eerdmans, 1975), pp. 195-212.

6. For more information on Jesus' view of the OT, see John Wenham, *Christ and the Bible* (Downers Grove: InterVarsity, 1972), pp. 11-37.

7. On the doctrine of Scripture, see Ted M. Dorman, *A Faith for All Seasons* (Nashville: Broadman and Holman, 1995), pp. 27-51.

8. For a popular discussion on the unity of the Bible, see Josh McDowell's *Evidence that Demands a Verdict* (n.p.: Campus Crusade for Christ, 1972), pp. 17-20.

9. See Robert Girdlestone, *Synonyms of the Old Testament* (Grand Rapids: Eerdmans, 1897), pp. 76-86.

10. For an instructive treatment of total depravity, see Donald G. Bloesch, *Essentials of Evangelical Theology*, vol. 1 (San Francisco: Harper and Row, 1978), pp. 88-119.

11. G. L. Archer, "Covenant," in *Baker's Dictionary of Theology*, ed. E. F. Harrison (Grand Rapids: Baker, 1960), p. 142.

12. For a helpful chart illustrating the various covenants, see *NIVSB*, p. 19.

13. See Kenneth Barker, "The Scope and Center of Old and New Testament Theology and Hope," in *Dispensationalism, Israel and the Church: The Search for Definition* (Grand Rapids: Zondervan, 1992), pp. 293-328.

14. Erich Sauer's trilogy is a clear exposition of the kingdom idea. *The Dawn of World Redemption*, trans. G. H. Long (Grand Rapids: Eerdmans, 1951); *The Triumph of the Crucified*, trans. G. H. Long (Grand Rapids: Eerdmans, 1951); *From Eternity to Eternity*, trans G. H. Long (Grand Rapids: Eerdmans, 1954).

15. See Gordon D. Fee and Douglas Stuart, *How to Read the Bible for All Its Worth*, 2d ed. (Grand Rapids: Zondervan, 1993), pp. 78-83 and Daniel M. Doriani, *Getting the Message: A Plan for Interpreting and Applying the Bible* (Phillipsburg, NJ: P & R Publishing, 1996), p. 170-186.

chapter **2**

The Old Testament Teaching on Creation

(Scripture reading: Genesis 1–2; Psalms 8; 33; 74:13; 89:10; 104; 148; Proverbs 8; Job 3:8; 26:12-13; 38; Isaiah 27:1; 40:12-31; 51:9-10)

Leading Questions

What do Old Testament references to creation tell us about the Creator and his creation?

Why was Genesis 1 written?

How does Genesis 1 provide the Christian with a correct understanding of reality?

Introduction

The first theme we take up is creation. Why was it not singled out as a major idea in the introductory chapter? The reason is that the biblical material does not focus upon the doctrine of creation. The number of texts dealing with creation is not large. However, as an underlying presupposition of redemptive history, the doctrine of creation is extremely important. The Hebrew Bible assumes a view of reality rooted in creation faith. The covenant-keeping God of redemption is also the creator-God; indeed, these two spheres of activity are intimately connected (see Col 1:15-20). For this reason we examine the OT teaching on this vital topic and reflect upon its implications.

The Interpretation of Genesis 1

The OT sets the stage for the drama of redemption by means of a creation account. The stage itself takes on form and shape in a majestic sequence of creative acts. Here we confront a problem: How are we to interpret this account? Some readers may wonder why such a question should even be raised. Why not just read it at face value as a straightforward, literal account of what actually happened "in the beginning?"

> **Substantial Numbers of Americans Continue to Doubt Evolution as Explanation for Origin of Humans**
>
> ***Some Americans appear uncertain as to meaning of terms, however.***
>
> Although most scientists subscribe to the theory of evolution as the best explanation for the origin of human begins, a recent Gallup poll shows that the American public is much more divided in its own beliefs. Americans choose "creationism" over "evolution" when asked which of these two terms best describes human origins, but slightly larger numbers of Americans choose one of two evolutionist explanations than choose a strict creationist explanation when given a choice between three specific views. At the same time, only about a third of the public say that Charles Darwin's theory of evolution is well supported by evidence.
>
> Taken from www.gallup.com, The Gallup Organization, 3-5-2001.

The problem is that we live in a scientific age, and this account was written in a pre-scientific age, in a culture vastly different from our own. We are in danger of reading it through our modern lenses and of assuming that it addresses scientific issues. In so doing, we may miss the original intention of the passage. The discovery of the meaning and intention of Genesis 1 is not nearly as easy as it may seem. We begin by surveying three major approaches employed by interpreters, all of whom accept the inspiration and the authority of the OT.[1]

The Completely Literal Approach

Genesis 1 as a historical narrative. The completely literal approach treats Genesis 1 as a historical narrative. That is, it describes what actually happened. Thus, not only the outline, but also the details, are taken at face value and treated as a straightforward account. This approach should not be confused with a rather naive, simplistic reading of the text. On the contrary, these interpreters are generally well informed about modern scientific facts and theories. They accept the statements made in the text at face value and make a sort of correlation with what they know about the discoveries of modern science; indeed, very often they appeal to scientific data as verification of the truthfulness of a completely literal interpretation.

It follows necessarily, if one interprets Genesis 1 in a completely literal fashion, that the heavens and the earth were created in six solar days. The expression "there was evening, and there was morning—the first (second, etc.) day" implies an ordinary day. This is further strengthened by reference to the seventh day, the Sabbath, which is clearly tied to the weekly cycle of days as we know it (Ex 20:8; 23:12).

This, however, raises a major problem about the age of the earth since consistency would require a relatively young earth. Genesis 1, read in connection with the rest of Genesis and the historical books, leads inevitably to calculations like that of Archbishop Ussher (A.D. 1581-1656). He set the date of creation at 4004 B.C. Bishop Robert Lightfoot refined this by setting the *exact time* at 9:00 a.m. October 23, 4004 B.C.! These scholars derived that date by working backwards from the time of David and Solomon using the genealogies (see e.g., Ge 5; 10). They assumed that the genealogies were all father-son links. Most current "complete literalists" recognize that the biblical genealogies often have missing links and do not always give father-son descent. They realize that the Hebrew word *bēn* can, in some contexts, mean "ancestor." Thus they infer "gaps" in the genealogies and allow some leeway in dating. Most advocates of the completely literal approach are comfortable with a dating of about 20,000-10,000 B.C. for creation. Even this refinement, however, is wildly out of agreement with current scientific estimates for the age of the earth and the universe. The former is usually set at about 4.5 billion years and the latter in the magnitude of 15-20 billion. This huge discrepancy constitutes a major problem for the completely literal approach.

Stance towards the modern scientific consensus. This discrepancy accounts for two features of the completely literal approach. In the first place, its stance toward the scientific consensus is generally one of *denial and distrust.* Much energy is spent in refutation of the validity of the scientific estimates and the methods and procedures used in obtaining these dates. Irregularities and contradictions in estimates employing scientific dating techniques are diligently collected and displayed as exhibits that, in their opinion, call into question the entire enterprise. It is not our purpose here to settle this controversy; we simply alert the reader that the issue is far from settled and is very often discussed in highly technical language.[2]

Advocacy of mature creationism. Another feature of this approach is the advocacy of mature creationism. That is, the proponents raise an interesting question: How old was Adam on the first Sabbath? On a completely literal interpretation, the answer would be—one day old! Yet they inquire further: How old did he appear to be? The answer is that he appeared to be an adult male. What about the trees? Did they have tree rings? Presumably they did. The point is that a literal reading of Genesis 1 seems to indicate an immediate, full-blown, mature creation. So the original creation had the *appearance of age*—it simply could not have been any other way.

There is a problem with this, however. The problem has to do with fossils. Fossils are the remnants of living things that have long since died and had their skeletal remains impressed upon rock. The scientific consensus holds that these fossils go way back into earth history and are part of the evidence used to date the earth to about 4.5 billion years. For example, beneath my office in Upland, Indiana, below the soil layers, one would undoubtedly come to fossil strata—some of the fossils being of animals and plants now extinct. What does mature creationism say about this? Why would God have created the earth with such fossil strata and so have conveyed the impression that these plants and animals once lived? A rather extreme response might be that the devil put them there to deceive human beings about the true age of the earth![3]

Theories to account for the fossil record. Since this is a crucial issue for the validity of mature creationism, we consider two suggested theories that attempt to alleviate the problem. The first theory we can call *the gap theory*. In the gap theory, Genesis 1:1 refers to the original, primeval creation, which may have been as much as 4.5 billion years ago in line with the scientific consensus. Verse two, however, refers to the aftermath of a cosmic judgment, which overwhelmed the original creation. Advocates of this view generally prefer to render verse 2 as follows: "Now the earth *became* formless and empty." (See NIV text note.) Ordinarily, this judgment is connected to the fall of Satan and his angels. Isaiah 14:12–15 is often appealed to as a description of this event (cf. also 2Pe 2:4; Jude 6). Genesis 1:3-31 then recounts God's re-creating the formless and empty earth, which had suffered catastrophe. The present earth is thus relatively recent. The fossils are evidence of the judgment that overtook the original creation of Genesis 1:1. Thus the theory can (1) maintain a relatively young earth view for the earth as we now know it, but also (2) account for the fossils in the earth's crust and allow for a date of the original creation on the order of 4.5 billion years, if necessary.

Despite its convenience in dealing with dating and fossils, one wonders if it is a fair reading *of the text itself.* Did the author intend for his readers to understand the existence of such a "gap" between verses one and two? Is the translation "became" instead of "was" justified? It looks like the theory is guilty of reading a lot into a little![4] I think it is fair to say that support for the gap theory among evangelicals has dwindled considerably of late.[5]

A more convincing theory has been resurrected and refurbished by the scientific creationism movement.[6] Spearheaded by Drs. Henry Morris and John Whitcomb (an engineer and OT specialist respectively), the theory attempts to solve the existence of fossils without giving in to the scientific consensus on the age of the earth. In short, the fossils are attributed to the great Noahic flood (Ge 7–8). Mature creationism (the appearance of age) allies itself with a sort of "flood geology" consistent with a completely literal interpretation of Genesis 1. Scientific creationism aggressively challenges the scientific consensus on the age of the earth and offers a number of other dating methods, which produce ages more in line with a relatively recent earth.

The theory, in a nutshell, operates as follows. On the second day of creation, the watery abyss covering the earth was divided into two great reservoirs: the oceans and a huge vapor canopy placed above the atmosphere of earth (Ge 1:6-7). In the Noahic flood, this vapor canopy condensed and collapsed upon earth in the form of torrential rainfall (Ge 7:11-12). In addition, there was a subterranean source of water that erupted onto the surface of the planet (Ge 7:11). This combination completely inundated the planet and destroyed land animals and plants. These were carried about and deposited through sedimentation and other geological processes in the earth's crust.

The vapor canopy theory explains two factors according to its defenders. In the first place, it accounts for the enormous longevity of the patriarchs in Genesis 5. The canopy acted as a radioactivity shield, protecting humans from the effects of radiation. After the flood, when the canopy was no longer in place, life spans significantly decreased (cf. Ge 5 with Ge 25:7; 35:28; 47:28; 50:22). This canopy also produced a greenhouse effect on the planet resulting in a semi-tropical climate over the entirety of the globe. The second, and most significant, factor relates to radioactive dating techniques. The argument states that the influx of radioactivity after the flood (because of the collapse of the canopy) has significantly altered the calibration of the "clocks." Radioactive dating assumes a constant rate of decay in its calculations. Flood geologists counter that such could not be the case assuming a literal, worldwide flood and a vapor canopy hypothesis. The detailed arguments are quite technical, and we will not overload the reader with the details.[7]

The important question to ask of flood geology is whether it can support the burden of explaining earth history. Flood geology has become a highly controversial and emotionally charged issue in some circles. One's view on this is almost a litmus test of orthodoxy. Again, it is not our purpose here to attempt a resolution. We simply call attention to the fact that many Bible-believing authorities are critical of flood geology and do not accept the idea of a relatively young earth.[8]

Before leaving the completely literal approach, consider the apparent discrepancies that arise just from a close reading of the text. According to Genesis 1:26-27, humankind, male and female, was created on day six. Following the literal approach, Genesis 2 would be a close-up of the sixth day of creation. But according to Genesis 2, Adam was first created, taken to Eden, and charged with its upkeep and protection. He subsequently experienced a deep loneliness, named "all the beasts of the field and all the birds of the air," and then—after all that—underwent surgery on his rib so that Eve might be created bone of his bones and flesh of his flesh. This is, to put it mildly, a full day!

Another discrepancy surfaces by carefully comparing Genesis 1:11-12 with Genesis 2:4b-6. The former passage, describing creative activity on the third day, indicates that the land produced vegetation. The latter speaks about a lack of rain and a man to work the ground. The vegetation was watered by ground water. Now it is this watering mechanism that causes the problem. The biblical text implies that this system had been operating for some time. If, however, one takes the two chapters literally and as complementary, only three days had elapsed! Despite various attempts to harmonize the discrepancies, these two chapters seem to be out of sync.[9] Perhaps this is a signal that we have misinterpreted one or both of them.

Essentially Literal

Genesis 1 contains figurative elements. The above-mentioned problems have led some interpreters to suggest that Genesis 1 may be better understood if some figurative elements are allowed in the account. These interpreters would opt for an essentially literal approach. That is, Genesis 1 is still a historical narrative, but some features of the narrative should be interpreted *figuratively*, not literally. The feature that is most often singled out as figurative is the word "day" (*yôm* in Hebrew); the days of Genesis 1 refer to extended periods of time or ages.

Stance towards the scientific consensus. One can see immediately that this approach has already provided an answer to the chief difficulty of the completely literal approach, namely, the problem of the age of the earth. *The essentially literal approach harmonizes science and the Bible.* In fact, this stance of harmonization is one of the clear differences between the completely literal and the essentially literal views. The latter has a generally open, non-combative attitude toward scientific theorizing about origins. Accepting the commonly voiced dictum that "all truth is God's truth," these interpreters are convinced that the Bible's version of creation and, at least some scientific theories, can be harmonized. In general, those adopting an essentially literal approach would not quarrel with the estimates of 4.5 billion years for the age of the earth.

Progressive creationism. A further distinction of the essentially literal view entails the adoption of some form of *progressive creationism.* Assuming a very old earth and recognizing some validity to the geological history of the earth as generally held by the scientific community, these interpreters maintain that God created the basic life forms and simultaneously endowed them with the capability of developing further. Though they may not be comfortable with the term, they recognize a form of evolution—an evolution or development that is divinely directed. Genesis 1, with its creative "days," presents a simplified version of God's intervention at key moments of earth history to create basic life forms. The variety of living things stems from the basic forms. One thinks of the numerous breeds of dogs, for example, as an illustration of the diversity possible from the basic forms.

Appeal is also made to a new version of evolution called *punctuated equilibrium.* This theory views the evolutionary process somewhat like a covered pot on a stove. When the heat builds up to a critical point, the contents boil over resulting in a creative surge of new life forms. Progressive creationists see these "boiling points" as God's direct intervention, rather than as random, purely natural occurrences.

Major theories. The most common version of the essentially literal view is the *day-age theory.* This theory holds that each day represents an era, epoch, or geological period. Scriptural passages may indeed be cited in which the

Hebrew word *yôm* refers to a period of time longer than a solar day (see Ge 2:4, NASB; Jdg 18:30, NASB). Many progressive creationists call attention to the remarkable correspondence of the geological ages with the order of the days of Genesis 1. This agreement is called *concordism*. They frequently appeal to concordism as evidence for the divine inspiration of Scripture.[10]

The essentially literal approach is not without its problems, however. One problem is that concordism works only in a very general way. For example, there is agreement on progression from the more simple to the more complex, and we have plant life preceding land animals in both versions. However, as soon as one tries to harmonize the particulars of the geological column (the sequence of strata in the earth's crust) with the days of Genesis 1, severe problems arise. According to Genesis 1, trees (day 3) preceded marine life (day 5), and birds (day 5) preceded insects (day 6). This flies in the face of the generally accepted interpretation of the geological column. Also problematic is the fact that apparently the sun was not created until the fourth era or epoch. How plants could survive for eons without sunlight is a major problem for concordism. Defenders of the view resort to the explanation that the sun was created on day one, but did not *appear* until day four. The text, however, says that God *made* two great lights on day four (1:16).

An interesting variation is the so-called *pictorial-revelatory* view. In short, this suggests that the days of Genesis 1 were not days of creation at all, but rather, revelatory days, in which God revealed to the narrator truths about the created order. Try to imagine the following scenario. God revealed himself to Moses (traditional author of the Pentateuch) on seven consecutive days. On each day some aspect of the created order, attributed to the Lord's creative power, was revealed to Moses. The days do not necessarily tell us the actual sequence of creation, rather, they inform us (perhaps in a very general chronological fashion) that all creation came from the hand of the creator. The Lord took seven days to reveal this to Moses. This seven-day sequence was then tied to the weekly cycle of Israel's life and so permanently commemorated.

In some respects this theory is a completely literal approach, since the days are ordinary, solar days. We have classified it as essentially literal, however, because it understands something other than what a face value reading would suggest about the nature of the days. This view has not garnered much support; the text itself does not use the language of revealing but of creating, making, dividing, separating, and causing. Furthermore, there can be little doubt about how later biblical writers interpreted the creation account (Ne 9:6).[11]

One other essentially literal theory merits consideration. The *framework hypothesis* agrees with the completely literal approach that the author was speaking of six ordinary days. However, the framework of an ordinary week was itself a *literary device* whereby a *logical* rather than chronological discussion might be presented. Thus the entire scheme of creation week served the author's primary purpose of providing a theology of the Sabbath. The sequence of creative acts is an artistic literary creation of the author, who provides a sort of meditation upon creation and its relationship to the Creator. It does not really intend to inform us about the how and the when; only the *why*.[12]

While this approach nicely sidesteps the dating problem and does not have to grapple with the discrepancies of the completely literal approach, it does not escape without shortcomings. Two main objections have been lodged against it: (1) The text itself gives no clues that the framework of a week is but a literary device. On the face of it, the text does say something about how and when. (2) Even more importantly, Exodus 20:11 indicates that the work week of Israel was patterned after that of God. How could this be valid unless God actually did as stated?[13]

Essentially Non-literal

Genesis 1 as a historical or symbolic story. The continuing problems of both the completely literal and essentially literal approaches have convinced some interpreters that the fallacy lies in assuming the text to be a historical narrative. If one reads the text in essentially non-literal terms, perhaps the remaining tensions can be alleviated. Two possibilities present themselves: Genesis 1 might be either a *historical story* or a *symbolic story*. Note carefully the substitution of the word "story" for "narrative."

A historical story is not a historical narrative. Historical features are present, but the work itself does not narrate something that actually happened as depicted. One might compare the historical story to a historical novel. While these novels are true to life and unfold within a historical setting, they are, nonetheless, creations of the author's imagination. In a similar fashion, it is suggested, Genesis 1 concerns something that happened—God did create the heavens and the earth—although not in the precise way described by the narrator.

A symbolic story, like the historical story, does not narrate events that actually happened in time and space. Unlike the historical story, however, neither is it set in a specific historical period. The intention of the symbolic story is to communicate something about present reality using the vehicle of the story form. In the case of Genesis 1, the intention is to teach Israel what is clearly true; namely, that God is the sovereign creator and humanity reflects his image. The creation account itself originated in Israelite tradition and has no validity as a work of history. Adam and Eve are not historical figures; they are *representative figures*. That is, they mirror the plight of all human beings in the real world.[14]

Stance towards the modern scientific consensus. Note that the essentially non-literal approach adopts a distinctive stance toward scientific theories about origins. There is generally an unquestioned acceptance of the scientific consensus. Proponents contend that religious truth and scientific truth operate on separate levels; they *dichotomize*, that is, *separate truth into different kinds or levels*. Given such a perspective, they can say that Genesis 1 is religiously true and the scientific explanation (some form of evolutionism) is scientifically true. Needless to say, there is no conflict here between the Bible and science. They are generally disdainful of attempts at harmonizing the two, since the effort is considered inappropriate and actually impossible.

Approaches to the biblical text. How, then, do essentially non-literalists treat Genesis 1? What kind of literary genre do they assign to it? Here we have no consensus, but rather, a range of suggestions. Some use the term historical myth. For many reared in evangelicalism, the term "myth" raises an immediate red flag. Part of the difficulty resides in the nuance essentially non-literalists give the term. As they understand it, historical myth describes a religious text that accounts for various natural and supernatural phenomena. Also involved in the notion of myth is an awareness that there must be something of real significance in the world, something beyond rational comprehension. One resorts to the language of myth in order to express the conviction that a reality transcends the created, visible order. So viewed as a historical myth, Genesis 1 affirms that behind the marvels of the material order stands one mysterious and majestic God. As a religious text, Genesis 1 tells us the truth about God and his relationship to the world.

The chief difficulty with this theory is that Genesis 1 has few, if any, characteristics of a myth when compared to ancient Near Eastern myths. The sophisticated definitions of myth one encounters in contemporary discussions owe more to modern philosophy than to comparative analysis of ancient Near

Eastern literature. One is hard-pressed to find even a remnant of myth in Genesis 1.[15]

A more convincing case can be argued for the category of parable. A parable is a true-to-life story, intended to convey a single point. Applied to Genesis 1, that point is God's sovereign creation of all things. That the OT and NT both utilize the parabolic form is, of course, a matter of simple observation. No one would accuse Jesus of being dishonest if there were no actual, historical, Good Samaritan or prodigal son (as indeed, it would seem there were not). Speaker and listener share an understanding about the nature of the relationship between a parable and reality. The principle objection to viewing Genesis 1 as a parable lies in the actual form of the text—it does not have the features of other biblical parables. One does not gain the impression from the text itself that this is a true-to-life story; one does gain the impression that it is an account of something that happened in time and space.

Some suggest that Genesis 1 is a form of prophecy. It functions as a counterpart to the book of Revelation, except that the vision is directed *backward* to beginnings rather than forward to final things. Since prophecy uses devices such as symbolic language, one must not insist on interpreting the text literally. Seen in the context of the entire Bible, one might appeal to symmetry and balance, whereby redemptive history is enclosed by a prophetic vision of past and future, like bookends.[16] Once again, however, Genesis 1 does not display the characteristics of prophetic or apocalyptic literature.[17]

We consider one more possibility. Suppose Genesis 1 was originally a confession of faith affirmed by the worshiping community of Israel as they assembled at the tabernacle or temple. The majestic cadence, the solemn and exalted tone, and the impressive repetition sound almost like a confession of faith—like an Apostles' Creed. One could even imagine that it was sung by priests and singers as part of Israel's liturgy.[18] Thus it may have been lifted out of its original context and placed at the beginning of Genesis as an appropriate introduction to the history of Israel. This suggestion has more plausibility than the others. Once again, however, it falls short of conviction on stylistic and contextual grounds. One may easily compare Genesis 1 and several psalms celebrating creation, most notably Psalm 104 (cf. also Ps 8; 19). Clearly the latter is a meditation based upon Genesis 1. The differences are readily apparent even in translation. From the standpoint of language, Genesis 1 is written in prose.[19] Psalm 104, by way of contrast, employs the devices and techniques of Hebrew poetry.

Problem with the non-literal approach. There is a troubling component in the essentially non-literal understanding of Genesis 1, and that is the dichotomy between religious and scientific truth. Is such a dichotomy valid? Are there different, apparently autonomous, orders of truth? In the opinion of this writer, while such a scheme may seem to afford a way out of the thicket, too much has been sacrificed in the exit. *At the heart of biblical faith stands the bedrock of historical events. These events cannot be withdrawn from the empirical world of historical and scientific investigation without seriously undermining the basis of religious certainty.* Read again Paul's carefully argued defense of the believer's resurrection in 1 Corinthians 15 to appreciate the inseparable connection between faith and history. In similar fashion, we are not yet convinced that one can sever the connection between the biblical account of creation and the "real" world of scientific investigation. There must be some correspondence between them.[20]

The following chart summarizes the three basic approaches we have considered.

Approaches to the Interpretation of Genesis 1

Issue	Completely Literal	Essentially Literal	Essentially Non-literal
Literary Genre of Genesis 1	Historical narrative	Historical narrative with figurative elements	Historical or symbolic story 1. Historical myth 2. Parable 3. Prophecy 4. Confession
Stance towards Scientific Consensus	Denies and distrusts the scientific consensus and advocates mature creationism	Harmonizes science and the Bible and advocates progressive creationism	Dichotomizes into separate "truth" categories and advocates theistic evolution
Theories to Account for Fossil Record	1. Gap theory 2. Flood geology	1. Day-age theory 2. Pictorial-revelatory theory 3. Framework hypothesis	Accepts scientific explanation of evolutionary theory
Problems	Seems to conflict with Genesis 2 and flies in the face of widely accepted scientific findings	Seems to make question-able concessions in order to hold both biblical and scientific data together	Accepts scientific theory uncritically and threatens to undermine religious certainty

Consensus on the Teaching of Genesis 1

At this point the reader may be coming up for air! Is there a view of Genesis 1 that resolves the tensions and answers all the questions? In my opinion, none of the three approaches is without problems.[21] Let me make a personal suggestion. In light of the rapidly changing views of scientific investigation and the complexities of interpreting Genesis 1, we might all be well advised to "hang loose" and not defend any one of the three major approaches as if the truthfulness of the Christian faith were at stake. Dogmatism on this issue seems premature.

It is, however, extremely important to establish a consensus on the doctrine of creation. To do this we must discern what is *essential* to creation faith and what is *peripheral*. In all three basic approaches to Genesis 1, there are three essential truths, which, I believe, must not be sacrificed if we are to be faithful to the biblical witness.[22]

The creation of all things by the one, true, and living God. This is *non-negotiable*. Compromise with thoroughgoing evolutionism, which leaves God out of the mechanism, constitutes a failure of nerve and results in a distorted, incorrect view of reality. It is also contrary to biblical faith that confesses: ". . . there is but one God, the Father, from whom all things came and for whom we live . . ." (1Co 8:6).[23]

The special creation of the first man and woman. The essentially non-literal approach must be careful here. To abandon the historicity of Adam and Eve undermines redemptive history. The apostle Paul sees humanity as consisting of only two divisions: those who are in the first Adam, the man from the earth, and those who, by a new creative work of the Spirit, are in the second Adam, Jesus Christ, the man from heaven (Ro 5:12-21; 1Co 15:20-23, 44-49). It seems precarious to permit a non-historical first Adam in one's thinking when all indications point to a complete acceptance by both Jesus and Paul of a historical Adam (Mk 10:6-9; Mt 19:4-6).

The unity of the human race. The creation account, joined as it is to the succeeding story of humankind, implies that all persons share a common, ancestral pair—Adam and Eve. The implications are profound. *All* are image-bearers of the divine glory. Even after the fall into sin, humans still reflect that image (Ge 9:6). No one race, nationality, language, or social class has a monopoly upon the inherent dignity bestowed by the creator. Racism, sexism, and nationalism, the bane of modern society, fall under the condemnation of creation faith. The new creation in Christ points the way back to a real, spiritual unity, which is based upon the original creation unity (Gal 3:26-28).

Principles in God's Creation

Creation and the Person of God

Isaiah 40:12-31 celebrates the awesome wisdom of God in his creative activity. Notice the skillful use of rhetorical questions, whereby the prophet is able to make us stop and reflect. In verse 12 the Lord strides through his universe like a cosmic Paul Bunyan, reducing to mere handbreadths the incredible distances. This effective figure of speech is called *anthropomorphism*, that is, a description of God in human terms. God the Father does not actually possess bodily parts, but we attribute these to him in order to convey the idea that he sees, hears, feels, and so on. In this passage, the anthropomorphism stresses God's transcendence; he is above and independent of the material universe. It also implies the omnipresence of God; he is everywhere present in the universe. As we proceed through our study of the OT, we will have occasion to point out many other examples of anthropomorphism. Verse 13 asks if anyone has ever understood God's mind. The expected answer, of course, is *no one*! In fact, the answer to each of the seven "who" questions in the chapter (vv. 12-14, 18, 25) is the same—no one. This section highlights the incomparability of God. No one possesses the kind and amount of wisdom he possesses. We thus ascribe omniscience to God. He knows all things that can be known. The created order is a continual testimony to this staggering fact (cf. Isa 42:5; 44:24; 45:18).

Creation and the Plan of God

The structure of the creation account. The structure of Genesis 1 tells us something very significant about the world in which we live. It displays a clear pattern. Each day can be broken down into five main components as follows:

Announcement	"And God said . . ."
Command	"Let there be . . ."
Report	"And it was so . . ."
Evaluation	"And God saw that it was good."
Temporal Framework	"And there was evening, and there was morning, the . . . day."

The effect of this stereotyped pattern is one of deliberateness and orderliness. Everything proceeds in a controlled and carefully thought out procedure. There is no room for randomness or experimentation; one senses the control of a firm hand guiding the entire process through a carefully planned program.

The climax of the creation account. Not only is there a distinct pattern evident in the unfolding days, but there is a stair-step or climactic structure in the sequence of the six creative "days." This can be visually grasped by the following layout.

Climactic Arrangement of the Creation Account

Cosmos

Day 6–Land Animals/Man

Day 5–Fish/Fowl

Day 4–Sun/Moon/Stars

Day 3–Land/Vegetation

Day 2–Sky/Sea

Day 1–Night/Day

Chaos

Conclusion:
Earth is made into a life-support system for human beings.

There can be little doubt about the supreme moment of creation. Only for human beings is the stereotyped pattern broken by divine deliberation; only they bear the stamp of his image. Clearly, then, *humans stand at the apex of the created order*. As Psalm 8:5 says, they are [only] "a little lower than the heavenly beings." As one moves from the foreboding chaos of Genesis 1:2 to the friendly cosmos (order) of day six, one senses that the created order has a distinct purpose. That purpose is to be a life-support system for humans. Only planet earth, in the known universe, is perfectly designed as a home for *homo sapiens*. Read the following reprinted article for a new appreciation for our amazing earth.

The following excerpt is from an article by William B. Tolar, Dean of the School of Theology at Southwestern Seminary, printed in the *Texas Baptist Standard*.

What Makes Life on Earth Possible?

The earth in relationship to the sun is not perpendicular; it is tilted at about a 23° angle. Could this have happened by accident or chance or was it so arranged?

While tilted at about a 23° angle, our world is rotating on its axis at about 1000 m.p.h. This rate, one scientist said, is just about right for you and me to exist. If our world turned at only 100 m.p.h. instead of 1000 m.p.h., our days and nights would be 10 times as long. Whatever survived the incredibly hot days would freeze in the night when temperatures would plummet to something like 240° below zero.

The world wobbles off of its 23° tilt about 3° with amazing regularity. Our seasons and our climates are affected by it.

If our world strayed up or down more than 3° off the 23° tilt, life might perish from the earth. Without the tilt to deflect the light and heat, the earth would absorb too much heat. Moisture would be pulled to the north and south poles and build up in tremendous ice caps.

Here are four things about the world working together in such a wonderful way: tilted just right, spinning just right, wobbling up just right, wobbling down just right. And the chance of my pulling four coins out of my pocket in perfect sequence by accident is 1 out of 10,000.

There is a fifth thing–the depth of the earth's oceans. If the earth's oceans had been deeper when the earth began, that much more water would have absorbed or would have dissolved the carbon dioxide and oxygen out of the air. Life could not have begun unless more air had been in the atmosphere originally. Thus, the earth's oceans are just about the right depth in relation to the amount of air in our atmosphere.

A sixth thing is the earth's crust. Not only are the earth's oceans about the right depth but the earth's crust is just the right thickness. If the earth were only 100' thicker on the outside than it is, that much additional matter would have oxidized all the free oxygen out of the air when the world began, and life-forms could not have begun.

There is a seventh thing. We are moving around the sun in an elliptical orbit at just about the right speed. If our world slowed down, it would be pulled so close to the sun at the shallow or narrow part of that football-like orbit that we would be burned to a crisp.

If our world were to slightly more than double its speed, it would throw us so far into space at the long point that we would freeze to death in the far reaches of space.

An eighth thing: our earth is about the right number of miles from the sun for us to be able to live–about 93 million miles. At this distance, our earth receives neither too much nor too little heat from the sun for us to live.

While the earth is tilted, wobbling, and racing about the sun, the moon is moving around the earth at just about the right distance! Averaging about 240,000 miles from the earth, the moon is just about right for our well being, controlling tides and keeping them within livable levels.

The correlation of creative activity. Besides the stereotyped pattern and the stair-step arrangement, there is also a careful correlation of creative activity on the several "days." The following chart visualizes this aspect of the creation account.

Days of Creation

Formless	Empty
Day 1 Light Day 2 Water/Sky Day 3 Land/Vegetation	Day 4 Luminaries Day 5 Fish/Fowl Day 6 Beasts/Humans
Realm	Ruler

There is both a vertical and horizontal correlation. Notice how Days 1-3 (vertical) answer the need for form in the earth. Form is provided through acts of separation or the introduction of boundaries and limits. Days 4-6 answer the need for filling the emptiness. Horizontally the juxtaposition of realm and ruler expresses nicely the correlation. Thus the luminaries (day 4) "rule over" the realm of light (day 1), the fish and fowl (day 5) "rule over" the realm of sea and sky (day 2), and beasts and humans (day 6) "rule over" land (day 3).

Such a careful, even meticulous, arrangement serves to underscore the *orderliness* with which creation proceeded. Behind the order and purposefulness stands the omniscient, omnipotent Creator-God. Thorough-going evolutionism, which reduces reality to the material order operating by random, chance processes, is inconceivable and has been demonstrated to be mathematically impossible. How much more satisfying is the majestic picture which unfolds in Genesis 1! How much more comforting to reflect upon a personal being who has imposed the order we constantly observe around us. We live in a cosmos, not a chaos.

Creation and the Power of God

There is another feature of Genesis 1 that deserves comment. Like a symphonic theme that returns again and again, we read the staccato phrase: "And God said. . . ." Creation by the word of God is an important idea in this chapter. Energy and power accompany God's word of command. Each command results in accomplishment. There is no struggle, no opposition, no strain. God's word invariably achieves its aims. This, of course, is an aspect of God's omnipotence (his unlimited power). Psalm 33:6, 9, 11 highlight the notion of creation by the word of God. God's will actualized in his word is supreme. As created beings, we can do nothing more important than submitting to the word of God. Order and harmony in our personal lives come about as a result of obedience to his word. The prophets and poets on occasion appeal to the "obedience" found in the realm of nature in order to shame disobedient Israel (see Isa 1:3; Job 12:7-9; Jer 4:22).

Creation and the People of God

Creation by the word of God also stresses the fact of his personal involvement. We have here no distant, delegated effort. God is personally involved in all of creation. Nothing in the created order is superfluous; nothing may be dispensed with and discarded. In other words, God's personal involvement in creation assures us that "it was good" (Ge 1:9, 12, 18, 21, 25); indeed, that "it was very good" (Ge 1: 31). We can affirm, then, that all of creation is valuable, indeed, *matter has value*.

Surprisingly, this truth has at times been distorted or denied. The motivation for this denial is usually the seeking of a deeper spiritual life. Thinking that sin somehow resides in the "stuff" of the created order, ascetic Christianity (a form of Christianity renouncing the comforts of society and practicing severe self-discipline) adopted an essentially Greek notion of the inferiority of matter. Spirituality consisted of a renunciation of the body and material things and a total preoccupation with the spirit. To be more specific, there was a lingering suspicion that sex was a hindrance to true spirituality. In certain segments of Christendom, the "higher spirituality" denied any outlet to sexual desires. The OT knows of no such spirituality. The creation account gives every encouragement to a joyful embracing of all creation—including the sexual dimension.

Like all good gifts, sex is enjoyed within certain limits and boundaries. The boundary for the enjoyment of sex is the marriage bond (cf. Ge 1:26-27; 2:20, 25 with Mt 19:4-6). The playboy philosophy argues that such a limitation kills all real enjoyment. Nothing could be further from the truth.[24] The biblical position holds that real freedom and joy are found within the guidelines of divine intention and permission.

Participation in the arts, scientific endeavors, politics, and many other aspects of modern society are not sinful per se. To be sure, the Christian must not adopt the point of view, the values, the behavioral standards, and attitudes of the unbelieving world (Col 3:1-2). But neither is he/she urged to withdraw from involvement in the created order. The mandate is to be salt and light *in the world* (Mt 5:13-16). The monastic movement (Christian movement that advocated withdrawal from society) lost its bearings because it had a faulty view of beginnings! The OT view of creation is a healthy corrective to the excesses of monasticism, asceticism, and extreme, negative views on "separation from the world."

Purpose of the Creation Account

We now take up the question of the purpose and intention of Genesis 1. Why was this account written? What was it intended to accomplish for its original audience, the nation of Israel? The answers to these questions will throw light on its significance for us today.

Genesis 1 as a Polemic

A polemic is an argument or dispute. A careful reading of the text reveals that there is a debate going on. What we have is an affirmation about beginnings that *denies and refutes false ideologies*. The major ideology refuted is polytheism. Polytheism (the belief that behind reality stands a number of gods and goddesses) was the consensus view of the ancient world.

At this point, we need to relate a creation story called *Enumah Elish* so that the reader can gain an appreciation for Genesis 1 against the backdrop of ancient Near Eastern thought. *Enumah Elish* was a version of origins held by the Sumerians, Babylonians, and Assyrians among others. In its Babylonian version, the epic poem celebrated the primacy of Marduk, the chief god of Babylon, in the pantheon of gods and goddesses. In the course of the story, there is a creation account having some rather close parallels to Genesis 1.[25]

The epic opens with a watery chaos personified as two deities—the fresh waters represented by the male god, Apsu, and the salt waters by the female goddess, Tiamat. Tiamat is portrayed as a dragon-like being. A third deity, Mummu, may represent the mists or clouds surrounding the abyss.

> When the heaven (-gods) above were as yet uncreated,
> The earth (-gods) below not yet brought into being,
> Alone there existed primordial Apsu who engendered them,
> Only Mummu, and Tiamat who brought all of them forth.[26]

The epic relates how the various gods were created. It is important to understand that this process was one of procreation. *The ancients could not conceive of beginnings apart from the act of sexual intercourse*. We will come back to this point later. Thus Apsu and Tiamat engender a succession of gods—who really are but personifications of some aspect of reality as perceived by the people of the Tigris-Euphrates river valley.

> Their [Apsu and Tiamat's] waters could mix together
> Into a single stream . . .
> In the depths of their waters, the gods were created. . . .[27]

Thus we have a theogony—an account of how the various deities came into being. As the various "godlets" began to fill the universe, a crisis occurred. The younger gods were very energetic and boisterous. In fact, they generated so much noise that Apsu (a sleep lover) could not rest. He decided upon a radical course of action—he would destroy the tumultuous brood and resume his sleep. Being resourceful, however, the gods decided on a bold counter-attack. Ea (the earth) cast a spell on Apsu and slew him.

Ea . . . tore off his [Apsu's] royal head-dress,
Removed his aura-cloak, put it on himself:
He bound him, even Apsu, and did kill him. . . .[28]

This act of patricide (murdering one's father) enraged Tiamat. She entered the fray and determined to avenge Apsu's death. She is a fierce, hideous dragon who spawns a whole series of serpents and monsters who assist her. The younger gods were really terrified now! In their desperation, they turned to one of the young gods, Marduk. He was implored to "take on" Tiamat and thus save them. He accepted the challenge only on the condition that, with his victory, he be acknowledged as the supreme god. This condition was granted and the epic next narrates the theomachy (divine combat) between Tiamat and Marduk.

So they came together—Tiamat and Marduk, Sage of the gods:
They advanced into conflict, they joined forces in battle.
He spread wide his net, the lord, and enveloped her,
The Evil Wind, the rearmost, unleashed in her face.
As she opened her mouth, Tiamat to devour him,
He made the Evil Wind to enter that she closed not her lips:
The Storm Winds, the furious, then filling her belly.
Her innards became distended, she opened fully wide her mouth.
He shot there through an arrow, it pierced her stomach,
Clave through her bowels, tore into her womb:
Thereat he strangled her, made her life-breath ebb away,
Cast her body to the ground, standing over it (in triumph).[29]

At this point, Marduk conceives of a brilliant idea—he will create a world. A series of creative acts follow in which the body of Tiamat is cut into two pieces, becoming the sky and earth. The stars and heavenly bodies are positioned, the seasons determined, the mountains and rivers situated, and so forth. Last of all, Marduk creates man. The gods request this creature in order to provide for their maintenance and sustenance (sacrifices were viewed as "feeding the gods").

Blood will I compose, bring a skeleton into being,
Produce a lowly, primitive creature. "Man" shall be his name
I will create *lullu-amelu*—an earthly "puppet"—man.
To him be charged the service that the gods may then have
rest. . . ."[30]

This creation story spread throughout the ancient Near East. Of course the leading characters vary depending upon location, but the essential story line is the same.[31] There are three basic movements to the story: (1) some sort of repressive monster who prevents creation, (2) divine combat (theomachy) between this repressive monster and the hero god and (3) a victorious hero who unleashes the vital forces of life and brings order out of chaos.

We now have enough background to draw attention to some fascinating poetic texts in the OT. Perhaps you have wondered what is going on in those texts speaking about Rahab and Leviathan, the great dragons in the sea. Is it possible there really was a "Puff the magic dragon [who] lived by the sea"?! Is Nessie, the Loch Ness monster, a descendant of Tiamat?

First of all, the Hebrews clearly were acquainted with the Babylonian creation epic and thus were familiar with the story about Tiamat. Those who held fast to Israelite faith, however, did not believe in the literal existence of Tiamat (=Rahab/Leviathan, names variously applied to the repressive dragon in the Hebrew Bible). But only in poetic texts do the allusions to the dragon appear. In other words, *for literary effect, the poets of Israel borrowed the imagery of the old dragon to make a theological point.* This is akin to a preacher alluding to classical mythology or fairy tales in a sermon. The theological point is the glorification of Yahweh (the personal name of Israel's God, translated as LORD in the NIV—see preface to *NIVSB*, p. xii). It was not Marduk, nor any other hero god, who brought order out of chaos; it was the Lord and the Lord alone. Isaiah, for example, makes it abundantly clear that there is no god but the Lord (Isa 44:6; 45:6-7). Isaiah can, however, employ the imagery of the old dragon in order to exalt Yahweh (27:1; 51:9-10).

Secondly, the Hebrew poets utilized the allusions to Tiamat in three ways:[32] (1) In texts like Job 26:12-13 and Psalm 89:10, the creation of the world is attributed to Yahweh who is portrayed as destroying the chaos monster. (2) Isaiah 51:9-10 and Psalm 74:13-14 creatively apply the dragon motif to Israel's historic enemy, Pharaoh. Pharaoh, by his opposition to the creation of God's people Israel, acts like the old repressive monster of the creation myth. Indeed, on the crown of the Pharaoh stood the Uraeus, the cobra (a snake), which represented his authority! Nonetheless, Pharaoh, the dragon, is vanquished in the great combat or test of strength (the ten plagues and the parting of the Red Sea) recorded in the book of Exodus. (3) A third use is illustrated by Isaiah 27:1, which prophesies a final and complete victory over "Leviathan the gliding serpent, Leviathan the coiling serpent." This victory occurs at the culmination of human history (see chapter 9 on eschatology).

What is fascinating is this: a comparison with Revelation 20:1-3, 7-10 makes clear that behind the figure of Leviathan is a real person—Satan. Whereas the pagan notions about Tiamat/Leviathan were wrong, the sinister forces of evil in the world are a grim reality. Satan, who exalts himself over God and opposes his kingdom, heads up these forces. In his character, he is a repressive monster. Isaiah prophesies, however, that the real hero will defeat this arch-enemy. The Lord will reign victorious!

We can now summarize these allusions to the old dragon Tiamat. The poets and prophets of Israel employ the allusions in order to highlight the sovereignty and ultimate victory of Yahweh. In so doing, they deny the theology of their pagan neighbors. The pagan myths are "broken" and "baptized" for use in Israel. As the Hebrews reflect upon beginnings, they realize that Yahweh has defeated the chaos monster and established cosmos. As they reflect upon their national history, they realize that Yahweh has intervened repeatedly to repress new eruptions of chaos under the guise of personal or national enemies. Finally, as they peer into the future, they are confident Yahweh will at last banish the chaos monster and establish ever-lasting cosmos.

We return to our discussion concerning the point of Genesis 1. There are clear signs that it was composed in order to respond to pagan notions. Let us reexamine the text in order to find these rebuttals.

Genesis 1:2 refers to a formless, empty, dark abyss. This is strikingly similar to *Enumah Elish*. The following chart illustrates the similarities.[33] On the other hand, it is dramatically different. Note that the abyss is not a god or goddess (like Apsu and Tiamat). The abyss is not a repressive force; in fact, it responds instantly to the hovering Spirit of God. There is no theomachy here. God effortlessly speaks the decree and "it was so." Philosophically, there is a great gulf between *Enumah Elish* and Genesis. Genesis posits a clear separation between God, a pure Spirit, and the material order. Polytheism is confused and contradictory about this. It advocates the eternity of matter.[34]

A Comparison of Genesis 1 and Enumah Elish		
Item	**Genesis Account**	**Enumah Elish**
Time of Chaos	Genesis 1:2 Earth	Represented by the gods Apsu and Tiamat
Watery Darkness	Formless and empty, darkness over the surface of the deep	Fresh water and salt water all that existed
Similar Order of Events	Begins with God, light before luminaries, man created near end, rest	Begins with primeval deities, light before luminaries, man created near end, rest
View of God	Strictly monotheistic	Extremely polytheistic
Nature of Account	Dignified, majestic, aesthetically pleasing, rational	Confused and contradictory, highly mythological
View of Spirit and Matter	Distinct separation of two concepts–matter created	Mythological inter-mixture 1. Tiamat's corpse made into the firmament 2. Deities represent natural forces 3. Eternality of matter

We also noted earlier that, for the composers of *Enumah Elish*, the only way they could conceive of origins was in terms of procreation. To put it bluntly, sex is what makes the world go round, so obviously, it was sex that got it started! Paganism operates by the slogan, "Do what comes naturally." Sexual immorality, with all its tragic consequences, necessarily exists where polytheism flourishes. An especially devastating consequence is that intimacy and sharing, which humans need, is eroded by emotional distance and disappointment, the inevitable by-products of sexual infidelity and perversion. A casual callousness becomes pervasive, with the disintegration of society as the final outcome. One can only lament that "modern paganism" has not advanced beyond this way of thinking. As prophesied in Hosea 8:7, we are reaping the whirlwind as a consequence.

By contrast, in Genesis, sexuality is a gift bestowed by the Creator. This gift has a unitive function. A man and a woman can experience a "one flesh" relationship. Sexuality is lifted above the level of doing what comes naturally. It is a tremendously bonding experience, which has at its heart a giving of oneself to another—a reflection of the self-giving way in which God relates to his people in Christ (cf. Eph 5:22-23). The net result is the integration of society where a monogamous pattern predominates.

The fourth day of Creation opens our eyes to more than sunlight and moonlight! Notice that the text avoids naming the heavenly luminaries. The sun and moon are called "the greater light" and "the lesser light." The stars are dismissed with a passing reference. Why this reluctance to speak about that which we are so prone to rhapsodize and romanticize? The polytheistic world surrounding Israel provides the answer. The worship of the sun, moons, stars, and other heavenly bodies goes back to the mists of antiquity. Who has not heard of the horoscope! Even Abram's father Terah was a moon-worshipper (Jos 24:2). The creation narrative quietly, but effectively, lays this idolatry to rest. The sun and moon are mere servants of God who do his bidding. Their primary significance for Israel concerns their function in reminding Israel of her sacred times, times set apart to celebrate the goodness, power, and faithfulness of the Creator-God. By no means are they to be revered or feared.

On the fifth day "God created the great creatures of the sea" (Ge 1: 21). The Hebrew word for these creatures is *tannîn*, a word used generally for various large, aquatic creatures. In a few texts, however, it refers to sea monsters like Rahab and Leviathan (Ps 74:13). Here the term simply refers to large creatures inhabiting the seas. The author deliberately undercuts the pagan notion of divine combat with a chaos monster as in *Enumah Elish*. The great sea creatures are not gods or goddesses; they are Yahweh's creatures who obey his will.

Lastly, we note the sublime narration of mankind's creation. What a contrast with *Enumah Elish* and other ancient creation accounts! Whereas *Enumah Elish* portrays humans as mere slaves of the gods, Genesis 1 endows the male and female with the very image of God—they are kings and queens of the entire earth. Humans are an afterthought in the pagan version—lackeys to meet the needs of gods who are overindulgent, selfish brats. The Hebrew version not only places mankind at the very climax of creation, but also bestows dignity and honor upon them—they rule as God's vice-regents. Not surprisingly, in the ancient world kings routinely treated their subjects as mere slaves, whose only purpose in life was to meet their regal whims and desires. After all, these kings were only imitating the behavior of their gods.[35]

More could be said on this topic, but the point has been established: Genesis 1 makes a bold affirmation about origins that is fundamentally at odds with the prevailing views. Not only did it refute wrong ideas about origins then, but it continues to speak the truth now in a world still beset by false cosmogonies (theories regarding the origins of the universe).

Two primary competitors challenge the Genesis version of origins today. The first of these is pantheism (the notion that the forces and workings of nature in their totality are "God," that is, all that is, is God). Unfortunately, this well-worn view has made a remarkable resurgence in North American culture of late, especially on college and university campuses. The primary vehicles have been various eastern religions and cults. It also underlies "New Age" thought, popularized and promoted by figures like Shirley MacLaine. The blurring of matter and God is a fundamental error of pantheism. Or to put it another way, pantheism denies or downplays the transcendence of God. This in turn leads to a virtual denial or radical redefinition of evil. If all reality is God, how does one account for the presence of evil? Is God evil or is evil an illusion? Pantheism generally affirms that what we all experience as evil in life—hardship, suffering, disease, death, natural disasters, and so on—is just an illusion. This is very difficult to maintain and is in fact a persuasive argument against pantheism.[36]

Genesis 1 affirms a radical disjunction between God, who is eternal, and matter, which is temporal. Nor does matter emanate (come forth) from God the pure Spirit. That is to say, matter is not of the same essence as God; rather, God spoke into existence that which had not previously existed, namely, matter. This doctrine is called *creatio ex nihilo*, creation out of nothing. *Note carefully that the doctrine does not say nothing produced something—a logical impossibility.* Rather, God, the eternally self-existent one, brought into being by his incomparable power that which had no prior existence or being. Scripture itself teaches this view: "By faith we understand that the universe was formed at God's command, so that what is seen was not made out of what was visible" (Heb 11:3). Furthermore, the Bible takes evil seriously—it has an actual existence in the universe. The source of evil is neither God nor matter as Genesis 1–3 makes clear. We will take up the question of the origin of evil in chapter three.

Another formidable challenge to creation faith is materialism or naturalism. This opinion holds that the only reality in the universe is physical matter in its various movements and modifications. Even thought and feelings are derived from the "stuff" of the universe. Those who subscribe to a thorough-going, cosmic evolution affirm this view. For them, Genesis 1:1 should be rewritten: "In the beginning was matter." As Carl Sagan intones during the opening line of the TV series "Cosmos": "The Cosmos is all that is, or ever was, or ever will be."[37] On the contrary, the scripture affirms the primacy of spirit—an eternal Spirit who created the universe freely and without the use of previously existing matter.

If you think about it, one is confronted with three fundamental options with regard to origins. Either 1) matter is eternal, or 2) God is eternal, or 3) nothing is eternal. The last view is absurd, so for all practical purposes, one is left with options one and two. Both boggle the mind because we cannot conceive of anything that has always been. Eternity is a category beyond our experience. We keep asking the child's question: But who made God?

There is a great difference, however, between options one and two. If matter is the supreme and ultimate reality, then what is to be made of personality, feelings, and thought? Are these aspects of our life mere accidents or by-products of nature? Do they have any real significance in an impersonal world? Only the view that a personal, eternal God brought into existence the temporal order, consisting of both personal beings and impersonal matter, can give ultimate meaning to our lives. Genesis 1 affirms that we are made in his image. That affirmation gives our lives significance. As such we are rational, volitional, emotional beings who are accountable and valuable to him. We are created for fellowship and communion with him; our highest aim in life is "to glorify God, and to enjoy him forever."[38] *Personality, then, is an essential, enduring aspect of life. Indeed, the universe makes no sense until one has discovered its ultimately personal dimension in the great Creator-God.*

The Genesis Account Is Doxological

Genesis 1 is doxological (having as its purpose the praise of God). In worship services we sing together "Praise God from whom all blessings flow. . . ." The Genesis account of beginnings was likewise designed to elicit from Israel praise to the great Creator. The chapter divisions of our English Bibles are a relatively late innovation; it was not until the 16th century A.D. that these were introduced. For the most part, the divisions are satisfactory; the creation narrative is an exception—the chapter division should have been placed after 2:3. When 1:1–2:3 is read as a unit, a most important aspect of the passage suddenly becomes evident—the climax of the account is the seventh day! Even though the creation of humans on day six is the apex of the creative acts, *the focus of the entire account is the Sabbath.*

Thus the creation week, climaxed by the Sabbath, serves as the pattern for the life of Israel. Man and woman work, just as God worked, for six days. Then there is a cessation from labor. Israel pauses and reflects, not only upon the work of her hands during the week past, but most importantly, upon the works of God's hands. There is a sacred rhythm to life, a dance, if you will, in which Creator and creature come together to celebrate the miracle of life. At the center of attention, adorned by the praises of his people, stands the majestic Creator-God. The hymns of Israel resound with creation faith:

> O LORD, our Lord, how majestic is your name in all the earth!
> You have set your glory above the heavens. . .
> When I consider your heavens,
> the work of your fingers,
> the moon and the stars,
> which you have set in place. . . (Ps 8:1, 3; 19:1-6; 33:6-9; and others)

So every Sabbath, Israel praises God for his power, wisdom, and love. Genesis 1:1–2:3 is foundational for this praise. The people of God today greatly impoverish their spiritual lives if there is not a corresponding sacred rhythm. On Sunday, the Lord's Day, the day of a "new creation," there still needs to be heard the confession of the early Church: "I believe in God the Father Almighty, creator of heaven and earth."

The Genesis Account Is Historical

A third purpose of the Genesis account of origins is historical. Since Genesis was written well before the rise of modern science, it obviously is not a scientific account. Neither is it historical in the same sense as the account of David's reign in 2 Samuel. There were no human observers of creation; the facts of creation are discovered by revelation rather than by scientific investigation. Still, it is presented as a sober statement summarizing what happened "in the beginning."[39]

It is a simple *phenomenological* description of origins. By phenomenological, we mean that Genesis 1 is written from the standpoint of an unassisted observer. Notice, for example, that nothing is enumerated in the heavens or on the earth that cannot be seen with the naked eye. For example, the multitudes of microscopic organisms, which teem on planet earth, are not even mentioned! Yet one must not equate simplicity with falsehood. The most knowledgeable physicists regularly speak of the sun rising and setting without anyone charging them with error! It is simply a matter of conventional language. Thus Genesis 1, viewed as a simple, phenomenological account of origins, communicates the basic and essential truths of creation. This was so for its original hearers/readers, as well as for our own day. God wisely chose a medium of revelation that did not require human beings to amass the knowledge they now possess before they could understand it![40] Modern science cannot improve upon the creation account.[41] This recognition already precludes many of the problems that have arisen in the so-called Bible-science controversy.

Viewed in the context of canonical Scripture, *Genesis 1 is the indispensable backdrop for salvation history*. Viewed as a part of Genesis, the creation account is inseparably linked to the whole. Genesis consists of ten "accounts" or main sections. These are easily discerned by a recurring formula: "This is the account of. . . ." The following chart illustrates this feature of Genesis.

The Ten Accounts of Genesis

The Account of the Heavens and the Earth	Genesis 2:4
The Written Account of Adam's Line	Genesis 5:1
The Account of Noah	Genesis 6:9
The Account of Shem, Ham and Japheth	Genesis 10:1
The Account of Shem	Genesis 11:10
The Account of Terah	Genesis 11:27
The Account of Abraham's Son Ishmael	Genesis 25:12
The Account of Abraham's Son Isaac	Genesis 25:19
The Account of Esau	Genesis 36:1
The Account of Jacob	Genesis 37:1

The author of Genesis gives no clues that 1:1–2:3 should be treated any differently than the other sections. It forms the indispensable prologue to the unfolding story of God's choice of Israel to be his special people. Consequently, we think it best to affirm the essential historicity of the creation account.

Provisions of the Biblical Teaching on Creation

We have already touched upon some important implications flowing out of creation faith. We now set out four provisions of the biblical teaching on creation that enable us to see reality from God's point of view.

Provides the Foundation for Scientific Inquiry

The biblical view of creation encourages us to discover God's footprints in the universe. We refer to the history of science. A number of philosophers have drawn attention to the intellectual environment in which modern science arose. It was in the West, steeped in Judeo-Christian tradition, where pioneering scientists formulated the scientific method that led to epochal discoveries. This was not an accident. Francis Bacon, Johannes Kepler, Galileo Galilei, and Sir Isaac Newton (among others) assumed something about the universe: it was an orderly system obeying laws and principles built in by the Creator. The universe was not divine, nor was it random and chaotic. These giants of the scientific enterprise, without reluctance, investigated nature because: (1) they did not view nature as infused by deity, and (2) they saw themselves as creatures encouraged and endowed to explore the world.

Both of these assumptions were problematic, if not inconceivable, in the East where pantheistic philosophy prevailed. In the polytheism of the ancient world, there was a dread of nature since the various gods/goddesses controlled different aspects of it. The ancients did everything they could to stay on good terms with Mother Nature, since Mother Nature was really the sum total of the various deities. Exploration into this realm was strictly a matter of "travel at your own risk!" In some respects, this dread still exists in pantheistic systems.

The Christian worldview, founded upon OT teaching, liberated people from such a baseless fear or from excessive reverence of nature. The contribution of the Bible to modern science can hardly be overemphasized. As Bruce Waltke, an OT theologian, has noted:

> By speaking the truth in a world of lies, God emancipated man from the fear of creation to the freedom to research it and bring it under his dominion. Here, then, was the sound, philosophical foundation on which true science could progress. Man could now stand at a distance from matter as an observer, calm and unafraid.[42]

These sentiments are echoed by Harvey Cox, another theologian: "Wherever nature is perceived as an extension of himself or his group, or as the embodiment of the divine, science, as we know it, is precluded."[43]

It is true that, in some instances, the Church appealed to a faulty interpretation of the Bible in order to squash certain scientific theories (for example, the heliocentric view of the solar system). Nonetheless, the overall development and progress of science would not have been possible without the Bible's liberating view of reality.

Provides an Understanding of Ourselves

We have already drawn attention to the significant difference between the view of *Enumah Elish* and Genesis regarding human beings. The OT has a lofty view of humanity. They are but a "little lower than the heavenly beings" (Ps 8:5); they are rulers over the works of God's hands (Ps 8:6a); and "everything is placed under their feet" (Ps 8:6b). While it is true that "all men are grass, and all their glory is like the flowers of the field" (Isa 40:6), it is also true that God has "set eternity in the hearts of men" (Ecc 3:11). This curious tension between the greatness and smallness of humans is graphically portrayed in Genesis 2:7. Human beings are a combination of dust and God's breath (more will be said about this in chapter nine). This composite, living being bears the stamp of God's image (Ge 1:26-27). As such he/she possesses dignity and honor. This image-bearing creature, alone of all God's creatures, is able to relate to, commune with, and express love for the great Creator-King. The worth of each individual is such that no one may murder a fellow human being without forfeiting one's own life (Ge 9:6). In a throwaway society such as ours, where numbers replace names, young people are deciding, in increasing numbers, that suicide is preferable to life. The message of the OT about the worth of each individual remains a beacon of hope for those who feel forgotten and forsaken by an impersonal world.

Provides Information Concerning the Nature of God

What is God like? The OT teaching on creation affords some mind-boggling insights into the nature of the one with whom we have to do—the God of the universe. We can summarize a large quantity of material here by focusing on four attributes of God, which the revelation dealing with creation underscores.

He transcends the natural order. Even if one were to explore every nook and cranny of the universe (impossible), and were to understand the workings of it all (unthinkable), one would not have exhausted the dimensions of God's essence, power, and knowledge. God is above and quite independent of creation. *He alone is self-existent*. This is what is meant by God's transcendence.

The OT expresses this truth in a number of ways. One way is through the concept of great height. Especially noteworthy is the appellation "Most High." Consider this: "Let them know that you, whose name is the LORD—that you alone are the Most High over all the earth" (Ps 83:18). "How awesome is the LORD Most High, the great King over all the earth" (Ps 47:2). Of course, the most frequent manner of describing God's transcendence is by the declaration that he inhabits heaven. The Hebrew word *sh_mayîm*, though sometimes used of the sky, or of the realm of the heavenly bodies, is most often used of God's dwelling place. This "place" is beyond all that has been made. We, at the beginning of the 21st century, have learned that the universe is incredibly large and—if the current theories are correct—is continuing to expand! Yet all lies within the scope and power of the God of "the heavens and the earth, the sea, and all that is in them" (Ex 20:11).

Another way of affirming God's transcendence relates to the notion of time and eternity. God is eternal. Though aware of time and acting within time, he is not subject to time as we are. Psalm 93:2 states that God is "from all eternity." Psalm 90:2, 4 reminds us that "from everlasting to everlasting you are God. . . . For a thousand years in your sight are like a day that has just gone by, or like a watch in the night." The OT clearly teaches the transcendence of God.

He is immanent in creation. The gospel song "He's Everything to Me" says: "Then I knew that he was more than just a God who didn't care, who lived away out there. And now he walks beside me, day by day." The OT repeatedly affirms the presence of God everywhere in his universe. This is not the same as pantheism. God is not literally in every object or substance in the cosmos; but *his spirit is everywhere present in the cosmos*.

No portion of the Hebrew Bible makes this point as profoundly as Psalm 139: "Where can I go from your Spirit? Where can I flee from your presence?" The implied answer is "nowhere." The psalmist finds great comfort and confidence in the God who is there—always there. In verses 1-6, the psalmist is awestruck at the complete knowledge God has concerning him all the time. In verses 7-13, there is no dimension, no direction and no darkness that shuts the psalmist off from the all-seeing, all-knowing God. Even as a developing embryo, the psalmist was in full view of God; indeed, God created him in his mother's womb, recapitulating the creation of the first Adam (vv. 13-16). These verses could be multiplied many times over.

He is sovereign over all creation. The old spiritual "He's Got the Whole World in His Hands" is right on target. So is the hymn "This Is My Father's World." Psalm 33:11 speaks for many passages in declaring that "the plans of the LORD stand firm forever, the purposes of his heart through all generations." Though Bildad the Shuhite held a defective theology with regard to evil, he was "right on" when it comes to God's sovereignty: "Dominion and awe belong to God; he establishes order in the heights of heaven" (Job 25:2).

The most frequent image, by far, in the OT representation of God, is that of king. He is the sovereign who reigns over his kingdom. Jewish prayers still address God as king of the universe. Today some theologians argue that such imagery is unfortunate. They suggest that it has contributed to oppression and injustice. They would rewrite theology using the paradigm of God as "lover."[44] This "new theology" feels free to make God in a new image rather than patiently listening to God's voice in Scripture. The biblical portrait of God as the great king, far from contributing to injustice in the world, exalts him as a faithful, loving benefactor whose rule *combines mercy and justice in precisely the right proportions*. His love and wrath are not mutually exclusive, and without both, moral government of the world would be impossible. Let us not be timid about God's sovereignty. This truth is the basis for courage and confidence in a not-always-so-nice world. (Why there are "bad things" in the world will be examined next in chapter three.) The eternal rule of God is our hope for all ages.

He is good. The goodness of God can be inferred from creation. We have all sensed this deeply. Who has not been moved by the grandeur, the marvels, the bounty of God's creation? Though we are troubled at times by the presence of evil, for the most part, North Americans enjoy the bounties of the good earth. As we saw earlier, the evidence for design in creation is unmistakable, and that design points to a near perfect life-support system for mankind. This cannot be an accident. The evidence points to a good God who has our welfare and well-being at heart.

The OT underscores this truth. Psalm 104 is a meditative hymn based upon Genesis 1. It celebrates the on-going providential control of the Lord over his creation. Note especially the emphasis upon the Lord's provision. The Lord supplies water, food, and shelter for all his creatures (vv. 11-23), and thus "these all look to [the Lord] to give them their food at the proper time" (v. 27). The upshot is that the psalmist exclaims "I will sing praise to my God as long as I live" (v. 33b). The goodness of God is not something reserved for the righteous, though it is certainly promised them (Ps 84:11). Even the unrighteous, the disobedient, are the beneficiaries of God's goodness (Ps 25:8). Jesus was not relating something unheard of when he reminded his disciples that "your Father in heaven . . . causes his sun to rise on the evil and the good, and sends rain on the righteous and the unrighteous" (Mt 5:45). The child's prayer cannot be improved: "God is great; God is good. Let us thank him for our food."

Provides a Partial Understanding of the Problem of Evil

The last provision of the biblical teaching about creation has to do with the problem of evil. *The problem of evil is the most difficult in Scripture.* We are not going to pretend to have an airtight solution. Furthermore, it is not our purpose here to delve into this issue—we will consider it in more depth in the next chapter. But we can affirm, based on the biblical view of creation, that the problem of evil is not located in the physical dimension of creation. That is to say, *evil is not inherent in the "stuff" of the universe.* There was no built-in flaw that was beyond God's capability to prevent; there was no engineering failure which tragically caused a catastrophe. God's wisdom and power absolutely rule out such an explanation. Indeed, we boldly say that to attempt a resolution of the problem by limiting God in either his wisdom, power, or goodness is a major failure of trust. A fair reading of Scripture simply will not permit us to scale back these attributes of God so that we can come up with what seems to us a satisfying answer to the question of evil.[45] When creation was finished, it was "very good" (Ge 1:31).

As we shall see in the next chapter, evil arises in the will of creatures having the power of contrary choice. To put it another way, evil was possible as soon as God made creatures with the ability to disobey. When Adam and Eve disobeyed God, evil became a reality on planet earth. Thus the spiritual dimension is where evil first appeared; from this realm it adversely affected the physical realm. For now we reiterate our earlier statement that biblical Christianity should not have a bias against the physical. Though not the ultimate principle in the universe—physical matter plays a subservient role to the spiritual dimension—neither is it the villain.

Perspective on the Biblical Teaching of Creation

We conclude this chapter by standing back and trying to get the big picture. No one can understand creation properly until Jesus Christ is taken into consideration. *Christ is the key to creation.* Why do we say that? Because *Christ is the Creator!* This astounding fact is not clearly perceived in the OT itself. There are, however, three passages that either intimate, or prepare the way for, the fuller revelation of the NT with regard to origins. They are Genesis 1:2, 26 and Proverbs 8:22-31.

The Genesis passage implies that there is a plurality of persons within the godhead. In verse two, the Spirit of God hovers over the pre-creation chaos. While one may object that this is a mere extension of the one God, comparison of Scripture with Scripture leads to the inference that the Spirit of God possesses a distinct personality. To be sure, this inference is heavily indebted to the NT.[46] We are assuming, however, that both Testaments originate by the self-same Holy Spirit. There is an essential harmony in the teaching of Scripture.

The passage in Proverbs uses the literary technique of personification. That is, God's wisdom is treated as a distinct personality, so much so that in verse 30, God's wisdom is called "the craftsman at his side" who was "filled with delight day after day; rejoicing always in his presence." In the NT, at least two writers, John and Paul, go a step further. God's wisdom is "fleshed out" in a real, distinct person. This person, the pre-existent Word of God (compare the repetition of the phrase "and God said" in Ge 1) is none other than Jesus of Nazareth "through whom all things were made" (Jn 1:1-14; 1Co 1:30; Col 1:15-20).

Thus we are confronted by a great mystery—*the Creator became part of his creation!* (Php 2:5-7). Just as modern cosmologists have rolled the cosmic clock back to the very moment of "the big bang," but cannot penetrate any further, so readers of Scripture are left standing in awe of the impenetrable mystery of incarnation: "Beyond all question, the mystery of godliness is great: He appeared in a body . . ." (1Ti 3:16). *The Scripture thus presents a triune God; Father, Son, and Holy Spirit who cooperate in the work of creation.* In this enterprise, the Father is the *source* of all things (1Co 8:6). The Son is accorded the role of *mediator*. He is the one through whom, by whom and for whom creation exists (Jn 1:3; Col 1:16; Heb 1:2). The Holy Spirit is the *executor* who carries out the plan (Ge 1:2). Paul's grandest vision comes into view when he says that God's ultimate will is "to bring all things in heaven and on earth together under one head, even Christ" (Eph 1:10).

For those who acknowledge Jesus as Lord, there can scarcely be a more comforting truth about creation than this: Jesus has become one with us in order that we might become one with the triune God. The oneness is not that of absorption into God, but rather of intimate fellowship and communion with God (Jn 17:21-23; Heb 2:14-18). This results in a robust sense of security. As Paul says: "I am convinced that [nothing] in all creation will be able to separate us from the love of God that is in Christ Jesus our Lord" (Ro 8:39). In short, the present created order is under the complete sovereignty of Christ, who not only created it, but has entered into it. Because of the entrance of sin, the present creation yearns to experience a re-creation (Ro 8:10-21; cf. Rev 21:1, 5). Christ also mediates the new creation (2Co 5:17). Thus the present order is not ultimate. One is foolish indeed to seek final significance in the universe (Mt 16:26). The universe is bounded by "the Alpha and the Omega, the Beginning and the End" (Rev 21:6); he alone can offer us that which is ultimate (Mt 24:35; 1Jn 2:17).

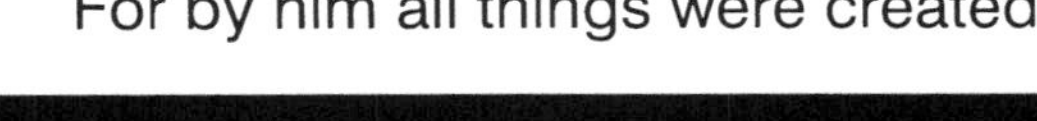
For by him all things were created

Relationship of Theme to the Core Concepts

The Unity of God's Plan of Salvation: The doctrine of creation establishes the framework for redemptive history. Beyond that, it establishes the rationale for redemptive history. Because humans, and only humans, bear God's image, they are uniquely related to the Creator. The image of God in each individual, though distorted and disfigured from what it was, gives a value and meaning to each life that cannot be compared to any other created thing or being. Here is a point where some animal rights activists have missed the boat (cf. Mt 10:31). God desires to save the masterpiece of his creative activity and to see his own image fully reflected in them. This is not to say that God is obligated by some psychological or moral necessity to save; only that *humans are worth saving*. Furthermore, the unity and solidarity of the human race establishes a means whereby God could effect a salvation sufficient for all. This means was through the incarnation, substitutionary death, and resurrection of Jesus Christ. He, as a Second Adam, now heads up a *new race*—which will be perfectly conformed to his image at his coming (Ro 8:29). The unity of the human race is thus a corollary to the unity of God's redemptive plan.

Faith and Politics: Politics, the art and science of exercising authority, is grounded in the creation mandate "let them rule" (Ge 1:26). *Christians should view politics not as a necessary evil, but as a necessary good.* The Creator provides both the capability and the model for this enterprise. As his vice-regents, we are obligated to reflect, within creaturely limits, his beneficent rule over all things. The ultimate aim of politics is that we might continue to experience God's creation blessings: "Be fruitful and increase in number; fill the earth and subdue it" (Ge 1:28).

Faith and Ethics: We have seen the crucial connection between one's view of reality and behavior. Polytheism could never sustain a truly ethical society because the gods worshiped were not consistently ethical. The Hebrew doctrine of creation is rooted in ethical monotheism: one, true, and living God who is the source of all things and who is good. As seen in the creation narratives, God desires that the crowning achievement of his creative work reflect his own goodness. Creation anchors the basic motivation for ethical living in personal accountability to a God who is good (Ge 2:17).

Faith and the Future: What God desires for humans in the end can be discerned in outline in the beginning. The creation mandate to subdue the earth remains the agenda for the future. There will be no escape of the spirit from the bondage and confines of the material order in God's completed salvation. *God's redemptive plan features a new earth as the ultimate residence of redeemed humanity.* Thus biblical eschatology is grounded in the doctrine of creation. There is, in the end, a return to the beginning.

For Further Discussion:

Does it really matter which view a Christian takes in regard to the interpretation of Genesis 1? Why or why not?

How does one's view of origins influence one's values and behavior?

Should sermons and Christian educational material make references to myth, fairy tales, legends and popular culture to illustrate spiritual and theological points?

For Further Reading:

Dyrness, William. *Themes in Old Testament Theology*, pp. 63-96. Downers Grove: InterVarsity, 1979. Discussion of theological issues involved in the biblical doctrine of creation.

Fuller, Daniel P. *The Unity of the Bible: Unfolding God's Plan for Humanity*, pp. 99-173. Grand Rapids: Zondervan, 1992. This section is an enlightening discussion about God's purpose in creation in light of the doctrine of the Trinity.

Sauer, Erich. *The Dawn of World Redemption*, pp. 17-31. Grand Rapids: Eerdmans, 1951. Helpful in showing how the biblical doctrine of creation provides the stage for the history of redemption.

There are many books written on the proper interpretation of Genesis 1 and the larger question of the relationship between the Bible and science. In addition to the works cited in the endnotes, we select the following, with an indication of the stance adopted.

Bube, Richard H. "Creation (A) How Should Genesis Be Interpreted?" *Journal of the American Scientific Affiliation* (March 1980): 34-39. Outlines the basic approaches, but holds the essentially non-literal approach.

Blocher, Henri. *In the Beginning: The Opening Chapters of Genesis*. Downers Grove: InterVarsity, 1984. Advocates the framework hypothesis and progressive creationism.

Carlson, Richard. Ed. *Science & Christianity: Four Views*. Downers Grove: InterVarsity, 2000. Surveys the various options mentioned in this chapter.

Davis, John Jefferson. *The Frontiers of Science and Faith: Examining Questions from the Big Bang to the End of the Universe*. Downers Grove: InterVarsity, 2002. Professor of Systematic Theology and Christian Ethics at Gordon Conwell Theological Seminary and winner of several Templeton Foundation awards for excellence in teaching on science and religion. Argues for a version of progressive creationism and addresses other science and faith issues.

Dembski, William A. *Intelligent Design: The Bridge Between Science and Theology*. Downers Grove: InterVarsity, 1999. Book by an articulate spokesman that challenges thoroughgoing Darwinism.

Fields, Weston. *Unformed and Unfilled*. Nutley, NJ: Presbyterian and Reformed, 1976. A defense of the gap theory.

Geisler, Norman. *Origin Science*. Grand Rapids: Baker, 1987. Defends the completely literal interpretation of Genesis 1.

Hyers, Conrad. *The Age of Creation: Genesis and Modern Science*. Atlanta: John Knox, 1984. Discusses the larger issues involved in the debate, and argues that one must recognize a dichotomy between religious and scientific truth. His approach is compatible with theistic evolution.

McGrath, Alister E. *Glimpsing the Face of God: The Search for Meaning in the Universe*. Grand Rapids: Eerdmans, 2002. A leading British evangelical philosopher and theologian provides an updated overview of the quest to understand origins.

Pun, Pattle P. T. *Evolution-Nature and Scripture in Conflict?* Grand Rapids: Zondervan, 1982. Argues for an essentially literal approach involving progressive creationism.

Ratzsch, Del. *The Battle of Beginnings*. Downers Grove: InterVarsity, 1996. Discusses the very contentious debate among evangelicals about origins.

Sauer, Erich. *The King of the Earth*, pp. 193-242. Grand Rapids: Eerdmans, 1962. Discussion of the various options with a defense of the day-age theory.

Stones, Don. *A New Look at an Old Earth: Resolving the Conflict Between the Bible and Science*. Updated and expanded. Eugene, OR: Harvest House, 1997.

Van Til, Howard J. *The Fourth Day*. Grand Rapids: Eerdmans, 1986. Argues against a completely literal interpretation of Genesis 1.

Youngblood, Ronald. *The Genesis Debate*, pp. 12-109. Grand Rapids: Baker, 1990. Reviews the various options for interpreting Genesis 1.

Endnotes

1. I am indebted to Richard H. Bube for his explanation of the three major approaches. See his "Creation (A) How Should Genesis Be Interpreted?" *Journal of the American Scientific Affiliation* (March 1980): 34-39.

2. Those interested may pursue the arguments further by consulting Henry M. Morris, *Biblical Cosmology and Modern Science* (Nutley, NJ: Craig, 1970); John C. Whitcomb Jr., *The Early Earth* (Grand Rapids: Baker, 1972); relevant issues of *Creation Research Society Quarterly*.

3. See Davis A. Young's *Christianity and the Age of the Earth* (Grand Rapids: Zondervan, 1982), pp. 27-40 for this and other explanations for fossils put forward by Christians.

4. Bruce Waltke provides a detailed refutation of the gap theory in *Creation and Chaos* (Portland, OR: Western Conservative Baptist Seminary, 1974), pp. 19-25.

5. See a stout defense in Arthur B. Custance, *Without Form and Void* (Brockville, Canada: Custance, 1970).

6. Bernard Ramm lists the early proponents of this theory in *The Christian View of Science and Scripture* (Grand Rapids: Eerdmans, 1955), p. 211. Modern adherents may be read by referring to n. 2, p. 211.

7. For further information, see Henry M. Morris and John C. Whitcomb, *The Genesis Flood* (Grand Rapids: Baker, 1965); John C. Whitcomb, *The World that Perished* (Grand Rapids: Baker, 1973) and Joseph C. Dillow, *The Waters Above: Earth's Pre-flood Vapor Canopy* (Chicago: Moody Press, 1981).

8. See Davis Young, *Creation and the Flood* (Grand Rapids: Baker, 1977) and *Christianity and the Age of the Earth* (Grand Rapids: Zondervan, 1982).

9. For more on this topic, see R. John Snow, *Genesis One and the Origin of the Earth* (Downers Grove: InterVarsity, 1977), pp. 125-135 and Meredith G. Kline, "Because It Had Not Rained," *WTJ* 20 (May 1958): 146-157.

10. For an example of this approach see Erich Sauer, *The King of the Earth* (Grand Rapids: Eerdmans, 1962), pp. 193-228.

11. See P. J. Wiseman, *Creation Revealed in Six Days* (London: Marshall, Morgan and Scott, 1948).

12. For a defense of this view, see Henri Blocher, *In the Beginning: The Opening Chapters of Genesis*, trans. David G. Preston (Downers Grove: InterVarsity, 1984).

13. See E. J. Young, "The Days of Genesis," *WTJ* 25 (Nov. 1962–May 1963): 1-34, 143-171.

14. For this discussion, I am indebted to Stephen B. Clark, *Man and Woman in Christ: An Examination of the Roles of Men and Women in Light of Scripture and the Social Sciences* (Ann Arbor: Servant, 1980).

15. See George W. Coats, *Genesis: With an Introduction to Narrative Literature* (Grand Rapids: Eerdmans, 1983), p. 47: "If ancient Near Eastern myths lie behind this unit, it is nonetheless clear that the unit is no longer myth. . . . " Compare Walter C. Kaiser Jr., "The Literary Form of Genesis 1–11," *New Perspectives on the Old Testament*, ed. J. Barton Payne (Waco: Word, 1970), pp. 54-55.

16. See Oscar Cullmann, "The Connection of Primal Events and End Events with the New Testament Redemptive History," in *The Old Testament and Christian Faith: A Theological Discussion,* ed. Bernhard W. Anderson (New York: Herder and Herder, 1969), pp. 115-123.

17. See Gordon Fee and Douglas Stuart, *How to Read the Bible for All Its Worth,* 2d ed. (Grand Rapids: Zondervan, 1993), chapters 10 and 13 for a definition and description of prophecy and apocalyptic.

18. This is defended by Jan Lever, *Where Are We Headed?* trans. Walter Lagerway (Grand Rapids: Eerdmans, 1970), pp. 22-23.

19. See Kaiser, "Literary Form," pp. 48-65.

20. See Blocher, *Beginning*, pp. 23-24:

> The fact that the primary purpose of Genesis is not to instruct us in geology does not exclude the possibility that it says something of relevance to the subject. In the last analysis, one cannot make an absolute separation between physics and metaphysics, and religion has to do with everything, precisely because all realms are created by God and continue to depend on

him. To oppose 'doctrine' and (factual) 'history' is to forget that biblical doctrine is first of all history. Faith rests on facts, objectively asserted.

21. For a survey of evangelical opinion on the subject of origins see Bill Durban Jr., "How It All Began: Why Can't Evangelical Scientists Agree?" *Christianity Today*, no. 32 (12 August 1988): 31-41.

22. Following William Sanford LaSor, David Allan Hubbard, and Frederich Wm. Bush, *Old Testament Survey* (Grand Rapids: Eerdmans, 1982), p. 74.

23. Compare Blocher, *Beginning*, p. 223.

24. See Clifford Penner, *A Gift for All Ages* (Waco: Word, 1986).

25. A useful translation and abridgement with explanatory notes is found in D. Winton Thomas, *Documents from Old Testament Times* (New York: Harper and Row, 1961), pp. 3-16.

26. Ibid., p. 5.

27. Ibid.

28. Ibid., p. 6.

29. Ibid., pp. 9-10.

30. Ibid., p. 12.

31. For further information, see Mary K. Wakeman, *God's Battle with the Monster: A Study in Biblical Imagery* (Leiden: E. J. Brill, 1973).

32. For the following, I am indebted to Waltke, *Creation*, pp. 13-15.

33. Taken from the book, *Chronological Charts of the Old Testament* by John H. Walton. Copyright © 1978 by The Zondervan Corporation. Used by permission of Zondervan Publishing House. Pg. 33.

34. For more information, see Walton, *Ancient Israelite Literature*, p. 26.

35. As A. W. Tozer has observed, "There is a spiritual law that we grow toward the mental image we have of God" (*Knowledge of the Holy* [New York: Harper, 1961], p. 9).

36. For a brief but helpful discussion of this issue, see Norman L. Geisler, *The Roots of Evil* (Grand Rapids: Zondervan, 1978), pp. 15-18.

37. See the book version *Cosmos* (New York: Random House, 1980), p. 4.

38. From *The Shorter Catechism*, question number one.

39. "To the author, it [Genesis 1] apparently constituted a sensible, unified record of the beginning of all things as made known by God through human and divine means." Samuel Schultz, *The Message of the Old Testament*, 3d abridged ed. (San Francisco: Harper and Row, 1986), p. 5.

40. Compare Ramm, *Christian View*, pp. 67-69.

41. Compare the statement of W. F. Albright:

> It is not, therefore, surprising that it [Genesis 1] stands comparison with ephemeral modern cosmogonies so well that it will endure, we confidently believe, long after they have perished. The current effort to "square Genesis with science" is as futile as the search for perpetual motion—and as lacking in philosophical insight ("Recent Discoveries in Bible Lands," a supplement to *Analytical Concordance to the Bible*, edited by Robert Young, 22d rev. ed. [Grand Rapids: Eerdmans, n.d.], p. 28).

42. *Creation*, p. 48.

43. *The Secular City* (New York: Macmillan, 1965), p. 24.

44. See, for example, Anna Case-Winters, *God's Power* (Louisville: Westminster/John Knox, 1990).

45. As in Harold S. Kushner, *When Bad Things Happen to Good People* (New York: Schoeken, 1981).

46. See the study notes listed in the index of the *NIVSB* under the heading "Holy Spirit."

chapter **3**

The Fall and the Flood

(Scripture reading: Genesis 3–11; Job 14:1-12; Psalms 14:1-3; 32; 51; 53:1-4; 90; Ecclesiastes 4:1-4; 9:3; Jeremiah 17:9-10)

Leading Questions

How did sin begin in the human race?
What was the essence of the original sin?
What were the consequences of the original sin?
What is the meaning and significance of the flood of Noah?
How does Genesis 1–11 relate to the rest of Scripture?

Introduction

The theme of sin and judgment pervades the OT. To synthesize this would require a considerable amount of space. We propose, therefore, to deal with this topic by examining Genesis 3–11. This section narrates the origin of sin in the human race and the dire consequences of its entrance; it also provides a microcosm of the entire problem of sin. By drawing out the truths of this section, we gain an understanding of the enormity of the problem.

The Prelude to the Flood

Thematically, Genesis 1–11 is a unit, constituting what scholars designate as the "Primeval History".[1] As such, chapters 2–11 are dominated by the account of the great flood of Noah. Diagrammatically, one can see the arrangement of the entire section in the following way.

Prelude to the Flood			The Flood	Postlude to the Flood
2:4-25 Setting for the story	3:1-24 Spawning of sin	4–5 Spread of sin	6–8 "Surgery" on a sinful world	9–11 Stubbornness of sin

The centerpiece of the section (chs. 6–8) is preceded by some key events leading up to this unprecedented judgment. Understanding this prelude is of utmost importance if we are to comprehend the nature and consequences of sin.

The Fall of Humankind (3:1-24)

The nature of the account. The account of the Fall is a literary masterpiece. It is one of the most profound stories in the Bible. The amazing thing about this narrative is its *artful simplicity coupled with its depth of theological and psychological insight.* With frugality of words, the narrator describes an event that resonates in the heart of the reader.

The nature of the narrative raises a question. Is this a historical narrative? Or is it a symbolic story? I think the answer lies somewhere in between. There is a historical core to the story. Paul appears to assume the historicity of Adam in his analogy between Adam and Christ in Romans 5. He also assumes the historicity of Eve's temptation in 2 Corinthians 11:3. On the other hand, there are symbolic features in the story: (1) The serpent is clearly identified by later biblical writers as Satan (2Co 11:3, 14; Rev 12:9; 20:2). (2) The tree of life and the tree of knowledge of good and evil are unknown to the present, created order. One would have to assume a completely different environment and setting for this period. Where in Genesis, however, are there indications of such a radical discontinuity between the pre-flood and post-flood eras? (3) The term "naked" carries a psychological nuance, and (4) the names of Adam and Eve have symbolic significance (3:19-20). What we have, then, is a unique kind of story which accomplishes two purposes: it tells about the historic introduction of sin into the human race and it describes the experience of each human being, who knows instinctively that he or she is guilty before God.[2]

The story itself has two basic foci: the temptation and the consequences of disobedience. First notice the temptation.

Satan's strategy. The sudden introduction of the serpent, a creature hostile to the Lord, raises a multitude of questions. We are not prepared for an evil being, coming unannounced into a scene of idyllic beauty and peace. Where did *he* come from? Why is he wicked if, as Genesis 1:31 says, everything was very good? Unfortunately, the answer is nowhere explicitly given in Scripture. *We are confronted with a deep mystery.*[3] Some early Church Fathers believed that Isaiah 14:12-15 and Ezekiel 28:12-17 narrated the pre-Adamic fall of Lucifer, the chief of the angels, now known as Satan. These texts were sometimes augmented by Luke 10:18 where Jesus said: "I saw Satan fall like lightning from heaven." But this interpretation of the above passages is doubtful.[4] That leaves us with little to go on. A plausible scenario, however, locates the origin of sin in the angelic realm. It makes sense to assume that Satan (like the tyrants in Isaiah 14 and Ezekiel 28) aspired to be like God (see 1Ti 3:6). In doing so, he became irrevocably opposed to God and his kingdom. We infer from Scripture that he is not alone in this endeavor; he is assisted by a host of fallen angels who are otherwise called demons. Though he is a creature, and thus limited in capability, he nevertheless is much more powerful than humans. He was acknowledged by our Lord as being the "prince of this world" (Jn 12:31).

Satan's strategy in the temptation is highly instructive. First, he attacks the wisdom of God (v. 1). Secondly, he attacks the word of God (v. 4). Finally, he attacks the will of God (v. 5).[5] The first two assaults are cleverly designed to "soften up" the human couple for the real objective of the temptation—to entice them to disobey God's will.

Look at the first attack. The question to the woman is couched in such a way as to instill doubt: "Did God really say. . . ?" How cunning is the question! In Genesis 2:16-17 God graciously invites Adam to enjoy the fruit of all the trees in the garden, *except one*. Adam is warned about the drastic results of eating from that one tree. Still, the mood of the invitation stresses God's liberality and goodness. However, the question of the serpent in 3:1 implies the stinginess and unreasonableness of God in not allowing the human pair to eat from *all* the fruit in the garden. One wonders if it was simply doubt about the factuality of the command that Satan was questioning. Perhaps Satan asks the question in a mocking, sarcastic tone so as to call into question the motivation of one who gave the command. In other words, to paraphrase, perhaps Satan is really saying this: "Eve, did God really give you such an unreasonable command? Does that not make you question God's wisdom?" The serpent focuses upon the motivation for the prohibition. He attempts to induce Eve to doubt that the Lord has her best interests at heart.

Satan then springs his second assault. This consists of an outright *denial* of God's word: "You will not surely die." For the first time we have a direct challenge to the word of God—his authority is questioned. One can only speculate how Eve felt as she heard this emphatic denial. Was she appalled at such a bold contradiction? Or was she enthralled with a creature who seemed to possess such self-assurance that he could contradict God himself? The narrator does not permit us to penetrate the thoughts of the actors.

Quickly, Satan follows up with an attack upon the will of God. According to Satan, God prevents anyone from being equal to himself. God, in short, cannot tolerate rivals. He is a jealous God who refuses to relinquish his unique power and position. Satan's argument is ironic. He, above all others, knows that it is impossible for a mere creature to become like God. That, however, is his greatest ambition, and *his first, futile attempt to achieve equality with God must have been the original sin in the universe*. Now, frustrated and banished, he entices Eve with the same prospect. How easy he makes it seem. Misled by half-truths, Eve imagines a golden opportunity to rise to a new level of existence.

Satan designs a blueprint for disobedience. To achieve his dark ambition, he sows seeds of doubt. These are germinated by a healthy dose of denial and fertilized by a liberal application of discontent. The result is to his liking: the humans disobey an explicit command of God.

What, after all, is the real essence of that first sin by the human pair? In Genesis 3:6, the text says "the woman saw that the fruit of the tree was good for food." Is physical appetite the essence of sin (food, sex, stimulation, etc.)? The Scripture does not locate it there (compare Jesus' words in Mk 7:14-23). Genesis 3:6 next says that the fruit was "pleasing to the eye"—the dimension of the aesthetic (that which appeals to our appreciation of beauty). Nor does Scripture single this out as the real culprit. What about the desirability for gaining wisdom? Are wisdom and knowledge the real source of the problem? Again, no real evidence can be found in Scripture indicating that this is the heart of the problem.

The specific sin is disobedience to the revealed will of God. This amounts to an act of rebellion. The rebellion must have been prompted by a lack of trust and by a sense of discontent. They no longer believe that God's will is best for them. We thus come to *unbelief* as a major factor.[6] However, if we probe further, is not the taproot of unbelief rooted in a wrong way of thinking? Why the discontent, envy, and lack of trust? For these attitudes to thrive there must be a perspective that evaluates everything with reference to self. We come, at last, to the ultimate issue of *pride*. Pride demands all our rights and privileges; we deserve them. Adam and Eve swallow the bait. In their minds, God is the selfish one, and they deserve to be on an equal footing. They do not want to be dependent upon God any longer; they want to be *independent, masters of their own destinies.*[7]

I think you will agree that there is no more powerful temptation than this. Who would not jump at the opportunity to be in full control of his or her life? In many ways, we succumb to this temptation all the time. Deep down we know that we cannot really be in complete control, but we certainly try hard at times—and pay for it dearly! Even eating disorders eventually come down to the issue of control. We could illustrate this same factor in a wide range of human activities. Let us be sure of one thing: the story of the Fall is our story too.

The consequences of disobedience. The staccato beat of the key verbs relates the fateful decision: *saw, took, ate,* and *gave*. Quickly, the rebellion unfolds. The consequences are both immediate and long-term. Verses seven and eight state that:

> . . . the eyes of both of them were opened, and they realized they were naked; so they sewed fig leaves together and made coverings for themselves . . . and they hid from the LORD God among the trees of the garden.

The act of disobedience results in a radical change of existence on planet earth. Disharmony and brokenness replace the harmony and unity of the garden. Disharmony cuts across all spheres of life and affects all relationships. *The fundamental relationships of life are now characterized by brokenness.*[8]

Notice, first of all, the relationship to God. Once the man and woman rebel, they attempt to escape from the presence of God. Fellowship and communion with the Deity give way to alienation and fear. Look at the sequence of verbs in verse 10: *heard, was afraid, was naked, hid.* The nakedness of the story is not mere physical nakedness; it is psychological nakedness as well. "Being exposed" is the heart of it. The man and his wife experience, for the first time, the emotion of guilt, that is, awareness of having done something wrong. The strong emotion of fear accompanies guilt.

Psychologically, humans do not handle guilt well at all. We try to erect defense mechanisms to deny or escape it. The human pair try to hide—but to no avail. They try to cover their "nakedness"—but with no success. They are exposed; they are guilty. Many psychologists and psychiatrists assert that a large percentage of their patients could be restored to sound mental health if they could only deal with guilt. Guilt is mental health enemy number one.

Unfortunately, too many health professionals try to talk their patients out of it. They treat guilt as if it were not a moral issue at all.[9]

The flight behavior of Adam and Eve demonstrates that spiritual death has occurred. Sin ruptures the relationship existing between the Creator and his crowning creation. Theologically, sin disrupts and divides. Similar to like-charged magnets, the sinful pair are repelled by the holiness of God. They cringe in fear expecting the worst, knowing they are culpable (deserving blame). The sense of alienation and estrangement from God, accompanied by anxiety and antagonism, are sure signs of spiritual death (see Eph 2:1; Col 1:21). The most important relationship in life has experienced brokenness—this spills over into the other relationships.

Interpersonal relationships are also affected. No human relationship is as intimate as that of husband and wife. Since it is foundational to all of society, it is a sort of miniature of all the others. Alas, sin mars even this. Whereas in 2:23 we hear Adam's joy over Eve, now we hear his accusation: "The woman you put here with me—she gave me some fruit from the tree and I ate it" (v. 12). How quickly he who would have given himself for his beloved is prepared to abandon her! Contrast Adam's attitude with that of Jesus Christ (the second Adam) in Ephesians 5:25. There could hardly be a clearer example of passing the buck than Adam's reply. Laying the blame elsewhere, or finding a scapegoat, is a well-established device humans employ in their futile effort to escape guilt. Notice that the man is not above implicating God in the blame as well. The woman raises the technique to a new level of sophistication when she is interrogated. Her response can be paraphrased: "The Devil made me do it!"

Those contemplating marriage need to ponder deeply the story of the Fall. Suddenly, the warmth, tenderness, and sense of oneness in Genesis 2:21-25 dissipate. From now on it is every man for himself or every woman for herself. Fallen human nature is such that romantic love alone can never survive the tendency toward selfishness. Marriage will not simply follow the script: "And they lived happily ever after." Marriage will require constant effort, adjustment, and commitment. Why is this? Because now that sin is a part of our very being, we have a tendency to be self-centered. Self-centered persons are prone to "cut and run" when they feel that they are not getting their needs met. They have a tendency to shut out those who obstruct their desires. These are the destructive tendencies that, left unchecked, will inevitably sever a "one flesh" relationship. Make no mistake about it—marriage will require, like earning a living (3:19), "the sweat of your brow!"

The breach of faith and loyalty between the first pair foreshadows a constantly replayed scenario in all other human relationships. Whether viewed at the level of children in a nursery or representatives convened at the United Nations General Assembly, one realizes the tragic consequences of that first rebellion. Rivalry, discord, bitterness, accusation, recrimination, and hatred (on and on the dreary recital goes) thrive in a fallen, divided, disharmonious world. No other known species destroys its own in such numbers and proportions as Homo sapiens. The closest competitors are rats!

To ignore this very pessimistic assessment of the human condition, apart from the grace of God, is a serious mistake. Starry-eyed optimism about the innate goodness of human beings must be countered by the consistent biblical teaching of the depravity of human beings. Sin affects all of life and every individual. This is the bad news; but until we have really grasped that fact, we are not ready for the good news.

There is one more major, broken relationship. Creation is not what it once was before the Fall. Disharmony characterizes our relationship to the environment. The curse upon the ground (v. 17) symbolizes a widespread devolution (degeneration). The present order, according to the Apostle Paul, is undergoing a process of decay. Elementary physics teaches us the same truth. The Second Law of Thermo- dynamics says that everything in a closed system tends toward a state of maximum entropy. Simply stated, everything is wearing out and running down! Paul calls this a "bondage" (Ro 8:20-21). In the Genesis story the necessity of painful toil and the appearance of thorns and thistles indicate this bondage (3:17).

Once again, we peer into mystery. Scientific studies of the cosmos make it abundantly clear that there is a dark side to the universe. Indeed, the vast reaches of space are positively hostile to life of any sort. The only known sanctuary is the glorious, blue planet earth, and even our "haven of rest" has its dark side. Hurricanes, earthquakes, tornadoes, and violent weather are reminders that we do not live in the Garden of Eden anymore. Chaos threatens to reassert its hold upon the earth. Even on the level of the microscopic, we encounter a whole host of germs, bacteria, and viruses that threaten to do us in. Add to all this the inherent dangers of living in a modern society (like flying, driving an automobile, riding a bicycle, or bungee-jumping), and you have the age of anxiety.

The other partner in the relationship is even more out of adjustment. The natural order has no greater enemy than Homo sapiens. We are greedy, unpredictable and wasteful. The plant and animal kingdoms are in grave danger from this bipedal mammal with the extraordinary brain. Our manner of operating, to judge by past history, is simply to take what we want when we want it. The result is tragic. Countless species of animals are extinct. Billions of tons of precious topsoil now lie in ocean shelves. Toxic chemicals threaten our water supply. Whole forests have disappeared and continue to do so at such an alarming rate that environmentalists fear a major climatological shift in the foreseeable future. Natural resources are fast disappearing from our "home." It is as if we have waged an all-out war against our own life-support system. Such a shortsighted approach is foolishness of the highest degree.[10]

In summary, Genesis 3 dramatically underscores the devastating consequences of the first human rebellion. Disharmony and brokenness have characterized life on planet earth from that moment until now. Furthermore, the consequences are seemingly irreversible. Genesis 3 concludes with cherubim and a flaming sword stationed at the entrance to the garden. The message is as clear as it is sobering—there is no apparent way back to Eden. The return home will be long and arduous and will necessitate the Lord's intervention.

The Fallenness of Humankind (Ge 4:1–6:8)

This section of the primeval history expands upon the consequences of sin. It graphically demonstrates the spread of sin throughout society. More deadly than the AIDS virus, sin, as a principle operating at the individual and societal level, mushrooms. We can label this section "the acceleration of sin." Like a snowball at the top of the hill, sin reaches avalanche proportions by the time we come to Genesis 6:8. Four episodes illustrate this avalanche.[11]

The murder of Abel (Ge 4:1-10). The first family produces the first fratricide (the murder of one's brother). Even though Adam and Eve experienced the forgiving grace of God (more will be said about this later), sin is still present in their lives. Sin, as a dominating force, passes in a mysterious way to their children. Cain and Abel are born with a sin nature (compare Ps 51:5). Abel recognizes his sinfulness and brings an animal sacrifice as an expression of his repentant attitude. Cain, on the other hand, demonstrates his sinful bent by deliberately not bringing a sin offering. The story implies that Cain refuses to acknowledge his sin and his need of God's forgiveness. His attitude could be epitomized by the slogan: "I'm OK, you're OK, we're all OK—OK!" But he is not OK. The Lord appeals to him and warns him: "If you do what is right, will you not be accepted? But if you do not do what is right, sin is crouching at your door; it desires to have you, but you must master it" (Ge 4:7).

Sin, here described as an animal of prey, preparing to pounce upon its victim, cannot be shrugged off. Cain, threatened by the evident blessing of God upon Abel, is obsessed by jealousy. Jealousy gives birth to hatred and hatred goads Cain to commit murder. Cain is not a victim in the sense that he cannot control his actions. On the contrary, the Lord holds him accountable for his deed (4:10). Because Cain stubbornly refuses to own up to his deep need of God's grace he is mastered by his sin nature. The result is the first murder in human history, and this in the very first family. Deeply shocked and grieved, Adam and Eve taste the bitter fruit of their disobedience. Their rebellion leads to their firstborn son becoming an accursed outcast. The future for the human family does not look bright.

The Saga of Lamech (4:19-24). The next major episode deals with a descendant of Cain. "Like father, like son," is never truer than in this case. Lamech is also a rebel. He is a law unto himself. Filled with an overweening sense of pride, he feels free to alter the divine guidelines for family life. Genesis 2:24 implies (and Jesus confirms in Mt 19:4-6) that God's original intention was monogamy (being married to only one person at a time) as the pattern for marriage. Lamech succumbs to lust (for sex, power, and prestige) by taking two wives (4:19). This introduces the practice of polygamy (being married to more than one person at a time) into society. Violating the creation ideal of a "one flesh" relationship, Lamech unleashes a number of unhealthy dynamics in family life. The scriptural accounts of polygamous relationships sufficiently demonstrate the destructive consequences (envy, jealousy, rivalry, bitterness, murder, and incest, to name but a few).

There is more. Lamech is not content to leave crime and punishment to divine determination. He becomes judge, jury, and executioner all in one. The first urban vigilante arises! He arrogantly boasts about his murder of a youthful offender. Lamech becomes the bully on the block and marks off his turf. That is a dangerous precedent. Suddenly, the other Lamechs of that first civilization assert their rights. Society is now up for grabs and the powerful dominate the weak. The warlords battle it out for supremacy. Violence becomes a way of life.

The "litany of death" (5:1-32). The insertion of a genealogy, at first sight, breaks off the acceleration of sin. While the genealogy performs a number of functions in the overall story, we notice its relevance to our theme. Genesis 5 makes a profound statement about one of the most fearful consequences of sin. Note the repetition of the phrase "and then he died" after each patriarch (5:5, 8,

11, 14, 17, 20, 27, 31). The only exception is Enoch (whose translation will be discussed later). Even if one should surpass the Guinness world record for longevity (969 years by Methuselah), the outcome is inevitable. One day it shall be said of each one of us "and then he/she died."

The Lord had warned the man: "but you must not eat from the tree of knowledge of good and evil, for when you eat of it you will surely die" (Ge 2:17). Adam and Eve did not die physically at the precise moment of transgression. They did, however, die spiritually at that moment. We have already seen the evidence for this. In time, however, their bodies ceased functioning and decayed. Evidently, the Fall set in motion a sort of internal "clock" that eventuates in the dissolution of body and spirit. Genesis 5 illustrates the universality of this experience. Short of divine intervention (extremely rare; only two known exceptions in all of history—Enoch and Elijah!), all will undergo death. The apostle Paul confirms that physical death in the human race began with the sin of Adam (Ro 5:12-21). Richard Adelman, a medical researcher at the University of Pennsylvania, arrived at this observation about human longevity:

> . . . the maximal life span of a human organism is about 120 years. Cells can reproduce themselves only a certain number of times and the replication process ceases. Even if cells are frozen, when thawed they "remember" how many replications they have already made.[12]

This is all the more remarkable when one reads God's verdict in Genesis 6:3: " . . . his days will be a hundred and twenty years" (but see *NIVSB* note). I think it safe to assume that no amount of medical research will ever be able to "reset the clock" in order to achieve a virtual immortality for the human body. Only the Creator can bestow everlasting life.

Demonic invasion (6:1-8). The last episode, which introduces the great flood, reads like a Stephen King horror story. At face value, the narrative describes aliens who cohabit with humans and produce bloodthirsty giants! Because of the difficulties this passage presents, alternative interpretations have been proposed. The following chart summarizes the three leading views.[13]

**Identity of the "Sons of God"
Genesis 6:1-2**

Items	Theory No. 1	Theory No. 2	Theory No. 3
Sons of God	Fallen angels	Godly line of Seth	Dynastic rulers
Daughters of men	Mortals	Line of Cain	Commoners
Sin	Cohabitation between super-natural and mortal	Marriage of holy to unholy	Polygamy

Without being dogmatic, let me suggest what I think is going on in this passage. Even though it raises considerable problems, my preference is for the fallen angels interpretation. I am assuming that demons are fallen angels. Since the Gospels in the NT present demon possession as a real possibility (something which many Christians think still occurs today), and since angels sometimes assume corporal form in Scriptural narratives (Ge 18–19), I have concluded that demons cohabited with women in Genesis 6. The wickedness of that era reaches such magnitude that the Lord reacts with alarm and grief. I would suggest that 2 Peter 2:4 and Jude 6 refer to this same incident.[14]

What is the meaning of this demonic invasion? A review of the flow of Genesis provides a helpful perspective. In Genesis 1:26-27 God creates human beings in his image. They are to rule planet earth in his name. In Genesis 3, however, the vice-regents become rebels. For a fateful moment they fall prey to the influence of the Evil One. The immediate aim of the Evil One (Satan) is to entice the first couple to transgress the divine boundaries ("but you must not eat from the tree"). This represents one of the devil's primary objectives in his constant opposition to God's kingdom—to confuse and break down the divine boundaries of life.[15] Satan is a sort of "chaos monster"; he delights in creating confusion, disorder, and disharmony. The episode in Genesis 6 is one of his more diabolical efforts. Satan tries to erase the image of God in humans and replace it with his own hideous likeness. He thinks he can turn the human race into a horde of demonically inspired beings. Seen in this light, the story represents a satanic parody (feeble imitation) on the image of God concept and a crisis of the first order. Will God's crowning creation become Satan's pawn?

The NT book of Revelation describes the terrible judgments befalling the earth just before Christ returns to establish his visible kingdom. This book may shed light on Genesis 6. In the series of trumpet judgments (Rev 8–11), the fifth trumpet (locusts, 9:1-11) could be interpreted as another (thankfully the last) demonic invasion.[16]

Regardless of the specific interpretation one may give to Genesis 6:1-8, the text plainly teaches the total depravity of humankind. Genesis 6:5 summarizes the tragedy resulting from one act of disobedience (cf. Ro 5:15, 17-19): "The LORD saw how great man's wickedness on the earth had become, and that every inclination of the thoughts of his heart was only evil all the time."

The Flood (6:9–8:22)

The Lord's response staggers the mind—the entire world deluged by a flood. All human life and most animal life perished, with the exception of the pitifully small remnant aboard the ark. Is such retribution justified? Does this not seem like a massive overreaction? What kind of God would do this? These are but a few of the questions that arise within the mind of the reader.

The Character of Sin

How does one vindicate God's actions in this account? We have already touched upon one line of argument. The human condition was critical. Life on planet earth was reverting to sheer chaos. Instead of sons and daughters of God, humans were beginning to act like sons and daughters of the devil. If the patient were to be saved, radical surgery was necessary. The analogy of a medical doctor is helpful. There are times when the doctor must hurt in order to heal; a deadly cancer must be excised. Accordingly, the pre-flood civilization had to be "surgically" removed if humanity were to survive the onslaught of sin. Viewed from this perspective, the flood was not the act of a selfish, vindictive deity (as was the case in ancient Near Eastern flood myths), but an act of mercy and grace. The judgment was remedial in its intention. Because God so loved his creatures, it was essential that there be a new beginning.

The Character of God

The other side of this issue has to do with the character of God. Many theologians understand the holiness of God as the core of his moral nature.[17] Holiness, applied to God, refers to his absolute uniqueness and majesty. It also denotes his absolute purity; God is separate from all evil. He does not participate in sin nor does sin exercise its baneful influence upon his moral nature (Ex 3:5; Job 34:12; Isa 6:1-4; cf. Jas 1:13). God's holiness is the basis for morality in the world.

This being so, one can better appreciate God's reaction to the pre-flood civilization. His image-bearers so corrupt themselves that they now reflect the monstrous evil of Satan. How could God remain unaffected by this perversion? God's holiness recoils against sin:

> The LORD was grieved that he had made man on the earth, and his heart was filled with pain. So the LORD said, 'I will wipe mankind, whom I have created, from the face of the earth . . . for I am grieved that I have made them' (Ge 6:6-7).

If the Lord had not been angry, he would have acted contrary to his own nature. Holiness must necessarily react against evil; to be indifferent to evil is ultimately satanic. Thankfully, God does not allow evil to triumph.

Historical Significance

The flood of Noah constitutes one of the major divisions of history. The pre-flood and post-flood eras are distinguished in 2 Peter 3:6-7 by the respective expressions "the world of that time" and "the present heavens and earth." There may have been far-reaching geographical, geological, and climatological changes brought about by the flood. An intriguing observation centers on a comparison of life spans in Genesis 5 and 11. After the flood (11:10-26), there is a dramatic drop in longevity. Noah, the last of the pre-flood generation, lived 950 years; Terah, the last post-flood link before the era of Abraham, lived 205 years. A number of speculative theories have offered plausible explanations for this decrease in longevity, most notably, the vapor canopy theory.[18]

Our primary interest in the flood, however, focuses upon this event as a singular act of divine judgment. This event is described in Genesis 6–8 as a truly worldwide phenomenon. For example, Noah constructed a very large ship (longer than a football field!). Such an enterprise hardly seems necessary to survive a local flood, in which case a relatively simple solution would be to move! The Lord warns Noah that the flood will "destroy all life under the heavens," and that "everything on earth will perish" (Ge 6:17). During the deluge "all the high mountains under the entire heavens were covered. . . . The waters rose and covered the mountains to a depth of more than twenty feet"

(7:19). The aftermath is described by saying "every living thing on the face of the earth was wiped out . . ." (7:22). This is the language of a universal flood.

Now some appeal to phenomenological language and interpret the passage in terms of a local flood. Thus from the standpoint of an unaided observer, the flood appeared to destroy all of life and cover all the surrounding mountains in the Tigris-Euphrates river valley.[19] It is difficult, however, to avoid the conclusion that the biblical writer had a truly worldwide flood in mind. This face value impression is strengthened by the manner in which NT writers refer to the flood of Noah. The Synoptic Gospels report Jesus as treating the flood story not only historically, but also in universal terms. He likens the pre-flood situation to the time before his Second Coming (Mt 24:37-38; Lk 17:26-27). Peter apparently understood the flood to be a worldwide catastrophe (2Pe 3:6-7). In fact, Peter viewed the flood as one of two universal judgments destined for the earth. The second judgment will be by fire at the end of the age. This analogous relationship between the two judgments tips the scales in favor of a universal flood. So, in spite of considerable scientific problems related to the flood, we think it best to adhere to a straightforward reading of the text.[20]

The Postlude to the Flood (9:18–11:26)

The conclusion to the Primeval History (chs. 1–11) makes a profound statement about sin and its consequences for the human race. It also poses an immense problem. This problem is set up by the narration of two episodes that "sandwich" another genealogy, the so-called Table of Nations (ch. 10).

Human Nature Unchanged (9:18-28)

The first episode occurs in the aftermath of the flood. The family of Noah had gained a healthy respect for God's sovereignty, having witnessed an awesome display of his wrath. One would assume that the great flood "scared the devil out of them"! Nonetheless, the first story narrated after the flood demonstrates its insufficiency to rid human beings of their sin nature; water could not wash it away. The crucial statement, which gives meaning to the entire postlude to the flood, is Genesis 8:21b: "Never again will I curse the ground because of man, even though every inclination of his heart is evil from childhood."

Once again this evil inclination manifests its presence and power in the family of God's redeemed people. First, Noah becomes intoxicated. We can scarcely excuse his behavior on the grounds of ignorance. The pre-flood civilization, of which Noah was a part, had surely discovered how to make wine. Though the account is abbreviated, the indications are that they had an advanced culture, including music and metallurgy (Ge 4:21-22). We must sadly acknowledge that the man who "found favor in the eyes of the LORD" (6:8) and "walked with God" (6:9) could also overindulge. Noah's lack of self-control led to even worse consequences than drunkenness.

The story that follows presents several difficulties. I will attempt an explanation, though I confess to considerable uncertainty. At face value, the story tells about Ham, the youngest of Noah's three sons, who discovers his drunken father lying naked in the tent. Ham then informs his two brothers. When Noah awakes, he proceeds to utter a curse upon Canaan, the son of Ham.

Several questions cry out for explanation. In the first place, we wonder what the exact offense was. What did Ham do to his father? The text says that Ham "saw his father's nakedness." Is it a sin for a grown son merely to see his father nude? In our culture this would not violate any moral code or social taboo. Perhaps in that culture it was considered wrong to see one's father naked, even if inadvertently. Still, in later portions of the OT one is hard-pressed to discover evidence for such a view. That is why most readers infer that Ham proceeded to mock his father. The basic sin is disrespect for one's parents. Ham's attitude and behavior dishonored Noah. This would be comprehensible were it not for another unanswered question in the text. If Ham dishonored his father, why was not he cursed rather than his son? What did Canaan do to deserve such a fearful curse? To compound matters, Canaan, seemingly, was not even present on that occasion. For some reason, Canaan plays a major role in this episode and is culpable of a grievous offense. What is it?

I suggest that the key to the passage is the phrase "saw his father's nakedness." This expression may be a euphemism (substitution of an inoffensive term for one considered offensively explicit). A comparison with Leviticus 18 may supply the intended meaning. This chapter contains a list of prohibited sexual relations. For example, in Lev 18:5, the NIV masks a literal rendering of the Hebrew by the forthright "to have sexual relations." In other words, if rendered literally, the latter expression would be "to uncover [someone's] nakedness." This seems to be synonymous with "to see [someone's] nakedness."

Now, if we plug this meaning back into Genesis 9:22, an entirely different scenario appears. The sin of Ham could be one of two options—both exceedingly reprehensible. Either he committed sodomy with his father or incest with his mother. Note that having sexual relations with one's mother is described as uncovering the nakedness of one's father (Lev 18:7). This could derive from the Hebrew notion of marriage being a "one flesh" relationship. Since, however, there is no mention of Noah's wife in the story, I take it that the offense was homosexual in nature.

The main difficulty with the view I have just proposed arises from the actions of Shem and Japheth. They back into the tent with a garment over their shoulders. "Their faces were turned the other way so that they would not see their father's nakedness" (9:23b). At face value, the point seems to be nakedness per se. On the other hand, the expression "to see someone's nakedness" might be a double entendre (an expression admitting of two interpretations, one often indelicate). Thus the text makes clear that Shem and Japheth are careful not to gaze upon their drunken father exposed immodestly in his tent; they do not share Ham's disrespectful, mocking attitude. However, Ham's sin goes beyond disrespect and entails the nuance of homosexual assault. We suggest that a native listener or reader would have recognized the double meaning of the expression.[21]

We still have not answered the question concerning Canaan's role. Most likely, he is not directly involved. The curse of 9:25-26 is a prophetic curse. The Canaan cursed here is not the immediate son of Ham, but the descendants of Canaan—the Canaanites of a much later time. The connection is this: Ham displays his sin nature by giving way to sexual perversion; Canaan may have emulated his father's behavior. In time, this baneful legacy would result in an ethnic group who reveled in sexual perversion. The religion of the Canaanites, as recovered through archaeology, was in fact one of the most degraded ever practiced.[22]

The curse itself would eventually be fulfilled when one branch of Shem's descendants, the Israelites, in the days of Joshua, invaded the land of the Canaanites, exterminating many of them. Later, David and Solomon subjected the remnant to slavery (1Ki 9:21). Noah saw, by the Holy Spirit, that the sexual perversion expressed by Ham would also characterize his son (Canaan) as well as his descendants (the Canaanites). "Like father, like son" has implications well beyond one's immediate family. Future generations are affected by our lives, for good or for evil.

Regardless of the precise interpretation of the passage, the episode does make this point: sin is still present in human beings. The flood did not eradicate it; the flood could only provide a new environment in which it might be better controlled.

Control is a key element in the post-flood world. The Lord institutes human government as a means of curbing the innate selfishness of individuals as well as groups. The agency of government with its regulations and laws restrain the Lamechs of the post-flood civilizations. Note that the highest function of government is capital punishment (the infliction of the death penalty, 9:5-6). Capital punishment is grounded in an important theological truth—every person is created in God's image. This being so, no one may presume to take away the life of another without forfeiting his or her own. More will be said on this in our discussion of the Siniatic covenant in chapter 5.

Another Attempt to Transgress Divine Boundaries (11:1-9)

The second major episode narrated in the post-flood era demonstrates that sin also manifests its presence throughout society. *There is a corporate or societal dimension to sin.* The Tower of Babel represents an attempt by the post-flood culture to become completely independent of God. It is the original temptation all over again, only this time, an entire civilization rebels against the Creator. Building a city is not sinful; nor is building a high tower. A tower that "reaches to the heavens," however, is not simply a high tower. That tower represents a concerted effort to gain control over their environment and circumstances. In other words, we have the emergence of technology designed to determine one's own destiny. The pride, insolence, and rebellion of this culture declare itself in the boast: "so that we may make a name for ourselves and not be scattered over the face of the whole earth" (11:4). After the flood, the human race was re-commissioned to rule planet earth in the name of the Lord (8:17; 9:1-3). These people, however, were determined to rule in their own name, that is, they would create a self-sufficient society and usurp the role of God. Technology would be their tool to enthrone themselves in their tower.

We are using the term "technology" broadly, as in the study of anthropology, to denote the body of knowledge available to a civilization. We should not picture that early civilization as primitive. They were highly intelligent and possessed technology, though, of course, nothing like our own. (Theories about interplanetary space travel during this time are fabricated out of thin air!)[23]

Reflect for a moment on the growth of technology. For example, if one were to graph the total body of knowledge available from about A.D. 1000 to the present, the result would be an exponential growth curve. A characteristic of an exponential curve is that it suddenly rises very sharply. This particular exponential curve illustrates the fact that for centuries the total body of knowledge did not significantly increase. Suddenly, in modern times, the amount exploded. It has been said that in the last 30 years, scientists have discovered more than all previous history combined! Another reason is the fact that 80% of all scientists who have ever lived are alive right now. The quantity and magnitude of research are enormous. Since discovery and research build upon the shoulders of those who have gone before, we can only expect a continued steep rise in technology.

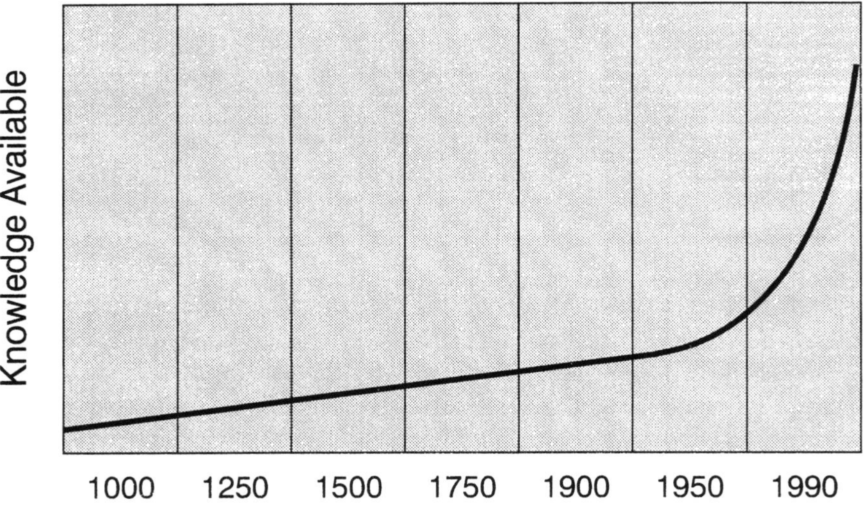

The point is simply this: the Tower of Babel generation was as inherently bright as our own (perhaps more so). All they lacked was the foundation upon which to build. This they were determined to establish. If the Lord had not intervened, within a relatively short period of time, they would have been in a position to acquire the kind of technology we possess today. The big difference, however, is this: they had a united purpose. There were no language barriers. There were no rivalries. In short, they could devote their entire resources to the achievement of their purposes. The text indicates that the Lord did not take this lightly. "If as one people speaking the same language they have begun to do this, *then nothing they plan to do will be impossible for them*" (11:6).

As in the demonic invasion of 6:1-8, the human race is at a crisis point. Genetic engineering, space travel, nuclear energy—all these things, which can be put to good use, can also be instruments of evil. Technology is not evil; the human heart is. The Tower of Babel generation, alienated from God, stood on the threshold of a "brave new world." Had the Lord allowed them to continue, in all likelihood, they would have proceeded rather rapidly to the stage of creating man in their own image. This brings us back to a leading idea in the primeval history. Being thwarted in his first attempt to create mankind in his image, Satan now influences humans to remake themselves in their own image. God, in his grace, resists (once again) the attempt to tamper with his special creation. He steps in and, in effect, retards the acceleration of technology.

His judgment is simple in execution. Suddenly, a multiplicity of languages spring up. The language barriers result in a lack of cooperation and the disintegration of the one-world government. Before long, misunderstanding, fear, hostility, rivalry, and war characterize human history. There would be no immediate acquisition of technology. To be sure, war generates its own technology, but the overall advance and concerted application of knowledge decisively slowed. God's act of confusion is a stay of execution.

In my opinion, the Tower of Babel episode will have a sequel at the end of the age—before Christ returns to establish his kingdom on earth. Revelation 13 symbolically portrays a one-world government headed up by the Antichrist. This individual will attempt, by Satanic power, to achieve what the Tower of Babel generation sought. He will claim to be God and will totally dominate the economic and political resources of the earth. Given the technology that is already operational, and that which is still in the planning stages, such a scenario is both plausible and frightening. The Antichrist may attempt to create a new "Master Race" in his image. As at ancient Babel, however, so this modern "Babylon the Great" will fail to "reach to the heavens." The Lamb (Jesus Christ) will destroy this rebellion and succeed in conforming his people perfectly to his own image (Rev 14:1-5; Ro 8:29).

The Problem of the Postlude (11:9)

The narrative of the Tower of Babel ends with a discouraging prospect: "From there the LORD scattered them over the face of the earth" (Ge 11:9b). The great question is this: What will happen to the peoples and nations? Has

God abandoned them to their fate? Will they regress further into ignorance, superstition, and idolatry? Will they be reached with the truth? The primeval history poses a problem that cries out for a solution. Genesis 12 answers by showing that God does have a plan to reach these scattered nations. "For God so loved the world . . ." (Jn 3:16). In fact, in light of the entire Scripture, one can see a clear relationship between Genesis 1–11 and the rest of the Bible. *Genesis 1–11 raises the problem; Genesis 12–Revelation 21 provides the solution*. Hannibal Smith was fond of saying on the TV show *A-Team*, "I love it when a plan comes together." Genesis 12–Revelation 22 sketches a plan that truly "comes together." The plan begins to take shape in our next chapter.

Relationship of the Fall and the Flood to the Core Concepts

The Unity of God's Plan of Salvation: Genesis 3 highlights a key principle in God's redemptive strategy: God's grace has priority; he always takes the initiative (Tit 2:11). If God does not take the first step, there is no possibility of salvation. Sin completely disables humans; they cannot save themselves. But Genesis 3 portrays a God who seeks out the sinner. He is, in Francis Thompson's words, "the Hound of Heaven."

The means whereby God saves sinners also first appears in Genesis 3. These include blood atonement and a descendant of Eve who will destroy the serpent (cf. Heb 2:14). These two ideas undergo development as we proceed through redemptive history.

Faith and Politics: The fallenness of humanity necessitates political endeavor. Our sinful tendencies invariably infringe upon the rights of others, if left uncurbed. The institution of human government is essential to prevent a return to the pre-flood chaos and violence. One of the most urgent issues of our time centers on the exercise of power in a fallen world. How should this be accomplished for the common good? Genesis 3 illustrates the following political realities bearing upon this question:

1. Fallen human beings still reflect God's image, though in distorted form: they still possess dignity and worth. Government, the agency and structure for exercising power, must protect this fundamental truth from erosion and assault. Racism, sexism, and extreme nationalism are modern ideologies that attack the essential dignity of human beings. Government must remain vigilant against them.

2. Sinful human beings naturally tend toward autonomy (being independent of authority). This manifests itself at both the individual and societal level.

Politics wrestles with the demanding task of preserving a balance between individual freedom and collective welfare. Lamech (Ge 4:19-24) and the Tower of Babel generation (Ge 11:1-9) illustrate, respectively, the two extremes of individualism (assumption that the individual is of first importance) and collectivism (the state has priority). Both undermine God's original intention. Achieving a balance has proven to be one of the most difficult political problems in history.

3. The responsible exercise of power requires theological resources. The task is beyond the capabilities of mere human wisdom. The generation of the Tower of Babel, by excluding God's revelation from consideration, condemned themselves to failure. Any government that follows suit will eventually become oppressive and self-destruct.

Faith and the Future: This section draws attention to an important but often-ignored, aspect of God's future plans. He will judge the world in righteousness and justice (Ac 17:31). Three great judgments in this section sober us by their severity. They are vivid reminders that "the wrath of God is being revealed from heaven against all the godlessness and wickedness of men who suppress the truth by their wickedness . . ." (Ro 1:17). The expulsion from Eden symbolizes the mortality and spiritual alienation characterizing fallen humanity. Life must now be lived east of Eden—a foretaste of final punishment (compare Ge 3:24 and Rev 21:27; 22:14-15). The great flood of Noah stands as the first of two universal acts of judgment. The world that now is awaits its final baptism by fire (2Pe 3:7). The Tower of Babel also casts a long shadow into the future. The rebellious intent to create a self-sufficient society anticipates another day when "the rebellion occurs and the man of lawlessness is revealed, the man doomed to destruction" (2Th 2:3). This rebellion, led by the Antichrist, culminates human history and, thankfully, climaxes in the return of the rightful "KING OF KINGS AND LORD OF LORDS" (Rev 19:16).

Faith and Ethics: Genesis 3–11 raises a fundamental problem for ethics. Why is it so difficult to do what we ought? The answer lies in the sin nature we all possess as an inheritance from our first parents (Ps 51:5). The primeval history graphically depicts the power of sin that dominates individuals and society. Only as God's grace is appropriated through faith and repentance can one "do what is right" (Ge 4:7). One does not achieve the truly ethical life by self-effort, but by divine enabling. Ethics flow out of redemption, not the other way around.

For Further Discussion:

Does Genesis 3 give a complete answer to the problem of the origin of sin?

What is your view on the precise nature of the original sin?

Do you think our contemporary society takes sin seriously? Why or why not?

What evidence is there to support the biblical teaching that sin is passed from parent to child?

Should Christians be opposed to technological advances since they may be employed for evil purposes?

For Further Reading:

Bloesch, Donald G. *Essentials of Evangelical Theology. Volume One: God, Authority, and Salvation*, pp. 88-119. New York: Harper and Row, 1982.
Bromiley, G. W. "Sin," *ISBE 4*, pp. 518-525.
Daane, James. "Sinner," *ZPEB 5*, pp. 444-447.
Dyrness, William. *Themes in Old Testament Theology*, pp. 99-110. Downers Grove: InterVarsity, 1979.
Fuller, Daniel P. *The Unity of the Bible*, pp. 175-247. Grand Rapids: Zondervan, 1992.
Ross, Allen. *Creation and Blessing*, pp. 130-220. Grand Rapids: Baker, 1988.
Sauer, Erich. *The Dawn of World Redemption*, pp. 32-54. Grand Rapids: Eerdmans, 1954.
_____. *The King of the Earth*, pp. 52-71. Grand Rapids: Eerdmans, 1962.
Van Gemeren, Willem. *The Progress of Redemption*. Grand Rapids: Zondervan, 1990.
Von Rad, Gerhard. *Old Testament Theology. Volume I: The Theology of Israel's Historical Traditions*, pp. 154-165. New York and Evanston: Harper & Row, 1962.
Youngblood, Ronald. *The Genesis Debate*, pp. 184-229. Grand Rapids: Baker, 1990.

Endnotes

1. See *NIVSB* outline, pp. 3-4.

2. See Bruce K. Waltke, "Historical Grammatical Problems," *Hermeneutics, Inerrancy and the Bible*, ed. Earl D. Radmacher and Robert D. Preus (Grand Rapids: Zondervan, 1984), p. 109.

3. James Daane nicely captures the mystery:

> The Bible no more explains the rise of sin in the world of the angels and its connection with the origin of sin in man's world, than it explains how man as God's creation could sin. There is neither a good moral reason nor a valid rational reason for the reality of sin. There can no more be a good moral reason for evil than there can be a valid reason for irrationality. Sin is both immoral and irrational ("Sinner," *ZPEB 5*, p. 445).

4. See Derek Kidner, "Isaiah," *The New Bible Commentary*, rev. ed. (Grand Rapids: Eerdmans, 1970), p. 600; John N. Oswalt, *The Book of Isaiah: Chapters 1–39* (*NICOT*, Grand Rapids: Eerdmans, 1986), pp. 320-322.

5. For this outline, I am indebted to David Allan Hubbard's lecture notes from "Themes in Old Testament Theology" (Pasadena: Fuller Theological Seminary, 1974).

6. Daniel Fuller argues that this is the essence of the original sin in his book, *Unity*, pp. 179-184.

7. For a thoughtful discussion on the essence of the original sin, see G. W. Bromiley, "Sin, " *ISBE 4*, p. 519.

8. On the consequences of sin, see ibid, pp. 520-521and Daane, "Sinner, " p. 446.

9. See Gary R. Collins, *A Psychologist Looks at Life* (Wheaton: Key Publishers, 1971), pp. 54-67 and Karl Menniger, *Whatever Became of Sin?* (New York: Hawthorn Books, 1973).

10. See Richard T. Wright, "The Environmental Revolution," *Biology Through the Eyes of Faith* (Grand Rapids: Zondervan, 1987), pp. 221-246 for a depressing survey of environmental degradation currently in progress.

11. Gerhard von Rad says that in Genesis 3-11, "sin broke in and spread like an avalanche. . ." (*Old Testament Theology. Volume I: The Theology of Israel's*

Historical Traditions (trans. D. M. G. Stalker; New York and Evanston: Harper & Row, 1962), p. 154.

12. Richard Adelman, "Neural Regulatory Mechanisms During Aging," *Age and Aging 11* (May 1982), p. 136.

13. Taken from the book, *Chronological Charts of the Old Testament* by John H. Walton. (Grand Rapids: Zondervan, 1978), p. 35. Used by permission of Zondervan.

14. The *NIVSB* note at 2Pe 2:4 states that "it appears impossible for angels, who are spirits, to have sexual relations with women . . .," p. 1900. Why this appears impossible is not stated. Walter C. Kaiser also argues against the fallen angel position in *More Hard Sayings of the Old Testament* (Downers Grove: InterVarsity, 1992), pp. 33-38.

15. Von Rad observes:

> The Elohim-beings [sons of God] of the upper world of God had intercourse with human kind, and this brought about a fresh impairment of the orders of creation which Jahweh had imposed upon mankind. This catastrophe was more serious than any of the previous ones, since it was much more than something which concerned the world of man alone; now the boundary between man and the heavenly beings was thrown down. (*Old Testament Theology*, pp. 155-156).

16. For this view, see Robert Mounce, "Revelation, " *New International Commentary* (Grand Rapids: Eerdmans, 1977), pp. 192-199.

17. See James Oliver Buswell, Jr., *A Systematic Theology of the Christian Religion, Vol. 1* (Grand Rapids: Zondervan, 1962), pp. 64-69; Donald G. Bloesch, *Essentials of Evangelical Theology. Volume One: God, Authority and Salvation* (San Francisco: Harper and Row, 1982), pp. 32-34; Millard J. Erickson, *Christian Theology, Vol. 1* (Grand Rapids: Baker, 1983), pp. 284-286.

18. Dillow, *Waters Above*, pp. 135-191.

19. See Ramm, *Science and Scripture*, pp. 238-249.

20. See Davis Young, *Creation and the Flood*, pp. 176-213 for a discussion of the difficulties.

21. For further discussion, see Victor P. Hamilton, *Handbook on the Pentateuch* (Grand Rapids: Baker, 1982), pp. 77-80.

22. See R. K. Harrison, *Old Testament Times* (Grand Rapids: Eerdmans, 1970), pp. 167-171.

23. As proposed by Erich Von Daniken, *Chariots of the Gods? Unsolved Mysteries of the Past* (New York: Putnam, 1969). For a convincing rebuttal, see Clifford A. Wilson, *Crash Go the Chariots*, rev. ed. (San Diego, CA: Master Books, 1976).

chapter **4**

The Promise to the Patriarchs

(Scripture reading: Genesis 11:27–25:11; Psalm 105:1-22)

Leading Questions

What literary technique does the narrator of the Abraham story employ?
What tension exists in the story of Abraham?
How does the story of Abraham fit into the overall structure of redemptive history?
What theological truths does this section convey?

Introduction

There are theologians who believe that God's promise of blessing and salvation is the leading theme in the OT.[1] Certainly it looms largely in any reckoning of its central message. Once again, to synthesize the promise theme throughout the entire OT revelation would require more than a chapter. I think we can, however, summarize it by an examination of the life of Abraham. The promise of God as covenanted to this man inaugurates a new chapter in salvation history. It also outlines the essentials of God's kingdom program. In many ways, all that follows the story of Abraham is but an elaboration of what God promised to and through this patriarch.

Literary Aspects of the Story

The patriarchal narratives (Genesis 12–50) are some of the best known and most skillfully told stories in the OT. The narrative art of the author places him among the finest literary figures of all time. Regrettably, we must limit our study to the Abraham narratives.

The story of Abraham covers the section Genesis 11:27–25:11. Genesis 11:27-32, in its formal characteristics, connects back to the genealogy of 11:10-26. It is, however, an important introduction to the Abraham cycle (a group of stories organized around a central theme or hero). This genealogical summary presents, at the outset, a sizable problem. Notice carefully verse 30: "Now Sarah was barren; she had no children." This, in a nutshell, constitutes the main problem that dominates this cycle of stories: Who will be Abraham's heir? Barrenness was a curse almost worse than death in Sarah's day (cf. Ge 30:1). Patriarchal society placed great importance upon male heirs and succession; it was a tragedy when a woman could not provide a male heir for her husband. Thus the story begins with Abraham and Sarah's misfortune.

The narrator not only begins by highlighting a major problem; he constantly weaves this problem throughout the entire cycle (Ge 16:1; 18:11). In fact, the literary technique employed is one familiar to most of us—the obstacle story. We may not recognize the terminology, but we do understand how it operates. In the obstacle story, each major episode revolves around a crisis for the hero or heroine. Very often an episode ends with the hero in dire straits, only to be rescued in the succeeding segment. Soap operas on television illustrate the point. Millions of Americans can scarcely wait to view the next episode of their favorite "soap!"

From a literary standpoint, the Abraham cycle is a skillfully composed story in which the tension increases by means of eight crises related to the problem of Abraham's heir. Standing in splendid contrast to the problem of childlessness is the promise of posterity—Abraham's seed will be as numerous as the stars of the heavens! Six times in the course of the story God affirms this promise to Abraham. Both Abraham and the reader experience the tension between these two realities. The issue is this: Will faith in the Lord's promise overcome the obstacles? What does Abraham's response teach us about faith in God's promises?[2]

Eight Crises Threatening the Promise

Crisis One: Threat to Abram's Wife

Setting for the crisis. Genesis 12:1-8 provides the setting for the first crisis. In these verses we have the heart of God's saving purpose, a dramatic and gracious answer to our question in Genesis 11:9: What will happen to the scattered nations? In short, the Lord made far-reaching promises to Abram (his original name—see 17:5 for the change). These promises were 1) a promise of an heir ("I will make you into a great nation"), 2) a promise of an inheritance ("To your offspring I will give this land"), and 3) a promise of a heritage ("I will make your name great" and "all peoples on earth will be blessed through you").[3]

It is striking that the wording of this promise deliberately recalls the Tower of Babel rebellion. In contrast to a generation who sought to "make a name for themselves," the Lord graciously promises to make a name for Abram. As David Clines has observed, a major idea in the Pentateuch has to do with the contrast between human initiatives, which end in disaster, and divine initiatives, which result in blessing.[4] The patriarchal narratives assume, and constantly demonstrate, the truth of Genesis 8:21; namely, that the human heart "is evil from childhood." Only God's grace can counteract this evil influence and bring blessing to sinful humanity. Furthermore, God desires that the nations experience his grace and blessing. The promise to Abraham launched a great missionary enterprise, which is still in progress.

With these great promises ringing in his ears, Abram leaves his pagan homeland and moves westward to Canaan. The comment in 12:4 "and Lot went with him" is not just window-dressing. According to 12:5 and the genealogy (11:27-31), Lot was Abram's nephew. In all likelihood, Abram views Lot as his heir. In that culture, the adoption of a near relative for inheritance purposes would have been quite acceptable. I assume that this represents a backup plan for Abram and Sarah. Since Sarah is barren, Abram adopts Lot as his heir. We will call this Plan A.

The narrative locates Abram's first settlement in Canaan at Shechem. Henceforth this site would possess a revered status as a "holy place." Another brief notice in 12:6 informs us that "at that time, the Canaanites were in the land." These descendants of the notorious Canaan, son of Ham, were the native inhabitants (see ch. 3, pp. 79-80). Abram, promised the entire land (v. 7), legally possesses not even the ground upon which he pitched his tent! This is another of the strong tension points between promise and fulfillment that works itself out in these narratives.

The story of the crisis. The stage is now set for the first crisis. This crisis is precipitated by a lack of precipitation! "Now there was a famine in the land . . ." (Ge 12:10). Canaan has a climate similar to that of southern California, essentially a two-season climate, rainy and dry. The rains normally begin in October/November and occur sporadically until about April/May. From May to October scarcely any rain falls. There is only dew. However, in order to have successful crops, it is essential that the "autumn and spring rains" (Dt 11:14) be of sufficient amount. Failure at either end usually spells trouble. Lack of sufficient rainfall at the critical periods is one of the hazards of agriculture in Canaan.[5] The result is periodic famines (we will have more to say about this phenomenon and its relationship to Canaanite religion later). Shortly after Abram begins his sojourn in Canaan, a famine afflicts the land. Abram does what countless other Semitic peoples living in Canaan would do periodically—he migrates to Egypt, the ancient breadbasket of the Near East.

The visit to Egypt thrusts Abram into a major crisis (Ge 12:14-16). Under the stress of fear and insecurity, Abram adopts a pretense that puts the Lord's plan at risk. Abram palms off his wife Sarah as his sister. As Genesis 20:12 makes clear, this is a half-truth; Sarah *is* Abram's half sister, but she is also his wife. Abram's fears are realized; Sarah's beauty comes to the attention of Pharaoh who promptly acquires her for his harem. For his part, Abram is greatly enriched by Pharaoh on account of Sarah. The barrenness of Sarah is academic now; she belongs to another. Is Sarah eliminated from God's promise to give Abram an heir?

The Lord comes to the rescue. Divine intervention in the form of diseases alerts Pharaoh to the true state of affairs. Pharaoh restores Sarah to Abram, but unceremoniously deports Abram back to Canaan. Surprisingly, however, he permits Abram to take all his newly acquired wealth back to Canaan. Keep this in mind—Abram's ill-fated sojourn in Egypt will not be the last time Hebrews experience Egyptian "hospitality" and depart with Egyptian loot! Thus the threat to Abram's wife is the first great crisis and a preview of things to come (cf. Ge 46–Ex 14). The Lord graciously delivers Sarah from Pharaoh's clutches.

Crisis Two: Lot's Separation from Abram

The setting of the crisis. The second crisis revolves around nephew Lot (ch. 13). Lot makes a decision that in effect *eliminates* him as Abram's heir. Remember that Abram probably has adopted Lot as his heir. The narrator seems to stress the fact of Lot's presence up to this point (13:1, 5).

In my opinion, the account of Lot's separation from Abram suffers from misunderstanding. Usually the wrong application is drawn from this story. A cursory survey of commentaries, Sunday school lessons and sermons sufficiently illustrates my point. Most often the lesson emphasized is the generosity of Abram in permitting Lot the first choice of pastureland. The following is typical of many commentaries: "Although the choice of territory rests with the older man, Abraham generously cedes this right to his ward."[6]

While Abram undoubtedly was a generous man, this is probably not the main point. A close reading of the text, in its larger context of the Abraham stories, and a careful consideration of geography affords a different interpretation.

The story indicates that owing to 1) the large number of animals belonging to both men, and 2) the presence of Canaanites and Perizzites, there simply is not enough grazing land available to permit the two men to live in proximity (13:5-7). At a "place between Bethel and Ai," Abram and Lot consider their options (13:3, 8). The location is approximately in the middle of Canaan. Crucial to understanding this story is the fact that the Hebrews oriented themselves with reference to the *east*, not the north.[7] Thus we need to envision the conversation between Abram and Lot within this framework. When Abram suggests to Lot, "Is not the whole land before you? Let's part company" (13:9), he is referring to the land of Canaan. Then Abram says: "If you go to the left, I'll go to the right; if you go to the right, I'll go to the left." For a Hebrew, *left is north; right is south*. In short, Abram simply suggests that they *divide* the land of Canaan between them. This is a perfectly reasonable plan.

The significance of Lot's choice. The response of Lot is the critical issue. According to the text, Lot chooses *neither* northern nor southern Canaan. Instead, he *leaves* the land of Canaan (13:11-12). The cities of the plain are clearly viewed as outside the boundaries of Canaan in the OT. Lot's departure from Canaan constitutes the second great crisis. By leaving, Lot demonstrates a failure to identify with the promise of an inheritance.

Abram must have been disappointed and frustrated—not because Lot chose the best pastureland—but because Lot, his heir apparent, left the land of promise. This interpretation is consistent with the conclusion of the episode (13:14-17). The Lord appeared to Abram "**after Lot had parted from him**" (v. 14), and reaffirmed his initial promise (Ge 12:1-3, 7). In spite of Lot's departure, the Lord would give Canaan to Abram's **offspring** (v. 15).

Crisis Three: Threat to a Potential Heir

Abram the warrior. The third crisis occurs as a consequence of Lot's departure. Lot pastures his flocks in the vicinity of Sodom (13:12). Unfortunately for Lot, a war breaks out and he is caught in the middle of it. An eastern Mesopotamian coalition invades the region of the Jordan Valley and, in the ensuing fighting, Lot becomes a prisoner of war. Abram, from his vantage point at Hebron some 4000 feet above the Jordan Valley, learns of Lot's capture (14:14). Abram is confronted with a threat to a potential heir, and now he faces a decision fraught with grave danger. If he intervenes and rescues Lot (by no means a sure thing), he runs the very real risk of becoming involved in an escalating cycle of retaliation, so characteristic of Middle Eastern wars (a tragic lesson learned by the United States in Lebanon in 1985). On the other hand, could he just sit back and let his nephew face his fate? Abram takes his courage in hand and springs into action. In a brilliant piece of strategy, he ambushes the careless raiders and recovers Lot as well as the stolen goods.

Abram the worrier. This bold action, however, haunts Abram's thoughts. He envisions another raiding party next year—only this time they come after *him!* It is not a comforting thought. Abram's fears are met by another visionary experience. The Lord appears to Abram with a word of assurance and security. "Do not be afraid Abram. I am your shield, your very great reward" (15:1). This comforting word promises Abram divine protection from the vengeful desires of the eastern kings. We read nothing more about them; the Lord of the universe prevents their exacting of revenge. The Lord is indeed Abram's shield.

With that need met, Abram pours out his heart's concern about an ongoing need—the need for an heir. We discover in chapters 18–19 that Lot, despite his indebtedness to Abram, has not returned to Canaan. He now lives in Sodom. Apparently, Lot does not share Abram's faith in God's promise. For his part, Abram desperately needs an heir. Following Lot's departure, Abram apparently puts into operation another backup plan—Plan B. This plan calls for the adoption of the faithful household servant, Eliezer of Damascus. Such a procedure has been verified from the family archives of recovered ancient Near Eastern documents.[8] Because of the necessity to provide male succession for inheritance purposes, even an heir not related by blood could be appointed, if all else failed.

The covenant with Abram. The Lord's response stuns Abram. "This man will not be your heir, but a son coming from your own body will be your heir. . . . Look up at the heavens and count the stars. . . . So shall your offspring be" (15:4-5). It is a measure of Abram's faith that he believes the promise. "Abram believed the LORD, and he credited it to him as righteousness" (15:6). This simple but profound act of trust becomes the hallmark of all who experience God's salvation. Rightly is Abram reckoned as "the father of all who believe . . ." (Ro 4:11).

There is, however, still another concern. What about the promise that Abram's seed would inherit the land of Canaan? After all, the Canaanites are already there and lay claim to it. The Lord's answer is as clear as the star-studded night: "To your descendants I give this land . . ." (15:18).

The Lord promises Canaan as an inheritance by an oath. This oath deserves special attention. In answer to Abram's question, "How can I know that I will gain possession of it?" the Lord asks Abram to prepare for a solemn oath-taking ceremony. In the ancient Near East, when two individuals entered into covenant, a ceremony symbolized the relationship (Ge 31:44-54; Jer 34:8-22). The parties to the covenant walked down an aisle between the pieces of the sacrificial animals, perhaps grasping each other's hand. This unusual ceremony symbolized the consequences of disloyalty and failure to keep covenant. If one of the parties should fail to uphold his obligation, his fate would be like that of the sacrificial animals. The oath sworn was in nature a self-maledictory oath (an oath calling upon oneself a curse for disobedience).

There is something even more unusual about the solemn oath sworn in Genesis 15:17-21. Who walked between the sacrificial pieces? Abram did not because he fell into a deep sleep (15:12). The only mention of something passing "between the pieces" is a "smoking firepot with a blazing torch" (15:17). In other portions of the OT, fire sometimes symbolizes or indicates the presence of the Lord (Ex 3:2; 14:24; 19:18; Jdg 6:21-22; 1Ki 18:38). The answer is made explicit in 15:18: "On that day the LORD made a covenant with Abram. . . ."

The theological significance of this ceremony lies in the nature of that which is sworn. Abram is virtually powerless to bring about the realization of the promise. Ten nations reside in Canaan and compete for domination (15:19). What can one man do against so many? The answer is that he can only exercise trust in "God Most High, Creator of heaven and earth" (14:19). The Lord alone walks between the pieces because he alone can accomplish the fulfillment of the oath. This is an unconditional promise. Remarkably, the Lord obligates himself by means of a self-maledictory oath. This act of condescension is an aid to Abram's faith as well as an inkling of the means whereby salvation is ultimately accomplished. God in Christ one day takes upon himself a curse. "Christ redeemed us from the curse of the law by becoming a curse for us . . ." (Gal 3:13).

Crisis Four: Helping God Out

Cultural background of the story. Some time passes. There is still no heir in spite of the solemn oath of Yahweh. The fourth crisis illustrates the great difficulty we have in simply waiting on God. It has now been ten years since

Abram arrived in Canaan (16:3)—he was 85 and Sarah was 75. Remember the old saying, "God helps those who help themselves"? (Many people believe this is in the Bible!) Sarah can wait no longer. She takes the initiative in a strategy designed to "help God out" in the accomplishment of his purpose. Another backup plan is devised—Plan C. This plan consists of a concubine (in this context, a secondary wife usually of inferior legal and social status) through whom an heir can be obtained. Sarah gave Hagar, an Egyptian slave, to Abram as a wife.

Our culture legally prohibits polygamy, but the practice was not uncommon in the ancient Near East and is still practiced in certain parts of the world today. Marriage documents, recovered from the general time period of Abram, sometimes contain a clause dealing with the problem of childlessness. If the primary wife is unable to produce a male heir, the husband is entitled to take a secondary wife for this purpose.[9] Such a custom must have prompted Sarah's action.

Consequences of the action. The consequences of this failure of faith soon surface. Domestic tranquility departs as soon as Hagar conceives. Doubtlessly hoping to replace Sarah as the primary wife, Hagar shows contempt for her mistress. This elicits an explosion of anger on Sarah's part. First, she unloads on Abram, and then she mauls Hagar. (The NIV translation "Sarai mistreated Hagar" [Ge 16:6] is an understatement.) Sarah's ill treatment of Hagar was not, by the way, without legal precedent. In the laws of Ur-Nammu (antedating Abram's time) a particular provision reads: "If a man's slave-woman, comparing herself to her mistress speaks insolently to her, her mouth shall be scoured with one quart of salt."[10] While Sarah may have resorted to that punishment, I think she preferred a more "hands on" approach! At any rate, Hagar flees the camp and would have perished with her child had not the Lord graciously intervened. He informs Hagar that her son shall bear the name Ishmael (God hears) and be hostile to all those around him. One wonders if Sarah's later rejection of Ishmael as Abraham's heir (21:8-21) played a role in this hostility towards others.

Our story, however, appears to have a happy resolution. In his 86th year Abram welcomes into the world his firstborn son. Seemingly, the Lord has fulfilled his promise of an heir. Abram must have been extremely pleased and grateful. Thirteen years later, the Lord drops another bombshell. In Abram's 99th year the Lord again appears to him and does three things. 1) He changes Abram's name to Abraham ("Exalted Father" becomes "Father of a Multitude" 17:5). 2) He institutes circumcision as a mandatory sign of the covenant relationship (17:11-14). 3) He announces that *Sarah* would bear a son—the heir (17:15-21). The last-named item effectively scraps Plan C and draws a protest from Abraham. "If only Ishmael might live under your blessing!" (17:18). The Lord answers that Ishmael will indeed be blessed, but the heir is Isaac—appropriately named because of Abraham's laughter of disbelief at the thought of Sarah bearing a child at age 90! (See *NIVSB* note on 17:17, p. 31.) In short, we are now back to square one—the Lord's original plan. Sarah will give birth, within one year, to the long-awaited heir. Abraham and Sarah hear the birth announcement, personally delivered by the Lord, in a remarkable theophany (an appearance of God) recorded in 18:1-10.

Historical interlude. Genesis 18:16–19:38 seems to digress from the main story line. Viewed at one level, however, this section maintains the tension by keeping us in suspense about Sarah's pregnancy. This is just good storytelling. On another level, the passage closes out the story on Lot and provides important background on the origin of Israel's immediate neighbors to the east. The story of Lot's escape from Sodom demonstrates the consequences of his wrong choice years before (ch. 13). The wickedness of the cities of the plain permeates his family. Only Lot and his two daughters survive the catastrophic destruction. The daughters, reflecting the behavior of Sodom and Gomorrah, induce their father to commit incest. Both of them conceive and give birth to sons—Moab and Ben-Ammi (Ammon). These sons become the progenitors of the two principle nations to the east of Israel. History informs us that, for the most part, conflict and violence marked the relationship.

This is a good spot to make some practical applications from the story of Abraham (see Ro 15:4). On the one hand, the story certainly contains an important reminder about the far-reaching consequences of wrong choices on the family level of society. What if Lot had exercised faith in the Lord and remained in the land of promise? Surely history would have been far different. Think of the tears and bloodshed resulting from the animosity between Israel and her neighbors Moab and Ammon. In fact, the consequences of one wrong choice by Lot ripple the surface of middle eastern history to this very day.

Think also of the Ishmael episode. What if Abram and Sarah had trusted God for an heir without the expedient of concubinage? In a sense, the current Middle East conflict between Arabs and Israelis is but another chapter in a continuing history, punctuated with hostility and animosity. Today the world watches anxiously lest the Third World War erupt in the Middle East. Who could have imagined such a consequence issuing from the birth of a son to a secondary wife?

These stories speak to us about the urgent need to establish strong Christian families: Our warfare against the forces of evil is fought at the level of the family as well as of society. If we are to overcome evil with good (Ro 12:21), we must forge committed Christian homes that pass on a godly legacy to succeeding generations.

However, these stories also demonstrate that the grace of God can overturn evil choices and bring good out of them. There were, in Bible times, Moabites, such as Ruth, who acknowledged the true and living God, and today many Arabs confess Jesus as Lord. The grace and mercy of our loving Father give grounds for hope. He can put back together the broken pieces of our lives and mend shattered families. In fact, one of the great projects continuing to unfold is the creation of one great spiritual family characterized by perfect love and unity (see Gal 3:26-29; Eph 1:5; 2:11-22; 4:14-19).

Crisis Five: Another Threat to Sarah

We resume the story of Abraham's heir in chapter 20. Moving into the region of Gerar, Abraham resorts to a familiar ruse—he once again pretends that Sarah is his sister. Abimelech, the local ruler, takes Sarah as a wife. Perhaps this was Abimelech's way of assuring good relations with a powerful chieftain—Abraham had a sizable number of servants at his disposal. (According to Ge 14:14, Abraham could muster 318 trained men.) Assuming a chronological order for chapters 18–20, we infer that Sarah was already pregnant or, if she was not, she became so within a year's time (compare 18:14 and 21:1). The crisis is this: To whom would the child be reckoned? The answer appears to be Abimelech. We are so close and yet so far from the fulfillment of God's promise!

Once again, the Lord rescues his covenant partner. The Lord afflicts the household of Abimelech with infertility (20:18). Then, in a dream, the Lord warns Abimelech not to have relations with Sarah because she belongs to Abraham. Abimelech confronts Abraham and gives compensation for the unintentional violation of Sarah's honor. Abraham in turn prays successfully for the household of Abimelech, and the crisis is averted.

Crisis Six: Ishmael or Isaac?

Genesis 21:1-7 brings us, at last, to the long-awaited moment. Incredibly, at the age of 100, Abraham becomes the father of a son born to Sarah who is 90! Truly, Isaac, the son of laughter, is a special child. Defying the ordinary biological processes, the Lord gives to Abraham a son whose conception was little short of supernatural. The question of Genesis 18:14 "Is anything too hard for the LORD?" has been emphatically answered. The birth of Isaac previews things to come. In the future a young virgin will conceive without a father (Mt 1:18; Lk 1:34-37)! To her astonished question "How will this be?" the answer comes back: "Nothing is impossible with God." This reply is a leitmotif of the Abraham cycle.

Seemingly, the story is now complete. Abraham has his heir. An unresolved issue still smolders, however. Isaac is not Abraham's firstborn son; Ishmael holds that distinction. Inevitably, a crisis brews until the status of these two sons is finally settled. Genesis 21:8-21 narrates the sixth crisis. The unresolved question is who is the principal heir—Ishmael or Isaac?

The crisis erupts on a festive occasion—the weaning of Isaac (21:8). In our culture, children are weaned at about one year old; in the ancient Near East, this could be as late as three! During the celebration, Sarah observes Ishmael (who was a teenager by now) mocking her child Isaac. The old bitterness rekindles and Sarah suddenly feels very jealous and protective of her son's status in Abraham's family. Sarah demands of Abraham that he disinherit Ishmael and dismiss both him and his mother. "Get rid of that slave woman and her son, for that slave woman's son will never share in the inheritance with my son Isaac" (21:10).

Emotionally torn between those he loves (21:11), Abraham agonizes over the crisis. He is doubtlessly aware of the legal standing of his firstborn Ishmael. Documents from Abraham's time stipulate that children born to concubines or slaves cannot be disinherited if the father acknowledges them, which Abraham clearly does in Ishmael's case.[11] Abraham desperately needs divine guidance. In response, the Lord directs him to give heed to Sarah's demand: "Listen to whatever Sarah tells you" (Ge 21:12). (By the way, this verse may be very useful for wives to show their husbands on occasion!) Ishmael will be blessed ("I will make the son of the maidservant into a nation" [21:13]), but "it is through Isaac that your offspring will be reckoned" (21:12). The sixth crisis establishes once and for all the status of Isaac: he is the sole heir. "Abraham left everything he owned to Isaac" (25:5). Isaac continues the line of promise.

Crisis Seven: The Near Sacrifice of Isaac

At last, it would seem, our story has run its course and we may now enjoy the resolution of the tension between promise and fulfillment. Such is not the case.

Just when we least expect it, the most severe crisis of all confronts us. *Chapter 22 is one of the most profound and mysterious portions of the entire Bible.* Suddenly, we encounter a story that bristles with questions—deep questions about God's nature and will.

Literary and psychological features of the narrative. The account is a masterpiece of Hebrew narrative. With few words the story unfolds, step by agonizing step, rising in tension right up to the awe-inspiring climax. Abraham is tested. So the narrator informs us in 22:1. Of course, Abraham is not informed about the meaning of the shocking command. (Note that a summarizing statement, which is then elaborated, typifies OT narratives.) The Lord orders Abraham to sacrifice his son Isaac without delay. The horror of this demand never fades with repeated reading. It seems incomprehensible. Notice how the repetition of key words heightens the psychological impact of this divine command. "Take your son, your only son, Isaac, whom you love, and go to the region of Moriah. Sacrifice him . . ." (22:2). As the story moves forward, the narrator creates an almost intolerable tension by repeating words and phrases like "his son," "my son," "father," "the two of them . . . together."

There are so many questions here. Did Abraham tell Sarah? One can scarcely entertain the possibility. Abraham, the father, must bear this trial alone. Did Abraham lie to his servants when he told them to wait until "we . . . come back to you" (22:5)? What did Abraham really think when he told Isaac "God himself will provide the lamb for the burnt offering" (22:8)? Why is there not the slightest bit of suspicion or resistance on the part of Isaac? Why no mention of pleas or cries on Isaac's part? In fact, the passiveness of Isaac throughout the story borders on the unreal. Is this how a teenager or young adult would react to being bound on an altar? Indeed, can we seriously consider the notion that a young man would even allow an old man (100+ years) to do this to him? These are but a few of the questions that flood our minds.

Typological features of the narrative. I will not pretend to have all the answers, but I do think some observations on the nature of the story provide some assistance in comprehension. At several points in the story of Abraham's heir, I sense foreshadowings of God's redemptive plan centered on Jesus of Nazareth. These foreshadowings or correspondences are not mere coincidences, but part of the divine outworking of redemption. We label such a phenomenon *typology*. An event, person, institution or object in the OT that foreshadows, anticipates, or corresponds to the NT teaching concerning the person and work of Christ is a *type*. An interpretation that draws such connections or correspondences is called *typological*. I believe this is a valid way of looking at Scripture (if used with caution), and we will consider more examples later on.[12]

The story of the near sacrifice of Isaac bears the earmarks of typology. It points beyond itself to another time when, on almost the exact location, another Father would in fact offer his only son as a sacrifice. In other words, as Christians, when we read the story, something familiar resonates in our hearts. John 3:16 is being acted out: "For God so loved the world that he gave his one and only Son. . . ." On Mount Moriah, time and eternity come together; we draw near to the Holy of Holies and catch a glimpse of the very heart of God our Father. It anticipates the central act in the drama of redemption; in so doing, it conveys a certain, timeless quality. In Isaac's passive behavior and quiet acceptance of his father's will, we have a picture of Jesus' own death—like that of a lamb being led to slaughter (Isa 53:7; Mt 27:41; Mk 14:36).

With regard to Abraham's own feelings, we can offer very little help. The narrator (as typical of Hebrew narration generally) does not allow us inside the characters' minds. We are, however, afforded some insight by an inspired interpreter of the story, namely, the writer of the letter to the Hebrews. In Hebrews 11, the author says concerning this great test: "Abraham reasoned that God could raise the dead, and figuratively speaking, he did receive Isaac back from death" (v. 19). This is a remarkable display of faith.

In my opinion, Jesus referred to this ordeal. In debate with the religious leaders of Jerusalem, he said: "Your father Abraham rejoiced at the thought of seeing my day; he saw it and was glad" (Jn 8:56).[13] Abraham's agony on Mount Moriah, a stone's throw from Golgotha, produced an overwhelming awareness of God the Father's redeeming love. Few, if any, will realize the depths of that love like Abraham.

Spiritual application of the narrative. Would the Lord ever make a similar demand on believers today? I can confidently answer no. The Lord does require "sacrifices" of those who would be disciples (Mk 8:34-38; Lk 14:25-27), but never that we sacrifice our children with our own hands. We may be called upon to bear the pain and anguish of losing a loved one to death; but never are we to be the executioner. Abraham's case was unique; it was part of redemptive history. As such, it manifested the once-for-all character of that ultimate sacrifice on Calvary, never to be repeated (Heb 9:26-28). We may trust God fully because he loves us unreservedly (Ro 5:5, 8). Abraham was commended because he did not withhold his only son (Ge 22:12, 15).

Christians are exhorted by the apostle Paul likewise to exercise complete trust in God "who did not spare his own Son, but gave him up for us all" (Ro 8:32).

Crisis Eight: A Bride for Isaac

The seventh crisis is of such a climactic nature that we can scarcely imagine another obstacle. Nonetheless, one more remains. If Isaac is the one through whom all the nations are to be blessed, then he must continue the line of promise. In order to do this he must marry. A bride for Isaac brings us to the eighth and last crisis in the life of Abraham (ch. 24). Now the question becomes: Who will be Isaac's heir?

A cultural difference: an arranged marriage. To western readers, this ought to be a problem for Isaac, not Abraham. We need to remind ourselves, however, that in the ancient Near East (and still in portions of the Near East today), parents arrange for marriages. Young men do not, on their own, initiate courtship and marriage. It is up to Abraham to secure a bride for Isaac and so insure continuity in the line of promise. Chapter 24 narrates one of the loveliest and most delightfully told stories in the OT.

The securing of a bride for Isaac involves no small obstacle. Abraham places important stipulations upon a prospective bride. Not least in difficulty is the absolute prohibition of a bride from among the native Canaanite population. Abraham's trustworthy chief servant takes a solemn oath promising not to obtain a wife from the Canaanites. Rather, he must find a woman from Abraham's clan back in the region of Haran (11:31; 12:4). The servant asks the question that brings us to the heart of the crisis: "What if the woman is unwilling to come back with me to this land?" Abraham issues a second prohibition—the servant must not take Isaac back to Abraham's homeland. If Isaac is to marry, a young woman, who is a relative, must be willing to leave her family and homeland and make the long trek out to the Wild West—Canaan. Abraham is confident that God will "send his angel" before the servant. Will his confidence be rewarded?

The narrator passes over the long journey itself (at least 400 miles by camel) and describes the servant's arrival in Nahor's town. The scene at the well affords a remarkable glimpse into the faith of this man. The influence of Abraham's faith shines through the narrative. The servant's prayer is simple and trusting. He requests a sign in order to select the right woman because he has arrived at the perfect time of day to check out the available candidates. (College students call this scoping!) Note that in the ancient Near East women carried the water. Role differences in patriarchal and pastoral-agrarian societies are usually quite pronounced.

The criterion for Isaac's bride. The sign, which involves a test, is worth pondering by those who are in the process of selecting a life partner. The reader may wonder what the nature of the test is. Virtually all the young girls who came to the well would probably have honored the request for a drink of water. The real test, however, goes well beyond that of supplying a thirsty traveler with water. Whoever among the young girls offers to water the servant's camels is the desired candidate. If you have ever seen a camel and know their capacity for water when thirsty, you will appreciate the test. This girl would have at least a 30- to 45-minute job on her hands trying to fill up 10 thirsty camels. They are like sponges! In short, which young girl is willing to go beyond ordinary courtesy? Who will go the extra mile (cf. Mt 5:41)? This test says something important about the character of the individual. She is not lazy and self-centered but industrious and self-giving.

These qualities are still vital to the making of a good marriage, and they apply to men as well. Most marriages that break up are those in which one or both of the partners is simply unwilling to go the extra mile. Especially worthy of note, before we leave this discussion, is the fact that the test does not involve superficial things like appearance of face and figure. Too many put the emphasis on the least important qualities (Pr 31:30). It is true that Rebekah was a very beautiful girl (v. 16), but that was not part of the test.

The consent of Rebekah's family. The next step for Abraham's servant is to obtain the consent of her family to the marriage. Rebekah's eldest brother Laban assumes a leading role in these discussions. Laban displays his craftiness later on when Cousin Jacob comes to live with him and marries his daughters Rachel and Leah (Ge 29–31). The repetition in the story is typical of Hebrew storytelling and is an aid to memory. The episode builds to a climactic moment. Laban and Bethuel give their consent: "This is from the LORD. . . . Here is Rebekah; take her and go, and let her become the wife of your master's son, as the LORD has directed" (24:50-51). The next morning, Laban and Rebekah's mother request that there be a ten-day period before Rebekah leaves for Canaan. The servant, however, insists upon leaving that very day. The issue is put to Rebekah: "Will you go with this man?" Her response displays considerable courage for a girl who could have been as young as 12 or 13: "I will go" (24:58).

The consummation of the marriage. Once again bypassing the long trek, the anticipated meeting between Rebekah and Isaac is touchingly narrated. Arranged sight unseen, this marriage was "made in heaven."[14] The sequence of verbs is instructive: Isaac married Rebekah "and he loved her." For those who have grown up in a culture steeped in the notion of romantic love and courtship, this story seems far removed. It serves, however, as a salutary reminder that lasting love is essentially an act of the will. Unfortunately, too many in North America marry on the basis of emotion and passion without a commitment of will. The divorce rates of the respective cultures speak for themselves. (It is much lower in cultures where marriages are arranged.)

The Conclusion of the Abraham Cycle

The story of Abraham has run its course. The narrator caps off the cycle in 25:1-11 with a brief coda (a passage bringing the story to a formal close). First, Abraham marries again, and not only marries, but fathers six more sons! God is fulfilling his promise to make Abraham's descendants as numerous as the stars of the heavens. Secondly, Isaac assumes the role of sole heir of Abraham's estate—the other sons are given gifts and sent away. There are no more rivals to Isaac and his future heir. Thirdly, the great patriarch dies and is buried in the family tomb at Machpelah. Finally, God blesses Isaac. The last named point brings to a satisfying resolution the tension winding itself through the Abraham cycle.

The entire cycle may be represented schematically by the chart on the following page.

The Theological Significance of the Abraham Narratives

We conclude by inquiring into the theological purposes of the Abraham narratives. Four main points stand out:

1. This cycle of stories highlights the faithfulness of God to his covenant promise. Yahweh, who added to his absolutely inviolable word of promise an oath (Heb 6:13-20), is the covenant-keeping God. Great is his faithfulness. At the end of his earthly pilgrimage we read of Abraham, "and the LORD had blessed him in every way" (24:1). This was in fulfillment of Yahweh's initial promise, "I will bless you." (12:2). The story ends with this statement: "God blessed his son Isaac" (25:11).

Structure of Genesis 11:27–25:11

Problem: "Now Sarai was barren; she had no child" (11:30).

Divine Promise	Crisis or Obstacle
1. Initial promise 12:1-3, 7	1. Threat to Sarai 12:10-20
2. Promise renewed 13:14-17	2. Prospective heir leaves 13
3. Promise ratified by covenant 15:7-21	3. Threat to Abram: Middle Eastern war 14
4. Covenant promise reaffirmed and signified by circumcision 17	4. Threat to another prospective heir 16
5. Promise of the heir born to Sarah 18	5. Threat to Sarah 20
6. Promise reaffirmed 22	6. Which heir? 21
	7. Threat to the heir 22
	8. A bride for the heir 24

2. The cycle underscores the necessity of obedience to the will of the covenant-making and covenant-keeping God. The climactic test of chapter 22 comes down to this: "Now I know that you fear God . . ." (22:12). Abraham was blessed because he obeyed. The old gospel song summarizes the life and example of Abraham: "Trust and obey, for there's no other way. . . ." Abraham demonstrated the genuineness of his faith by obedience—a point repeatedly made by the Apostle Paul (1Th 1:3; Ro 1:5; 6:17; Gal 5:6) as well as James (Jas 2:21-24) and John (1Jn 2:3-5).

3. The call of Abraham represents a decisive moment in the unfolding history of redemption. The great question of Genesis 11 concerning the scattered nations begins to receive an answer. The Lord will bless these nations through the offspring of Abraham. *Thus Genesis 1–11 stands over against Genesis 12–Revelation 22 in the relationship of problem to solution*. God's saving plan, remarkably, begins with the call of a solitary man and his family. God's strategy comes down to this: it is through the *one* that the many will be reached. The *one* is the promised seed of Abraham (Ro 5:12-21).

4. The story of Abraham and his heir has typological dimensions. What we mean is that, at several points, the story points beyond Abraham and Isaac and anticipates the coming of Jesus Christ. As Abraham's only heir, conceived by divine intervention and bringing laughter and joy, *Isaac is a type of Jesus Christ* who also is an only son, the heir of all things (Heb 1:2), miraculously conceived (Mt 1:18; Lk 1:35), and bringing great joy to all people (Lk 2:10). Just as it was through Isaac that Abraham's offspring was reckoned (21:12), so it is through Jesus, the ultimate heir, that membership into the family of God is reckoned (Jn 14:6; Ro 8:17).

Relationship of Theme to Core Concepts

Unity of God's Plan of Salvation: This section, like the Fall and Flood, stresses the priority of God's grace. The Lord calls, promises, and fulfills his oath; Abraham simply responds in faithful obedience to these divine overtures. This pattern remains a constant in redemptive history.

The significant contribution of this portion, however, centers on the doctrine of justification by faith. Genesis 15:6 answers for all time the question: How can one be in a right relationship with a holy God? "Abram believed the LORD, and he credited it to him as righteousness." In the book of Acts, the Philippian jailer asked Paul and Silas the question: "Sirs, what must I do to be saved?" Their response sounds the same chords as Genesis 15:6: "Believe in the Lord Jesus, and you will be saved . . ." (Ac 16:30b-31). The principle of salvation by grace through faith characterizes redemptive history from Adam and Eve until the number of the elect is finally complete. (For appeal to Ge 15:6 by the Apostle Paul in defense of justification by faith compare Ro 4:1-12, 20-24 and Gal 3:6-9).

Faith and Politics/Faith and Ethics: Politics and ethics impinge upon each other. The story of Abraham reminds us that one cannot neatly separate politics from one's private life. The family histories of Lot, Ishmael, and Isaac have evolved into one of the most complex and dangerous political dilemmas of our time. Moral and ethical choices made in private eventually spill over into the public arena. The continuing parade of fallen political figures, disgraced by moral indiscretions, dramatically illustrates the point. The lesson for those who would exercise political power is simply this: *character is the bedrock of politics*; and the foundation of character is faith in God Most High. The challenge for Christians in politics—and in the broadest sense of the term, most of us are involved to some degree in politics—is the same as confronted Abram: "I am God Almighty; walk before me and be blameless" (Ge 17:16).

Faith and the Future: The promise to Abram in Genesis 12:3b sketches in outline the shape of the future: "All peoples on earth will be blessed through you." The Lord's redemptive plan incorporates the salvation of the Gentile nations. When history ends in judgment and the Kingdom of God appears triumphant, around the throne of God appears "a great multitude that no one could count, from every nation, tribe, people and language, . . . " (Rev 7:9). Not all Gentiles, but all kinds of Gentiles, will be redeemed. The future of missions and evangelism is bright; the Lord desires many people to gather round his throne.

The promise to Abram in Genesis 12:7 also includes the specific grant of the land of Canaan as an inheritance. In 15:8-19 the Lord guaranteed this promise by a self-maledictory oath. Any discussion of eschatology must take into account the irrevocable promise of Canaan to the descendants of Abraham (Ro 11:29). The particularity of the promise may be puzzling, but the prospect of the Jewish people in their "Promised Land" appears repeatedly in the prophetic writings. Jeremiah's prophecy of future national restoration in Chapters 31–33 read in conjunction with the remarkable rebirth of the modern state of Israel inspires confidence in God's prophetic word. We will speak more of this in chapter nine.

For Further Discussion:

Why did Lot refuse to share in God's promise to Abraham?

Why did the Lord allow Abraham to experience so many difficulties?

Are tests of faith necessary for growth in the Christian life?

How does the life of Sarah speak to us as Christians?

Are all believers guaranteed ultimate blessing and prosperity like Abraham?

For Further Reading:

Bright, John. *A History of Israel.* 3d ed, pp. 60-93. Philadelphia: Westminster, 1981.

Dyrness, William A. *Themes in Old Testament Theology*, pp. 113-142. Downers Grove: InterVarsity, 1979.

Fuller, Daniel P. *The Unity of the Bible*, pp. 251-344. Grand Rapids: Zondervan, 1992.

Helyer, Larry R. "Abraham's Eight Crises: The Bumpy Road to Fulfilling God's Promise of an Heir," *Abraham and Family: New Insights into the Patriarchal Narratives*, pp. 41-52. Edited by Hershel Shanks. Washington, DC: Biblical Archaeological Society, 2000.

Hess, R. S., P. E. Satterthwaite, and G. J. Wenham. *He Swore An Oath: Biblical Themes from Genesis 12–50.* Cambridge: Tyndale Fellowship for Biblical and Theological Study, 1993.

Kaiser, Jr., Walter C. *Toward an Old Testament Theology*, pp. 84-99. Grand Rapids: Zondervan, 1978.

Millard, Alan R. "Abraham," *ABD* 1:35-40. Fine overview of the historical, literary, and theological dimensions of the Abraham stories.

Millard, Alan R. and Donald J. Wiseman, eds. *Essays on the Patriarchal Narratives.* Winona Lake, IN: Eisenbrauns, 1983. The authors defend the historicity and reliability of the patriarchal narratives.

Sauer, Erich. *The Dawn of World Redemption*, pp. 89-107. Grand Rapids: Eerdmans, 1960. Sauer writes from a moderately dispensational viewpoint.

Van Gemeren, Willem A. *The Progress of Redemption.* Grand Rapids: Zondervan, 1988. Van Gemeren writes from the perspective of covenant theology.

Endnotes

---

1. See Walter C. Kaiser Jr., *Toward an Old Testament Theology* (Grand Rapids: Zondervan, 1978).

2. "The story-teller makes the reader himself live through and suffer through the various situations in which the recipient of the promise was tried. There can be no doubt that, though the key word "faith" occurs only once in them, it is the problem of faith which lies at the back of these stories about Abraham" (Von Rad, *Theology*, p. 171).

3. I am indebted to Kaiser, *Old Testament Theology*, pp. 52, 86-94, for this formulation of the patriarchal promise to Abraham. See also ibid., pp 168-169.

4. See *The Theme of the Pentateuch* (Sheffield: *JSOT,* 1978).

---

5. Of course, in the modern state of Israel, this problem has been offset to some extent by heavy reliance upon irrigation. Nonetheless, a recent severe drought (2000-2001) taxed even the resources of the Sea of Galilee, and there were extensive agricultural losses.

6. E. A. Speiser, *Genesis* (*Anchor Bible*; New York: Doubleday, 1964), p. 98. The *NIVSB* also misses the point, p. 26. See Larry R. Helyer, "The Separation of Abram and Lot: Its Significance in the Patriarchal Narratives." *JSOT* 26 (1983): 77-88 and, more popularly written, "Abraham's Eight Crises: The Bumpy Road to Fulfilling God's Promise of an Heir," *Bible Review* (October 1995): 20-27, 44.

7. See Helyer, "Separation," p. 87 n. 12 for references.

8. See *ANET*, p. 220, and Harrison, *Old Testament Times*, pp. 74-76.

9. See the series of laws in *The Code of Hammurabi*, *ANET*, p. 172, #144-146.

10. *ANET*, p. 525a.

11. *ANET*, p. 173, #170.

12. For further information see John Goldingay, *Approaches to Old Testament Interpretation* (Downers Grove: InterVarsity, 1981), pp. 97-122.

13. In agreement is Kaiser, *Hard Sayings*, pp. 52-56. See *NIVSB* note on John 8:56 for a different view.

14. In the Book of Tobit (an apocryphal work dated to about the third century B.C.) the notion that marriages are ordained in heaven is clearly expressed (Tob 6:18; 7:11).

chapter **5**

The Exodus from Egypt and the Sinai Covenant

(Scripture reading: Exodus; Leviticus 1–19; 26; Numbers 6; 9–25; 30–36; Deuteronomy 1; 4–8; 13; 17–18; 27–34)

Leading Questions

What does the exodus teach us about the character of God and his redemptive program?
How did the Mosaic Law as a whole function in Israel?
What are the three primary aspects of the Law?
What was the heart of the Mosaic Law?
What was the purpose of the sacrificial ritual?
What was the rationale behind the laws of uncleanness?
How was the Mosaic Law code different from other ancient Near Eastern law codes?
How does the Sinai Covenant relate to second millennium suzerainty treaties and what is the theological significance of this?
How does the Tabernacle fit into the Sinai Covenant?
What does the Tabernacle teach us about God's plan of salvation?

The Exodus

Exodus means "a going out, a departure." The great "going out" in the OT, which was the central event of Israel's history, was the departure from Egypt under Moses. This event established the descendants of Jacob as a nation. Approximately 120 references to the exodus underscore its importance in the Hebrew Bible; the exodus theme constitutes a major idea in the entire Bible.

The Character of the Deliverer

The exodus was a major self-manifestation of God. As such it pointed to certain characteristics and attributes of Yahweh, the great "I AM WHO I AM" (Ex 3:14). Three attributes in particular display themselves in the narrative of the exodus: the sovereignty, faithfulness and mercy of the Lord.

His sovereignty. Sovereignty refers to the state or quality of being absolutely supreme and dominant. In the context of our discussion, God's sovereignty means that he alone possesses all authority and power in the world he has created. He has no rivals. He accomplishes his will and purpose and nothing thwarts his plan (Ps 115:3; 135:6; cf. Eph 1:11). The story of the exodus makes this point in an unforgettable way.

A good starting point is the "Song of the Sea," a victory hymn celebrating the Lord's triumph over Pharaoh's army at the Red Sea (Ex 15). Notice the use of height to convey the notion of the Lord's control (". . . he is highly exalted" 15:1). The imagery of a warrior (15:3) is especially noteworthy. In fact, verse six recalls many palace and temple reliefs in ancient Egypt, portraying the victorious Pharaoh standing over a fallen foe, ready to deliver the *coup de grâce* with his battle axe.[1] In this case, however, Yahweh stands over the defeated Pharaoh!

The narrative of the exodus also makes the same point. The phenomena of the 10 plagues demonstrate convincingly Yahweh's complete control of nature.[2] The timing, severity and selective location place them in a unique category of events. As Exodus 15:11 asks: "Who is like you . . . working wonders?" One recalls the impact upon Jesus' disciples when he, exercising the authority his Father gave him, calmed a storm by a mere word: "Who is this? Even the wind and the waves obey him!" (Mk 4:41).

Another aspect of the plagues relates to the theology of ancient Egypt. The Nile valley, like the Tigris-Euphrates system, spawned a highly complex polytheistic religion. Inasmuch as the Nile river made life possible in the midst of an otherwise barren desert, the ancient Egyptians worshiped it as a deity. Khnum was designated as guardian of the Nile; Hopi, the spirit of the Nile; and Osiris, its bloodstream. These were only a few of the deities venerated in ancient Egypt. The following chart lists some of these gods and goddesses.[3]

The Plagues and the Gods of Egypt

Plague	Reference	Possible Egyptian Deity
Nile turned to blood	Ex 7:14-25	Khnum: guardian of the Nile Hapi: spirit of the Nile Osiris: Nile was bloodstream
Frogs	Ex 8:1-15	Heqt: form of frog; god of resurrection
Gnats	Ex 8:16-19	
Flies	Ex 8:20-32	
Plague on cattle	Ex 9:1-7	Hathor: mother-goddess; form of cow Apis: bull of god Ptah; symbol of fertility Mnevis: sacred bull of Heliopolis
Boils	Ex 9:8-12	Imhotep: god of medicine
Hail	Ex 9:13-35	Nut: sky goddess Isis: goddess of life Seth: protector of crops
Locusts	Ex 10:1-20	Isis: goddess of life Seth: protector of crops
Darkness	Ex 10:21-29	Re, Aten, Atum, Horus: all sun gods of sorts
Death of firstborn	Ex 11:12-36	The deity of Pharaoh: Osiris, the giver of life

The chart brings into focus an interesting correlation between the deities and the plagues. Nearly every plague was directed at a supposed deity. Egyptians conceived of their deities as controlling a particular aspect of nature. Against the will of Yahweh, however, these deities were absolutely impotent. When the plagues had run their course, Egypt was in shambles and her religion discredited. None of these reputed powers could resist the will of Yahweh, the God of the wretched and powerless Hebrews. The irony of this situation illustrates a leading idea in Scriptures: the Lord is the champion of the powerless and oppressed. (See Ps 35:10; 1Co 1:26-29; 2Co 12:7-10.)

Especially devastating was the last plague—the death of the firstborn. The ideology of statehood in ancient Egypt assumed the deity of Pharaoh. At various periods of Egypt's history, Pharaoh was the incarnation of the sun god, Re, and at death he was transformed into Osiris, god of the underworld. The plagues were a divine contest or combat (recall the Tiamat myth) between Yahweh and Pharaoh. The bone of contention concerned the status of Israel. Yahweh told Pharaoh: "Israel is my firstborn son. . . . Let my son go, so he may worship me" (Ex 4:22-23). Pharaoh's response was: "Who is the LORD, that I should obey him and let Israel go?" (Ex 5:2) Pharaoh probably viewed the Israelites as state slaves. They were under contract to produce a certain quota of bricks for his public works program (Ex 5:6-9).[4]

Each succeeding plague 1) demolished a plank in the ideology and theology of Egypt, 2) devastated the land and thus requited Egypt for its violation of human rights and crimes against humanity, and 3) demoted Pharaoh to the level of a mere mortal—and a stubbornly sinful one at that! Fittingly, Pharaoh forfeited his own firstborn (a supposed god!) to Yahweh as punishment for his refusal to let Yahweh's firstborn go. The "Song of the Sea" has it right: "In the greatness of your majesty you threw down those who opposed you" (15:7). When the smoke of conflict cleared, no rivals remained. "The LORD will reign for ever and ever" (15:18).

Exodus 2:1-10 narrates the account of Moses' birth and early childhood. This story likewise exhibits Yahweh's sovereignty. Continuing a theme in the Joseph cycle (Ge 37–50), the narrator stresses the Lord's providential control over all that unfolds—even the seemingly inconsequential things. Moses' life is spared, ironically, by Pharaoh's own daughter! Apparently she adopts Moses. Yet, in God's providence his real mother nurses him and undoubtedly teaches him the Hebrew traditions (Ex 2:9-10). Moses receives the advantages of all the "wisdom of the Egyptians" (Ac 7:22), but never forgets his Hebrew heritage, so that he eventually "refused to be known as the son of Pharaoh's daughter" (Heb 11:23). The entire episode (Ex 2:11–3:10) demonstrates the Lord's providential preparation of a leader. Think of it—40 years spent as a fugitive herding sheep in the very region where he would spend 40 more years leading a very stiff-necked people on the way to Canaan!

His faithfulness and mercy. We treat these "twin" attributes together. The setting of the exodus is the brutal oppression of Israel, the "dark night" revealed to Abram centuries earlier. In the famous covenant ceremony of Genesis 15, Abram was told: "Know for certain that your descendants will be strangers in a country not their own, and they will be enslaved and mistreated four hundred years. But I will punish the nation they serve as slaves, and afterward they will come out with great possessions" (Ge 15:13-14). The people of Israel are now in the "ironsmelting furnace" of affliction (Dt 4:20). Do the Hebrews remember the prophecy given to Abram? Do they look expectantly for Yahweh's rescue? The narrative is silent about this. Apparently the Hebrews harbor no hope for deliverance. As the repressive measures grow more severe and cruel, as forced labor is augmented by a barbaric form of birth control (1:15-22), the Hebrews turn to the God of Abraham, Isaac and Jacob:

> The Israelites groaned in their slavery and cried out, and their cry for help because of their slavery went up to God. God heard their groaning and he remembered his covenant with Abraham, with Isaac, and with Jacob. So God looked on the Israelites and was concerned about them (Ex 2:23b-25; also 3:6-10, 16-17; 4:31).

The covenant-keeping God has not forgotten. He will fulfill his promise to rescue and bring them back to Canaan—but in his own time. Abraham had waited 25 years for his son Isaac. Israel would have to wait four hundred years before the time of deliverance came. Similarly, the people of God would have to wait until "the time had fully come" (Gal 4:4) before the ultimate "heir of all things" (Heb 1:2) appeared. Abraham learned patience and perseverance; Israel multiplied and became numerous; after all, the Israelites would eventually have to dislodge the Canaanites by force. The hard labor toughened the people of Israel physically (Ex 1:12, 19); it prepared them for the struggle in the promised land. This observation applies generally to God's dealings with his people. One of the most difficult spiritual lessons to learn is that of waiting on the Lord. "Be still before the LORD and wait patiently for him; do not fret when men succeed in their ways, when they carry out their wicked schemes. Refrain from anger and turn from wrath; do not fret—it leads only to evil. For evil men will be cut off, but those who hope in the LORD will inherit the land" (Ps 37:7-9).

The Character of Deliverance

A careful study of the exodus throws light upon God's redemptive program. The various aspects of that deliverance from Egypt enable us to glimpse the grand unity of God's plan of salvation.

Liberation and redemption. Notice, first of all, that the deliverance is from bondage; it is essentially an act of liberation and redemption. We have already suggested that the Hebrews were state slaves under contract to supply Pharaoh's government with cheap labor. This involved a cruel, political and economic exploitation. Yahweh's liberation alters the status of the Hebrews dramatically. As the rest of the Pentateuch and the book of Joshua make clear, the family of Jacob becomes a distinct nation. They emerge from their oppressed beginnings to become by David's time (1 and 2Sa) the leading state in the ancient Near East. Furthermore, the Law of Moses reflects a deep concern for various forms of oppression and injustice. In principle and precept, the Hebrew nation/state reflects Yahweh's demand for righteousness, justice, and mercy in the economic, social, and legal spheres (more will be said about this later in chs. 6–8).

Political bondage is not, however, the only, or even the primary, evil inflicted upon the children of Israel. More devastating by far is the spiritual bondage. The Israelites for over 400 years are immersed in a thoroughly polytheistic culture. The powers of darkness bound that ancient civilization in its grasp, with the attendant conditions of fear, superstition and ignorance. Inevitably, the influence of this system infiltrates Hebrew thought. Erosion of faith in the God of the Fathers displays itself in the generally dismal record of the wilderness wanderings. How quickly many revert to pagan ways! Joshua, in his great farewell address, refers to the apostasy of the Hebrews during their tenure in Egypt (Jos 24:14) and Amos seemingly refers to idolatry during the desert experience (Am 5:25-26; but see *NIVSB* note on 5:26). As the Lord called Abram out of the polytheism of Mesopotamia (Ge 12:1), so Moses led Israel out of Egyptian polytheism.

Spiritual and political bondage are not two separate spheres unrelated to each other. In fact, a survey of political history reveals that spiritual bondage lies at the taproot of politically oppressive systems. A true knowledge of God and man is absolutely essential for any semblance of good government.

Creation of a people of God. Secondly, the primary objective of the deliverance is the formation of a unique people of God. "I will take you as my own people, and I will be your God" (Ex 6:7). This election of the children of Israel to be God's people shapes the rest of the OT. There were secondary objectives in the exodus; for example, that Pharaoh and all Egypt might know that Yahweh was God. But the primary objective is the creation of a people who know the true and living God and witness to the truth in the midst of error. Israel's mission from the exodus onward is summarized by a much later text outlining Israel's mission in the era of the Exile.

> You are my witnesses, declares the LORD,
> and my servant whom I have chosen,
> so that you may know and believe me
> and understand that I am he.
> Before me no god was formed.
> I, even I, am the LORD,
> and apart from me there is no savior.
> I have revealed and saved and proclaimed—
> I, and not some foreign god among you.
> You are my witnesses, declares the LORD,
> that I am God. (Isa 43:10-12)
>
> I will also make you a light for the Gentiles,
> that you may bring my salvation to the
> ends of the earth. (Isa 49:6)

Dependence upon divine intervention. The deliverance from Egypt depended entirely upon divine intervention. Moses could never lead Israel out of Egypt by force of personality or arms. Egypt was the most powerful state in the known world. Military options were futile, as were negotiations or diplomacy. The narrative makes plain that redemption was achieved through an unprecedented display of divine power. Even Pharaoh's magicians acknowledged that "this is the finger of God" (Ex 8:19). The Lord told Moses at the burning bush: "I have come down to rescue them [Israel] from the hand of the Egyptians. . . . But I know that the king of Egypt will not let you go unless a mighty hand compels him. So I will stretch out my hand and strike the Egyptians with all the wonders that I will perform among them" (Ex 3:8, 19-20). Yahweh is the great liberator—he sets his people free from the oppressive powers of darkness.

Involvement of human agency. Despite the necessity of divine intervention, Yahweh's deliverance did involve human agency. The Lord raised up Moses and Aaron to effect the rescue; he commissioned them to announce to Pharaoh the release of Israel. They were God's mouthpiece and mediator in the negotiations with Pharaoh. Some actors in the drama of redemption played unwitting (Pharaoh's daughter) or even hostile (Egyptian foremen) roles; yet they freely contributed to the overall objective, which was the rescue of Israel.

Correspondence to NT. As we reflect on these four characteristics of the Lord's deliverance of Israel, it is striking how this pattern recurs in the NT teaching on salvation. The NT describes the salvation accomplished for us in Christ in terms of an exodus. "For he has rescued us from the dominion of darkness and brought us into the kingdom of the Son he loves, in whom we have redemption, the forgiveness of sins" (Col 1:13). The purpose or goal of NT salvation is also peoplehood. In a remarkable passage, applying Exodus 19:5-6 to the Church, Peter reminds his Christian readers that "you are a chosen people, a royal priesthood, a holy nation, a people belonging to God, that you may declare the praises of him who called you out of darkness into his wonderful light. Once you were not a people, but now you are the people of God . . ." (1Pe 2:9-10). No point is more insisted upon in the NT than the necessity of divine initiative and intervention. As was the case in Moses' day, so in the Messianic era, salvation absolutely depends upon a gracious God who comes to us. There is no room for auto-emancipation in the gospel. "For it is by grace you have been saved, through faith—and this not from yourselves, it is the gift of God—not by works, so that no one can boast" (Eph 2:8-9). Finally, we have a corresponding involvement of human agents in NT salvation—those who proclaim the good news of deliverance. In a passage based upon Isaiah 52:7, the Apostle Paul points out that the Lord uses human preachers in the saving of a people. "How, then, can they call on the one they have not believed in? And how can they believe in the one of whom they have not heard? And how can they hear without someone preaching to them? And how can they preach unless they are sent? As it is written, 'How beautiful are the feet of those who bring good news!'" (Ro 10:14-15)

Clearly a fundamental harmony and unity mark the Lord's plan of salvation. People in OT times were not saved in a different way than those in the new age. The four characteristics outlined apply to salvation at all times in God's redemptive program. The notion that the OT teaches salvation by works and the NT salvation by grace is in error. God has one plan of salvation and that one plan is portrayed in both testaments. To be sure, there is a greater elaboration and an advanced experience of "such a great salvation" (Heb 2:3) in the NT, but there is an undergirding continuity that binds the people of God together from Adam and Eve to the last sinner who shall be saved by grace.

The Community of the Delivered

We turn our attention now to this redeemed people called Israel. What was their mission in the world? How were they to function in the overall strategy of God's redemptive program? The titles given Israel at the time of the exodus inform us about certain aspects of Israel's mission.[5]

The firstborn son. The title "firstborn son" in Exodus 4:22 is a good starting point. The notion of the firstborn played a prominent role in the patriarchal narratives. What was involved in that culture in being a firstborn son? In Hebrew society (as well as most ancient Near East cultures) the firstborn son enjoyed certain privileges and advantages over other siblings. In terms of rank and standing in the family, the firstborn had priority. For example, in Genesis 43:33, Reuben, the firstborn, was seated at the place of honor at a meal. Presumably, this was customary. In terms of inheritance, an even more pronounced advantage existed. Hebrew family law accorded the firstborn a larger share of the inheritance. In the Mosaic law code this was stipulated as a double portion; that is, the firstborn received twice as much of the family estate as any other sibling (Dt 21:17). The reason for this larger share is never explained in the OT; but since the eldest son would also become the head of the family/clan, he would be responsible for unmarried and widowed sisters. The increased inheritance allowed for increased expenditures and responsibilities. Thirdly, in terms of leadership and priestly duties, the father generally groomed his eldest son as successor. Of course, in the patriarchal narratives, one of the leading themes is how the firstborn was consistently bypassed for a younger son. These exceptions, however, only prove the rule and demonstrate the Lord's sovereign choice. In general the father treated his firstborn with special sanctity and affection (Ge 49:3). All of this added up to considerable privilege.

Privilege, however, entailed great responsibility. The story of Joseph's sale into slavery demonstrates the burden of responsibility. Reuben tries to prevent the brothers from harming Joseph since he, Reuben, is answerable to his father for the rest of the brothers and family members (Ge 37:21-22, 29-30; 42:22, 37). Unfortunately for Reuben, a moral failure results in the loss of his standing in Jacob's family (Ge 35:22; 49:3-4; 1Chr 5:1). So, when applied to Israel the expression conveys the ideas of special love and affection, privilege, and responsibility. Implicit in the term is the understanding that the firstborn—

who might, of course, be an only son—is generally the first among other brothers. They, too, are entitled to inheritance rights.

Three titles occur together at the important 19th chapter of Exodus. In the setting of the Sinai Covenant, Yahweh calls Israel "my treasured possession," "a kingdom of priests," and "a holy nation" (Ex 19:5-6).

A treasured possession. What does it mean to be Yahweh's "treasured possession?" The background appears to be that of kings and their royal treasuries (Isa 39:2). A victorious king plundered the crown jewels and riches of his vanquished foe and transferred them to his own palace treasury. These would, of course, be kept under close guard and displayed on occasions of great importance and pomp. Similarly, Yahweh vanquished Pharaoh; he plundered the wealth of Egypt (Ex 3:21-22; 12:36). From the Lord's perspective no treasure is more precious and meaningful to him than Israel. Once transferred to the sovereignty of Yahweh, Israel is placed under special protection. To appropriate Yahweh's "treasured possession" without his permission is to court disaster. Yahweh is exceedingly jealous of his people. The expression, then, conveys the ideas of the value and worth of Israel as well as the special protection set over them. The promise to Abram "I will bless those who bless you, and whoever curses you I will curse" extended to the descendants of Abram, the children of Israel. Egypt, Syria, Assyria, Babylon, Persia, the Seleucid kings, among others, discovered, to their shame and humiliation, the consequences of harming the Lord's "treasured possession." In my opinion, this status of the Jewish people still exists; they still "are loved on account of the patriarchs, for God's gifts and his call are irrevocable" (Ro 11:28). We will say more about this in chapter nine.

A kingdom of priests. A priest represents the people before God; he offers prayers, praise, and gifts on behalf of the people. He also mediates God's forgiveness and blessing to the people. This position of standing between God and his people typifies Israel's role in the world. Israel channels blessing to the world by bearing witness to the true and living God. Yahweh had promised that "all peoples on earth will be blessed through you" (Ge 12:3). This blessing is now mediated through the nation descended from Abram. One of the important functions of the OT priesthood was that of teaching the Law to the people. In the promised land, the priests inherited no portion as their own (Jos 13:14, 33; 21:1-42; Dt 18:1-8), but settled throughout the entire land with the Levites. In this way they served as teachers of the Law. Viewed in larger perspective, Israel as a nation mediates the truth of God to the Gentiles. There are several notable stories about Gentiles who came to know the Lord through the witness of Israelites (Ruth, Ru 1:16; Rahab, Jos 2; Naaman, 2Ki 5).

A holy nation. The notion of holiness is very important in Scripture. That which is "holy" is separated from the sphere of the common and ordinary and devoted to the Lord for his special use. As a nation, Israel was to be separate from the world of the Gentiles (characterized by error, fear, and superstition) and wholly consecrated to Yahweh. They were given a detailed pattern for living, a pattern which embodied holiness. (We will take this up below).

Continuity between Israel and the Church. Once again, notice the continuity between Israel and the Church. All the above titles apply to the Church, demonstrating that the basic function and role of the Church is the same as that of Israel. In Hebrews 12:23 Christians are called "the church of the firstborn [plural], whose names are written in heaven." Whereas Paul referred to Christ as "the firstborn [singular] among many brothers" in Romans 8:29, he also styled believers "heirs of God and co-heirs with Christ" (Ro 8:17). Christ thus shares with his people the status of firstborn.[6] The Lord of the Church bestows special affection, sanctity and privilege upon his people; he also requires of them a heavy responsibility. This responsibility entails bearing a powerful witness in the world to the greatest of the mighty acts of God—the revelation of God himself in the person of Jesus of Nazareth (2Co 5:17-21). See 1 Peter 2:9-10 for the other three titles reapplied to the Church.

Election and the people of God. These titles point to an important theological truth: Israel is a chosen people—they are an elect people. This chosenness is not an exclusivist, racist, or nationalistic privilege; it is an election open to all who confess the faith of Israel. In the Bible, *election links up inseparably with mission*. There are no imposed limits on the people of God apart from personal trust in the great "I Am." This is true in both Testaments. Furthermore, chosenness never results from human merit or achievement whether actual or potential. As the Lord reminds Israel in Deuteronomy 7:7-8 and 9:4-6, it is not because of her greatness or righteousness that she is chosen. Quite the contrary, she is weak and stiff-necked. So also the Church needs reminding that election is based upon the

Lord's sheer grace towards us who are deserving of wrath and judgment (Eph 2:1-13).

The Code of the Delivered (The Mosaic Law)

The way of life required of a holy nation is spelled out in a truly remarkable document—the Mosaic or Sinaitic law code. There are in fact five great legal collections (all of which are considered Mosaic by Jewish tradition) now incorporated into the Pentateuch. These are as follows:

1. The Decalogue (literally the "ten words," or as it is better known, the Ten Commandments), Exodus 20:1-17
2. The Book of the Covenant, Exodus 21–23
3. The Priestly Code, Exodus 25–Numbers 10
4. The Holiness Code, Leviticus 17–26
5. The Deuteronomic Code, Deuteronomy 12–26

Scholars have differing opinions as to the relationship between these five collections. For our purposes we will consider them part of a unified religious-legal tradition (showing some growth and development) set in a narrative framework of Israel's origins.[7]

The constitution of Israel. To understand this material, we must recognize that the Mosaic Law was essentially the constitution of the nation Israel. We have an analogy in the United States' constitution, though, of course, there are important differences. Israel was a theocracy, that is, a government ruled by God through the mediatorship of specially sanctioned leaders and agents. The law code expressed the will of the monarch, Yahweh, for his people Israel. In such a government there is no clear separation of church and state as in the American constitution. For example, in the Book of the Covenant and the Deuteronomic Code, we have a mingling of civil and religious laws. There is no indication in the present texts that the Hebrews distinguished between these categories. The Law of Moses was viewed as a unified collection. Still, for the purposes of analysis, it is useful for us to make distinctions. Accordingly, the legal materials, in terms of content, fall into three main categories.

The moral law. The moral law is distilled in the Ten Words or Ten Commandments (Ex 20:1-17; Dt 5:6-21). Actually, the entire Mosaic legal corpus could be viewed as but commentary and explication of the Ten Commandments. Here we have the heart of Israel's faith and life.[8]

The Ten Words divide into two main divisions: commandments 1-4 focus upon relationship to God; commandments 5-10 focus upon relationship to neighbor. The first four deal with the vertical dimension of life; the second six, the horizontal. The order is not indifferent; only as one is right with God can there be any hope of living rightly with one's neighbor. When asked to identify which of the commandments was most important, Jesus summarized the Ten Commandments under two main ones: "'Love the Lord your God with all your heart and with all your soul and with all your mind.' This is the first and greatest commandment. And the second is like it: 'Love your neighbor as yourself.' All the Law and Prophets hang on these two commandments" (Mt 22:37-40). Thus our analysis is indebted to Jesus' own understanding of the Law.

Three positive statements are included among the prohibitions. These positive declarations establish the basis or provide a context for the prohibitions. Thus the prohibitions against disloyalty, the making of idols or images and the misuse of God's name are all predicated upon the grand declaration of the existence and redeeming activity of the Lord. Commitment to this saving God is strengthened by Sabbath observance (commandment four). The fifth commandment, a positive declaration concerning parents, heads the list of prohibitions that treat the horizontal relationships of life. The family forms the core of any society; if one has difficulty with the authority of one's parents, there is almost inevitably difficulty in other relationships (husband-wife, employer-employee, teacher-student, and so on). Honoring one's parents goes a long way towards the establishment of a proper context for relating to one's neighbor.

Finally, notice that there are no sanctions mentioned for failure to comply. These statements stand as categorical imperatives—they are the expression of God's will for his people. They are founded not upon social wisdom, political expediency or royal preference. They are a transcript of the character of Yahweh. As such they possess divine authority. In this regard, Israel's law code was unique in the ancient Near East. Furthermore, the Ten Commandments continue to exercise a powerful influence upon the conscience of human beings. As H. L. Ellison has so well stated:

> . . . the Ten Commandments contain a statement of the great basic principles of character that must exist if a man wishes to be in fellowship with God; all the rest is commentary and a guide towards the creation of this character.[9]

The ceremonial law. A large portion of Israel's law code deals with matters pertaining to the cult. We are using the term "cult" in its technical sense to refer to actions, words and objects employed in the worship of a deity or deities. Cult involves established forms, rites, feasts, times, and sacred places. (This meaning should not be confused with popular usage in which it refers to various groups deviating from mainstream Christianity, such as Mormons, Jehovah's Witnesses, and non-Christian groups like Hare Krishna). Cultic regulations, then, deal with the rituals of a particular religion. There are three main areas of Israel's cult that we examine.

1. Sacrifice. The Israelite sacrificial ritual involved several different kinds of sacrifices, and these were rigidly prescribed for various settings or circumstances. In regard to the number and amount of sacrifices, the Hebrews were not exceptional. Cultic and ritual texts from as early as the third millennium B.C. have as many, or more, different kinds of sacrifice than the Israelites.[10] The following chart is a summary of the various sacrifices.

The Hebrew Sacrificial System[11]

Offering	Disposition	Animals	Occasion	Passage
Burnt	Completely burned	Unblemished male	Demonstrates dedication	Lev 1
Meal or tribute	Token portion burned; rest eaten by priest	Unleavened cakes or grain	General thankfulness	Lev 2
Peace a. Thank b. Vow c. Free will	Fat portions burned; rest shared by priest and offerer	Male or female without blemish	Fellowship a. Blessing b. Deliverance c. Thanks	Lev 3; 22:18-20
Sin	Fat portions burned; rest eaten by priest	Bull, male or female goat, female lamb (depends on status)	Purification needed	Lev 4–5:13
Guilt	Fat portions burned; rest eaten by priest	Ram without blemish	Ritual or objective guilt	Lev 5:14–6:7

The purpose of Israel's sacrificial system lies in a provision for failure to achieve the standards required of a holy people.[12] The sacrifices restore a harmonious relationship between Yahweh and the individual Israelite or the community at large. This point is crucial.

At face value, the Mosaic cult conveys the impression that animal sacrifices did in fact remove sin. Leviticus 17:11 reads: "For the life of a creature is in the blood, and I have given it to you to make atonement for one's life" (see also Lev 4:20, 26; 5:10; 12:8). But Hebrews 10:4, in the NT, states that "it is impossible for the blood of bulls and goats to take away sins." How do we harmonize these two statements?

First of all, sin is an offense or affront against a holy God; it involves an intensely personal and relational dimension. God our creator made us in his image, innocent of all sin. We were not created with a sinful nature—that is entirely our own doing and has no justification (see chapter three). Consequently, God is the injured or aggrieved party in this matter (Ge 6:6). This means that God alone can forgive sin (Isa 43:25; Mk 2:7). The ground of forgiveness must, therefore, lie in the merciful character of God himself (see Ex 34:6-7; Ps 51:1; 130:3-4). The question then becomes: Upon what conditions can a holy God forgive human sin? This brings us to the heart of the human predicament and to the biblical teaching on salvation.

The biblical answer is clear: since human beings, from the Fall onward, are sinful, they can do nothing about their condition. There is simply no way to rid themselves of the sin nature (Ro 3:9-18, 23; 7:24). As the Teacher in Ecclesiastes said: "What is twisted cannot be straightened . . ." (Ecc 1:15a). No ritual, ceremony, magic or self-reformation can avail; forgiveness must be granted by a holy God. Herein lies a profound difference between pagan religion (ancient and modern) and Hebrew religion. The former consists of some system or method of wringing it out of the deity; the latter celebrates the undeserved, gracious bestowal of forgiveness by a loving and merciful God. Israel's faith proclaimed that a holy God made available forgiveness; he desired to live among a sinful, impure people (Ex 6:7). What he required was heartfelt repentance (Ps 32:5; 51:1-12). Sacrifice, sincerely performed, was an expression of this repentance. This was the condition upon which a holy God met with guilty sinners. Repentance, accompanied by a proper sacrifice, expressed the faith of the sinner in God's gracious promise of forgiveness.

So what did the sacrifice itself effect? The sacrificial ritual symbolized the transfer of contamination and pollution from the sinner to an innocent substitute. The moment of transfer was when the sinner laid his hands on the head of a unblemished animal (Lev 4:29). Presumably, a confession of sin accompanied this act. The medium of transfer was the animal's blood. The blood of the victim (whether ox, sheep, goat, or pigeon) was then brought into contact with the altar or the sacred furniture within the tabernacle/temple. The result of this contact symbolized either that God's holiness annihilated the contagion or contained it, thus preventing further contamination.[13]

In spiritual terms, the sinner, by laying his hands on an innocent victim and confessing his sin, dissociates himself from his sin. The sinner acknowledges that something offensive to God has intruded into the relationship and needs to be remedied. God in his grace provides a means whereby the relationship can be restored to full communion and harmony. That means is the transfer of sin's guilt and pollution to an innocent victim. Certainly a supplicant is profoundly moved by this ritual. How could one personally kill an animal, flay it and watch it be consumed on the altar without reflecting on the tragedy and consequences of one's sin? The principle of substitution— the innocent for the guilty—seems undeniable.

Seen in the larger perspective of redemptive history, animal sacrifices were a stop-gap measure. The blood of a sacrificial animal cannot deal with the source of a particular sin, namely, the sin nature, an invasive force that controls the core of one's being (as seen in Paul's depiction of it in Romans 6–7). Sacrifices had to be repeated over and over again since sin incessantly spawns sins. So how could the source of the problem be dealt with according to the OT? No answer seems forthcoming. The prophets, however, were confident that in the future, God would deal decisively with the problem of sin (see Isa 4:3-4; 26:2; 60:21; Jer 31:33-34).

According to the NT, God in Christ resolved the problem once and for all. He accomplished this by providing an infinitely superior substitute or ransom. A sinless human being (Heb 2:9-18; 4:15) who was, at the same time, the very image of God (Col 1:15; 2Co 4:4) replaced the innocent animal. The moment of transfer took place on the cross (2Co 5:21). The sinless one absorbed all the guilt, pollution and contamination of sin—a real transfer took place (Ro 8:1-4). The altar was the cross; the victim was the Son of God. God the Father condemned sin in that moment of deep mystery (Mk 15:33-34; 2Co 5:21). The penalty that such guilt entailed was exacted in the person of Jesus Christ. As a result there was complete satisfaction on the part of a holy God since the guilt, penalty, and pollution of sin had been dealt with once and for all (see Heb 1:3; 2:9; 7:26-28; 8:6; 9:7-15; 10:1-14).

The sacrifice of Jesus Christ was not, however, an impersonal, magical operation which now makes everyone "all right" regardless of one's attitude toward sin. The sinner appropriates this provision by faith and repentance. "If we confess our sins, he is faithful and just and will forgive our sins and purify us from all unrighteousness" (1Jn 1:9).

One last question remains. Since OT sacrifices were inadequate to deal finally and completely with sin, how could God truly forgive sinners who lived before the coming of Christ? The answer would appear to be that the death of Christ has always been the underlying basis of atonement. This event, planned before the creation of the world (1Pe 1:20; Eph 1:4), made it possible for God to forgive the repentant sinner who confessed his/her sin and offered a ransom in the form of an animal sacrifice. One might say that the sins of pre-cross saints were atoned for on credit. The symbolic transfer of guilt and pollution in the sacrificial ritual anticipated the real transfer at Golgotha (Ro 3:24-26). The temporary gave way to the eternal.

2. *Sacred seasons.* Much of the ceremonial law deals with the observance of a religious calendar. Israel experienced a sense of rhythm in life—a rhythm dictated by the God of Israel.[14]

Special Days	Hebrew Name	Reference	Commemoration
Passover (un-leavened bread)	Pesach	Ex 12 (Lev 23:4-8)	Deliverance from Egypt
Pentecost	Shavuoth	Dt 16:9-12 (Lev 23:9-14)	Celebration of harvest
9th of Av	Tish'ah be'av	No direct reference	Destruction of first and second temple
Day of Atonement	Yom Kippur	Lev 16 (Lev 23:26-32)	Sacrifices for sins of the nation
Tabernacles	Succoth	Neh 8 (Lev 23:33-36)	Wilderness wanderings
Dedication	Chanukah	John 10:22	Cleansing of temple
Lots	Purim	Esther 9	Deliverance from Haman's plot

As can be seen in the chart, the sacred seasons encouraged Israel to remember God's goodness. Memory of past events is a powerful factor in shaping present behavior. Unpleasant experiences make us take steps, consciously or unconsciously, to avoid a recurrence, while pleasant experiences generally create in us a relaxed and trusting attitude.

Significantly, the Mosaic Law, and later the psalmists (Ps 105–106), continually call for the Israelites to reflect upon the goodness and greatness of God and to recall all his benefits. Because the Lord has created his people and redeemed them out of Egypt, he has full claim upon them. They are his children and ought to experience their greatest delight in praising and blessing his name.

Of special interest are the three pilgrimage festivals. The Feast of Unleavened Bread (Passover), the Feast of Harvest (Pentecost) and the Feast of Ingathering (Tabernacles) required the presence of all the men (Ex 23:14-17). This required attendance came at a very busy time of the year for the Israelite farmer. The necessity of meeting together to reaffirm commitment, to encourage each other, and to offer collective praise and thanksgiving overrode all other needs and priorities. It was a way of proving where one's priorities really were. It further illustrates the truth that faith is lived out in community and that communal worship is essential for a vital, growing faith.

One of the most important functions of the Israelite religious festivals involved reciting together the Lord's mighty deeds. The early Christian church likewise observed special occasions that recalled events in the life of Jesus. The apostolic church met on the first day of the week to commemorate the Resurrection. That became the day of corporate worship (Jn 20:19, 26; Ac 20:7; 1Co 16:2; Rev 1:10). Though not yet referred to in the NT, there was a gradual development of a church calendar in which the saving activity of Jesus was celebrated throughout the year. Furthermore, the NT makes clear that the early Christians viewed the history of Israel as their story too (1Co 10:1).

Virtually all Christian churches today exhibit an awareness of the importance of remembering God's saving deeds. In most liturgical churches there is a carefully developed scheme; in other churches, it is less formal, but unmistakably present. Our hymns, prayers, Scripture readings, sermons, and pageants reflect the importance of reminding ourselves how faithful God has been to us collectively and individually.

3. Separation. Perhaps the most difficult portion of the ceremonial law for the modern Christian to understand deals with the various categories of "clean" and "unclean." Certain actions, conditions, or objects rendered one "unclean" and consequently unfit to participate in the worshiping community.

As a first step in grasping this entire concept, we need to be clear on the definition. "Uncleanness" is a ritual or ceremonial idea in the Mosaic Law.

Ritual refers to a prescribed form or order of worship. Uncleanness, in a ritual sense, is not primarily referring to filth or refuse, though physical cleanliness was enjoined upon Israel. Rather, uncleanness signifies a condition of separation between a holy God and sinful human beings. Thus "the standard of ritual purity in Israel is built on the view of God's holiness and of man's alienation from God because of his sin."[15] Uncleanness is not necessarily sinful itself, but is symptomatic of sin and may lead to sin. Essentially uncleanness is that which renders one *unqualified or unfit to approach a holy God*. One may not casually or indifferently draw near to God; to do so is to invite destruction.

Holiness is dynamically opposed to sin, and uncleanness is precariously close to sin. "The laws of uncleanness prevented false approaches to the true God."[16] Conversely, cleanness speaks of fitness to approach God in worship. "Cleanness has to do with fidelity to cultic laws . . . [it] is a condition of being obedient to the statutes and ordinances of the law, which allow one to encounter the holy without danger."[17]

For the sake of clarity we organize these various laws of uncleanness into five basic categories. They are as follows:

1. Contact with a corpse
2. Contagious skin diseases
3. Processes connected with sex and reproduction
4. Consumption of a forbidden food
5. Physical impairments[18]

In each of these categories, circumstances or situations might arise which rendered one "unclean," that is, unfit to worship. Obviously uncleanness was a recurring experience for every Israelite; in particular, death and sexual activity would affect everyone sooner or later. Remember, uncleanness did not mean that one was guilty of sin—only that one lacked ritual purity. To remedy this deficiency there were steps by which one could achieve the requisite ritual purity in most cases. Sadly, there were a few instances in which no remedy was available. These will be mentioned shortly. Becoming "clean" might entail immersing and/or washing, burning with fire, cleansing agents, the passage of time, and in some instances, the offering of sacrifice.

The most difficult aspect of uncleanness is trying to ascertain the rationale for these forbidden categories. Some say that the laws were arbitrary in nature; they were simply imposed as a test of Israel's loyalty and obedience to the Lord.[19] As such they served to separate Israel from her neighbors and so to create a barrier against pagan influences. While it is true that these guidelines did separate Israel from her neighbors, arbitrariness does not seem in keeping with God's character and dealings with Israel as revealed in other portions of the great law code of Moses. In fact the motivation for observing God's laws in Leviticus is repeatedly stated: "I am the Lord your God"; arbitrariness does not seem consonant with this. We probe more deeply for an underlying rationale.

A popular idea focuses on hygienic factors; that is, these regulations protected Israel against various diseases. According to this view, even though the Hebrews knew nothing about germs and bacteria, God gave them rules that would greatly diminish the health risks involved in various activities and circumstances. Proponents appeal to Exodus 15:26: "If you listen carefully to the voice of the LORD your God and do what is right in his eyes, if you pay attention to his commands and keep all his decrees, I will not bring on you any of the diseases I brought on the Egyptians, for I am the LORD who heals you."[20] There is a certain plausibility in this approach. We know, for example, that corpses spread disease, sick people infect others, and certain animals transmit parasites.

As a comprehensive explanation, however, hygiene seems inadequate. For example, why are the food laws no longer applicable to Christians? The NT clearly indicates that they are no longer binding (Mk 7:14-23; Ac 10:9-16; Col 2:16-17; 1Ti 4:3-5). If hygiene were the issue for Israel, why is it no longer so for the Church?

Another possible explanation centers on Canaanite cultic practices. Some of the forbidden animals figured prominently in Canaanite sacrificial rituals. Sacred prostitution flourished, and occult practices, including attempts to communicate with the dead, found wide acceptance. To prevent pagan influence, the Lord created barriers to social intercourse with pagans. The laws dealing with food, sexual processes, and death functioned in precisely this way. While throwing some welcome light on this issue, we must admit, however, that it falls short of explaining all the regulations. For example, Canaanites, like the Hebrews, offered sheep and cattle, yet these were not prohibited to the Israelites.

Perhaps the best comprehensive explanation for the laws of uncleanness is the symbolism. The various things that rendered one unclean are symbolic or typical of sin, which separates from a holy God. Within this general conception Mary Douglas has advanced a systematic understanding of these laws that makes sense. She suggests that wholeness, integrity and conformity to a norm or type is the fundamental rationale. Whatever falls short of this ideal is treated as unclean.[21] Thus Israel is taught to make distinctions and discriminations. The standard for this elaborate symbolism is the holiness of God and the perfect salvation that he provides.

In light of this, one can easily perceive that death is the most vivid reminder and symbol of sin in the world (Ge 2:17; 3:19; Ro 5:12). Death is the opposite of what God intends for his people (Dt 30:19). It is the withdrawal of life from the body. Consequently, contact with a corpse is the most defiling of all the categories.

Disease, especially skin disease, which visibly mars God's special creation, demonstrates the presence of sin in humanity. Since anyone suffering from this condition falls short of the divine ideal for humanity, the individual becomes ritually unclean and cannot worship with the community until the condition clears up.

Bodily emissions connected with reproduction also render one unclean in that there is a loss of fluids. This is not to say that sex as such is sinful, but the restraint such a system places upon sexuality does promote a circumspect relationship between the sexes. Furthermore, such a system prevents sexual acts from being introduced into the worship of the community, as it was among the Canaanites. Thus, a couple who had intercourse must bathe with water and wait until sunset (Lev 15:16-18). Since participation in communal worship was prohibited to those who were unclean, this effectively prevented ritual prostitution, part of the destructive fertility cult of the Canaanites. The uncleanness connected to childbirth and the menstrual cycle derives from the loss of blood. Since blood was the medium of atonement, it was holy. Loss of blood immediately rendered one unclean until a certain period of time elapsed.

With regard to unclean food, the idea is once again that of conformity to a standard of wholeness and normality. As Wenham observes:

> The animal world is divided into three spheres; those that fly in the air, those that walk on the land, and those that swim in the seas (cf. Gen. 1:20-30). Each sphere has a particular mode of motion associated with it. Birds have two wings with which to fly, and two feet for walking; fish have fins and scales with which to swim; land animals have hoofs to run with. The clean animals are those that conform to these standard pure types. Those creatures which in some way transgress the boundaries are unclean.[22]

The last category is physical impairments. This applied primarily to the priests. No priest could serve at the sanctuary who lacked a limb, was mutilated, or had any defect (Lev 21:16-24). The point seems to have been that the one who mediates between the holy God and his people must reflect the image of wholeness and integrity that is the goal for every believer in the Lord.

In summary, the necessity of making fine distinctions between what is holy and common, clean and unclean, serves to impress upon Israel the danger of being separated from a holy God.[23] The cult, however, provides a means to overcome uncleanness and to resume communal worship. This results in a sense of acceptance and assurance. Uncleanness is not necessarily sinful; rather, it is a recurring fact of life. Nothing is more basic than bed and board! Since the laws of uncleanness permeate all of life, the system fosters a constant awareness of God's claims upon his people.

The NT, while no longer requiring ritual purity, nonetheless urges upon the new people of God moral purity. It too seeks to promote an awareness of the Holy One (2Co 7:1; 1Ti 2:2; Heb 12:10, 14). The ultimate intent of the laws of uncleanness still applies to the Christian Church. Paul's prayer for the Philippians focuses on that abiding concern: ". . . that you may be able to discern what is best and may be pure and blameless until the day of Christ" (Php 1:10).

The civil law.

1. Contents. The third main aspect of the Mosaic Law pertains to the civil law. Here we find those miscellaneous laws that cover such mundane matters as property rights, personal injury, slaves, litigation, and social responsibility. Most of this legislation is of the nature of case law, that is, law based on judicial decision and precedent. Case law is framed in the conditional mood with an *if . . . then* construction (if you buy . . . if men quarrel . . . if a man hits . . . if a man steals . . . then . . .). These laws probably served as guidelines for priests and elders in the settlement of actual cases brought before them.

2. Comparison with other ancient law codes. Archaeological investigation has revealed that Hebrew laws have numerous parallels to ancient law codes that, in many cases, antedate those of Moses by several centuries. To take but one example, the *Code of Hammurabi* discovered in 1901 and dating to around 1728-1676 B.C. (about three centuries at least before Moses), has several very close parallels to the Law of Moses. In matters of false witness, kidnapping, and loss of animals entrusted to one's care, the offense and penalty in the respective codes are identical. (cf. Ex 23:1-3; Hammurabi 1, 3, 4; Ex 21:16; Hammurabi 14; Ex 22:10-13; Hammurabi 266-267).[24] The examples multiply when one considers parallels that are similar in wording.

This similarity has led to the inference that the Hebrews simply borrowed their legal system from the more advanced cultures that preceded and/or surrounded them. Often this has coincided with a devaluing of the unique and revelatory character of biblical law.

We need to remind ourselves that God's revelation has come to us in the garb of humanity. There must be accommodation to the audience if there is to be meaningful communication. As we saw in the opening chapter, Scripture bears the earmarks of humanity. Here is a case in point. There is no doubt that correspondences between ancient law codes and the biblical laws exist. We should be surprised if there were not! The fact is that the resemblances stem from a similar intellectual and cultural heritage. The Hebrews were a Semitic people who lived in the ancient Near East. "It is only natural that in codes dealing with peoples in somewhat similar conditions, related racially and culturally, that there should be some likeness in the incidents leading to litigation and likewise in the penalties imposed for infringement of common statutes."[25]

Having acknowledged similarities, however, we should also point out significant differences. Beginning with the least important, we observe that the biblical laws regulate a simple farming and pastoral society. The law codes of Mesopotamia pertain to a more urbanized and commercial society. More importantly, the Mosaic Law code is characterized by many purely religious injunctions. By contrast, the law of Hammurabi is strictly civil. There are no injunctions pertaining to the worship of deities.

The respective codes also display a marked difference in the level of morality. The Mosaic code is more humane than any of its counterparts. This humaneness is especially manifest in regard to the type of punishments inflicted and the status of the powerless. With regard to the former, the code of Hammurabi specified at least ten varieties of bodily mutilation. Nearly anything that could be cut off, might be! Only one instance of mutilation was sanctioned in the Law of Moses (Dt 25:11-12). Of special interest is the fact that the Mosaic Law placed more value on human life than on property. In certain cases, theft was a capital offense in Hammurabi's code; in the OT, it never was. Instead, restitution was prescribed. For example, Hammurabi's Code paragraph 22 reads: "If a citizen has committed a robbery and is caught, that man shall die."[26] This should be contrasted to Exodus 22:1-14. Furthermore, there was a sliding scale of justice in Hammurabi's code according to class distinction.[27] No such class distinctions existed in Israel. In principle, there was justice for all (Lev 24:22). As for the powerless—the orphans, widows, women generally, and slaves—they were treated with more compassion and equity than in the pagan law codes. The OT Law, for example, provides for emancipation of slaves, whereas this rarely occurs in Hammurabi's Code.[28]

This differing morality points to an even more fundamental distinction. The law code of Hammurabi is essentially secular in nature. Its overriding concern is for the efficient functioning of the economic and commercial interests of the city-state. Inefficiency and negligence are as criminal as theft. Over against this stands the essentially religious nature of the Law of Moses. *The golden thread throughout its regulations is the two-fold foci of love for God* (Dt 6:4-5) *and love for neighbor* (Lev 19:18). Quite alien to the ethos of Hammurabi's Code, the Law of Moses enjoins the curbing of lust (Ex 20:17) and seeks to limit selfishness. Indeed, charity is an obligation (Ex 22:21-27, 29; 23:4-11).

This brings us to the heart of the matter. The Law of Moses has as its foundational principle *the will of a holy God*. Such cannot be said for the Code of Hammurabi. Now, to be sure, Hammurabi claimed that his law code had divine authority. His god Shamash (the sun-god) was represented at the top of the stele (an upright stone with an inscribed surface) on which the code was written as handing a copy to Hammurabi personally. This kind of after-the-fact legitimization was undoubtedly essential for widespread acceptance. Yet, as we have already seen, the code itself was essentially secular. The will of Shamash is not appealed to once, nor is it even a presupposition for the various enactments. By contrast, the "Ten Words" were inscribed by Yahweh's own finger; the Book of the Covenant was dictated by Yahweh himself (Ex 20:1; 21:1; 24:2, 12; 34:1, 27-28); and furthermore, the Sinai Code was stamped by Yahweh's own character—it is theological through and through. This theological basis accounts for the most significant difference; indeed, *the moral perfection of the God of Israel makes all the difference in the world*.

Does the civil law of ancient Israel have any abiding relevance? Since we are obviously not members of the theocratic kingdom of Israel, we are instead bound by the civil laws of our own nation, state, county, and community.[29] Still, the ancient laws of Moses continue to impact our lives. In the United States, our legal tradition is greatly indebted to English common law. English common law is in turn much indebted to the OT laws. There is then some continuity with regard to the principles of jurisprudence (philosophy of law). Yet it must be acknowledged that we are culturally far removed from the times of ancient Israel and our society has a vastly more complex legal system. We should be careful, however, in thinking that we cannot learn anything from the civil laws of ancient Israel that would guide us as we live in the 21st century. As a matter of fact, there are a number of principles implicit in the civil laws that we would do well to recapture for our own day. I will give but one example and challenge you to discover others.

We mentioned earlier that in ancient Israel more value resides in people than in property. Capital punishment was not imposed as a deterrent—it was a recognition that every human being is made in God's image. To take another's life intrudes into a sphere of authority that only God possesses. Each person has worth as an image-bearer. To take away a human life is to forfeit one's own right to bear the image of God in life. Consequently, crimes against persons were treated with utmost seriousness and severity. The intention was to uphold human dignity and worth.

On the other hand, crimes dealing with property were not punished as severely. The reason seems clear: *things are not nearly as important as persons*. Inasmuch as property does, however, reflect the values and concerns of personhood, there are rights to be recognized and protected. Still, the degree of punishment is not the same as crimes against people themselves. There is no capital punishment for theft; restitution is the prescribed sentence. The offender restores (and adds to) the property of the owner. Restitution emphasizes that property is an extension of a person who reflects the image of God. As image-bearers all are commissioned with work. By means of productive effort as stewards of God's good gifts, we give an accounting of our efforts to rule over the earth. Theft is a means of acquiring at the expense of others and violates the notion of stewardship.

In short, capital punishment for theft is much too severe—no lesson about stewardship can be learned that way! More to the point in our society, incarceration (imprisonment) also fails—how can the dignity of victim and offender be restored? As a matter of fact, the victim usually pays more than the value of the goods stolen. Not only does he/she lose the property stolen, he/she must also pay taxes to support the thief during his period of incarceration! The offender suffers the indignity of dehumanizing forces while in prison, and, all too often, only learns how to be a better criminal. The statistics on repeat offenders are appalling.

What we are arguing for is a system whereby thieves recompense their victims—the OT principle of restitution. This, we think, restores the proper balance between people and things. Our penal system all too often places those guilty of theft in the same prisons as those guilty of murder. This reveals our values; things are becoming more important than persons. We should try to reverse this through a process of prison and penal justice reform.

Furthermore, the notion that the penal system, as it presently exists, functions as a remedial institution is belied by the facts. The incidence of repeat offenders remains discouragingly high. Those sent to prison typically emerge angrier and more clever in crime than before. The prison system actually serves as a training ground in crime!

A major problem in this regard is public apathy. Individuals who have family members, relatives or friends in this dehumanizing system soon realize the appalling conditions. But unfortunately, there is scant awareness and concern by the larger society. The general approach appears to be "out of sight, out of mind." The price paid by the public for this indifference can scarcely be calculated. Our prisons are full to overflowing; surely there is a better way. The ancient Law of Moses points us toward this better way. The prophets of Israel and the teachings of Jesus and his apostles assist us even more to provide a climate for criminal justice that combines justice and mercy in just the right proportions.[30]

The Sinai Covenant

Introduction

At the heart of Israelite religion stands the covenant Yahweh made with Israel at Mt. Sinai. In 1954 George Mendenhall of the University of Michigan demonstrated that the Sinai Covenant had close parallels to suzerainty treaties of the second millennium B.C. This observation cast an entirely new light on the subject.[31] A suzerainty treaty was an agreement imposed by a powerful ruler (a suzerain) upon a weaker ruler (a vassal). The overlord or suzerain promised certain benefactions (benefits or gifts) to his vassal if specific stipulations were obeyed. These suzerainty treaties of the mid-second millennium displayed regularity in their components. They contained six main sections in the written text itself. We will illustrate these parts by quoting from an actual treaty imposed by the Hittite king Mursilis II on his vassal Duppi-Tessub of Amurru sometime between 1339-1309 B.C.[32]

Components of a Second Millennium Suzerainty Treaty

Preamble. The first part of the suzerainty treaty is the preamble or title. This portion identifies the author of the treaty, the suzerain. It is often in very flowery language, which, of course, is highly flattering to the overlord. Here is how Mursilis II began:

> These are the words of the Sun Mursilis,
> the great king, the king of the Hatti land,
> the valiant, the favorite of the Storm-god,
> the son of Suppiluliumus, the great king,
> the king of the Hatti land, the valiant.[33]

Humility is obviously not considered a virtue!

Historical prologue. Next comes the historical prologue. This section reviews previous relations between the two parties. Past benefactions by the Suzerain are enumerated in order to impress upon the vassal the reasons why he should be grateful and loyal. Here is how Mursilis expresses it:

> Aziras was the grandfather of you, Duppi-Tessub. He rebelled against my father, but submitted again to my father. When the kings of Nuhasse land and the kings of Kinza rebelled against my father, Aziras did not rebel. As he was bound by treaty, he remained bound by treaty. As my father fought against his enemies, in the same manner fought Aziras. Aziras remained loyal toward my father [as his overlord] and did not incite my father's anger. My father was loyal toward Aziras and his country. . . .
>
> When my father became god [i.e. died] and I seated myself on the throne of my father, Aziras behaved toward me just as he had behaved toward my father. . . .
>
> When your father died, in accordance with your father's word I did not drop you. Since your father had mentioned to me your name *with great praise,* I sought after you. To be sure, you were sick and ailing, but, though you were ailing, I, the Sun, put you in the place of your father and took your brothers (and) sisters and the Amurru land in oath for you.[34]

Stipulations. Next comes the most important part of the suzerainty treaty—the stipulations. This section consists of the obligations laid upon the vassal by the overlord. The obligation above all others is loyalty. Thus the purpose of the treaty comes down to this: the securing of the entire allegiance of a vassal to the suzerain. The stipulations portion of the treaty generally falls into two categories. There are the basic or general stipulations followed by an elaboration into detailed and specific stipulations. Here are examples from Mursilis' treaty:

a. Basic stipulation:

> . . . So honor the oath (of loyalty) to the king and the king's *kin!* And I, the king, will be loyal toward you, Duppi-Tessub. When you take a wife, and when you beget an heir, he shall be king in the Amurru land likewise. And just as I shall be loyal toward you, even so shall I be loyal toward your son. But you, Duppi-Tessub remain loyal toward the king of Hatti land. . . Do not turn your eyes to anyone else!

b. Detailed stipulations:

> With my friend you shall be friend, and with my enemy you shall be enemy. . . .
>
> As I, the Sun, am loyal toward you, do you extend military help to the Sun and the Hatti land. . . . (If) anyone should revolt against you, (if) you then write to the king of Hatti land, and the king of Hatti land dispatches foot soldiers and charioteers to your aid—<if you treat them in an unfair manner>, you act in disregard of the gods of the oath.
>
> If anyone of the deportees from the Nuhasse land . . . escapes and comes to you, (if) you do not seize him and turn him back to the king of the Hatti land . . . you act in disregard of your oath.
>
> If anyone utters words unfriendly toward the king or the Hatti land before you, Duppi-Tessub, you shall not withhold his name from the king. . . .
>
> If a fugitive comes to your country seize him. . . .[35]

Provisions relating to the treaty document. There is also a section containing provisions relating to the treaty document. The text itself is deposited in the sanctuary of the vassal. There are two copies—one for the suzerain and one for the vassal. Furthermore, the text of the treaty must be read aloud in public periodically by the vassal. Though missing in Mursilis' treaty, this section appears in a similar treaty made by Suppiluliumas.

> A duplicate of this tablet has been deposited before the Sun-goddess of Arinna, because the Sun-goddess of Arinna regulates kingship and queenship.
>
> In the Mitanni land (a duplicate) has been deposited before Tessub, the lord of the *kurinnu* [a kind of sanctuary or shrine] of Kahat. At regular intervals shall they read it in the presence of the king of the Mitanni land and in the presence of the sons of the Hurri country. . . .[36]

Witnesses to the treaty. The fifth element of a second millennium suzerainty treaty consists of a long list of gods/goddesses who are invoked as witnesses to the covenant. This section can be quite lengthy and demonstrates how numerous the gods were in these ancient polytheistic religions. Here are some of the deities appealed to by Mursilis II:

> The Sun-god of Heaven, the Sun-goddess of Arinna, the Storm-god of Heaven, the Hattian Storm-god, Seris (and) Hurris, Mount Nanni (and) Mount Hazzi. . . .
>
> Sin, lord of the oath, Ishara, queen of the oath, Hebat queen of heaven, Ishtar, Ishtar of the battlefield, Ishtar of Nineveh. . . .
>
> . . . all the olden gods, Naras, Napsaras, Minki, Tuhusi, Ammunki, Ammizadu, Allalu . . . the mountains, the rivers, the springs, the great Sea, heaven and earth, the winds (and) the clouds—let these be witnesses to this treaty and to the oath.[37]

Curses and blessings. The last item consists of a series of curses and blessings. The curses are invoked upon the vassal if he breaks the treaty by acts of disloyalty. On the other hand, the blessings are invoked as a reward for faithful obedience to the treaty stipulations.

> The words of the treaty and the oath that are inscribed on this tablet—should Duppi-Tessub not honor these words of the treaty and the oath, may these gods of the oath destroy Duppi-Tessub together with his person, his wife, his son, his grandson, his house, his land and together with everything that he owns.
>
> But if Duppi-Tessub honors these words of the treaty and the oath that are inscribed on this tablet, may these gods of the oath protect him together

> with his person, his wife, his son, his grandson, his house (and) his country.[38]

Unwritten components. Besides these six written elements, there are two other components of the suzerainty treaty. First, at the ratification of the treaty, the vassal comes to the palace of the suzerain and participates in a solemn ceremony. Central to this solemn ceremony is a formal oath of obedience sworn by the vassal. Secondly, there is a formal procedure for acting against rebellious vassals. If, in the course of time, the overlord receives word that the vassal has acted with disloyalty, a specially delegated messenger urges the vassal to rectify his behavior and warns him of the consequences of continued disobedience. This, then, constituted a suzerainty treaty of the mid-second millennium B.C.

Analysis of Sinai Covenant

Similarities. We turn now to a comparative analysis of the covenant Yahweh made with Israel at Mt. Sinai. The parallels suddenly stand out in sharp relief.

The preamble of the Sinai Covenant is succinct. It also lacks the unnecessary self-congratulations so evident in the pagan suzerainty treaties. "And God spoke all these words" (Ex 20:1). Note that two other portions of the OT display suzerainty treaty features, and both of these, the book of Deuteronomy and Joshua 24, are occasions of covenant renewal. Deuteronomy 1:1-5 and Joshua 24:2 function as preambles in their literary contexts.

The historical prologue follows in Exodus 20:2: "I am the LORD your God, who brought you out of Egypt, out of the land of slavery." This brief retrospect indicates the grounds for Israel's gratitude as a loyal vassal to Yahweh; she was completely indebted to Yahweh for her existence as a distinct people. The historical prologue is much more extensive and impressive in Deuteronomy 1:6–3:29 where a long rehearsal of all Yahweh's blessings occurs. See also Joshua 24:2-13 for a historical review going all the way back to Abraham.

The stipulations fall neatly into the two categories of basic and detailed. The basic stipulations are summarized in the Ten Words (or Ten Commandments), but even these are epitomized in the essential requirement for enjoying the protection and blessing of Yahweh: "You shall have no other gods before me" (Ex 20:3). Yahweh demands exclusive loyalty. Following the Ten Words (20:1-17), chapters 21–23, designated by scholars "the Covenant Code," spell out the detailed stipulations. Similarly, Deuteronomy 4–11 answers to the basic stipulations followed by chapters 12–26 which list the detailed stipulations. The considerable expansion in Deuteronomy derives from the fact that the Sinai Covenant is incorporated into a series of sermons delivered on the occasion of a covenant renewal ceremony. Joshua 24:14-25 also reflects a covenant renewal ceremony.

With regard to the provisions for the covenant document we find a precise parallel to the suzerainty treaties. In Exodus 25:16 (and 34:1, 28-29) the deposition of the text is specified: "Then put in the ark the Testimony which I will give you." The "Testimony" refers to the text of the covenant—at least the preamble, historical prologue and basic stipulations (Ten Words), though it may also have included the detailed stipulations (Covenant Code), provisions for deposition, witnesses and curses and blessings. Compare Deuteronomy 31:24-26:

> After Moses finished writing in a book the words of this law from beginning to end, he gave this command to the Levites who carried the ark of the covenant of the LORD: "Take this Book of the Law and place it beside the ark of the covenant of the LORD your God. There it will remain as a witness against you."

With regard to the public reading there is a very good parallel in Deuteronomy 31:10-13:

> Then Moses commanded them: "At the end of every seven years, in the year for canceling debts, during the Feast of Tabernacles, when all Israel comes to appear before the LORD your God at the place he will choose, you shall read this law before them in their hearing. Assemble the people—men, women and children, and the aliens living in your towns—so they can listen and learn to fear the LORD your God and follow carefully all the words of this law. Their children, who do not know this law, must hear it and learn to fear the LORD your God as long as you live in the land you are crossing the Jordan to possess."

It is with the witnesses that we have a *major departure* from the standard suzerainty treaty format. As one would expect, no other gods/goddesses are appealed to as witnesses. Instead, a memorial stone serves as a silent witness (Ex 24:4; Jos 24:27). In addition, Moses composes a song, somewhat like our national anthem, which functions as a constant witness (Dt 31:19–32:43). Even the law book itself and the people as participants bear witness to the covenant (Dt 31:26; Jos 24:22). The song of Moses also refers to the heavens and the earth as silent witnesses to this epoch-making event (Dt 32:1).

An interesting variation occurs with respect to the curses and blessings. *In the Sinai Covenant the order is reversed:* the blessings come first, followed by a much longer section enumerating the curses for disobedience. This section can be seen in Leviticus 26:3-13 (blessings) and 14-20 (curses). In Deuteronomy 28:1-68 we also have the blessings (1-14) followed by the curses (15-68). This section is implicit in Joshua 24:19-20.

The parallel goes beyond even the written elements, however. One can also detect the other three elements of a suzerainty treaty. The solemn ceremony is narrated in Exodus 24. (A covenant renewal ceremony also occurs in Deuteronomy 27 and Joshua 24.) Here, in a most impressive setting, Israel stands before her suzerain, listens to the reading of the covenant document, and swears allegiance: "Everything the LORD has said we will do" (24:3). The suzerain's palace is the awesome Mt. Sinai. A private audience takes place on the summit where Moses and Aaron, Nadab and Abihu, and the seventy elders, as representatives of the nation, stand before their suzerain ("they saw God and they ate and drank," 24:11). At the foot of the mountain, an altar and twelve stone pillars representing the twelve tribes of Israel add to the solemnity of the occasion. Significantly, sacrificial blood is sprinkled on both the altar and people. Only by means of shed blood could they come into the presence of a holy God. Thus the oath and ceremony of the suzerainty treaty had their counterparts in the Sinai Covenant.

One last feature remains: notification of treaty violation. This, too, appears in the prophetic literature. As we will explore in more detail in chapter eight, the prophets of Israel function as delegates of Yahweh warning her repeatedly of covenant violations. Their messages ring with the authority of the suzerain and constantly refer to the relationship that exists between Yahweh and Israel; in form and terminology they are similar to lawsuits (See Hos 4:1-3; Am 3:1-2). This, then, is the formal procedure for acting against rebellious vassals. *Thus in virtually every respect the Sinai Covenant conforms to the essential elements of the second-millennium suzerainty treaties*. These can be summarized in chart form.

Differences. The Sinai Covenant, however, does entail three significant adaptations of the suzerainty treaty format. In the first place, suzerainty treaties are always enacted between the heads of two already-existing states. In the case of Israel, we have a unique circumstance—she is a brand new people without a prehistory. Her suzerain first creates her and then places her under covenant obligations. Secondly, the covenant between Yahweh and Israel is much more comprehensive than a typical suzerainty treaty—it regulates both Israel's internal and external affairs. By contrast, a suzerainty treaty controls only the foreign policy of a vassal state. Finally, the Sinai Covenant represents a unique arrangement. Israel is the sole people in the privileged relationship of knowing Yahweh, the overlord. By contrast, a second-millennium suzerainty treaty was not restricted to a single vassal state; a particular overlord might be in treaty with two or more vassals at the same time.

The Sinai Covenant and Suzerainty Treaties

Component (Written)	Component (Unwritten)	Function	Biblical Parallel
Preamble		Identifies the author of the treaty	Ex 20:1; Dt 1:1-5; Jos 24:1-2
Historical prologue		Reviews previous relations between parties	Ex 20:2; Dt 1:6-3:29; Jos 24:2-13
Stipulations		Lists obligations laid upon vassal	Ex 20:3-17; 20:22-23:17; Dt 4-26; Jos 24: 14-25
Disposition of document		Specifies the deposition and reading of treaty	Ex 25:16; 34:1, 28-29; Dt 31:1-13, 24-26
Witnesses		Lists the various witnesses to the treaty	Ex 24:4; Jos 24:27 (stone); Dt 31:19-32:43 (song); Dt 32:1 (heaven and earth)
Curses and blessings		Lists penalties and benefits	Lev 26:1-33; Dt 28; Jos 24:20
	Solemn ceremony	Formal oath of obedience in the presence of suzerain	Ex 24; renewed in Dt 27 and Jos 24
	Treaty violation	Formal procedure for acting against rebellious vassal. Lawsuit or indictment.	Am 3:1-2; Hos 4:1-3; Isa 1:2-31; Mic 6:1-16

Theological Significance of the Sinai Covenant

We inquire now into the theological implications of the suzerainty treaty between Yahweh and Israel.[39] Seven theological principles flow out of the relationship.

Unilateral in nature. God and Israel do not stand on equal footing in this relationship. To put it another way, there is no parity between the covenant partners. The Sinai Covenant is unilateral in that Yahweh establishes the relationship; he takes the initiative and dictates the terms. This principle is still valid. The Church, likewise, stands in a similar relationship. Certainly believers today do not negotiate the terms of relationship with God; they do not suggest compromises or trade-offs. On the contrary, the New Covenant established by the blood of Jesus Christ comes to us in an unconditional form; either we accept his terms or we have no relationship. "I am the way and the truth and the life. No one comes to the Father except through me" (Jn 14:6).

Required response. God's people are required to respond with faith, obedience, and love. In this sense there is a human component to the covenant relationship. In a word, the response demanded is *loyalty*. Undivided allegiance is still obligatory for the NT believer. Jesus said: "No one can serve two masters. . . . You cannot serve both God and Money" (Mt 6:24). "If anyone would come after me, he must deny himself and take up his cross and follow me" (Mk 8:34). "If you love me, you will obey what I command" (Jn 14:15).

Faith and history. The Sinai Covenant involves God in the history of his people. This notion of a God who acts in history, indeed, who guides the course of history for a particular people is distinctive in ancient Israel. The Church also confesses that the Lord of the universe directs the course of history for each individual believer as well as for the corporate body. "I will be with you always, to the very end of the age" (Mt 28:20). "His intent was that now, through the church, the manifold wisdom of God should be made known to the rulers and authorities in the heavenly realms . . ." (Eph 3:10).

Security and assurance. For God's people there is now a real security in life. Real trust between God and his people is possible. This contrasts markedly with the pagans and their gods. The pagans were always running scared because they never knew for sure if their gods were pleased with them or not. Furthermore, even if all the right rituals and ceremonies have been observed, there was always the possibility that fate would overrule the god and disaster would still strike. The faith of Israel did not allow an independent force or power to operate in the universe; Yahweh is supreme, and he is committed to the protection and blessing of Israel. The same is true of the Church. Listen to these words of assurance from the Apostle Paul:

> For I am convinced that neither death nor life, neither angels nor demons, neither the present nor the future, nor any powers, neither heights nor depth, nor anything else in all creation, will be able to separate us from the love of God that is in Christ Jesus our Lord. (Ro 8:38-39).

Morality and ethics. The Sinai Covenant makes possible a well-defined moral and social order based upon the covenant stipulations. At the heart of the covenant are the Ten Words which function as a transcript of God's character. For Israel and for the Church morality is not determined by sociological consensus or by legislative and judicial process; the will of Yahweh governs the behavior and ethics of his people. This means that, for the believer today in the United States, just because 51% of the population decide by ballot that a certain action is legal, it does not necessarily mean that it is permissible for the Christian. A law passed by Congress or a ruling handed down by the Supreme Court must never take precedence over the clear teaching of Scripture. God's Word is the final court of appeal for faith and ethics in the life of a Christian (Ac 5:29). God's people know what is expected and required of them.

Fundamental benefit. The fundamental benefit of the covenant is the knowledge of the Lord. No price can be set on such knowledge—it is beyond calculation. All of life now becomes a response to God's will. Knowing God is not mere intellectual awareness of his attributes and laws—it involves a deepening, personal experience of fellowship and communion. For the faithful Israelite, and for the Christian, there is no artificial distinction between the sacred and secular. Sanctity permeates all of life—the routine as well as those special moments of worship and exaltation.

Scope of the covenant. Finally, we note that this covenant between God and his people hints at a universal application. True, only Israel is a vassal nation under the suzerainty of Yahweh, but Israel is not limited to a specific ethnic, national group. In principle, anyone may join the covenant community. There is here no racism. The same should hold true for the Church. The Gospel reaches out to the ends of the earth and creates a new community of faith (cf. Ac 1:8; Eph 2:11–4:16). As in our discussion of election earlier, God's salvation is as wide as his mercy: "Turn to me and be saved, all you ends of the earth; for I am God, and there is no other" (Isa 45:23). Once again, note the symmetry and harmony in God's plan of salvation. The covenant between God and Israel has clear correspondences to the New Covenant between God and the Church. He is unchanging in his dealings with sinful human beings. Great is his faithfulness!

The Tabernacle

Introduction

The last question we take up is this: How did the tabernacle fit into the framework of the exodus and the Sinai Covenant? The answer appears in the basic promise of Exodus 6:7: "I will take you as my own people, and I will be your God." Notice that the first part of the verse summarizes the essence of the Sinai Covenant viewed as a form of suzerainty treaty. The second part of the verse, however, relates to the worship of Israel. The tabernacle, in other words, is the focus of Israel's cult in that the worship of Yahweh centers on this structure. Much insight can be gained by looking more closely at this meeting place between Yahweh and his people.[40]

A Description of the Tabernacle

Chapters 25–31 and 35–40 provide abundant material for analysis of this worship center.[41] However, the description surprises us in several particulars. In the first place, the order of description proceeds by *starting from the inside and working outward*. Secondly, we are surprised, and perhaps a bit bored, by what seems to western readers as the unnecessary repetition. Why was it important to narrate verbatim in chapters 35–40 that Moses made everything in accordance with God's commands, chapters 25–31. The whole section could have been summarized by saying that Moses did as he was ordered! Finally, the most surprising feature of all to Israel's neighbors concerns a significant omission. The tabernacle was best known to the pagans for what was *not* inside the sanctuary! The omission, of course, is an image of the Deity. Nowhere is any representation of Yahweh to be found, not even in abstract form. The term *anaconic* refers to this phenomenon and means that there were no images or visual representations of God in Israel's religion. So far as we know, only Israel's cult was anaconic among all the peoples of the ancient Near East.

Theological Significance of the Description

God's nature determines true worship. What then are the significant implications that follow from the above observations? The order of description stresses that which is most important first. In terms of function the tabernacle serves as a sort of "wrapping" for the invisible God. All the furnishings, utensils, furniture, vestments, and assorted equipment are secondary to the astounding fact that Yahweh's presence resides in this simple shelter. Thus the account in Exodus starts with that which is most important in the tabernacle—the ark of the Testimony. This chest contains the covenant document between the great suzerain and his vassal. It also represents the footstool of the great king (see Ps 99:1-5; 1Ch 28:2). His presence with his people is indicated by a glowing light, the Shekinah, appearing just above the two cherubim who hovered over the ark. *Thus it is God's nature rather than anything in the created order that determines the nature of true worship.*

Consequently, the people of God need to get their priorities straight when they come before his presence. To put it another way, not our needs, but God's nature determines true worship. Modern worship practices need to be re-examined in light of this fundamental truth. Next time you are in a worship service, ask yourself whether what is being done reflects primarily the emotional and entertainment needs of the worshipers or the nature of God. The answer may be quite revealing.[42]

God's will determines true worship. The repetition in the description does more than simply take up space. Characteristically, repetition in Hebrew narrative serves to drive home an important point. We need to remember that the Hebrews were oriented to the oral rather than the visual dimension of storytelling. The repetition makes the point that true religion must conform to the express will of God. The importance of this principle is underscored in an unforgettable way by the story of Nadab and Abihu in Leviticus 10. These two young priests "took their censers, put fire in them and added incense; and they offered unauthorized fire before the LORD, contrary to his command. So fire came out from the presence of the LORD and consumed them . . ." (Lev 10:1-2). Precisely what the unauthorized fire was we do not know; we do know that it was contrary to the clear instructions given them. Deviation from the divine liturgy was not tolerated.

This probably strikes modern readers as disappointing. The hallmark of much contemporary Christian worship is variety and spontaneity. Does Leviticus 10 mean that there is only one set form of worship? I do not think so. Remember, at this point in redemptive history, Israel is surrounded by pagan neighbors who practice many immoral and degrading things as part of their religious rituals. Against that backdrop, the Lord sought to establish barriers that would prevent true worship from being slowly submerged in the orgies of Canaanite fertility rituals.

The fertility cult of Canaan was a form of magic. The Canaanites practiced sacred prostitution in order to stimulate Baal to have intercourse with his heavenly consorts (which were many). The rationale was that since Baal was the god of storm and rain, anything stimulating his sexual activity would bring rain and fruitful seasons upon the land. (Recall that in *Enumah Elish*, origins are connected to sexual intercourse). In the Canaanite cult, sacred prostitution assures the needed rain. Add to this the power of the sensual nature and you have a religion capable of exercising a powerful hold over the minds and bodies of people. The Canaanites also sacrificed firstborn children under the same misguided thinking that if one gave one's first or best to the deity, then the deity would give back other children to take their place. This whole business is akin to a genie in a bottle. The pagans thought they could manipulate their deities to get what they wanted. It is against such notions that the Nadab and Abihu episode should probably be viewed. I suspect that their innovation into the worship of Yahweh was similar to something the Canaanites practiced, and thus was punished so severely and summarily.

Now, with regard to modern Christian worship, I think there is still a relevant principle. Christian worship, worthy of the name, certainly may include considerable variety. This variety, however, should never compromise the theological integrity of Christian worship. The content of the "faith once for all delivered to the saints" must be preserved. Some practices introduced into Christian worship undermine a genuine meeting of God and his people. One thinks of certain meditation techniques, which are really based on a pantheistic worldview and focus more upon one's feelings than upon the true object of worship. The attempts by a few in some mainline denominations to "re-image" God as the divine *Sophia*, a feminine deity of paganism, are subversive and heretical. I also wonder if a modern form of the ancient fertility cult is being slipped in the back door in some forms of "Christian" hard rock, which appeal more to beat than beatitude! (I realize this labels me as an "old fogy," but it seems to me that careful discrimination is in order with regard to the controversial issue of acceptable church music.) Whatever one may think of the examples chosen, anything that usurps the centrality of the triune God in worship, is in danger of repeating the error of Nadab and Abihu.

God's spirituality determines true worship. The third implication arising from the description of the Tabernacle centers upon the lack of an image. This omission testifies to the spirituality of God; that is, God is a pure spirit and has no bodily parts. Not only is he a pure spirit, he is the eternal, self-existent Spirit who created all things. To represent him in any created form whatsoever is to restrict him greatly in his attributes. In the words of Isaiah, "To whom will you compare God?" (40:18). Nothing in the universe can represent Yahweh without reducing him immensely. Of course the pagans thought the Israelites were foolish in worshiping a God who could not be seen. For their part they never left home without their gods! They carried about their necks images of their god, thinking thereby that the deity was present. Israel knew better.

Modern believers need to rethink their position on this. Christians generally have not represented God the Father in human form—though one thinks of exceptions right away, like the famous paintings of Michelangelo on the ceiling of the Sistine Chapel. The Protestant tradition, however, has generally avoided this practice based upon the second commandment. Should we, however, incorporate pictures of Jesus in our churches and religious literature? The majority of Christians do, but should they?

The rationale is that the incarnation radically altered the situation. God, in the person of his son, entered into our existence. Jesus of Nazareth is truly a human being. As the writer to the Hebrews says: "Since the children have flesh and blood, he too shared in their humanity. . ." (Heb 2:14). It is this fact that has prompted Christians to represent Jesus in human form. The problem is that we tend to represent him like ourselves! The reaction of white Christians to a picture of a black Jesus is worth pondering. Though he is truly a human being, he is a truly unique human being—one who freely gave his life for all human beings (cf. Php 2:5-11). To be sure, his historic experience upon earth was lived out in a thoroughly Jewish context. This should not be denied or ignored.

It is a remarkable fact, however, that nowhere in the canonical Gospels do we have a physical description of Jesus. The only description of our Lord, in the NT, is found in the book of Revelation—a highly symbolic, visionary description. We can perhaps add Isaiah 53, which prophesies the ministry and death of Jesus: "He had no beauty or majesty to attract us to him, nothing in his appearance that we should desire him" (53:2). This biblical reluctance to describe the historical Jesus should probably be followed today. We are on firmer ground when we avoid representing any person of the triune God pictorially. Rather, on a positive note, we need to uphold and value God's transcendence, majesty, and incomparability.[43] Our best theologizing cannot adequately describe and explain him. He is bigger and greater and more wonderful than all that we can imagine! This seems to be the main point in the fact that there were no images in the tabernacle.

Typological Significance of the Tabernacle

Finally, we comment on the enduring spiritual significance of this mobile shrine. We have already indicated the presence of a typological dimension to the OT, namely, persons, places, events, and institutions that foreshadow NT truth. Without indulging in unwarranted flights of fancy, we can nonetheless see in the tabernacle the outlines of God's plan of salvation. The arrangement of the tabernacle and its furnishings illustrate how one can approach a holy God. We might say that the path to the holy of holies illuminates the way the people of God must always come to him.

The altar and justification. When one enters the outer courtyard, further progress is arrested by the imposing bronze altar. The first matter that must be settled, if one is to approach any further, is the problem of sin. The altar of burnt offering speaks of the necessity of atonement as a prerequisite for fellowship with a holy God. The penalty for sin must be paid and the sinner pardoned. This typifies the doctrine of justification.

The laver and daily cleansing. Beyond the altar stands the bronze laver, used daily by the priests for cleansing in connection with their sacrificial duties. The laver speaks of the need for confession and cleansing in our lives.

We need to be washed and renewed on a regular basis. 1 John 1:9 nicely summarizes this station on the way to the holy of holies: "If we confess our sins, he is faithful and just and will forgive us our sins and purify us from all unrighteousness."

The Holy Place and sanctification. We are now ready to enter the Holy Place, the anteroom to the Most Holy Place. Here we encounter three pieces of furniture: the table of bread on the north, the lampstand on the south, and, to the east, in front of the curtain separating the Holy Place from the Most Holy Place, the altar of incense. These pieces typify an advanced stage of spiritual development. If the courtyard illustrates one's initial conversion experience, and the need for daily forgiveness and cleansing, the Holy Place portrays an ongoing process of becoming holy. This is the doctrine of sanctification.

The three pieces of furniture in the Holy Place typify the means of becoming holy. The twelve loaves of bread, representing the entire people of God, speak of spiritual sustenance that comes by communing with God. His words are a source of spiritual nourishment and sustain us in our walk with him, a point made in Deuteronomy 8:3: ". . . man does not live on bread alone but on every word that comes from the mouth of the LORD" (cf. Mt 4:4). The lampstand speaks of spiritual illumination. Using the word of God, the Spirit of God quickens our conscience and mind and makes us sensitive to the things of the Spirit (see 1Co 2:12-15). Lastly, we see the altar of incense, symbolizing the ascending prayers of God's people (cf. Rev 5:8). Through prayer the people of God commune with their great King and heavenly Father. By these means of grace, there is an ever-deepening experience of fellowship with the holy God and with other members of the spiritual family.

The holy of holies and glorification. We come at last to the Most Holy Place. Inside this room, which is a perfect cube symbolizing the perfection of God, stands the centerpiece of the tabernacle, the ark of the covenant. This chest, surmounted by a lid consisting of two cherubim, contains the two copies of the covenant between Yahweh and Israel. Above the lid, conceived as the footstool of the Lord, shines the Shekinah, the visible radiance of God's presence. The ark is where the high priest sprinkles the blood of atonement on the Day of Atonement. The lid is called the mercy seat and typifies the truth that only through the effectiveness of the shed blood may a worshiper come to God. This room, symbolizing the culmination of God's saving plan whereby the sinner is conformed entirely to the moral image of Christ, is the ultimate experience of seeing God face to face (Mt 5:8). In NT terms this represents the doctrine of glorification (cf. Ro 8:17, 29-30). In short, *the tabernacle represents the completion and climax of God's redemption of his people.*

Accordingly, when the NT depicts the consummation of God's redemptive program, it does so by portraying a city in the shape of a cube. This perfect city, the New Jerusalem, is the place where God dwells with his people on a new, redeemed earth (Rev 21:1-27). Of course the student of the NT recognizes that the tabernacle falls short of the fellowship with God now available in Christ. In the OT era, only the high priest could venture into the Most Holy Place, and then only once a year on the Day of Atonement (Lev 16). Now access is provided on an unprecedented scale and scope (Ro 5:1). The book of Hebrews makes the repeated point that the New Covenant far exceeds the privileges and experiences of the Old.

> Therefore, brothers, since we have confidence to enter the Most Holy Place by the blood of Jesus, by a new and living way opened for us through the curtain, that is, his body, and since we have a great priest over the house of God, let us draw near to God with a sincere heart in full assurance of faith, having our bodies washed with pure water. (Heb 10:19-22)

Even this, however, pales in comparison to the glory that yet awaits the people of God at the Second Coming of Christ. As the Apostle John so memorably expresses it:

> Dear friends, now we are children of God, and what we will be has not yet been made known. But we know that when he appears, we shall be like him, for we shall see him as he is. Everyone who has this hope in him, purifies himself, just as he is pure. (1Jn 3:23)

Relationship of Theme to Core Concepts

Faith and Ethics: As we conclude our discussion of the exodus and the Sinai Covenant, we sketch in large brush strokes the leading theological ideas that emerge.[44] Viewed as a literary unit, the book of Exodus divides neatly into three divisions. These divisions afford an insight into the theological lessons which dominate the story of the exodus. In chapters 1–18 the narrative focuses upon the historic event of liberation from bondage. Theologically the idea of redemption is uppermost. In chapters 19–24 the narrative recounts the inauguration of the Sinai Covenant. The content of this covenant is spelled out.

The dominating concept throughout is morality. Then in chapters 25–40, with an interruption to describe the apostasy of the golden calf (chs. 32–34), we have a lengthy section giving detailed instruction about the construction of the tabernacle with its priesthood and furnishings. The keynote in this section is worship.

The chronological relationship of these three key concepts is not accidental. *The sequence of redemption, morality, and worship constitutes a theological paradigm for one's approach to a holy God.* There can be no worship until the problem of relationship is resolved. The people of God must first be set free from the bondage of sin. Redemption is a prerequisite for worship. As Jesus would say centuries later, "the true worshipers will worship the Father in spirit and truth, for they are the kind of worshipers the Father seeks" (Jn 4:23). Redemption produces morality. The attempt to live a life in accordance with the standard of a holy God, apart from being redeemed from the power of sin, is fruitless (Ro 7:21–8:4). Once liberated from the guilt and power of sin, however, the child of God delights in doing his will (Eph 5:1). Morality is a consequence of redemption, not a prerequisite. There are no self-made men and women in the kingdom of God!

The Unity of God's Plan of Salvation: This chapter has focused on the covenant and cult of Israel. As such it has demonstrated that there is a significant continuity between the Old Covenant people of God and the New Covenant people. There is an underlying unity and harmony in God's dealings with human beings. The Christian Church has always confessed that in the cult of Israel, we see types and symbols of the completed work of Christ. The notion of substitutionary atonement is rooted in the sacrificial system of ancient Israel. Israel and the Church both experience God's grace by means of a relationship defined in terms of covenant. The principles whereby a holy God saves a sinful people are constant in salvation history, thereby assuring us that God is faithful and can be trusted.

Faith and the Future: The tabernacle, in its arrangement and services, hints at God's ultimate objective for his people. The holy of holies was inaccessible to all but a select few. Yet it speaks of something better. The writer to the Hebrews says, "The Holy Spirit was showing by this that the way into the Most Holy Place had not yet been disclosed as long as the first tabernacle was still standing" (Heb 9:8). With the coming of our great High Priest, we may now "approach the throne of grace with confidence" (Heb 4:16). The new temple of God consists of believers in whom the Holy Spirit takes up residence (cf. 1Co 3:16; 6:19; 2Co 6:16). But there is more. The holy of holies, a cubic room, anticipates the glorification of all believers and their eternal dwelling with God in the New Jerusalem, portrayed in the book of Revelation as a perfect cube (Rev 21:15-17). Perfection and glory await every believer in Christ (cf. Ro 8:29-30).

For Further Discussion:

Does the United States of America have a covenantal relationship with the Lord? Defend your answer.

Should the constitution of the United States be amended by deleting the separation of Church and State from its principles and structure? Why or why not?

What relationship does the Mosaic Law have to the modern Christian?

Are there abiding principles in the Mosaic Law that apply to the modern Christian and to society at large? If so, how do we discover them?

Can animal sacrifice play any meaningful part in the life of a Christian? Why or why not?

How much of the detail involved in the tabernacle should be viewed as typological, i.e. as pointing toward the work of Christ on our behalf?

What do the exodus and the Sinai Covenant imply about God's ultimate purpose for his people?

For Further Reading:

Carpenter, E. E. "Sacrifices and Offerings in the OT," *ISBE*. 3d ed. 4:260-273.
Davis, J. J. *Moses and the God of Egypt*. Grand Rapids: Baker, 1971.
Dyrness, William. *Themes in Old Testament Theology*, pp. 113-160, 171-188. Downers Grove: InterVarsity, 1979.
Fee, Gordon D., and Douglas Stuart. *How to Read the Bible for All Its Worth*. 2d ed., pp. 149-164. Grand Rapids: Zondervan, 1993.
Feinberg, Charles Lee. "Clean and Unclean," pp. 238-241. *NBD*, 1962.

Fuller, Daniel P. *Unity of the Bible*, pp. 345-386. Grand Rapids: Zondervan, 1992.
Hartley, J. E. "Clean and Unclean," *ISBE*. 3d ed. 1:718-723.
Kaiser, Jr., Walter C. *Toward Old Testament Ethics*, pp. 81-111. Grand Rapids: Zondervan, 1983.
Kaiser, Jr., Walter C. *Toward an Old Testament Theology*, pp. 122-164. Grand Rapids: Zondervan, 1978.
Kline, Meredith G. *The Treaty of the Great King*. Grand Rapids: Eerdmans, 1963.
Sauer, Erich. *The Dawn of World Redemption*, pp. 113-120. Grand Rapids: Eerdmans, 1951 [rpt 1965].
Soltau, Henry W. *The Tabernacle, the Priesthood and the Offerings*. Harrisburg, PA: Christian Publications, 1965.
Westerholm, Stephen. "Tabernacle," *ISBE*. 3d ed. 4:698-706.
Wright, C. J. H. "The Ten Commandments," *ISBE*. 3d ed. 4:786-790.
______. *God's People in God's Land*. Grand Rapids: Eerdmans, 1990.

Endnotes

1. See James B. Pritchard, ed., *The Ancient Near East: An Anthology of Texts and Pictures* (Princeton: Princeton University Press, 1958), plate 84.

2. See K. A. Kitchen, "Plagues of Egypt," *NBD* (1962), pp. 1001-1003, for more discussion.

3. Taken from the book, *Chronological Charts of the Old Testament* by John H. Walton. Copyright © 1978 by The Zondervan Corporation. Used by permission of Zondervan Publishing House. Pg. 85.

4. See Peter Craigie for elaboration of this notion. *The Book of Deuteronomy* (*NICOT*; Grand Rapids: Eerdmans, 1976), pp. 19-83.

5. I am indebted to Kaiser, *Theology*, pp. 100-113 for the outline and much of the substance of this discussion.

6. See further Larry R. Helyer, *The Prototokos Title in the New Testament*, unpublished doctoral dissertation, Fuller Theological Seminary, Pasadena, CA, 1979, pp. 167-202.

7. A. van Selms, "Law," *NBD* (1962), pp. 718-721.

8. See Walter C. Kaiser, Jr., *Toward Old Testament Ethics* (Grand Rapids: Zondervan, 1983), pp. 81-95 for a helpful overview of the Ten Commandments.

Also helpful are articles by Vernon C. Grounds, "Commandments, Ten," *Zondervan Pictorial Encyclopedia of the Bible*, ed. Merrill C. Tenney (Grand Rapids: Zondervan, 1963), pp. 177-179; R. A. Cole, "Law in the Old Testament," *ZPEB* (1975), 3:883-894; Derek Kidner, "Ten Commandments," *ZPEB* (1975), 5:672-676; C. J. H. Wright, "Ten Commandments," *ISBE,* 3d ed., 4:786-790.

9. *The Message of the Old Testament* (Grand Rapids: Eerdmans, 1969), p. 40.

10. As may be seen in the Ebla texts from Syria. See Giovanni Pettinato, *The Archives of Ebla: An Empire Inscribed in Clay* (New York: Doubleday, 1981). See also Anson F. Rainey, "The Order of Sacrifices in Old Testament Ritual Texts," *Biblica* 51 (1970): 485-498.

11. Adapted from Walton, *Charts*, p. 22.

12. See further R. T. Beckwith, "Sacrifice and Offering," *NBD* (1962), pp. 1113-1123; Philip Budd, "The Sacrificial System," *Eerdmans' Handbook to the Bible*, ed. David Alexander and Pat Alexander (Grand Rapids: Eerdmans, 1973), pp. 174-175; J. A. Motyer, "The Meaning of Blood Sacrifice," ibid., p. 178; A. F. Rainey, "Sacrifices and Offerings," *ZPEB,* 5:194-211; E. E. Carpenter, "Sacrifices and Offerings in the OT," *ISBE*, 3d ed., 4:260-273.

13. For further study of this concept see Noam Zohar, "Repentance and Purification: The Significance and Semantics of *hattā't* in the Pentateuch," *JBL* 107 (Dec 1988): 609-618.

14. Adapted from Walton, *Charts*, p. 20.

15. J. E. Hartley, "Clean and Unclean," *ISBE,* 3d ed., 1:720.

16. Ibid.

17. Ibid.

18. I am indebted to Charles Lee Feinberg, "Clean and Unclean," *NBD* (1962), p. 239.

19. Ibid.

20. For a popular presentation of this view see S. I. McMillen, *None of These Diseases* (Spire Book, Old Tappan, NJ: Revell, 1967). A more scholarly treatment

may be found in Edward Neufeld, "Hygiene Conditions in Ancient Israel (Iron Age)," *BA* 34 (1971): 42-66.

21. *Purity and Danger: An Analysis of Concepts of Pollution and Taboo.* (Boston: Routlege and Kegan, 1966). This view is, for the most part, accepted by Gordon Wenham, *The Book of Leviticus (NICOT:* Grand Rapids: Eerdmans, 1979), pp. 18-25, 165-225.

22. Ibid., p. 169.

23. Ibid., pp. 170-171.

24. See S. Greengus, "Law in the Old Testament," *IDBS*, p. 533. For an English translation of the laws of Hammurabi see *ANET*, pp. 163-180.

25. Merrill F. Unger, *Archaeology and the Old Testament* (Grand Rapids: Zondervan, 1954), p. 155. I am indebted to Unger for this entire discussion. See pp. 154-157.

26. *DOTT*, p. 20. See also pp. 6-8.

27. Ibid., pp. 196-205.

28. Ibid., p. 37.

29. This is not how Christian theonomists, i.e., those who believe the Law of Moses should still be authoritative for civil life, view the matter. See Greg L. Bahnsen, "The Theonomic Reformed Approach to Law and Gospel," in Wayne G. Strickland, ed., *The Law, the Gospel, and the Modern Christian* (Grand Rapids: Zondervan, 1993), pp. 124-143 and the responses to this by non-theonomists.

30. For a more thorough study of this issue, see Daniel W. Van Ness, *Crime and Its Victims* (Downers Grove: InterVarsity, 1986) and Charles Colson, *America's Prison Crisis* (Washington DC: Prison Fellowship Ministries, 1987).

31. "Covenant Forms in Israelite Tradition," *BA* 17 (1954): 26-46, 50-76.

32. For the complete text see *ANET*, pp. 203-206. See also J. A. Thompson, *The Ancient Near Eastern Treaties and the Old Testament* (London: Tyndale 1964), pp. 9-17; K. A. Kitchen, *Ancient Orient and Old Testament* (Chicago:

InterVarsity, 1966), pp. 90-102; id., *The Bible in Its World* (Downers Grove: InterVarsity, 1977), pp. 79-86.

33. *ANET*, p. 203.

34. Ibid., pp. 203-204.

35. Ibid., pp. 204-205.

36. Ibid., p. 205.

37. Ibid.

38. Ibid.

39. I am indebted to Dyrness, *Themes*, pp. 124-126 for this discussion.

40. For further details see Laurence T. Chambers, *Tabernacle Studies* (Grand Rapids: Zondervan, 1958).

41. I am indebted to J. A. Motyer, "The Tabernacle," *Handbook*, pp. 167-168 for the following discussion. See also C. L. Feinberg, "Tabernacle," *ZPEB*, 5:572-583 and S. Westerholm, "Tabernacle," *ISBE*, 3d ed., 4:698-706.

42. For a helpful evaluation of modern worship see Robert E. Webber, *Worship Old and New* (Grand Rapids: Zondervan, 1982), pp. 11-20.

43. J. I. Packer, *Knowing God* (Downers Grove: InterVarsity, 1973), pp. 38- 44 has some very helpful observations on this issue.

44. I am indebted to Bernard Ramm, *His Way Out* (Glendale, CA: Gospel Light, 1974) for this section.

chapter 6

The Kingdom of God: Part One

(Scripture reading: Joshua 1–11; 23–24; Judges; Ruth; Psalms 93–99)

Leading Questions

Why is the theme of the kingdom of God so important for understanding redemptive history?

What significance did this theme have for ancient Israel and what continuing significance does it have for Christians today?

What is one of the most persistent and difficult tensions in scripture?

What features of Hebrew culture need to be understood for a proper grasp of faith and politics in Israel?

What is the overriding problem of faith and politics?

How did the pattern of leadership in Israel change in the days of Samuel and what pitfalls did this transition entail?

What parallels are there between American and Hebrew political history?

How did God use kingship in Israel to prepare for the coming of Messiah?

Introduction

The most comprehensive theme that best unites Old and New Testaments is the kingdom of God. This theme helps us understand the unfolding of redemptive history.[1] The kingdom of God is the active, dynamic rule of God over the universe.[2] As we saw in chapter three, Satan and his seed are in rebellion against the rule of God. Redemptive history climaxes with a glorious vindication of God's rule and the removal of all rebellion from his Kingdom (cf. Rev 11:15–18; 19–20). Exodus 15:18

expresses the essence of the idea when it states: "The LORD will reign for ever and ever." Recall that this affirmation occurs in the aftermath of the contest with Pharaoh in which the issue revolved around who held control over Israel. The outcome, of course, demonstrated that Yahweh was in control of more than just Israel. Yahweh was Lord of all creation. The kingdom of God is thus an aspect of God's sovereignty.

The Significance of the Theme

This theme has considerable significance for the history of Israel. It influenced in a positive way the course of Israel's national history, as well as the course of individual Israelites who were committed to the kingdom of God. We can see this in at least three ways.

Hope for Tomorrow

First, the notion of the kingdom of God sustains the nation in times of distress and affliction. It is significant that during times of oppression the prophets portray the coming kingdom in glowing terms, infusing the people with hope. They do not cast off their trust in the Lord, but endure the hardships, knowing that better days are coming if they will but repent and live in obedience to the Law of the Lord. The Lord will triumph against all forces and foes arrayed against his kingdom. One thinks here of Daniel's prophecies in Daniel 4:3, 34–35; 7:13–14. The kingdoms of this world give way to the kingdom of God (cf. Rev 11:15). The saints receive their reward and share in that reign (Rev 11:18). The prophets speak of "birth pangs" which precede the glorious appearing of the kingdom. Micah 5:3 is representative of this line of thought: " . . . Israel will be abandoned until the time when she who is in labor gives birth and the rest of his brothers return to join the Israelites." When the nation was plunged into times of deep suffering, there was always the hope that the ultimate phase of the kingdom of God could not be far off. This idea of a time of "great tribulation" preceding the glorious appearing of the kingdom underwent significant development during the intertestamental period (ca. 400 B.C.–A.D. 30) and reappears in the NT (cf. Mt 24:6–8, 15–25; 2Th 2:3–12; Rev 3:10; 6:12–17; 13).

Fear of the Lord

Secondly, the idea of the kingdom of God promotes a deep moral tone in Israelite faith and practice. The concept of God's rule as a present reality and a future prospect reminds Israel of her responsibility and accountability. The kingdom involves judgment. It is this constant reminder of Judgment Day that tends to keep Israelite morality on a much higher plane than her pagan neighbors. This is not to say that Israelites were always moral and ethical—the Scriptures depict quite the opposite (cf. Isa 1:1–4; 65:2–5). But it is to say that, in comparison to the pagans, Israelites were generally more upright. This is owing to the notion of a God who expects his people to reflect his own goodness (cf. Lev 19:2 et al.). Failure to do so invites both temporal and eternal judgment (Dt 4–6; Ps 73).

Optimistic View of History

Thirdly, the idea of the kingdom of God shapes Israel's view of history. The Hebrew view of history is linear rather than cyclical as may be seen in the following figure. A linear view understands history as moving toward a goal; a cyclical view conceives of history as constantly moving in great circles.[3] There is no real progression in a cyclical view in that what has been will be and what will be has already been. A pagan view of history is usually some form of a cyclical view and is dominated by the notion of fate. It is a sort of *que será será* (whatever will be, will be) mechanism which even the gods are not able to control or avoid—some things simply must be.

Such an understanding of history naturally leads to a very pessimistic view of life. Little effort is expended to rectify evils or champion justice since all is predetermined, and one has no real power to alter fate.[4] Over against this stands the robust faith of Israel that perceives God's hand and will behind the vicissitudes of history. God controls all things and is guiding history toward a glorious consummation. On this understanding history is really His Story! The upshot in the response of believing Israel to this understanding was a lively sense of hope and optimism. The optimism was not based on human achievement or capability, but on the certainty of God's plan for the universe and for human beings, his special creation. Furthermore, the Lord involved himself in the history of his people. There was encouragement to resist evil and to make a difference in society because the Lord so willed it and rewarded such efforts (Ps 126:5–6; cf. Gal 6:9).

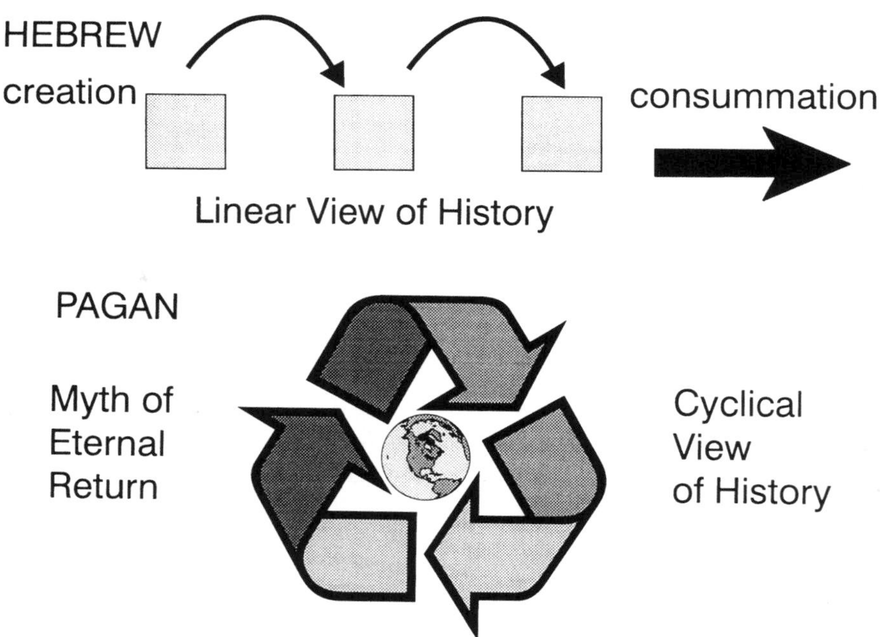

The Scripture everywhere displays this sense of an on-going history driven by the sovereign Lord of all things. No wonder the faith of Israel contrasts so markedly with that of her neighbors. The prophets assume a view of history in which the Lord is directing it toward the goal of his choosing. That goal is worth pursuing. As Isaiah sketches the goal and climax, it still elicits hope: "Of the increase of his government and peace there will be no end. He will reign on David's throne and over his kingdom, establishing and upholding it with justice and righteousness from that time on and forever. The zeal of the LORD Almighty will accomplish this" (Isa 9:7).

Relevance for Today

The theme of the kingdom of God also has continuing significance for modern believers in Jesus Christ. Many of the issues raised during Israel's national history as a theocracy are still vitally important to our own day. Not least among these issues are those connected with faith and politics. For example, how does one live as an obedient member of the kingdom of God while at the same time being a responsible member of one of the kingdoms of this world? *Herein lies one of the most persistent and difficult tensions found in Scripture.* How does one exercise faith and bring it to bear upon politics? Should one's faith have any bearing upon the conduct of politics? What should one do if a particular political policy conflicts with moral and ethical values derived from one's faith?

For some the answer is that faith and politics have nothing to do with each other—one must eschew politics since they are contradictory. The argument is that politics relates to this world that is passing away and is under the dominion of Satan. To engage in politics is to compromise one's faith. The biblical position, according to adherents of this view, is to forsake politics and confine oneself to the spiritual kingdom of God. For others a quite different answer is forthcoming. They advocate active involvement in the political process. One must attempt to influence positively the political process by the application of moral and ethical principles derived from Scripture and Christian tradition. It is not my purpose here to argue the relative merits of these two stances. In either case, the problem becomes one of determining precisely how believers relate to the various political processes, since *a total separation from politics is impossible.*

We develop the problem of faith and politics in the form of a case study. We will survey Israel's political history with an eye to discerning transferable concepts applying to our own governmental system. The fundamental tension between faith and politics is the primary focus of the next two chapters. This tension clearly emerges from the text of Scripture itself. For the believing Israelite, who lived under a monarchy from the days of David onward, the problem is memorably expressed by the Psalmist who asked "Can a corrupt throne be allied with you—one that brings on misery by its decrees?" (Ps 94:20)

A problem begins to develop in Israel's political history: the more power is centralized, the more difficult it is to embody the kingdom of God on earth. The reason is that power corrupts those who wield it, and one can no longer simply equate national policy with the rule of God. In fact, these two are at times diametrically opposed. The prophets, Yahweh's emissaries, sound the alarm repeatedly in this connection. When God enters into a covenant with Israel, the kingdom of God takes on tangible shape in the nation of Israel. In no time at all, however, reality falls short of the ideal. The vassal nation rebels repeatedly against her overlord and non-compliance more often becomes the norm than compliance.

Especially during the days of the judges one has great difficulty identifying the federated tribes with the kingdom of God. Still, in his mercy and patience, the Lord continues to forgive and bless his people. Nonetheless, we discern a gradual displacement of the kingdom of Israel from the kingdom of God. If the reigns of David and Solomon represent the high water mark for the fortunes of Israel, they also introduce features that put the country on a collision course with her great overlord. Later kings of Israel and Judah seek to establish their own kingdoms, in direct opposition to the kingdom of God.

The history of the theocratic kingdom, then, provides the setting for our focus upon the tension between faith and politics. How does one accomplish the will of God in politics when the leadership pursues policies disregarding the will of God? The answer was not easy then, nor is it today.

The Pattern of Leadership in the Old Testament

Before we trace the development of the kingdom of God in the OT, we need to explore how the cultural background of ancient Israel impinged upon political theory and practice. Once again we consciously recognize the cultural distance separating us from biblical times. Politics took place in a different cultural context than our own, and *we need to recover the original, biblical context before we bring the biblical witness to bear on the political issues of today.*[5] This recovery involves a consideration of how leadership was exercised throughout the OT era. Two features of Israelite culture are important here.

The Patriarchal Structure

First, one must grasp how Israelite society was structured. Hebrew society was organized around a powerful patriarch who wielded authority over his entire family. This family is an extended family, not a nuclear family as in our own society. The extended family includes father and mother with all their children whether married or not and all their children. In other words, several generations live together. The patriarchal narratives of Genesis reflect just such a pattern. There we note, for example, that Jacob's extended family consists of no fewer than 70 individuals (Ge 46:8–26). This is quite a crew for dinner! By contrast, the typical American family consists of something like 4.5 members.

Around this patriarch of an extended family are other extended families related by blood ties and marriage. These families form the next larger social grouping, the clan. Several clans constitute a still larger kinship group known as the tribe. In Israel a federation of tribes are bound together by their common allegiance to the Sinai Covenant. Several 12-tribe federations are mentioned in the OT (Ge 22:20–24, the Ishmaelites; 25:12–18, the Arameans). At the core of such tribal organizations, however, are the powerful patriarchs who function as the elders of the tribe. They make the decisions affecting the entire federation. Within each family the patriarch exercises nearly absolute control. In the pre-tribal days reflected in Genesis, even matters affecting life and death are decided by the patriarch (cf. Ge 38:24). The following diagram helps visualize the structure of Israelite society in its pre-monarchic phase, covering the books of Joshua, Judges, Ruth and much of 1 Samuel.

In the OT God uses strong leaders to accomplish his purposes. The word of God comes to a leader and, through him, to the larger group. In the pre-monarchic era, this strong leader is either a patriarch, such as Abraham, Isaac and Jacob, or a judge, such as Gideon and Jephthah (Moses and Joshua are hard to classify). The Lord works through these powerful individuals because, once again, they are the ones who make decisions affecting the entire group.

Structure of Israelite Society

Patriarch

Extended Family

Clan

Tribe

Corporate Solidarity

One other feature of Hebrew culture affects our understanding of the political dimensions of the OT. That feature is corporate personality or corporate solidarity. This expression describes a culture in which the individual thinks of himself/herself as part of a group, be it extended family, clan or tribe. *The rugged individualism of our own North American culture is scarcely discernible in the OT.* The individual does not think in terms of individual goals or aspirations, but rather, in group terms. The good and goal of the group is uppermost.[6]

This means that the life of the clan is so intertwined with that of the clan leader, a powerful elder, that he embodies the entire clan in himself. This is a two-way process in that the values and traditions of the tribe and clan also affect the leader. His decisions, in other words, are rarely independently exercised, but reflect the ethos (beliefs, customs, ideals) of the community. The connection between patriarch and clan/tribe is so integral that the Hebrews view their ancestors as living on in the lives of their descendants.

This relationship may be seen in a number of OT passages of which Hosea 12 is representative. Here, starting in verse two, the prophet indicts Israel for their apostasy. Notice in this passage that there is a connection between the actions of Jacob and the actions of his descendants living some 1,000 years later! In other words, the Israelites of Hosea's day continue to behave like their eponymous ancestor (a person from whom a people is supposed to have taken its name). This is not a mere metaphor either. They view the connection realistically.

Modern psychology and sociology have taught us to appreciate what the Hebrews took for granted, namely, that we are greatly affected by our forebears. There is validity to the notion of corporate solidarity and we moderns are beginning to rediscover it. As North Americans, we must constantly "slip into the sandals" of the Hebrews if we are to participate meaningfully in dialogue with the OT. This is especially so when it comes to correlating the Word of God and modern politics. Representative democracy and individualism are alien categories to the OT. Nevertheless, as we shall argue, the basic and crucial issues of politics have not significantly changed from their day to our own.

The New Pattern of Leadership in the Days of Samuel

The old patriarchal pattern of leadership and its sequel in the charismatic judges come to an end in the days of Samuel the prophet. The changeover occurs rather suddenly, though dissatisfaction with the old structures had existed for some time. The crisis that precipitates this change is narrated in 1 Samuel 8:1–22. We will discuss later, in more detail, the background of the crisis, but for now we simply draw attention to the nature of the change. The people of Israel request a king like the other nations. The issue in dispute concerns the manner in which authority and power are exercised in Israel. Kingship still continues the long-standing tradition of strong centralized leadership. The major difference revolves around two changes in the pattern of leadership.

Continuity of power. The first difference between the old tribal federation and the new pattern of kingship concerns the issue of continuity of power. In other words, how is power passed on? The judges are charismatically selected—that is, they are selected by Yahweh and endowed with the Holy Spirit to carry out their function of deliverance. Kings operate on the dynastic principle; that is, the successor to the throne belongs to the royal family, usually the firstborn son. The father and his royal advisers groom the heir apparent for his task.

Concentration of power. The second difference relates to the concentration of power. Kingship concentrates power in the hands of a few. The king and his officials make decisions previously made by tribal and clan leaders. The apparatus of government gravitates to the city of the king. As time goes on, this concentration of power tends to increase rather than diminish. The number of government officials and programs typically proliferate, resulting in further centralization of power. (Does this sound familiar?)

The Israelites identify their crisis as essentially a political problem. They reason that their military and economic setbacks stem from incompetent leadership and an ineffective tribal federation. There are good grounds for both complaints. But, instead of inquiring into the theological roots of their dilemma and learning a lesson from their history, *they attempt to correct an essentially spiritual problem by means of a political solution.* The people really are rejecting the rule of Yahweh over their lives—that is the root problem.[7] In spite of this, the Lord grants a change in the pattern of leadership. This new pattern, in fact, figures prominently in the ongoing kingdom of God.

The Problem of Leadership in the Old Testament

Israel's request for a king exposes the root problem lurking beneath the change in leadership style and pattern. What dangers are inherent in kingship? Notice that the Israelites demand of Samuel that he "appoint a king to lead us, such as all the other nations have." The question now becomes: What kind of king did the other nations have?

Kingship Among Israel's Neighbors[8]

The neighbors of Israel all subscribed to some form of sacral kingship. That is, the king partakes of some measure of divinity. The degree of divinity varied, and, in the measure of divinity claimed lay the degree of power wielded.

The Egyptians practiced the most extreme form of sacral kingship. In Egypt Pharaoh is a god, as we have already seen in the discussion of the exodus. He is the son of Ra, the supreme creator god. During his life, he is the incarnation of Horus or Seth, and after his death, he becomes Osiris, the god of the underworld. Given this status, it is no wonder that no law code has ever been discovered in ancient Egypt since Pharaoh's word *was* law. In principle Pharaoh was an absolute dictator. The Joseph stories in Genesis 39–50 reflect just such a concentration of power.

According to the ideology of kingship in Syria and Mesopotamia, the gods choose kings. The king thus manifests a divine unction or supernatural power. The god/goddess adopts him as son—hence the notion of "divine sonship." Palace reliefs of Mesopotamian kings symbolically convey the ideology of divine sonship. These reliefs depict the king suckling the breasts of a goddess. This represents the transformation whereby he is endued with divine power and elevated above the capabilities of mere mortals.

Needless to say, such a conception of the king also leads to enormous power and veneration, constituting the essential problem with the system. *Power concentrated in the hands of a few can become a curse.*[9] This is what alarmed Samuel by the Israelite request. He knew what dangers lurked in the adoption of kingship for Israel. As we shall see, his worst fears were eventually realized.

The Position of the King in Israel

In contrast to Israel's pagan neighbors, the position of the Hebrew king is carefully defined and limited. Deuteronomy 17:14-20 clearly specifies the qualifications and prohibitions of kingship. Several items are of special interest.

Qualifications. The king is, first and foremost, divinely chosen. This, as we saw in 1 Samuel 8, is the real problem in the people's rejection of the system of judges—they want to choose their own leaders. This is tantamount to rejecting Yahweh's rule over them. The Lord grants the request for a king, but reserves the right to choose the candidate. In fact the Lord explicitly chooses the first three kings of Israel. After Solomon, however, we hear no more of a divine choice; the dynastic principle of succession takes over.

Besides divine choice, the king must be a native Israelite. Compare our own constitution, which specifies that the president must also be a native-born citizen. Here is one example among many of how the Bible influenced the framing of the constitution.

Prohibitions and stipulations. There are three prohibitions, each one worth careful reflection. The king must not acquire great numbers of horses, take many wives, or accumulate large amounts of silver and gold. Positively, he must make a personal copy of the Law and read it all the days of his life.

What is the intent of each of the prohibitions? The prohibition against horses checks a tendency toward militarism. Militarism is a policy whereby national interests are secured and advanced through the aggressive use of military force. The chariot formed the main striking force in the armies of the ancient Near East. It is equivalent to the battle tank so vital to modern armies. Thus, the prohibition effectively discourages the incorporation of militarism into national policy. The Hebrew state must not build its foreign or domestic policy around the application of military force. They are to walk in conformity to the Sinai Covenant and trust Yahweh to prosper their affairs and protect them from enemies. Of course, provision is made for the development and defensive use of the military. They are not, however, to covet the lands and wealth of neighbors, for the Lord has given them a good land and he will richly bless them if they obey his commands (Dt 15:4).

The second prohibition about the number of wives speaks to the issue of pride and sexuality as it relates to power. Near Eastern monarchs measured their prestige and power by the size of their harems. The seductive power of unrestrained sex upon spirituality is clearly recognized ("his heart will be led astray").[10] Sex per se is not sinful, but it needs to be expressed within the confines of covenant faithfulness—a condition hardly compatible with a large number of wives. To be sure, the king is not limited to one wife, but there is a warning that moderation be the order of the day. Apparently Saul, the first king of Israel, had only one wife, Ahinoam (1Sa 14:50).[11] David, who reigned over a powerful state, had eight wives and an unspecified number of concubines (1Ch 3:1–9). This may have contributed to his moral failure in the Bathsheba affair (2Sa 11).

The third prohibition limits the amount of personal wealth the king may accumulate owing to his position as head of state. Pagan kings sought to amass great personal fortunes by a rapacious policy of taxation and militarism. The root problem with wealth is that it tends to turn the heart away from the source of all good things and to focus upon the created order as the source of happiness (Ps 73, cf. 1Ti 6:10).

The requirement that the king possess a personal copy of the law and that he read it all the days of his life brings us to the real heart of kingship in Israel. Clearly, in Hebrew kingship, the king does not possess the kind and extent of power most Near Eastern monarchs exercised. The ideology of Hebrew kingship is dramatically different. In Israel the king is the leading citizen, not a divine or semi-divine being whose thoughts, plans and intentions are superior to the average citizen. The underlying principle is that *power is a gift and must be used to serve God, not exploit human beings*. The great problem constantly besetting the Hebrew kings, however, is the same as their pagan neighbors, namely, *the abuse of power*.

Report card of Hebrew kings. It is a sobering fact that not one Hebrew king avoids this pitfall. Beginning with Saul, we discover that each one abuses the power granted by the Lord to be king over his people. Let us briefly review the royal report cards.

When we first encounter the impressive Saul, he appears self-effacing and timid, certainly not power-hungry (see 1Sa 9–10). The transformation of Saul's character illuminates the seductive nature of political power. After Saul receives a second chance and again fails (cf. 1Sa 13:7–14), Samuel announces his final rejection (1Sa 15:23). Does Saul accept this divine demotion? No. Instead, he strives desperately to hang on to power and pass it on to his son. Saul's reign concludes with bouts of paranoia, mental instability, brutality, deep depression, national defeat and, finally, suicide. He is one of the most tragic figures in the OT and affords a classic case study in the problem of power and politics.

David's career as king is the high point in the history of kingship in Israel. Here is the man after God's own heart; yet even he did not escape the tempter's snare. The Bathsheba affair blots an otherwise remarkable career. Second Samuel 11 and 12 narrate the infamous affair and Nathan's ringing accusation "You are the man!" David considers himself more worthy and important than the citizens over whom he rules. As a result, he rationalizes the taking of another man's wife. This act flagrantly violates the Covenant. To make matters worse, he attempts to cover up his deed with deceit and murder. He thus breaks three of the Ten Commandments (adultery, murder and lying). David's reign from then on is rocked by internal dissension, most of it coming from his own family.

Solomon's reign is both instructive and perplexing. A quick survey of 1Kings 10–11 reveals that he breaks each Mosaic prohibition with regard to kingship: he accumulates chariots and horses, he acquires many wives (700 wives plus 300 concubines!) and he amasses a huge personal fortune. Little wonder that his empire collapses after his death and divides into two warring states (1Ki 12). What happened to all that wisdom? Unparalleled power must have eroded the foundations of good moral judgment.

Limitations on the power of Hebrew kings. This is a good point at which to consider how the Sinai Covenant addresses the problem of abuse of power. Notice in the following diagram that there are checks upon the king's power built into the governmental structure. The king and his cabinet are not allowed to intrude into the office of the priest. This is what got Saul into trouble with Samuel (1Sa 13:5–14). It was also Uzziah's downfall (cf. 2Ch 26:16–21). The prophet serves as an independent auditor of the king's performance. If the king violates the provisions of the Sinai Covenant, a prophet soon threatens disciplinary action. Nathan the prophet demonstrates precisely the role of Yahweh's emissary (2Sa 12:1–14. For other examples see 2Sa 24:11; 1Ki 16:7; 16:29–17:1; 21:17–19; 2Ki 21:10–16). Yahweh is the true king of Israel under whom, in principle, the king of Israel faithfully serves as a vassal. In short, the king of Israel is under *an unconditional obligation to uphold the Sinai Covenant.* In our own government, when a new president is inaugurated, he takes an oath to uphold and defend the constitution of the United States of America.

It is helpful to realize that the founding fathers of our own country grappled with the same basic problem of concentration of power. Having experienced in England the problems of monarchy, especially the relationship of Church and State, they made sure that there was a separation of powers. In this they had good theological precedent in the OT. Our own system of representative government has three main branches: the executive, legislative and judicial. In this way, the problem of concentrating too much power in the hands of a few individuals is minimized.

Titles of Hebrew kings. Note the various titles accorded the Hebrew king. Although he is at times referred to as "son of God," this does not carry the meaning it has among Israel's neighbors. The notion of a divine conception or birth plays no role in Israel's ideology of kingship. The term instead points to the covenanted relationship the king enjoys with Yahweh.

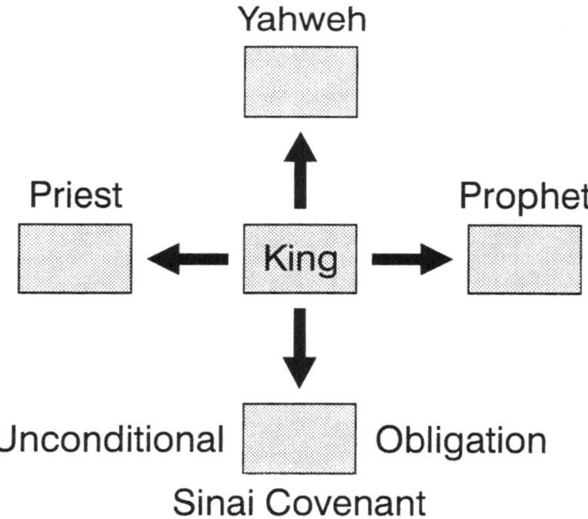

All the rights of sonship in the human sphere, such as protection, care and inheritance, accrue to the king. The relationship is not based upon the mythological idea of a divine procreating, but upon trust and obedience. The personal dimension of faith in the covenant-keeping God of Israel is decisive.

A second title is actually the most prominent and frequent. The king is the Lord's anointed. The term "anointed" comes from the Hebrew verb *māshach*, meaning "to rub with oil, pour oil over." In the noun form we have the derivative *māshîach*, meaning "one who has oil rubbed or poured over him." The act of pouring oil over the head of the king-to-be signifies divine endowment and authority. The king does not thereby become semi-divine, as in Mesopotamian or Canaanite kingship, but he does receive divine assistance. The act is regarded as a gift of God and in several passages is associated with the coming of the Spirit of God upon an individual (see 1Sa 10:9; 16:13; Isa 61:1). This title plays a leading role in the development of the Messianic hope—indeed, the term "Messiah" is the Greek equivalent of the Hebrew *māshîaḥ*. We take this up later in chapter nine.

The third title, "servant," focuses on the role and function of the king. The king is a servant of the Lord. His task is to serve Yahweh's people. He is always to remember that he rules as Yahweh's vice regent—the very throne he sits on is really the Lord's (cf. 2Ch 9:8). To be a servant of the Lord does not carry a servile connotation—it is a great honor. Only those entrusted with important tasks from the Lord receive this exalted status. In 2 Samuel 7:5 the Lord instructs the prophet Nathan: "Go and tell my servant David . . ." The prophets themselves bear the title "my servants the prophets" (see ch. 8).

Finally, the kings of Israel are styled as "shepherds." This term stresses the kind of relationship the king ought to maintain between himself and his people. In short, he protects and provides for them. A divine oracle decrees David's destiny: "You will shepherd my people Israel, and you will become their ruler" (2Sa 5:2).

The Problem of Power Today

The prophets were acutely aware of the abuse of power. We should not think such a problem no longer exists. In fact, the problem is of major proportions in virtually all governmental systems and societies, our own representative democracy being no exception. Former Senator Mark Hatfield has written eloquently about this problem in our government. Listen to his words in his book *Between a Rock and a Hard Place*:

> The allurement of power and honor subtly but malignantly grows within the politician, often gaining control of one's whole being before it is discovered.
>
> An important, but often ignored, factor is the essentially dehumanizing character of relationships in the political world. People relate to a Senator's prestige, title, and

> influence. They assume that his opinions must automatically be more accurate than their own. A Senator grows accustomed to being treated in this reverential way. Within, this can breed the belief that he is more important, more virtuous, and wiser than the average citizens whom he represents.[12]

Chuck Colson, who served time in prison as a result of involvement in the Watergate scandal during the Nixon administration, has also written pointedly about the problem of political power:

> Last month marked the two-hundredth anniversary of George Washington's inauguration as the first president of the United States. And 200 years ago, the first Congress convened—a body of citizens with a bold vision for a new republic.
>
> Today I fear many of those visionaries might not recognize their Congress. For what was originally intended to be a government made up of citizens representing their peers has gradually become an elitist body of professional career politicians. And this has not been for the good of the nation.
>
> Granted, that first Congress of 1789 got off to a slow start. The Senate's president, Vice President John Adams, occupied most of that body's first month in debate over titles for the government's new leaders. George Washington narrowly escaped being christened "His Mightiness," "His Highness, the President of the United States of America and Protector of the Rights of the Same," or "His Magnificence."
>
> Senators were to be "His Highness of the Upper House," Congressmen, "His Highness of the Lower House." Happily, no such titles were approved—though one senator dubbed John Adams, a short, fat, and haughty man, "His Rotundity."
>
> Eventually, the new experiment in government for the people, of the people, and by the people got off the ground. Its Congress was to be truly "representative." The colonial farmers, lawyers, and merchants were to leave their plows, law books, and shops to spend two years serving in the House of Representatives. It was part of their duty of citizenship.

> Thus the House reflected as nearly as possible true democracy, with citizens participating in their own self-government. Senators, on the other hand, were to be appointed by the states as a restraint upon the passions of the majority.
>
> Today, however, our elected representatives, both senators and congressmen, are for the most part far from the heartbeat of the people. Most are used to power and privilege, coming from upper- or middle-class backgrounds, higher educations, and high church. And any elitist sensibilities they already have are accentuated upon their arrival on Capitol Hill.
>
> Power, privilege, position, prestige, and parties—these are the perks of politics. They tend to intoxicate even the most sober-minded.
>
> With such perks as free mailing privileges, travel, and honoraria from favor-seeking special interests, many of our elected officials in Washington lose touch with real life in the heartland. They have become career professionals intent on two priorities: retaining their tenure and rise in seniority. Reelection campaigns cost up to $15 million—and 96% of them are successful. Their pay raise debate last winter showed how little is left of the founders' spirit of sacrificial public service. Those reigning in today's "imperial Congress" have come a long way from our humble beginnings.[13]

The last line of Colson's remarks reminds one sadly of the career of Israel's first King—Saul of Benjamin.

The Paradigm of Israel's Ideal King

Positive Role Models in the Royal Psalms

Besides explicit instructions in the Law of Moses about the role and qualifications of a Hebrew king, the prophetic and hymnic literature also address this important matter of the exercise of power. For example, the book of Psalms contains a category of compositions called the "Royal Psalms." They focus on the function, role and ideals of a Hebrew king.

These psalms include the following: 2, 18, 20, 21, 45, 72, 89, 101, 110, 132 and 144. From these we single out three primary functions of a Hebrew king.

Military leader. The first function is military leader. Recall that the initial request for a king, in the days of Samuel (1Sa 8), involved precisely this role. Both Saul and David were necessarily preoccupied in their reigns with the conduct of war and military operations. In this connection, it is worth noting that David never suffered a military defeat in his many wars as the supreme commander of the forces of Israel.

Two Psalms in particular picture for us the military role of a Hebrew king. Psalms 20 and 21 both assume as their setting a conflict in which the king takes a leading role. In the first psalm we have a prayer before battle. One may envision the Levitical choir invoking blessing and protection upon the king and his army (vv. 1–4) and anticipating the Lord's victory (vv. 5–6). Not to be overlooked is the underlying philosophy of war from a Hebrew perspective: neither machines of war nor tactics ultimately bring victory—that is in the hands of God. Trust in God, not in the devices of human beings, is the prerequisite for success, even in this most violent of enterprises. The Psalm ends with a heartfelt petition that the king would be delivered and the victory secured. The sequel, Psalm 21, portrays the victorious forces of Israel, celebrating their triumph in the Lord's presence at the temple.

Here one senses the great difference between a militaristic state like Assyria and the state of Israel under David. The Assyrians gloried in recounting the exploits of its warriors and generals, as well as the gruesome tally of victims. The Psalmist, by contrast, celebrates the gracious God who gives his people victory when they trust in him. In this connection, one should also note that the Mosaic Law gives instructions concerning the conduct of war (Dt 20). In contrast to their pagan neighbors, Israel conducted war in as humane a manner as possible. The Geneva Conventions of our own century owe some of their foundational principles to the Mosaic Law.

Administrator and champion of justice. Psalm 72 highlights another function. Here we see the ideal of justice forming a major plank in the political platform of the king. *The king must be one who upholds justice and provides a climate for righteousness among his citizens.* It is incumbent upon the king to protect the rights of the weak and powerless. Special consideration must be extended to widows and orphans. The king is their "public defender." "He will defend the afflicted among the people and save the children of the needy; he will crush the oppressor" (v. 4).

A celebrated example of this role occurs in 1 Kings 3:16–28, where Solomon renders a difficult decision. The case involves a maternity dispute between two prostitutes. In Israel the king functions as the Supreme Court in legal and judicial matters (cf. 2Sa 12:1–14). The end of this account draws attention to Solomon's fitness to be a king over Israel: "When all Israel heard the verdict the king had given, they held the king in awe, because they saw that he had wisdom from God to administer justice" (v. 28).

As will be seen in the prophetic literature, the prophets repeatedly indict kings for their failure to provide for justice and righteousness (cf. 1Ki 21:19; Isa 1:10, 15–17, 23; 32:1–8). It is a major factor in the collapse of the Hebrew kingdoms. Thus the charge of being the chief administrative officer in Israel involves rendering and insuring justice in the land.

Leader in faith and worship. A third primary function is that of cultic leader. The king must be the leading worshiper of Yahweh. He is also entrusted with the maintenance of the temple and its worship. Psalms 110 and 132 reflect this understanding, as well as the narrative sections of 1 Kings 8 and especially 1 Chronicles 22–26; 28–29. In 1 Kings 8 Solomon leads the nation in the dedication ceremonies for the new temple. Although it says that "the king and all Israel with him offered sacrifices before the LORD" (v. 62), this does not mean that Solomon actually officiated as a priest; it simply means that he presented sacrifices to the priests. One should also recall that David drew up the plans for the temple and actually began acquiring the materials to be used in its construction (1Ch 22). David had a leading hand in the hymns and songs sung during worship. He was known as "Israel's singer of songs" (2Sa 23:1). He also organized and assigned duties to the Levites among which was the ministry of music and singing (1Ch 24–25). The chronicler also singles out Josiah and Hezekiah for their highly visible piety (cf. 1Ch 29–31; 34–35). It is important to grasp the role the king plays in the area of worship. The people must see him as a man of prayer and faith.

Psalm 110 also celebrates the divine appointment of the Davidic line to the status of priest-king after the pattern of Melchizedek (cf. Ge 14:18). In this psalm, the king acquires a higher status than the Aaronic high priest, even though, under the Old Covenant, he was excluded from certain priestly prerogatives, namely the offering of sacrifice. This prophecy of the combination of the kingly and priestly office becomes another important factor in the development of the messianic hope, culminating in Jesus of Nazareth (cf. Hebrews).[14] The Royal Psalms thus serve as a pattern held up before the reigning Davidic king to remind him of the ideal to which he should aspire. As H. H. Rowley has observed:

> There is reason to believe that while they may have been royal psalms, used in the royal rites of the temple, they were also "messianic." They held before the king the ideal king, both as his inspiration and guide for the present, and as the hope of the future.[15]

Negative Role Models

Besides these positive role models found in the Royal Psalms, negative examples occur in the prophetic literature. Two such examples come to mind.

A Babylonian king. The first occurs in Isaiah 14 and portrays a Babylonian king. Obviously, no Hebrew king should conduct himself like this despot. The excesses and vices for which the Babylonian king is indicted are placed in the literary setting of a "taunt song." A taunt song celebrates the downfall of the wicked. Beginning at verse four, note some of the descriptions of this dictator. He was an oppressor who "struck down peoples with unceasing blows and in fury subdued nations with relentless aggression."

In verse seven, in a nice example of personification, even the trees of Lebanon break out in singing at the fall of this tyrant. The background of the song lies in the extensive logging operations of the Assyrian and Babylonian kings in the mountains of Lebanon. The great palaces and temples of Assyria and Babylon were paneled with the beautiful and fragrant cedars and pines of the Lebanese mountains. Now that the tyrant is dead, the trees celebrate! There is a respite from the logging crews cutting down vast tracts of timber and hauling them across the desert to Mesopotamia.[16] This calls to mind a continuing problem of environmental protection. Just as despotic kings plundered the surrounding lands for their own enrichment and pleasure, so in our modern world, the greedy squander natural resources. God's displeasure with this lack of good stewardship is as real today as it was in the days of the Babylonian kings.

We should also note the arrogance and pride of this monarch. In vv. 12–14, his inflated notion of himself recalls the idea of divine kingship. This tyrant imagines that he is a god, that he is privy to the council chambers of the gods. In reality he is a weak, frail human being who has succumbed to the abuse of power. Death is the great leveler and he now discovers belatedly the truth about himself and all his so-called achievements—"maggots are spread out beneath you and worms cover you" (v. 11b).

A Canaanite king. A second example of how a Hebrew king should *not* function is taken from the world of Canaanite kings. In Ezekiel 28 we read another taunt song, this time celebrating the demise of a king of Tyre. Again we pick out descriptions of this tyrant. He is characterized by pride (v. 2), excess (vv. 4–5), violence (v. 16), and covetousness (v. 5). He too thinks he is a god—he imagines himself in the garden of God. Some interpreters of scripture think that the description of this king shades off into a description of the fall of Satan. While this may be, we probably should not lose sight of the very human king of Tyre throughout as the principal figure. Once again, power has transformed this ruler into a selfish and degenerate individual. He, like his Babylonian counterpart, serves as a salutary warning to Israel about the perils of kingship.

The Promise of the Ideal King

In spite of the negative aspects of kingship in Israel, God uses this institution to advance his kingdom purposes. In fact, kingship becomes part of the emerging messianic hope, a hope that receives its greatest impetus through the divinely appointed Davidic dynasty. The Lord promises David that an ideal king would rise up from his dynasty. The story of this promise is one of the most important passages of the OT. We need to consider more fully this account.

The Davidic Covenant

Second Samuel 7 is the setting of this promise. David successfully frees Israel from her enemies and creates, really for the first time, a unified state controlling the entire region of Canaan. David's army captures Jerusalem, which had been a Jebusite enclave since the days of the conquest (2Sa 5:6–10). As a city not occupied by Judah, Benjamin or Ephraim, it becomes the "City of David." Besides being the political center of this fledgling state, David also centralizes religious authority in Jerusalem by transferring the Ark of the Covenant and tabernacle (2Sa 6:1–19). Thus a concentration of power exists in Jerusalem with David firmly in control. Against this backdrop we read of the Lord's promise to David.

Chapter seven opens with David sensing the disparity between his luxurious palace and the rather weather-beaten and unimposing tabernacle. He desires to construct a temple giving visible expression to the greatness of Israel's God. One should remember that the surrounding states built impressive temples in honor of their national deities. David's desire, however, is not granted. First Chronicles 28:3 gives the reason: David has shed much blood as a warrior. Instead, Solomon (whose name means "peaceable") will be the actual builder (v. 6). As already noted, however, David did take a leading role in drawing up plans and in providing for the materials in its construction.

The Lord follows up this denial, however, with a promise far exceeding David's wildest expectations. The promise is essentially threefold in nature (cf. the tripartite Abrahamic Covenant in Ge 12:1–3, 7). Verse 16 contains the threefold promise: "Your house and your kingdom will endure forever before me; your throne will be established forever." The "house" is a reference to the Davidic dynasty; the "kingdom" is the right to rule over the kingdom of God on earth; and the "throne" refers to the outward trappings of sovereignty.

What makes this announcement extraordinary—even supernatural—is the stated duration of the investiture. All three items endure "forever," an attribute usually connected with the divine. The promise can hardly be explained away as court hyperbole. On the contrary, the promise ultimately finds fulfillment in the perfect, ideal king. Jesus Christ realizes the aims of the Kingdom of God for Israel and the nations (cf. Mt 1:1; Lk 1:32–33, 69; Ac 2:30; 13:28; Ro 1:2–3; 2Ti 2:8; Rev 3:7; 22:16).

The Davidic Covenant becomes a major feature of redemptive history. As we shall see, later prophets and psalmists hark back to and enlarge upon this promise to David. Note, for example, how Psalms 2, 89, and 132 recall and reaffirm this divine promise. "Once for all, I have sworn by my holiness—and I will not lie to David—that his line will continue forever and his throne endure before me like the sun; it will be established forever like the moon, the faithful witness in the sky" (89:35–37).

The Portrait of an Ideal King

The promise of an ideal king, however, seemed mocked by reality. The kings who succeeded David fell far short of this glowing portrait. Even Solomon, the immediate successor and most powerful, in terms of military might, wealth and prestige, is a bitter disappointment. His ruinous policies even precipitate the division between north and south. The Hebrew historians do not reckon most of the monarchs of Judah as good kings. As for the northern kingdom of Israel, not one of its kings receives a favorable rating. Did this failure of the Hebrew kings diminish hope in the coming of the Messiah? To judge by the inspired Scripture, the Lord used precisely their failure to lift the sight of the people (at least the faithful) to the ideal messianic king.

Isaiah's contribution. In this regard Isaiah 11:1–5, 10–11 is instructive. During a time of deep national humiliation, the prophet Isaiah sketches a portrait of a Davidic descendant who rules in accord with the will of the Lord. In verse one his pedigree is confirmed—he is a scion [heir] of the house of Jesse (David's father). Verses two and three document the true requisites for exercising power—the Spirit of the Lord and the fear of the Lord. In verses four and five we see at last the great ideals of justice and righteousness fleshed out. No wonder that peace, prosperity and, supremely, the knowledge of God flourish in such a kingdom (vv. 6–9).

Jeremiah's contribution. Jeremiah also adds to this emerging portrait with some deft pen strokes. During his tenure as prophet, Judah came under the ultimate sanction of the great Sinai Covenant—she was expelled from her land. In spite of enormous human suffering, Jeremiah peers beyond the disaster of national collapse to the brighter day when at last the promised heir of David resumes the reins of power. The last kings of Judah after Josiah are spiritual failures and their administrations mirror their deficiencies. In contrast to them, Jeremiah sees a day when the Lord will

> raise up to David a righteous Branch. A king who will reign wisely and do what is just and right in the land. In his days Judah will be saved and Israel will live in safety. This is the name by which he will be called: The LORD Our Righteousness (23:5–6).

Ezekiel's contribution. We add one more prophetic voice to our chorus singing Messiah's praises. Ezekiel, like Jeremiah, lived through the harrowing days of Judah's destruction. In fact, Ezekiel was carried away in the deportation of 597 B.C. In a refugee camp along the Chebar canal, Ezekiel keeps alive the hopes of the righteous remnant by sketching more lines of the messianic portrait. For Ezekiel, the image and title of shepherd stand out in stark contrast to the greed and callousness of Judah's last kings. "I will place over them one shepherd, my servant David, and he will tend them; he will tend them and be their shepherd. I the LORD will be their God, and my servant David will be prince among them. I the LORD have spoken" (Eze 34:23–24).

The psalmists' contribution. In addition to the prophets, the Psalms also contain passages describing a king who possesses ideal qualities and rules over an ideal kingdom. These are the "Royal Psalms" mentioned earlier. In Psalm 2 the Lord promises the Davidic king that he will "make the nations your inheritance, the ends of the earth your possession. You will rule them with an iron scepter; you will dash them to pieces like pottery" (vv. 8–9). Of course no historical king of Israel or Judah ever ruled over such an empire. To write off such language as mere court hyperbole does not do justice to the hope and expectation that develops around such grand visions of the future. During a time of apparent humiliation, Psalm 89 recalls the promise made to the house of David long ago:

> I will not violate my covenant or alter what my lips have uttered. Once for all, I have sworn by my holiness—and I will

> not lie to David—that his line will continue forever and his throne endure before me like the sun; it will be established forever like the moon, the faithful witness in the sky" (vv. 34–37, cf. Ps 132).

According to Helmer Ringgren, "this idea of divine kingship is the background and the necessary condition of the belief in the coming Messiah, it is the soil, from which the messianic hope has grown."[17] This notion is, he goes on to say, "part of the preparations that were necessary for the realization of God's plan of salvation."[18]

The Fulfillment of the Promise to David

The promise of an ideal king does not die with the OT. The NT picks up this hope, transforms and enlarges it, and presents a finished portrait—he is none other than Jesus of Nazareth! *The remarkable thing about the NT witness is that it draws together the three primary offices of the OT and unifies them in the person of Jesus.* Thus the NT presents Jesus as the final prophet, who speaks the last saving word of God's grace (Heb 1:1–2), the great High Priest in the order of Melchizedek (Heb 6:20–7:28) and the "KING OF KINGS AND LORD OF LORDS" (Rev 19:16). Many other passages could be cited to illustrate the point; in Jesus there is a convergence of these OT offices. Fallen human beings cannot be trusted with such power; but the man from heaven provides humanity with the perfect king. This King is a shepherd who gives his life for his sheep (cf. Jn 10:11). And he is the Savior of all who entrust themselves to him (1Ti 2:3–6).

Endnotes

1. Chapters 6 and 7 are greatly influenced by lecture notes taken in the class "Themes in Old Testament Theology." The class was taught by Dr. Allan Hubbard, President and Professor of Old Testament at Fuller Theological seminary, in the spring of 1974. Other works that have been helpful in developing this theme are: John Bright, *The Kingdom of God* (Nashville: Abingdon, 1953); Erich Sauer, *The Dawn of World Redemption* (Grand Rapids: Eerdmans, 1951); F. F. Bruce, *The New Testament Development of Old Testament Themes* (Grand Rapids: Eerdmans, 1968); Daniel P. Fuller, *The Unity of the Bible* (Grand Rapids: Zondervan, 1992).

2. This notion has been carefully developed by George E. Ladd in *Jesus and the Kingdom* (New York: Harper and Row, 1964).

3. See further Th. C. Vriezen, *An Outline of Old Testament Theology* (Oxford: Basil Blackwell, 1966), pp. 370-372.

4. See David Bebbington, *Patterns in History: A Christian Perspective on Historical Thought* (Grand Rapids: Baker, 1979), pp. 21–42. Note his statement on p. 25: "It followed that people must resign themselves to a pattern of perpetual recurrence. Human activity is in the last resort futile, since all will take place exactly as it did before."

5. For further discussion of the necessity for such an undertaking, see Fee and Stuart, *How to Read*, chs. 4 and 5.

6. See further John J. Pilch and Bruce J. Malina, eds., *Biblical Social Values and Their Meaning* (Peabody, MA: Hendrickson, 1993), pp. 49–53, 88–91.

7. See *NIVSB* note on 1Sa 8:5 and 8:7, p. 385.

8. See W. White, Jr., "King, Kingship," *ZPEB*, 3:795–801.

9. To Lord Acton is attributed the aphorism: "Power corrupts, and absolute power corrupts absolutely."

10. Henry Kissinger reportedly once said "political power is the strongest aphrodisiac known to man." Media reports of those in high places tend to confirm the sad accuracy of Kissinger's remark.

11. See the *NIVSB* footnote on 2Sa 12:8, p. 439.

12. Mark Hatfield, *Between a Rock and a Hard Place* (Waco: Word, 1976), p. 16.

13. Charles Colson, "Reigning in the Imperial Congress," in *Jubilee*, the monthly newsletter of the Prison Fellowship (May 1989): 7.

14. See *NIVSB* notes on v. 4, p. 907.

15. *The Faith of Israel: Aspects of Old Testament Thought* (Philadelphia: Westminster, 1956), p. 192.

16. See *ANET*, pp. 274–276, 278, 291, 307 for examples.

17. "The Messiah in the Old Testament," *Studies in Biblical Theology* (London: SCM, 1956), pp. 11–24 (here 21). See also J. Jocz, "Messiah," *ZPEB*, 4:198–207 and O. A. Piper, "Messiah," *ISBE*, 3d ed., 3:330–338.

18. Ibid., p. 24.

chapter 7

The Kingdom of God: Part Two

(Scripture reading: 1–2 Samuel; 1–2 Kings; Lamentations; Ezra 1; 5:1–2; 7:6–10; Nehemiah 1–2; 4; 6:1–16; 8; Esther; Daniel 1–6)

Leading Questions

How does the Primeval History (Ge 1–11) establish the theme of the kingdom of God?

Why is the election of Israel a crucial moment in the kingdom of God?

How did the struggle with the Philistines lead to a major transformation in the life of Israel?

How did the monarchy change Israelite history and society?

What sicknesses began to develop during the monarchy and what parallels are there to our own country?

What were the factors in the division of the kingdom?

What political issues do the reigns of Jeroboam I, Ahab and Jeroboam II raise that are still relevant to our own government?

How do the reigns of Hezekiah and Josiah illustrate the tension between faith and politics?

Why did Israel survive the destruction of the two kingdoms?

What changes took place among the Jewish people during the exilic and post-exilic periods?

The Prelude in the Primeval History

The Setting for the Kingdom of God

The idea of the kingdom of God already appears in the creation narrative of Genesis 1. We recall that the climax of God's creative acts is the creation of human beings. As God's image they are entrusted with ruling over planet earth in his name. "Rule over the fish of the sea and the birds of the air and over every living creature that moves on the ground" (Ge 1:28). Thus it was God's original intention that humans should exercise power over a portion (a rather small portion at that!) of his vast domain. The Lord of the Universe wished to share with his image-bearers an aspect of his very nature. This high calling is celebrated in Psalm 8: "You made him ruler over the works of your hands; you put everything under his feet: all flocks and herds, and the beasts of the field, the birds of the air, and the fish of the sea, all that swim the paths of the seas" (vv. 6–7). Human beings, then, were created as God's vice-regents.

The Sabotage of the Kingdom of God

This happy situation apparently did not last long. Into this tranquil scene slithers the serpent. We have already discussed this episode in chapter three. Satan's intention was to turn the first human couple into rebels and to lay claim to this planet. In the mystery of God's wisdom, this takeover was permitted, though it should be noted that Satan's sovereignty over earth is not absolute. Still, he possesses considerable power and was acknowledged by Jesus himself as the "prince of this world" (Jn 12:31; 14:30; 16:11).

The Struggle to Re-establish the Kingdom of God

In overview, the rest of the Bible (Ge 3:8–Rev 22:6) recounts the re-establishment of the rule of God over a rebellious planet, which is under the malign influence of sin, death and the devil (see above in chapter one). The biblical story line traces the vicissitudes of this cosmic struggle and the thrilling conclusion, fulfilling the prayer of Christians for nearly 2,000 years: "your kingdom come, your will be done on earth as it is in heaven" (Mt 6:10).

The Preparation in the Patriarchal Era

As we saw in chapter four, the struggle to re-establish the kingdom of God on earth took a new and important turn with the call of Abraham (Ge

12:1–3). God's amazing plan, as sketched in the OT, focuses upon one man and his descendants—the people of Israel. The three-fold promise of an heir, an inheritance and a heritage becomes the road map to the rest of the highway of redemption. The patriarchal stories conclude with the extended family of Jacob in Egypt, sustained providentially by the faithful son Joseph. This deliverance remarkably foreshadows the work of Jesus on behalf of his people, the Church, in the NT.

The Program in Israel's Election at Sinai

At Mount Sinai, Israel becomes the instrument for the establishment of the Kingdom. They are the visible embodiment of God's rule on earth. As discussed earlier, their election has an inclusive intention—that is, it is designed to reach out and invite other peoples to abandon their paganism and to embrace the one, true and living God. We may illustrate how Israel's election functions in the plan of God by the following chart. Their mission is to extend the boundaries of God's visible kingdom so that the whole earth may be filled with a knowledge of God: "For the earth will be filled with the knowledge of the glory of the LORD, as the waters cover the sea" (Hab 2:14).

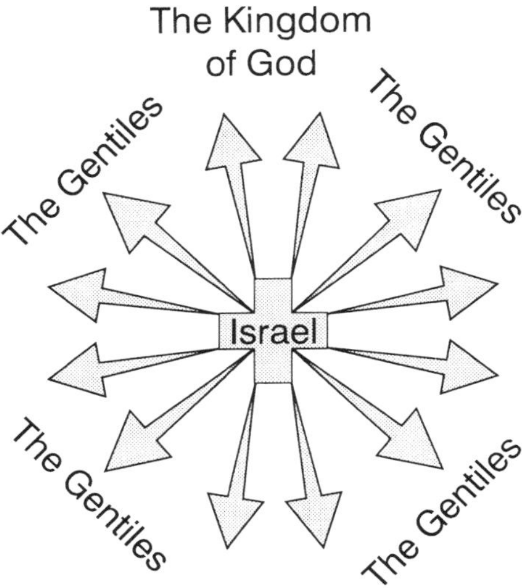

The Great Experiment: The Theocratic Kingdom

We will briefly trace the course of Israel's political history as recorded in the OT. As noted in chapter five, the form of government, instituted for Israel by the Lord himself at Mount Sinai, is a theocracy. That is, the Lord is the rightful King who rules over his people by divinely appointed representatives. These leaders are accountable to the Lord as well as to the tribal leaders and elders.

The Tribal Federation

That brings us to an important observation. The specific form of theocracy is that of a tribal federation. The Sinai Covenant is the constitution to which the 12 tribes swear allegiance. The tribes are held together by a common faith expressed at a central shrine.

This governmental pattern stands in stark contrast to that of the established peoples living in the land of Canaan. Prior to Israel's arrival, there had never been a central government in the region. Owing to the unique geographical and geological features of Canaan, the tendency was for small territorial zones of influence centered on fortified cities. Even when Egypt exercised hegemony over the region, that authority was fragmented by competing city-states. The city-states were located primarily along the coastal plain and the main thoroughfare running from Egypt to Damascus and points eastward.

When the Israelites invade the land of Canaan, they establish their own sphere of influence—essentially the central mountain ridge, running like a backbone down the western flank of the Jordan Valley. Two and a half tribes remain on the east side of the Jordan.

After Joshua's initial conquest, the Hebrews gradually adopt a form of co-existence with the indigenous peoples. For the most part, they stay up on the central ridge, in the hill country, and carve out settlements in the forests that covered much of the land in those days (Jos 17:15–18). The Canaanites remain along the coastal plain and the interior valleys, adjacent to the trunk route between Egypt and Mesopotamia. The Hebrews are a pastoral, agrarian (pertaining to agriculture) society with minimal involvement in commerce and trade, such as existed along the main trunk route. Still, there appears to have been significant interaction between these two cultures:

> The Israelites lived among the Canaanites, Hittites, Amorites, Perizzites, Hivites and Jebusites. They took their daughters in marriage and gave their own daughters to their sons, and served their gods. The Israelites did evil in the eyes of the LORD; they forgot the LORD their God and served the Baals and the Asherahs (Jdg 3:5–7).

This interaction results in apostasy, provoking the Lord into punitive action in accordance with the Sinai Covenant. Recall the curses of the suzerainty treaties. The book of Judges records a series of apostasies and punishments for disloyalty—indeed, the book consists of a cyclical pattern of apostasy, punishment, repentance and deliverance.[1]

The Struggle Against the Philistines

Background of the struggle. One ethnic group whom the Lord uses to discipline his people calls for special mention. In the Bible this group is called the Philistines.[2] They appear to be one tribe of a larger federation whom the Egyptians called the Sea Peoples. These were peoples of Aegean origin (Greece and the surrounding islands). Sometime in the 13th and 12th century B.C. there was a massive invasion of Dorian Greeks into the region of present day Greece and Turkey. The so-called Sea Peoples were dislodged from their homelands and set sail in their swift ships to the eastern Mediterranean. Egyptian records describe a series of desperate struggles between Rameses III and the Sea Peoples for control of a portion of the Nile Delta and coastal regions of Egypt. For the most part Rameses repulsed the onslaught, although he did permit some of them to settle and serve as mercenaries in his army and navy.[3]

Egypt was not the only portion of the eastern Mediterranean to be visited by these invaders, however. Canaan presented a choice new homeland and was relatively easy to overcome militarily. All along the coast pockets of Sea Peoples established enclaves. One such enclave was in the area known today as the Gaza Strip. Here a sizable contingent of the Sea Peoples, the Philistines, settled down. This group confronts the Hebrews with their greatest threat. The books of Judges and Samuel reflect the life and death struggle between these two groups over the control of the land of Canaan.

Let us take a moment and review this struggle, a struggle instrumental in bringing about a fundamental change in the political history of Israel. Although there is a brief mention of Philistines subdued by Shamgar in Judges 3:31, they do not figure prominently in the stories until we get to the judgeship of Samson in chapters 13–16.

If one looks at a map and then reads the stories of Samson, it is evident what is happening. The conflicts between Samson and the Philistines take place in the Shephelah. This is a region of low foothills between the coastal plain, where the Philistines were, and the hill country up on the central ridge. The Philistines were, in all likelihood, feeling insecure within their restricted coastal enclave. They attempt to maintain their presence by controlling the foothills looming to the east. The inevitable tension between the two groups flares up in periodic armed conflict. The conflict escalates into a prolonged military struggle to determine who will control all of Canaan. In the days of Samuel the prophet, we hear of Philistine military action taking place on the central ridge (1Sa 4:1–11; 7:7–17). In Saul's tenure as the first king of Israel a series of battles are fought in order to drive the Philistines off the central ridge (1Sa 13:2–14:23). Clearly the contest has taken on momentous proportions for the combatants.

Advantages of the Philistines. In this struggle to control the land of Canaan, certain advantages reside with the Philistines. In the first place, they spring from a culture that has a strong military tradition and glories in combat. If one has read Homer's *Iliad*, the mind-set of the Philistines can more easily be appreciated. Young Philistine boys aspire to be fearless warriors, proficient in the art of warfare. Early on in life they learn to handle sword, spear, shield, bow and arrow. This is a far cry from the background and training of a typical Hebrew boy. To be sure, Hebrew boys knew how to fight—that is part of human nature! But Hebrew youths were taught how to tend flocks, to cultivate the olive and vine, and to live peaceably with their neighbors. Indeed, even the aliens living among them were to be well treated: "And you are to love those who are aliens, for you yourselves were aliens in Egypt" (Dt 10:19).

The weapons of the Hebrews are relatively simple instruments, like slingshots and homemade swords and spears. By contrast, the Philistines possess the most technologically advanced weapons of the day. They have mastered the art of smelting iron. Much of the Mediterranean world is still in the bronze age. The Philistines, however, produce iron weapons far superior to bronze weapons. Iron is harder and holds its edge, that is, its sharpness, better than bronze. The Bible calls attention to the disparity in weaponry. In fact, one passage dramatically illustrates the superiority of Philistine weaponry:

> Not a blacksmith could be found in the whole land of Israel, because the Philistines had said, "Otherwise the Hebrews will make swords or spears!" So all Israel went down to the Philistines to have their plowshares, mattocks, axes and sickles sharpened. The price was two-thirds of a shekel for sharpening plowshares and mattocks, and a third of a shekel for sharpening forks and axes and for repointing goads. So on the day of the battle not a soldier with Saul and Jonathan bad a sword or spear in his hand; only Saul and his son Jonathan had them (1Sa 13:19–22).

Another advantage of the Philistines has to do with their political organization. They were organized into five city-states, each of which was headed up by virtual dictators. These city-states were a sort of Philistine Pentapolis, consisting of Gaza, Ashkelon, and Ashdod along the coast, and Gath and Ekron further inland, not far from the Shephelah. These five cities could quickly mobilize for war and cooperate under the leadership of an appointed commander-in-chief. Once again, the *Iliad* provides an instructive parallel in that the various Greek contingents fought under the general direction of Agamemnon. The upshot is that the Philistines present a strong, unified front with superior tactics and weapons. They are a formidable foe.

Besides their lack of military tradition, training and advanced weapons, the Hebrews suffer a severe handicap of disunity. Even a cursory reading of Judges demonstrates that rarely, if ever, do the tribes fight as a unified nation against a common enemy. After the death of Joshua and the generation contemporaneous with him, the cohesion among the tribes breaks down—this is basically a spiritual problem with political consequences. Participation in confronting invaders is determined more by regional self-interest rather than by the common good of the tribal federation. As the refrain in Judges has it: "In those days Israel had no king; everyone did as he saw fit" (Jdg 21:25).

Advantages of the Hebrews. On the basis of the foregoing assessment, one would have little reason to think that the Hebrews could possibly overcome the Philistine threat. In fact they did, and the reasons are fascinating.

The first advantage Israel possesses is geographical in nature. The Hebrews occupy the central ridge—the geographical backbone of the country. Any group or nation wishing to dominate the land of Canaan must control the central ridge. All traffic to the east must somehow negotiate the passes of the central ridge. Furthermore, the main coastal route can never be truly secure so long as a powerful, hostile force exists, entrenched up on the ridge. There are numerous points at which the main lines of communication can be cut. Penetrating up onto the ridge is no easy matter, as the Philistines repeatedly find out.

The Hebrews do not live in large, fortified cities. Siege warfare simply cannot dislodge the Hebrews. Narrow, steep wadis [canyons] make invasion by large numbers of soldiers a dangerous proposition because of the threat of ambush. In short, it is extremely difficult to deliver a decisive blow against the Hebrews—they just melt away into the wadis and caves only to return another day for battle.

Thus the picture that emerges in 1 Samuel resembles a standoff. The Philistines, by virtue of a superior military, are securely entrenched on the coastal plain, while the Hebrews cling tenaciously to their superior position. David, son of Jesse, however, decisively breaks this stalemate. In short, David, fleeing from Saul's insane jealousy, offers himself to the Philistines as a mercenary. While among the Philistines, David learns some valuable lessons in military strategy and tactics. Perhaps he also learns the secret of iron smelting.[4] In any case, during his time of exile, he surrounds himself with what becomes the nucleus of a professional army, or at least, the nucleus of his officer corps. When David becomes king over all Israel, and the Philistines realize that he is a real threat to their national security, he delivers several crushing blows to their military machine. They are finally forced to submit to David as a tribute nation and to relinquish any ambitions to control the newly emerging state of Israel. In the end, only one of the contenders unifies the land of Canaan. Henceforth, it is known as the land of Israel.

The deciding advantage. There is one more well-known story in 1 Samuel that draws attention to the ultimate advantage Israel possesses in her struggle with the Philistines. It also illustrates how what appears to be a mismatch, humanly speaking, is an opportunity for the Lord to demonstrate his power to deliver those who truly trust him. The story is the duel between David and Goliath (1Sa 17). The account opens by setting the stage for the conflict. The Philistines, in keeping with their policy of consolidating their foothold on the coast of Canaan and of ultimate control of the entire land, have penetrated up into the Shephelah, into the Valley of Elah. Saul seeks to block this invasion and mobilizes his forces opposite the Philistines.

In the midst of this confrontation and stalemate, there suddenly emerges the great champion of Gath. It is as if he has walked out of the pages of the *Iliad*. The description of his armor and weapons is precisely that of a warrior in the Trojan War. Everything down to his bronze greaves matches that of Homer's classic! This giant (the NIV translates six cubits and a span as "over nine feet tall") even has an armor-bearer going in front of him. The iron point on his spear alone weighs nearly as much as a shot (16 lbs.) in track and field! In typical Greek heroic style, Goliath challenges the Hebrews to select a champion and fight him in single-handed combat. Once again, this comports with the Greek traditions of war and valor. Several times in the *Iliad* the siege comes to a halt as two warriors accept a challenge to fight to the death. Indeed, the *Iliad* climaxes with the combat between Achilles and Hector, two heroes from the opposing armies of the Trojan War.

None of the Hebrews accept the challenge. Even Saul, the great hero of earlier days, shrinks back with fear. Of course this highlights Saul's real problem: because of disobedience, the Holy Spirit has departed from him and he is bereft of divine assistance. Into this "dispirited" army steps the rising star of Israel's future—young David. Sensing keenly the shame and humiliation of the nation and its king, David volunteers to fight the Philistine hero. Note his credentials for this contest: he had killed both a lion and a bear, which had attacked his father's flocks, and he had faith.

"The LORD who delivered me from the paw of the lion and the paw of the bear will deliver me from the hand of the Philistine" (v. 37). The difference between Saul and David is that the Holy Spirit rests upon David. Remember that Samuel "took the horn of oil and anointed him in the presence of his brothers, and from that day on the Spirit of the LORD came upon David in power" (1Sa 16:13).

When Saul attempts to outfit David in his own armor, the result is almost comic: "I cannot go in these" (v. 39). Instead, he uses what he has grown up with—his shepherd's staff and his trusty slingshot. This latter weapon should not be underrated. The sling of ancient times was a long leather strap with a pouch attached. The rock or similar projectile was inserted into the pouch and the leather strap hurled above one's head until sufficient velocity was attained. At that moment, the rock was released from its pouch. A trained slinger can easily attain velocities in excess of 100 mph. (A major league pitcher can usually throw a fastball at about 90 mph.)[5] As to accuracy, the biblical description of the seven hundred left-handed Benjamite slingers "each of whom could sling a stone at a hair and not miss" (Jdg 20:16) is probably only a slight exaggeration. The story of David's encounter with Goliath assumes he had attained a comparable capability with his sling. David places the smooth rock in the only location possible to kill Goliath—just below his helmet on the forehead and just above the shield over which Goliath peered down at his adolescent foe! To borrow an expression from NFL commentator John Madden, "Boom! Bam!" and Goliath goes down!

This great victory over the Philistines brings David to national prominence and, indeed, into the royal family itself. In his providence, the Lord raises up the one who will achieve complete victory over the Philistines. It does not happen overnight, but the handwriting is on the wall for the Philistines. We thus conclude this section with the ultimate weapon of Israel—their God who promised this land long ago to Abraham, Isaac and Jacob. The Philistines could never overturn that royal grant to Israel. They could and did retard Israel's full occupation and dominion over the land, but that was basically Israel's fault. Israel's disobedience brought on the Philistine oppression in the first place. In his great faithfulness, however, the Lord raises up for Israel a "man after his own heart" (1Sa 13:14). Under his leadership there comes into existence, for the first time, a powerful nation state, controlling the entire land of Canaan.

The Changes Brought About by the Monarchy

David's unification of the twelve tribes of Israel into a nation, which functioned under a monarchic form of government, permanently changed Hebrew culture and society. In one generation we have the emergence of a Middle Eastern power dominating the region. The Israelites enter the larger world of commerce, industry, foreign relations, trade and, unfortunately, war. No longer are they isolated in outlook. They are forced to be aware of and interact with the surrounding national states. They become more sophisticated, urbane and acquisitive. Higher standards of living and pursuit of pleasure characterize an increasing number of Israelites. We will list some of the changes which David's administration brings about and discuss their impact.

Dynastic succession. The first change concerns the transfer of power, always a crucial issue in government and politics. With the rise of David and the divine promise accorded him concerning his dynasty (cf. 2Sa 7:16 and discussion above), there is a transition from charismatic to dynastic succession. That is, after the reign of Solomon, we no longer hear of the Spirit of the Lord coming upon an individual to be king (as was the case with Saul and David). Rather, the king in power grooms one of his sons to succeed him on the throne. The problem here is that the heir to the throne may not be anointed by the Holy Spirit (cf. 1Sa 10:6–9; 16:13; 1Ki 1:28–40; 11:43). He may not even be a man of faith (cf. Isa 7:9b). Many of the Hebrew kings were unfit to reign—their only qualification being their royal descent or a successful coup.

Centralization of power. A second change is even more significant for the life of Israel. This relates to centralization of power. Under David and, to an even greater degree, under Solomon, power gravitates from the outlying tribal areas to the city of Jerusalem. Here officials appointed by the king make decisions formerly made by village elders and tribal leaders. In place of the old tribal federation, Solomon reorganizes the nation into districts. The new structure appears in 1 Kings 4:7–19, where we find a list of district governors who replace the tribal leaders.

A careful reading of the text suggests that Solomon did not simply replace the 12 tribes with 12 districts. Rather, the districts reflect overlapping of the older tribal territories and a redrawing of economic and political units.[6] One suspects the reorganization did not sit well with all the citizens of the state of Israel!

An interesting and instructive observation about the various district governors is the relationship two of them have to Solomon. Both Ben-Abinadab and Ahimaaz are Solomon's sons-in-law. This illustrates an all-too-frequent feature of governments, namely, that relatives of those in power very often benefit from their family ties. Those two officials take the place of tribal leaders who previously made decisions affecting their own tribes. One wonders how well-accepted the sons-in-law were!

This process of centralization of power parallels a similar trend in American political history. You may remember from your study of American history that a contentious debate swirled around the problem of apportioning decision-making between the federal government and the individual states. The issue of states' rights versus federal government still continues; each election the political rhetoric reaches fever pitch. Many candidates decry the concentration of power in the federal government. They promise to restore to the people their eroded rights and power; they urge a swing of the pendulum back to the grassroots. Of course, veteran observers of the political scene also know that, historically, federal government has steadily increased. Furthermore, this regularly transpires under the administration of the very officials who promise to reduce government and bureaucracy! Generally, there is an inexorable trend toward more concentration of power under a central governing agency.

Institution of forced labor. A third fundamental change during David and Solomon's reign is creation of the corvée. Corvée is forced labor under the direction of the government. This work force is paid little, if anything, and provides a source of cheap labor for public works projects and government spending projects. The corvée of Solomon's empire has two distinct divisions. One section comprises Israelite young men who are drafted to serve in the various projects authorized by the government. In 1 Kings 4:6 we read of a certain Adoniram, son of Abda, who is in charge of forced labor. According to 1 Kings 5:13–18, 30,000 Israelites are enlisted as lumberjacks in the mountains of Lebanon, where they log the beautiful cedars of Lebanon and the pine trees (cf. ch. 6, p. 181). Another 70,000 transport the logs to Israel. Finally, 80,000 stonecutters chisel out the massive limestone blocks used in the temple, palaces, public buildings and defensive towers and walls. These workers are Israelite conscripts. Eventually they serve their time and then pursue their own trades and occupations.

The second division of the corvée, however, does not have any future options. These are the remnants of the Canaanite peoples who lived among the Hebrews since the days of Joshua. According to 1 Kings 9:20–23, Solomon conscripts them as slave laborers. They provide a source of cheap labor, performing menial work beneath the dignity of Israelites.

Professional army. A fourth innovation is the appearance of a professional, standing army. Throughout the days of the tribal federation, the army was essentially a citizens' all-volunteer force. This changes during David's tenure. Now we note the presence of trained soldiers and generals (2Sa 8:18). David begins to employ mercenaries (hired, professional soldiers) and drafts young Israelite men into military service (1Ki 9:22). The army that takes shape toward the end of David's reign and into Solomon's is the most formidable in the entire Middle East. One cannot resist a comparison to the current Middle East in which the Israeli armed forces, once again, are the best in the region.[7]

International relations. Israel becomes a nation among nations. This necessitates the institution of a diplomatic corps and the cultivation of international relations. Israel's economic and political interests require representatives in foreign capitals. Israelite young men are trained in the art of diplomacy and international relations. This in turn means a steady flow of ambassadors and diplomats from neighboring states to and from Jerusalem. As a result of contact with the larger world, the horizons of Israel's cultural world expand considerably. One thinks of the state visit by the Queen of Sheba recorded in 1 Kings 10. Such contacts must have become increasingly common.

Emergence of a middle class. Another new development with considerable consequences is the emergence of a middle class of businessmen, merchants, small industrialists, and landholders. Remember that in the early years of Israel's history, the typical Israelite is a herdsman or farmer. While many still follow that way of life during the monarchy, a middle class begins to appear. Since the latter's prosperity depends upon a stable government, which was supportive of investment and trade, the middle class generally supports the government and often has spokespersons involved in the government at various levels and in various capacities. Note that in 1 Kings 10:28 there is mention of royal merchants who engage in international trade. Of course the leader in the export-import business was none other than Solomon himself. He has a lucrative business importing horses and chariots from Egypt and Kue (probably Cilicia, in modern Turkey) and exporting them to the Hittites (in modern Turkey) and to the Arameans (in modern Syria and Iraq). Since the chariot was the mainstay of the ancient armies of those days, this was really a version of arms sales.[8]

Jerusalem as political and religious center. A seventh major change in the days of the early monarchy involves concentration of power in the city of Jerusalem. Up until the early days of David's reign, this city was a Jebusite enclave right in the heart of the hill country of Judah. In fact, it effectively controlled traffic in both a north-south and east-west direction. No real unification of the country is possible without Jerusalem being an integral part of the land of Israel.[9] Not surprisingly, one of the first things David does as king of all Israel, is capture Jerusalem and make it his capital (2Sa 5:6–10, cf. 1Ch 11:4–9). Since neither Judah nor Ephraim previously occupied the city, these two powerful and jealous tribes cannot "cash in" on its new status. Thus David's selection of a neutral site for his capital is a stroke of genius.

Recent archaeological work on the site of ancient Jebus (Jerusalem) illuminates the account of the capture. Today, one may see the tunnel dug by the Jebusites in order to have a continual source of water within the walls of the city. One may also visualize how Joab was able, with extraordinary physical agility, to climb up the shaft of the tunnel in order to attack the defenders within the imposing walls of Jebus.[10]

Jerusalem now becomes the focal point of Israelite religion. Not long after making Jerusalem his capital, David orders the Ark of the Covenant transferred to Jerusalem (1Sa 6:12–19; 1Ch 15:26–16:3). Later he moves the tabernacle to the threshing floor of Arunah on the summit above Jerusalem (2Sa 24:18–24). The temple built by Solomon creates a national and religious shrine, which served as a symbol of national unity. Henceforth Jerusalem's significance for the faith of Israel soars. We may even speak of the beginnings of a Zion tradition, taking its place alongside the exodus and Mount Sinai traditions. The Zion tradition thus links the promise of an eternal Davidic dynasty with the site of the temple, the place where the visible glory of God resided.

Summary. These seven changes in the days of David and Solomon have far-reaching effects for the life and faith of the average Israelite. Some of these changes are unquestionably positive. They result in a higher standard of living and in a stronger sense of unity than in the days of Joshua. Other changes, however, bring in harmful and destructive tendencies. We turn now to an examination of the "downside" of the monarchy.

The Sicknesses of the Monarchy

Unequal distribution of wealth. The first of these sicknesses has to do with the unequal distribution of wealth. What happens is that fewer and fewer citizens possess more and more of the wealth. The number of aristocrats is relatively small; the number of peasants great. In contrast to the days of the tribal federation, when there was comparatively little difference in terms of wealth and possessions, a few families amass fortunes. There were always those who were poor in Israel's history, but now, during the days of the monarchy and afterwards, the numbers of the indigent soar. Several reasons for this widening gulf between the haves and the have-nots deserve mention.

The old laws specifying the remission of debt every seven years and the return of land to the original tenants in the fiftieth or Jubilee year are conveniently ignored by the ruling class (cf. Dt 15:1–3; Lev 25:8–24). Powerful families control most of the productive land. The prophet Isaiah laments: "Woe to you who add house to house and join field to field till no space is left and you live alone in the land" (Isa 5:8).

The rich and powerful also control the courts to their own advantage. The powerless have no advocate or any means of securing justice. Isaiah castigates the officials of his day: "Your rulers are rebels, companions of thieves, they all love bribes and chase after gifts. They do not defend the cause of the fatherless; the widow's case does not come before them" (Isa 1:23). Amos, a little earlier than Isaiah, denounces conditions in the northern kingdom of Israel in these words: "They trample on the heads of the poor as upon the dust of the ground and deny justice to the oppressed" (Am 2:7). He pleads with his generation to "hate evil, love good; maintain justice in the courts" (Am 5:15).

The primary problem is the failure to observe the stipulations of the Sinai Covenant. An interesting line from Deuteronomy underscores this failure. The Mosaic Law has built into it features that tend to prevent undue concentration of wealth in the hands of a few (see Ex 23:1–13; Lev 25; Dt 15:1–11). Complete obedience to the Law of Moses carried with it a guarantee of general prosperity for all citizens.

> However, there should be no poor among you, for in the land the LORD your God is giving you to possess as your inheritance, he will richly bless you, if only you fully obey the LORD your God and are careful to follow all these commands I am giving you today (Dt 15:4–5).

Of course, therein lay the problem. Isaiah relays the Suzerain's complaint: "I reared children and brought them up, but they have rebelled against me" (Isa 1:2). Rebellion against the Lord results in social upheaval and tension.

High cost of economic and military security. A second sickness stems from the high price tag for military security and economic prosperity. As the saying goes, there is no such thing as a free lunch. In order to provide for the military security of his kingdom, Solomon invested enormous sums into the building and maintaining of a formidable military machine. One of the hazards with being located on a major land bridge between Africa, Asia, and Europe is the desirability factor from the standpoint of neighboring nations. Sitting astride the major trade routes, Solomon controlled an extremely lucrative business. According to 1 Kings 10:15, he levied taxes and tariffs on the merchants and traders who passed through his kingdom. He also engaged in commerce and trade by means of a merchant marine fleet with the assistance of the Phoenicians to the north (1Ki 10:22). As Solomon's wealth and fame increased, envy by neighbors kept pace.

To ensure his position in the international economic network, Solomon had to be able to defend his interests militarily. In 1 Kings 9:15–19 we learn of three fortified cities: Hazor, Megiddo, and Gezer. They function as choke points on the international highway, running from the Tigris-Euphrates river valley to the Nile river valley. Here Solomon could, and undoubtedly did, install levy and excise stations. He garrisoned these stations with strong contingents of troops and chariots. Only massive military force would have been able to dislodge him. For the time being, he was "king of the mountain" and he intended to stay there. This, however, meant a constant commitment to maintaining a military presence—an expensive undertaking. One study estimates that, in terms of per capita cost, each Israelite forked over about an ounce of gold per year just to pay for the military part of Solomon's budget. Of course this is but a portion of the total budget. In addition, the massive public building projects, the agricultural development of the Negev (the southern region in the area around Beersheba), and the merchant marine all required large sums of money.[11]

There is even evidence that Solomon's administration ran into a problem familiar to Americans—namely, deficit spending! According to 1 Kings 9:11–14, Solomon ceded territory to Hiram, King of Tyre. This was probably in order to pay for the large amounts of cedar and pine purchased for the temple and palace. The point is that in order to maintain his position in the region, he has to tax his citizens heavily. This tax burden appears to escalate steadily throughout Solomon's reign. As the tax rate increases, so do complaints—especially from the middle class who shoulder an ever-increasing load of the taxes.

Infiltration of paganism. The third sickness is even more devastating in its effects than the first two. This is the infiltration of paganism into the fabric of religious life in Israel. We noted above how Solomon violated the three prohibitions of the Mosaic Law regarding kingship. According to

1 Kings 11:1–8, Solomon's many wives turned his heart away from steadfast commitment to the Lord. "He followed Ashtoreth the goddess of the Sidonians, and Molech the detestable god of the Ammonites" (v. 5). He even built high places in Jerusalem for the gods of his wives. One can imagine the impact of this upon the average Israelite. The king is supposed to be the leading citizen and the role model of faith and commitment. This act of apostasy by Solomon is like the proverbial small hole in the dike. Before long the hole becomes a huge chasm through which the moral pollution of paganism sweeps over the land. The values and traditions of the Sinai Covenant are under assault by a revival of Canaanite religion. This sickness more than anything else spells the doom of the empire. Indeed, it is the leading cause of the dissolution of the grand experiment that began at Mount Sinai.

As we conclude this section, we have seen how three sicknesses, which became especially prominent during the long 40-year reign of Solomon, spelled the demise of the united monarchy. According to 1 Kings 11:9, "The LORD became angry with Solomon." Furthermore, the Lord conveyed his displeasure to Solomon by announcing:

> Since this is your attitude and you have not kept my covenant and my decrees, which I commanded you, I will most certainly tear the kingdom away from you and give it to one of your subordinates. Nevertheless, for the sake of David your father, I will not do it during your lifetime. I will tear it out of the hand of your son. (1Ki 11:11–12)

Relevance for today. Does this all sound vaguely familiar? It should. As we reflect upon the parallels, we realize that our country was not begun, like Israel, by entering into a covenant with the Lord and by promising to live in accordance with clearly defined stipulations. Still, this nation was founded upon principles based upon and derived from the Judeo-Christian tradition. That being the case, *we should be able to apply the lessons learned from the history of Israel to our own situation.*

Consider unequal distribution of wealth. In the United States there is a widening gap between the haves and the have-nots. Increasingly, a smaller segment of society controls the wealth and resources of our nation. Back in 1984 a study by the Federal Reserve found that the wealthiest 2 percent of American families own most of the tax-free bonds, half of the stock and

20 percent of the nation's real estate,[12] a trend that has accelerated, not declined.[13] This kind of disparity leads to social unrest and violence. Riots in depressed areas of our major cities are indications of dangerous social problems. Racial inequities and injustice exacerbate the situation.[14] Issues like this cry out for just and fair resolution.

Christians need to ask whether we have contributed to the problem by consciously or unconsciously identifying with the interests of the powerful and wealthy. The challenge lies in working through solutions that more equitably share the wealth of this great land, which itself exploits far more than its share of the earth's resources. Make no mistake about it, this problem is monumental in proportions and the solution is not obvious or easy. The OT demands that Israelites provide for the poor; our society would rather forget about them. The Bible urges sharing; we seem bent on hoarding. The Bible enjoins equal justice for all—regardless of race or color. We may pride ourselves on being "color blind," but our actions belie our words. Surely this is a place to begin.

Americans have the most expensive government in the history of mankind! Like Solomon, we find ourselves spending huge amounts on defense and the military in order to secure our economic future. Of course, outstripping our military budget are numerous (and necessary) social programs, Social Security and Medicare. Add to this waste, fraud, mismanagement, interest on the national debt, special interest group appropriations and subsidies for everything from soup to nuts and you have a formula for financial failure.

There are many difficult questions here to which I will not pretend to have answers. But should not Christians, with faith commitments anchored in the message of the Bible, be asking some hard questions at this point? In an age of consumerism, just how much is enough? Is it true that what's good for big business is good for America? Do we have a double standard when it comes to "white collar" crime? Should we flex our military muscles in order to defend our "right" to a disproportionately large share of the world's dwindling resources? Does being "king of the mountain" clash with Christian values of sharing and concern for others? Can our government continue to spend more than it takes in? How can we deal more fairly and compassionately with those below the poverty line? How can we equitably right the wrongs of ongoing racism? These are not easy questions. *They demonstrate a fundamental problem: the tension between faith and politics.*[15]

As Christians beginning the 21st century, we can all agree that many of the values of the founding generation have been eroded. Are we not, as a nation, accountable to basic moral and ethical standards? One thinks here of Amos' sweeping indictments against the neighboring nations for their crimes against humanity (Am 1:3–2:3). We, living in North America, are confronted by a new wave of paganism. This presents special problems for believers because of our pluralistic society. Nonetheless, we sense deeply that some practices, if widely adopted, cannot but destroy the fabric and well-being of our society. The war against the unborn, the violence permeating all aspects of society and the breakdown of the family are siren calls for repentance. This should impel us to work within the existing structures for a truly just, moral and compassionate society.

The Divided Kingdom

Rupture between north and south. Solomon was dead. Forty years of peace and prosperity were over. Never again would there be a similar period in Israel's history. Rehoboam, Solomon's firstborn, began his reign over the most powerful state in the Middle East. Things went wrong on his inauguration and he never really recovered. In the account of his coronation, we discover serious shortcomings in his character and capabilities.

According to 1 Kings 12:1, "Rehoboam went to Shechem, for all the Israelites had gone there to make him king." This seems strange. Why would Rehoboam go to Shechem for his coronation when the capital was in Jerusalem with its splendid palace and temple? The rest of the chapter enables us to surmise why. Evidently the northern tribal areas feel that under Solomon they are shortchanged in terms of representation and services. They probably resent the fact that the tribe of Judah seems to benefit most from the central government. As a gesture of protest, and as an opportunity to deliver a strong message to Jerusalem, the north insists that Rehoboam come up to Shechem, in the north, for his coronation. Shechem was, of course, a revered site in Israelite memory as the first place where Abram pitched his tent and where Jacob purchased a plot of land (cf. Ge 12:6–7; 33:18–20).

We also learn that a certain Jeroboam attended the coronation at the insistence of the northern tribes. Jeroboam is no stranger to Jerusalem. In fact, he had been a high official in Solomon's administration serving in the hated post of director of forced labor for the house of Joseph (1Ki 11:26–28). Following an extraordinary word of prophecy promising him rule over the house of Israel, Jeroboam rebels against Solomon (1Ki 11:26–39). When Solomon finds out, Jeroboam must flee to Egypt for sanctuary. Perhaps Jeroboam realized that the forced labor and taxation had become too burdensome and that the north needed relief from the oppressive measures of Solomon. At any rate, Jeroboam forms a government in exile while in Egypt and keeps in touch with other dissidents in the north. The coronation affords Jeroboam the perfect opportunity to challenge the young king away from his power base in Judah.

The incident at Shechem provides a case study in ambition and power. As soon as Rehoboam arrives at Shechem, a welcoming committee, tossing complaints not garlands, meets him. They make demands, not oaths of loyalty. Their complaints are primarily twofold: they demand a cut in taxes and a cutback in the manpower allotted to the forced labor gangs (1Ki 12:4). Rehoboam, taken by surprise, requests a delay of three days so that he could sort out the issues involved in this demand. As it turns out, that is about the only sensible thing he does in the entire episode! What follows is a sad commentary on the young man's maturity and character.

First, he confers with his experienced advisors who have served under his father Solomon. These men give him the best advice he could have sought. They tell him, in effect, that the key to success is to adopt the attitude of a servant. In short, they urge him to embrace the ideals of kingship enshrined in the Mosaic Law (cf. Dt 17:14–20). They know from personal experience that Solomon oppressed the people with his grandiose projects and self-aggrandizement. Their advice is worth quoting: "If today you will be a servant to these people and serve them and give them a favorable answer, they will always be your servants" (1Ki 11:7). Unfortunately, he rejects that sound counsel and turns to his young advisors (v. 8).

The young men who have grown up with Rehoboam have a different agenda. To them, the demands of the northerners are a direct challenge to the legitimacy of Rehoboam's reign. Their approach is: "show these people who's boss." According to them, this is no time to back down or show leniency. Rehoboam must assert his power in no uncertain terms. Only in this way will the protesters be silenced.

Of course, it is not incidental that the young advisors are the ones with the most to gain by more governmental projects and spending, since they are the ones administering the programs! Reputations and promotions as leaders and administrators are at stake for these young men in days ahead. They have grown up in relative luxury and abundance. They have little understanding of living conditions for the average Israelite, who is trying to make ends meet with an ever-increasing tax burden. They do not have to live with the discouraging prospect of being conscripted into the labor gangs. In short, pampered and sheltered individuals, growing up in a climate that insists "more is better," are ill equipped to advise Rehoboam at this critical juncture. Rehoboam lets his peers guide his decisions—and it is a fateful decision.

> When all Israel saw that the king refused to listen to them, they answered the king: "What share do we have in David, what part in Jesse's son? To your tents, O Israel! Look after your own house O David!" So the Israelites went home (1Ki 12:16).

The nation of Israel suffers a schism that is never healed. From henceforth we will refer to the northern tribes as *Israel* and the southern tribes as *Judah* (Judah, Benjamin and Simeon with remnants of the scattered tribe of Levi). Although Rehoboam contemplates a forcible reunification, the people are spared the agony of a bloody civil war. Shemaiah the prophet conveys the Lord's warning not to contest the division (vv. 22–24). *The division of the kingdom is a divine judgment upon the people of Israel.*

One thinks of the American Civil War and the factors precipitating that great crisis, arguably the greatest in our history. Surely, that too was a divine judgment upon the United States of America. While there are many differences between these two historical events, there are some common threads. For example, the northern tribes' discontent over feeling excluded from political power has its counterpart in the South's similar discontent over the issue of states' rights versus the federal government. Of course economic issues figured heavily in both revolts. The hated corvée of

Solomon's day relates to the institution of American slavery, with its essentially dehumanizing effect upon both enslaved and enslaver.

Beneath these factors, however, lay the issue of power. Abuse of power introduces a destabilizing force into political systems. Flagrant violations inevitably create conflict and dissolution. The division of the kingdom of Israel is a warning to all political systems.

Redefinition of the kingdom of God. With the division an accomplished fact, we are faced with the problem of definition. How are we to identify the kingdom of God on earth? Is it to be found only in the southern kingdom of Judah? Or does it also continue on in the north? In fact, we can no longer identify the kingdom with either of these states. At times, the uneasy truce erupts in open and violent hostility. Rather, *we must now redefine the kingdom in terms of a righteous remnant who still maintain a commitment to the covenant obligations.* Thus we have a remnant community of Israelites from both north and south. This theme of the remnant becomes increasingly important as we proceed in our story.

Retrograde Course of the North

We summarize a large amount of material dealing with the northern kingdom of Israel by selecting three representative kings. We could call this section: "We three kings of Israel are!" These three examples demonstrate the generally downward spiral of the north, spiritually and morally. The viewpoint of the historian responsible for 1 and 2 Kings is clear: he considers the rebellion of Israel to be wrong. "So Israel has been in rebellion against the house of David to this day" (1Ki 12:19).

Jeroboam 1: the slippery slope. We begin with the founder of the first dynasty in the north, Jeroboam 1. His dates are 931–910 B.C. Two features of his reign deserve special attention. These illustrate our primary concern in this chapter with the tension between faith and politics.

In the first place, Jeroboam establishes a new center of political power. Obviously, he cannot claim Jerusalem without military force, nor is that advisable anyway, since the northern tribes wanted the center of power in their region. Shechem is the obvious choice with its historic associations going back to the patriarchs.

The problem with Shechem, however, is its location at a site not easily defended. The city lies in a valley between two mountains, Gerizim and Ebal (cf. Dt 27). The strategic shortcoming of Shechem is matched by another. Jeroboam's kingdom suffers from a problem evident already in the days of the judges. The great rift valley of the Jordan is more than just a geographical boundary. It also marks a dialectal and regional boundary. That is to say, the Israelite tribes, living on the east side of the Jordan Valley, over a long period of time developed their own dialect. One remembers from the book of Judges that west-bankers or Ephraimites pronounced the Hebrew word for a flowing stream or flood as *sibbôleth*, with an "s" sound, whereas east-bankers or Gileadites pronounced it as *shibbôleth*, with an "sh" sound. (Jdg 12:4–6). If you drive south from central Indiana and cross the Ohio River, you likewise cross a major regional boundary. With this comes a dialectal difference as well; you now hear English spoken with a distinctive southern drawl.

Jeroboam is an astute politician. He knows that a long-standing problem is lack of real unity among the northern tribes. There is too much fragmentation. He seeks to remedy this by establishing a second capital on the eastern side of the Jordan at the ancient site of Peniel, which also possesses historic and sacred overtones (1Ki 12:25; cf. Ge 32:22–32).

Even more significant than a new set of capitals, however, is the other feature of Jeroboam's reign. Sensing the strong pull of religious tradition upon his people, Jeroboam acts to create a new religious tradition, which he can exploit for his own political purposes. "If these people go up to offer sacrifices at the temple of the LORD in Jerusalem, they will again give their allegiance to their lord, Rehoboam king of Judah. They will kill me and return to King Rehoboam" (v. 27). He thus sets out to create a new religious system complete with sacred places, persons, and rituals.

By design he installs two cultic centers, each of which is strategically located. People living in the north can make pilgrimages to the sanctuary in Dan, and those living in the southern portion of Israel can worship at Bethel. The latter site possessed sacred associations from the days of the patriarchs (cf. Ge 13:3–4; 28:10–22). The ostensible reason for designating these two sites is to make travel easier. The biblical historian gives the ulterior motive—to ensure his political survival.

He then proceeds to rehabilitate the old golden calf cult. The calf or bull idol represents Yahweh. This, of course, violates the prohibition about images. Worse still, the calf or bull image in Canaanite worship represents the fertility god Baal. In the course of time the distinction between Yahweh and Baal blurs. As the sacred historian never tires of informing us, "this thing became sin" (v. 30). Jeroboam also institutes a new priesthood—not restricted to the Aaronides, but rather, determined by royal appointment. He further enacts new religious festivals, deliberately juxtaposing them to the traditional ones of the Mosaic Law.

All of this is calculated to undergird his new state with a religious legitimacy. Jeroboam is not the first, nor certainly the last, political leader to recognize the power of religion to achieve political objectives. Indeed, political leaders generally are adept at tapping the religious sensibilities of people in the exercise of power.

Look closely at the American presidency and you will find examples galore. American presidents, or those who would be president, consistently appeal to what may be called civil religion (i.e., love for God and country). No one can be elected as president of the United States presently, nor in the foreseeable future, who openly avows atheism. Every American president to date has had some religious affiliation and has appealed to religious sentiment in the performance of his duties.

Heads of state in modern Muslim nations are not always devout Muslims. Nevertheless, they make sure they are regularly seen in public praying or engaging in pious acts. This assures the public that they are "good Muslims" and thus worthy to lead the country. Many other examples of this could be cited.

In short, Jeroboam is a consummate politician who makes decisions out of political expediency. He employs religion to secure and maintain his political power. From the standpoint of the biblical historian, he led the north into grave sin and all his successors simply followed suit.

Ahab: syncretism. Our second king is the infamous Ahab and his brazen wife Jezebel. Ahab reigned from 874–853 B.C. The historian of 1 Kings tersely evaluates him:

> He did more evil in the eyes of the LORD that any of those before him. He not only considered it trivial to commit the sins of Jeroboam son of Nebat, but he also married Jezebel daughter of Ethbaal king of the Sidonians, and began to serve Baal and worship him (1Ki 16:30–31).

A rising tide of syncretism characterized Ahab's reign. *Syncretism refers to the combining or merging of two or more religious traditions to create a new one.* The infusion of foreign elements came chiefly from the Canaanite religion practiced by the Phoenicians and so fervently advocated by Jezebel. The cults of Baal and Asherah were essentially fertility cults. The essence of the ritual was the practice of sacred prostitution in order to stimulate Baal to have sexual intercourse with his many heavenly consorts, among whom was the goddess Asherah. This was thought to produce storms and rain, so important to the agriculture of Canaan. Baal was represented as standing astride a bull with thunderbolts in his hand. Asherah was identified, at various times, as either a goddess of love or war and was represented as standing nude on the back of a lion.[16] In real life, Jezebel personified this combination of eroticism and violence. Evidently she exercised considerable power over Ahab. During Ahab's tenure the old faith of Mount Sinai was nearly submerged by the Canaanite cult of the Tyrian Baal. Note that there were many local versions of Baal among the various peoples living in the eastern Mediterranean, hence the reference in the Bible to the "Baals."

1. Champion of the covenant. One of the most famous and colorful biblical characters lived during these threatening days of Ahab and Jezebel. The Lord raised up a champion of the Sinai Covenant in the person of Elijah. This courageous prophet challenged the syncretistic faith of the northern kingdom and called the people back to the Mosaic foundations. The story of this confrontation requires further elaboration.

In 1 Kings 17 Elijah, a Gileadite, suddenly appears at Ahab's splendid palace at Samaria and issues a proclamation of judgment: "As the LORD, the God of Israel, lives whom I serve, there will be neither dew nor rain in the next few years except at my word" (v. 1). As suddenly as he appears, he disappears. Soon, however, his word of judgment unfolds with devastating results. Three years and six months pass. The usual rainy season (October–April) produces nothing. The dew, which ordinarily soaks the hill country of Samaria and Judah during the dry season (May–September) and enables the grape crop to come to maturity, does not appear. The country sinks into a devastating drought with mounting losses in terms of both animal and human life. The irony of this severe drought should not be missed. Baal is supposed to be the god of storm and rain, who provides fruitful seasons. Ahab, under Jezebel's prodding, has sold himself to serve Baal. Where is Baal when you need him? This is precisely the point Elijah wants to drive home. To make this even clearer, Elijah suddenly reappears and throws down the gauntlet—he issues a challenge to Baal.

2. Contest on a mountain. Elijah proposes a contest on Mount Carmel. The object of the contest is to determine which God, Yahweh or Baal, can produce the desperately needed rain and break the drought. This great contest on Mount Carmel is one of the most dramatic scenes in the Bible. Representing Baal are 450 prophets; Asherah has 400. Elijah alone champions the cause of Yahweh. Elijah dictates the terms of the contest to good advantage. He desires that the prophets of Baal offer sacrifice first. He wants the people to see the spectacle and abject futility of Baalism. Even the location is deliberately chosen. There had long been a Canaanite sanctuary on Mount Carmel. If Baal could accomplish anything, he should be able to do it there. One might say that, in effect, Elijah allows the game to be played on Baal's home court! He is counting on Yahweh to humiliate Baal before the home crowd.

Elijah's question to the people before the contest began demonstrates what has happened in the north since the division of the kingdom. "How long will you waver between two opinions? If the LORD is God, follow him; but if Baal is God, follow him" (1Ki 18:21). Erosion of faith and commitment has taken its toll. We are at a crisis point in the history of the north.

The prophets of Baal go first. Here we see appalling rituals based upon the even more appalling theology of paganism. They cry and shout attempting to get the attention of their god. *The Living Bible* captures Elijah's biting sarcasm very nicely in its paraphrase: "Perhaps he is talking to someone, or he is out sitting on the toilet, or maybe he is away on a trip, or is asleep and needs to be wakened!" (1Ki 18:27). The biblical historian obviously takes some delight in recounting the story and in informing the reader about the results: "But there was no response; no one answered" (v. 26). This failure called for more intense efforts. Assuming that actions done on earth stimulate the deity to act on one's behalf, the prophets whip themselves into a frenzy. The dancing mentioned in the text was performed in a rhythmic and repetitious manner designed to induce a trance. They also slash their veins and bleed profusely. All of this is what anthropologists call mimetic magic, the belief that ritual actions can influence and obtain aid from the deity. They thought that such actions would elicit Baal's sympathy. But as the historian laconically notes: "no one paid attention" (v. 29).

One may still see in various religions of the world similar, ritual practices. In modern Lebanon there is a sect of Islam in which, on the anniversary of the death of their cult founder, all the males from about five years old and up have their foreheads slashed with a barber's razor. They proceed in a loud procession to the mosque for prayers and services with the blood streaming profusely down their faces. The rationale is that Allah recognizes and rewards such acts of extreme devotion.

Comparable practices even exist within Christendom, especially where influenced by indigenous pagan religions. For example, in the Philippines, a few young men are nailed to crosses, for a short time, during Good Friday observances. This practice is not officially recognized by the Roman Catholic Church, but it continues anyway. Our point is that even in Christendom, syncretism still threatens true faith. In fact, evangelicals are under great pressure from theological liberalism to abandon the finality of Christ and embrace the various religious traditions of the world.[17] Elijah's challenge to his people is still applicable: "How long will you waver between two opinions? If the LORD is God, follow him; but if Baal is God, follow him."(1Ki 18:21; cf. Ac 4:12).

In contrast to the vain attempts to gain Baal's attention and favor, Elijah's approach stands out in solemn simplicity. To head off any charges of fraud, he orders the sacrifice and the entire area doused in water. He then sets up a simple altar of 12 stones—representing the 12 tribes of Israel and consciously invoking the memory of the Lord's election of Israel at Mount Sinai. Elijah's attitude is one of repentance and humility. His only action is a sincere petition—no vain repetitions here. His motive is that the Lord be recognized for who he really is. The divine response is one of the great moments in the history of salvation. "Then the fire of the LORD fell and burned up the sacrifice, the wood, the stones and the soil, and also licked up the water in the trench" (v. 38). The people's response underscores the truth Elijah champions: "The LORD—he is God! The LORD—he is God!" (v. 39).

The contest on Carmel by no means breaks the hold of Baalism upon the northern kingdom. Elijah and his successor Elisha spend their entire lives battling this false religion. This episode, however, serves to illustrate the tendencies at work in the north.

3. *Confrontation in a vineyard.* Another event further illustrates the erosion and breakdown of Mosaic values in the north. Chapter 21 narrates the story of Ahab's appropriation of Naboth's vineyard. As such it shows how the old values and traditions of the Mosaic Law are being supplanted by Canaanite ideas of kingship and the state. As the story opens, Ahab is spending time at his second palace at Jezreel. We recall that Ahab's father Omri had founded a new capital at Samaria (1Ki 16:24) located up on the central ridge. Ahab established a second palace at Jezreel overlooking the fertile Jezreel Valley, the location of the major highway from Egypt to Mesopotamia.

As Ahab looks out from his palace, he notices a vineyard adjoining his property. It occurs to him how convenient that piece of property is as a vegetable garden. It is a surprise to discover that Ahab enjoyed gardening! He makes a generous offer to the owner, a certain Naboth. The offer is flatly refused on the ground that the portion of land has been in the family since the days of the division of the land by Joshua. As the Mosaic law makes clear, all the land of Canaan belongs to the Lord (Lev 25:23). The Israelites are simply tenants. Each ancestral portion remains in the possession of the families assigned. If they lose some or all of it because of indebtedness, it reverts back to them in the Year of Jubilee (cf. Lev 25:8–55). Naboth reflects an Israelite who still adheres to the ancestral law. This sets up a clash of values: the old Mosaic values versus the Canaanite notions of kingship and the supremacy of the state over the individual.

Ahab is not yet a thoroughgoing Canaanite. He still has a conscience informed by the Mosaic Covenant, which will not let him run roughshod over his citizens. The result is a frustrated monarch who does not manage a very mature response—sulking, pouting, and refusing to eat! Into the picture enters his Canaanite wife. She has no sympathy for Ahab's behavior. In her view, kings take what they want, when they want it. No doubt her father was her role model. Losing patience with Ahab, she takes matters into her own hands. "Is this how you act as king over Israel" (v. 7)? Acting just like a Canaanite king, she brings to bear the powers of state to remove the obstacle.

First, she convenes an assembly on the pretext of an emergency requiring divine intervention. She makes sure that Naboth is not only summoned as a leading citizen to this day of fasting, but is also seated in a prominent position among the people. She then plants two false witnesses in the group of nobles who rise to bring charges of blasphemy against the man (cf. Lev 24:15–16). He is summarily executed. Receiving word that all went according to plan, she informs Ahab that the plot of land is his—Naboth is dead. He does not bother to inquire about the circumstances; he probably suspects, but thinks it best not to know the details of this sudden acquisition.

The whole account is a tragic commentary on the steady erosion of traditional values. The episode serves also as a continuing warning that any state, if unrestrained by morality and ethics, can become the instrument of the powerful to advance and protect their own interests. American history provides a multitude of examples in which the wealthy and powerful manipulate the system to their own advantage. One thinks of the collapse of Enron and the Arthur Andersen and WorldCom scandals to mention but a few.

Jeroboam II: spiritual rot. We consider the last of our northern kings, Jeroboam II, who reigned from 800–743 B.C., the longest reign of all the northern kings. Named after the founder of the first king of the northern kingdom, this man's administration allows us to understand why the kingdom of Israel finally collapsed.

1. Recovery and resurgence. The first noteworthy feature of this regime is recovery and resurgence in the economic and military sphere. 2 Kings 14:23–29 outlines briefly his accomplishments. After Ahab's death in battle and the violent death of his wife Jezebel, Israel falls increasingly under the power of Aram (located in approximately the area of modern Syria). Things hit an all-time low during the reign of Jehoahaz when the Arameans reduce the Israelite army to a mere 50 horsemen, 10 chariots and 10,000 foot soldiers (2Ki 13:7).

But under Jeroboam II there is a recovery of military power and territory seized by Damascus (capital of Aram). In part, the reason is that Assyria (approximately the area of modern Iraq) begins a revival of military might and expansionism. As the biblical historian tells us, "The LORD provided a deliverer for Israel, and they escaped from the power of

Aram" (2Ki 13:5). The Arameans, being just to the west of Assyria, first feel the pressure. The Assyrians overwhelm them and this allows Israel to recover lost territory and military clout. As a matter of fact, inasmuch as Jeroboam II is at peace with Uzziah king of Judah during this period, between the two of them, they control most of what had been "Greater Israel" in the days of Solomon. Coupled with renewed military strength, the two Hebrew kingdoms prosper economically, being able to control trade routes as Solomon had earlier. It would seem that the good old days were back again.

2. Spiritual rot. The biblical historian, with an eye to what really matters, lays the same charge against Jeroboam II as he does all the other kings of the north: "He did evil in the eyes of the LORD and did not turn away from any of the sins of Jeroboam son of Nebat . . ." (v. 24). From an outward perspective, things seem much better during Jeroboam's reign—and they are. But the recovery and resurgence mask spiritual rot. The biblical historian gives little space to the shortcomings of these days, but fortunately, we have a valuable supplement in the writings of the prophets Amos and Hosea. These 8th century prophets preach to the northern kingdom precisely during these gilded days. Their perspective tells us how the Lord views the situation.

3. Rise of the classical prophets. In our discussion of the Sinai Covenant, we pointed out how the Hebrew prophets function as Yahweh's official delegates sent to warn of covenant violations. Samuel and Elijah stand out as prime figures in this regard. Beginning in the days of Jeroboam II, a steady succession of prophets appears with an urgent warning: Israel is living on borrowed time. The covenant violations are of such magnitude and frequency that the sovereign Lord is about to invoke the ultimate covenant curse—expulsion from the land (cf. Am 7:11, 17). The prophets Amos and Hosea give us a distressing picture of social and spiritual conditions in the northern kingdom in the middle of the 8th century B.C.

Amos is our first witness. The Lord directs this shepherd and sycamore-fig tree dresser from the southern kingdom of Judah to the cult center at Bethel right across the border in Israel (Am 7:10–15). There he thunders a message of imminent judgment. Notice how his sermons have the character of lawsuits and indictments. In effect, *he is a prosecuting attorney representing the great overlord, Yahweh.*

> Hear this word the LORD has spoken against you, O people of Israel—against the whole family I brought up out of Egypt: You only have I chosen of all the families of the earth, therefore I will punish you for all your sins (Am 3:1–2).

The language recalls the election of Israel at Mount Sinai. What were the specific charges? Here are some samples gleaned from Amos's sermons:

> They sell the righteous for silver, and the needy for a pair of sandals. They trample on the heads of the poor as upon the dust of the ground and deny justice to the oppressed. Father and son use the same girl and so profane my holy name (Amos 2:6b–7). They do not know how to do right (3:10). You who turn justice into bitterness and cast righteousness to the ground (5:7). You oppress the righteous and take bribes and you deprive the poor of justice in the courts (5:12).

Hosea adds his voice to the litany of complaints uttered by Amos. In language clearly recalling a courtroom, in which the Lord is the litigant, Israel the defendant, and Hosea the prosecuting attorney, we hear the charges being filed.

> Hear the word of the LORD, you Israelites, because the LORD has a charge to bring against you who live in the land: There is no faithfulness, no love, no acknowledgment of God in the land. There is only cursing, lying and murder, stealing and adultery: they break all bounds, and bloodshed follows bloodshed (Hos 4:1–2).

Hosea proceeds right down the list of Ten Commandments and cites Israel for violating five of them—50 percent is hardly a passing grade! In all likelihood there was failure for all ten. Their fundamental failure is simply this: they are unfaithful to their God (4:12). Remember that the primary stipulation the suzerain insisted upon was loyalty.

Isaiah and Micah lodge lawsuits against Judah not long after Amos and Hosea. Once again we hear the language of the courtroom as Judah is now brought before the bar of justice. Here is how Micah arraigns Judah:

> Listen to what the LORD says: "Stand up, plead your case before the mountains; let the hills hear what you have to say, Hear, O mountains, the LORD's accusation; listen, you everlasting foundations of the earth. For the LORD has a case against his people; he is lodging a charge against Israel" (Mic 6:1–2).

In similar fashion, Isaiah levels a series of broadsides against rebellious Judah in his opening messages (1:2–31): "Hear, O heavens! Listen, O Earth! For the LORD has spoken; 'I reared children and brought them up, but they have rebelled against me . . .'"(1:2).

4. Dichotomy between faith and practice. As these prophets make clear, the failure of Israel and Judah is not their lack of religion and ritual. On the contrary, both nations are very "religious." Unfortunately, there is a dichotomy, a separation, between religious activity, (participating in worship, liturgy, and sacrifice) and a genuine faith and piety anchored in obedience to the revealed word of God. This leads to an important theological observation: *whenever you have a dichotomy between faith and ethics, you cannot have the kingdom of God.* Or, to express it another way, what one professes, one should practice. Belief and behavior are intertwined. This is the basic complaint of the prophets in the 8th century—Israel has compartmentalized her life such that religious affirmations are divorced from everyday life. Consequently, she only fools herself when she thinks the Lord is watching over her for good. In fact, the Lord is about to requite her for disloyalty through a devastating national judgment.

Before we proceed to examine this judgment, a word is in order about our own times. Polls taken by the George Gallup organization show consistently that a sizable majority of Americans consider themselves to be Christians—80 percent in fact. The same polls consistently show increased interest and activity in religion and church attendance. Nonetheless, moral standards continue to decline. This paradox is similar to the days of Jeroboam II and Uzziah. Americans are apparently equally adept at being religious without it really affecting their daily lives. One encouraging fact did emerge from the pollsters: They found that among the "deeply committed," moral standards are significantly higher. Therein lies the challenge. We who call ourselves Christians must be deeply committed, which, among other things, means there should be no dichotomy between faith and ethics. Only as these two are held tightly together can we really experience the kingdom of God. Furthermore, ethics must not be construed as merely personal, but must include a social and corporate dimension as well.

We summarize the reigns of the above three kings in terms of the tension between faith and politics.

King	Description	Problem of Faith and Politics
Jeroboam I	Political expediency	Using religion to achieve political aims and ambitions
Ahab	Syncretism	Combining elements of false religions with revealed truth resulting in erosion of fundamental values and beliefs
Jeroboam II	Dichotomy	Separating religious practice from biblical morality and ethics

Imminent judgment. Both Amos and Hosea announce imminent judgment. If Israel does not immediately repent, the result will be the wrath of God. As both prophets make increasingly clear, this wrath entails the end of the nation.

Notice how Amos more sharply focuses on the nature of this national catastrophe as the book unfolds. Chapter two describes the judgment in terms of a major military defeat, although no invader is mentioned by name (2:13–16). In 3:11–12 there is the further elaboration of the military invasion, with the terrifying prospect of only a small remnant surviving the onslaught. In 4:2–3, the self-indulgent, wealthy women of Samaria are warned that they will be carried off as prisoners of war. At 5:7, for the first time, Amos explicitly informs us that Israel will be exiled beyond Damascus. Though not mentioned, the powerful state of Assyria lay to the east of Damascus. Amos' listeners probably understood this as alluding to the Assyrians. At 6:14 we learn that the invaders will wreak havoc upon the entire land. In 7:17 Amos solemnly proclaims that the nation will be exited. Finally, Amos concludes with the somber oath of the Lord himself: "Surely the eyes of the Sovereign LORD are on the sinful kingdom. I will destroy it from the face of the earth—" (9:8).

Hosea likewise announces *the rejection of the northern state as the people of God.* His message flows out of a personal tragedy. His wife was unfaithful and he divorced her. This experience parallels that of the Lord and his bride, Israel. Israel is also unfaithful and chases after other gods. Reluctantly, the Lord divorces his people (Hos 2:2). Hosea's prophecy clearly names Assyria as the instrument of the Lord's anger (8:9–10; 9:3; 10:6; 11:5).

Sadly, the people of Israel and their leaders do not take the message of Amos and Hosea to heart. In the case of Amos, the authorities prohibit him from speaking anymore and send him back to Judah (7:10–13). The message of judgment fell on deaf ears. To the listeners it seemed so unlikely; things were so promising. Prosperity and power had returned. Was this not sufficient evidence that the Lord was pleased with Israel? The last chance to repent passed without a response. The sovereign Lord put in motion the gears of judgment.

The Collapse of the North: Hope for the Remnant

A ravager. Assyria was the instrument of the Lord's judgment upon Israel (cf. Isa 10:5–11). In 745 B.C., about 15 years after Amos preached at Bethel, Tiglath-Pileser III ascended the throne of Assyria and embarked upon a far-reaching and aggressive foreign policy. Unifying the areas along the Tigris-Euphrates River valleys—approximately the region today occupied by modern Iraq—he forged the most formidable war machine the ancient world had ever witnessed. Furthermore, the Assyrians conducted war in a manner that defies imagination in cruelty and barbarism. Each spring the Assyrian armies were on the move, pillaging and destroying cities and villages. They perfected the use of siege engines and sappers to breach and undermine walls. (Sappers were engineers who dug beneath foundations in order to undermine walls.) Their cavalry was deployed with great effectiveness, sweeping behind enemy lines and scouring the countryside. Assyrian generals issued ultimatums to besieged cities: they could surrender and be deported to another region; or they could resist and face utter annihilation. The Assyrian soldiers stacked the mutilated body parts of the inhabitants in great piles. As a means of demoralizing the defenders of a city, they impaled prisoners alive on wooden stakes outside the walls in clear view and allowed them to die slowly in agony. The

Assyrians gloried in their victories and celebrated their achievements on great reliefs in their palaces. From these reliefs we learn of their inhumane treatment of their unfortunate victims.[18]

In 743 B.C., Tiglath-Pileser III campaigned in the west and reached Israel, which was ruled by Menahem. Judgment had begun. But the full brunt of the assault was yet to come. In the rule of Pekah, the Assyrian juggernaut rolled through the northern part of Israel and annexed it to the expanding Assyrian Empire. The biblical historian comments: "In the time of Pekah king of Israel, Tiglath-Pileser king of Assyria came and took Ijon, Abel Beth Maacah, Janoah, Kedesh and Hazor. He took Gilead and Galilee, including all the land of Naphtali, and deported the people to Assyria" (2Ki 15:29). All that remained was the central ridge of Samaria. Israel paid exorbitant tribute in order to avoid being totally dismembered and absorbed into Assyria. Hoshea, the last king of Israel, apparently was disloyal to his overlord and suffered the consequences. Shalmanezer attacked Israel. According to the Bible:

> The king of Assyria invaded the entire land, marched against Samaria and laid siege to it for three years. In the ninth year of Hoshea, the king of Assyria captured Samaria and deported the Israelites to Assyria. He settled them in Halah, in Gozan on the Habor River and in the towns of the Medes (2Ki 17:5–6).

It was all over for Israel. The northern kingdom of Israel, which began in about 931 B.C., lasted until 722/21 B.C. Some of the survivors of the Assyrian onslaught were deported to the Tigris-Euphrates region. Here they began life as a minority community among other ethnic groups similarly deported by the Assyrians. They continued, however, as a distinct people and never lost their identity as part of the 12 tribes of Israel, contrary to the various theories, which have grown up over the centuries, about the so-called "lost tribes of Israel."

A ray of hope. Almost all of Amos' preaching was gloom and doom. But right at the end of his book, a ray of light breaks through the storm clouds. Amos said that the Lord would destroy the sinful kingdom of Israel, but the destruction would not be total (Am 9:8b). The survivors would be scattered among the nations (9:9), but that was not the last word on the matter. Like the Phoenix rising from the ashes, there would be a revival of national life at some distant time called the Day of the Lord. (See chapter nine for further discussion of this important concept.) The Lord would raise up the Davidic dynasty (9:11); he would bring the exiles back to their homeland (9:14); and he would plant them in their land permanently (9:15). Hosea, likewise, saw a day when the Israelites would seek the Lord's forgiveness, and the Lord would once again settle them in their homes (11:11). The very prophets who proclaimed imminent judgment also promised future repentance and restoration.

A remnant. During this time the notion of a remnant becomes prominent and may be traced through the various prophets. Pride of place, however, goes to Isaiah, who, more than any other prophet, develops the theme of the righteous remnant. Through this remnant, the Lord continues to work out his kingdom purposes. Isaiah personally experienced the major upheavals of the Assyrian invasions. Several passages in his book graphically describe the aftermath of those incursions (cf. 1:7–9; 3:1–3; 4:1–2; 10:28–32; et al.). What is of interest to us, however, are those passages speaking of a glorious future. In 11:10–16 we read a remarkable prophecy about a regathering and an exodus from exile, surpassing that from Egypt in the days of Moses. In fact, the passage contains clear echoes of the exodus from Egypt:

> The LORD will dry up the gulf of the Egyptian sea; with a scorching wind he will sweep his hand over the Euphrates River. He will break it up into seven streams so that men can cross over in sandals. There will be a highway for the remnant of his people that is left from Assyria, as there was for Israel when they came up from Egypt (vv. 15–16).

Another passage, chapter 35, in matchless poetic imagery and power, depicts a return of the people of Israel across the burning desert. Like the lifting of an ancient curse, the desert is transformed into a veritable Garden of Eden. The culmination of the return to Zion exceeds all expectations: "They will enter Zion with singing; everlasting joy will crown their heads. Gladness and joy will overtake them, and sorrow and sighing will flee away" (v. 10).

A ruler. In addition to the motif of a Second Exodus, the prophet Isaiah and his colleagues begin sketching a portrait of the coming messianic king and his kingdom (see ch. 6). Pride of place once again belongs to Isaiah. He adds more brush strokes to the portrait of David's great descendant and his glorious reign than any other single prophet. In chapter two Isaiah pictures a Jerusalem that, like a magnet, draws the nations of the world. The attraction is the power of truth, justice, and peace. One can only long for such a world in our time—a world where war is forgotten and weapons are transformed into tools for cultivation. This reminds us of humanity's original vocation, to till and take care of the Garden. Chapter 7 adds to the messianic profile, hinting at a birth characterized by the supernatural: "The virgin will be with child and will give birth to a son, and will call him Immanuel" (v. 14b; cf. Mt 1:18–25). Chapter 9 announces the throne names of messiah and gives a breathtaking glimpse of the extent and duration of his kingdom (9:6–7). The transformation that accompanies the messiah's reign is nowhere more strikingly portrayed than in 11:1–9. Again, it is like stepping back into the beauty and serenity of the Garden of Eden. All of nature experiences a lifting of the curse of Genesis 3. The thorns and thistles, and all the travails and frustrations they represent, no longer torment a rebellious humanity.

A reminder. An important observation about these messianic prophecies concerns *the earthly and concrete nature of the future kingdom.* We should not overlook the fact that, although the coming kingdom is spiritual, it never loses contact with the realm of the temporal and material. That is to say, we are dealing with a political entity having a capital in Jerusalem. Jerusalem is not, in these prophecies, a symbol or metaphor for spiritual realities. Rather, the future spiritual kingdom manifests itself in time and space. Much Christian theology has "spiritualized" these prophecies and, in the opinion of this writer, lost a certain dimension of God's ultimate purposes. We will argue in chapter nine that a literal, earthly reign of Jesus the Messiah is one of those purposes.

The Collapse of Judah: A New Covenant Prospect

From vassal to province (722–586). Judah survived the Assyrian onslaught, but at a very heavy price. She became a tribute nation, a vassal state of the great kings of Assyria. As such she had to swear loyalty to the Assyrian king and provide assistance as he might require (recall the discussion of suzerainty treaties in chapter five). In addition, Judah had to pay heavy tribute, which was, in effect, the price of maintaining internal autonomy over her own affairs. Part of the expected loyalty to be shown to Assyria raises the problem of faith and politics in an especially acute fashion. The great overlord required that the gods of Assyria be honored by Judeans. Their images should be prominently displayed—thus creating a major problem for a Judean king. Could he, in good conscience, permit such a thing, since the fundamental requirement of the Sinai Covenant prohibited acknowledgment of any other god? The kings of Judah were in a "catch-22." They were torn between two competing loyalties. The dilemma was solved by most of the kings of Judah during this period with a religious compromise—they did allow images of Assyrian deities to be erected in Jerusalem and other sites in their kingdom. King Ahaz demonstrates this concession:

> Then King Ahaz went to Damascus to meet Tiglath-Pileser king of Assyria. He saw an altar in Damascus and sent to Uriah the Priest a sketch of the altar, with detailed plans for its construction. So Uriah the priest built an altar in accordance with all the plans that King Ahaz had sent from Damascus and finished it before King Ahaz returned (2Ki 16:10–11).

Ahaz also removed the bronze altar from before the temple and put it on the north side. The new altar was used for morning and evening offerings, but the old bronze altar was still used for seeking guidance from the Lord (16:15–16). Note that these things were done "in deference to the king of Assyria" (v. 18). Not surprisingly, the biblical historian assigns bad marks to most of the Judean kings. Still, one might ask, what other choice did they have, realistically, since Assyria possessed such overwhelming power and insisted upon this requirement?

Struggling with faith and politics. We will select two of the good kings of Judah (the only two so designated during this period), and seek to understand how they grappled with this tension between faith and politics.

1. Hezekiah versus Sennacherib. The first is Hezekiah who reigned from 716–687 B.C. In the fourth year of Hezekiah's reign, Samaria fell and Israel ceased to exist as a nation. Hezekiah's father, Ahaz, had already submitted to Assyria as a vassal. After Ahaz died, Hezekiah became sole ruler of Judah and took the courageous step of rebelling against Assyria. This may have been provoked by his strong objection to images of Assyrian gods in Jerusalem. Remember that his rule was characterized by religious reform, including the destruction of Canaanite cultic images. He probably destroyed the Assyrian idols as well (2Ki 18:4).[19]

The consequence of this rebellion was devastating. According to 2 Kings 18:13–15, the valiant attempt to be free of both political and religious coercion failed:

> In the fourteenth year of King Hezekiah's reign, Sennacherib king of Assyria attacked all the fortified cities of Judah and captured them. So Hezekiah king of Judah sent this message to the king of Assyria at Lachish: "I have done wrong. Withdraw from me, and I will pay whatever you demand of me." The king of Assyria exacted from Hezekiah king of Judah three hundred talents of silver and thirty talents of gold. So Hezekiah gave him all the silver that was found in the temple of the LORD and in the treasuries of the royal palace.

Archaeology has thrown light upon this episode. The great palace of Sennacherib at Nineveh yielded, among other things, a clay prism on which was inscribed an account of the invasion of Judah. Sennacherib boasts of destroying 46 fortified cities, countless villages and taking 200,150 prisoners. Sennacherib also boasted that he shut up Hezekiah the Jew in Jerusalem "like a bird in a cage."[20] The Bible narrates this siege in 2 Kings 18:17–19:36. From the Bible we learn that Sennacherib did *not* take Jerusalem. Interestingly, the prism makes no mention either of the taking of Jerusalem. The Lord humbled the pride of Assyria.

> That night the angel of the LORD went out and put to death a hundred and eighty-five thousand men in the Assyrian camp. When the people got up the next morning—there were all the dead bodies! So Sennacherib king of Assyria broke camp and withdrew. He returned to Nineveh and stayed there (19:35–36).

Although Sennacherib failed to take Jerusalem, he did wreak havoc upon the nation. Thousands must have perished and over 200,000 were reduced to slavery in Assyria. Judah was brought back into the orbit of Assyrian power by becoming a vassal state once again.

What should Hezekiah have done? Should he have put his nation at risk by defying the powerful Assyrians? Should he have allowed his religious scruples to force a nation to bear the brunt of devastating war? Why did the Lord permit Judah to suffer such a calamity, especially when Hezekiah had tried to be loyal to the King of Heaven rather than to the arrogant king of Assyria? These are questions not easily answered and they illustrate the difficulties believers face while living as citizens of two kingdoms—the Kingdom of God and the kingdom of this world.

2. Josiah versus Neco. We turn now to the other good king of Judah. Josiah's reign (640–609) is narrated in 2 Kings 22–23. He comes to power when he is a mere eight years old. During his first years as regent, he presumably rules under the tutelage of advisers.

Noteworthy about this young man is his yearning for God. At age 26, he requests that the temple be repaired. This repair leads to the discovery of the law book of Moses. When its contents are read to Josiah, his conscience is smitten; Judah is not in compliance with the stipulations of their great king, Yahweh (2Ki 22:11–13). Soon thereafter, Huldah the prophetess delivers an oracle of judgment upon the nation. Josiah himself, however, is commended for his repentant attitude and is promised he will not live to see the coming devastation (vv. 15–20). Josiah throws himself into a reform effort unlike any before. He calls the nation together for a covenant renewal ceremony at the temple. He sets about destroying cult centers and high places, not only in Judah, but also in what had been Israel in the north (2Ki 23:1–25).

This raises a question: How could he carry out such a reform effort while maintaining loyalty to the king of Assyria? The answer is that Assyria no longer exerted her power and influence over neighboring states. A rapid change was occurring in the Middle East and a new superpower was emerging. In 625 B.C., Babylon wrested independence from Assyria. In alliance with the Medes and other peoples, the Neo-Babylonian kingdom waged an unrelenting war against Assyria. Note that about three years after Babylon's independence, Josiah began his reformation of Judah's religion. By 612 B.C., Nineveh, the capital of Assyria, fell to the Babylonian onslaught. The Assyrians were in full-scale retreat, struggling to maintain a foothold on the upper Euphrates. It is precisely in this period of a power vacuum that Josiah expands the borders of his rule up into what had been the northern kingdom of Israel.

To some, it may have seemed that the golden days of Solomon were returning once again. Such was not the case. Josiah's reform movement and his own piety were not enough. It was a case of being too little, too late. The sacred historian makes this observation:

> Nevertheless, the LORD did not turn away from the heat of his fierce anger, which burned against Judah because of all that Manasseh had done to provoke him to anger. So the LORD said, "I will remove Judah also from my presence as I removed Israel, and I will reject Jerusalem, the city I chose, and this temple, about which I said, 'There shall my Name be'" (2Ki 23:26–27).

The end came when Josiah got caught in the power politics of his day. As the Assyrians were reeling and trying to stave off the coup de grâce by Nebuchadnezzar—the Babylonian general and heir apparent to the throne—the Egyptians made a bold move to reassert control over Canaan. A vigorous and ambitious Pharaoh named Neco intervened in the war on the side of Assyria, even though these two countries had been bitter enemies. You may recall the saying, "Politics makes strange bedfellows." Neco sought to prop up the Assyrians, not out of goodwill or loyalty, but simply out of self-interest. He sensed, correctly, that the new superpower in the Tigris-Euphrates was Babylon. What concerned him was whether Babylon would have designs on Egypt as Assyria had earlier. In order to provide for a buffer state between himself and Babylon, and in order to dominate the trade routes then falling under the authority of Josiah, Neco moved a large army up the trunk route, right through Josiah's newly independent state of Judah.

Josiah confronts an agonizing decision. To let Neco come through uncontested is tantamount to capitulation to Egypt.[21] Judah would become a vassal state to Egypt. For about 800 years, Israel had been free from the clutches of Egypt. The prospect of becoming subject to Egypt is unthinkable. Josiah risks all in a military confrontation. Perhaps the outward success of his reform effort gave him false hope. Perhaps he thought the Lord would regard his commitment and relent from the word of judgment uttered by the prophetess Huldah. Josiah makes a stand and trusts the Lord for the outcome. Unfortunately for Josiah, there is no divine intervention, such as occurred in Hezekiah's day.

The historian laconically narrates the result: "King Josiah marched out to meet him in battle, but Neco faced him and killed him at Megiddo" (2Ki 23:29). For all practical purposes, Judah becomes a vassal state of Egypt. Neco even replaces Josiah's successor, Jehoahaz, with another son of Josiah's, Eliakim. Neco changes his name to Jehoiakim, showing further his complete control over his vassal king. The brief period of independence is over. Indeed, there would be no more peaceful days left in Judah's history. The end was only about 22 turbulent and violent years away.

Two prophetic voices on the kingdom of God: Jeremiah and Ezekiel. At this point in our survey, we listen to the voices of two of the Lord's choice servants. They preach the Word of God during those last terrible years of Judah's national existence. Jeremiah and Ezekiel represent the Lord's last word to rebellious Judah. In spite of hostility and rejection, both men remain steadfast to their prophetic call. We will discuss their ministries in more detail in chapter eight.

Jeremiah lived in the vicinity of Jerusalem, in the village of Anathoth, an easy walk from the temple. He may have been a priest, since Anathoth was a priestly village. He survived the carnage of the siege of Jerusalem in 588–586 B.C. Fellow survivors took him to Egypt against his will where, it appears, he died.

Ezekiel, on the other hand, was actually deported as a young man in 597 B.C. to a refugee camp along the Chebar canal, in the general vicinity of modern Baghdad.[22] He was from a priestly family, but never served in that capacity because of his deportation and the ensuing destruction of the temple in 586. Even though these two men were separated by over 500 miles and ministered in quite different settings, their messages share some common themes and concerns. These we explore briefly.

1. Both Jeremiah and Ezekiel announce the imminent destruction of Judah. They maintain this stance in the face of hostility and ridicule by the false prophets, government leaders, and the general populace—it was definitely a minority report! Even though they both agree on God's verdict upon the state, each conveys the dreaded message in his own distinctive manner.

Jeremiah, for example, describes a boiling pot tilting away from the north and scalding the inhabitants of Judah (Jer 1:13–14). On one occasion he speaks of a scorching wind from the desert, which sweeps away everything in its path (4:11). Jeremiah's basic message to Judah is summed up in his initial call: "See, today I appoint you over nations and kingdoms to uproot and tear down, to destroy and overthrow, to build and to plant" (Jer 1:10).

Ezekiel, on the other hand, addresses the mountains and hills of Judah in a striking instance of personification. He calls down upon them a horrifying curse of invasion, with the corpses of the slain littering the hills. The panic-stricken people of Judah seek vainly to resist and flee from the overwhelming tide. Ezekiel stresses the certainty of judgment: "The end has come upon the four corners of the land. . . . Disaster! An unheard-of disaster is coming. The end has come! . . . The day is here! It has come!" (Eze 7:2, 5, 10).

For both prophets, the message was as difficult to accept as it was to deliver. They loved their country and wanted to see it survive. In Jeremiah's words, "Since my people are crushed, I am crushed; I mourn, and horror grips me" (8:21). Ezekiel cried out: "Ah, Sovereign LORD! Will you completely destroy the remnant of Israel?" (11:13).

2. Both prophets focus upon the righteous remnant, the hope for the future. Jeremiah sees a day when the Lord gathers this remnant (described as a flock of sheep) from all the nations where they have been scattered (Jer 23:3). Ezekiel's visions of a glorious future for people and land occupy much of his book (Eze 40–48). Both deliver words of hope and encouragement to the remnant.

They also challenge wrong notions about God's ways and purposes. In the aftermath of the destruction of Nebuchadnezzar's invasion, the survivors tended to blame the judgment on their ancestors. Neither prophet allows such an idea to go unchallenged. Their messages stress rather that each individual must take responsibility for his or her own sin. A proverb was widely circulated at that time, which was really an attempt to rationalize and lay the blame elsewhere. "In those days people will no longer say, 'The fathers have eaten sour grapes, and the children's teeth are set on edge'" (Jer 31:29–30). The proverb thus traces the problem back to parents and ancestors. Against this idea Jeremiah counters with: "Instead, everyone will die for his own sin; whoever eats sour grapes—his own teeth will be set on edge" (v. 30). Ezekiel encounters the very same proverb and deals with it like Jeremiah (cf. Eze 18:2–4).

Neither prophet denies that we are influenced greatly for good or evil by our heredity. We cannot, however, succumb to the notion that we are mere victims and can do nothing about these influences. On the contrary, we can and ought to resist sinful tendencies and examples. This doctrine of individual responsibility is foundational for the Gospel of Jesus Christ. "Whosoever will, may come" is firmly rooted in Jeremiah and Ezekiel's preaching.

3. Both prophets also make it clear that the remnant will endure much suffering. They do not promise a life of ease for the righteous. As their own lives so powerfully testify, "we must go through many hardships to enter the kingdom of God" (Ac 14:22). Jeremiah was perhaps the most unpopular and hated of all the prophets. Many viewed him as a traitor. Even his family and village turned against him (11:21; 12:6). This personal rejection is reflected in many of his messages.

Ezekiel may have been viewed as mentally unbalanced. Many probably shunned him because of rather bizarre behavior. (See chapter eight for discussion of symbolic actions.) For both men the cost of discipleship was extremely high. Jeremiah was not permitted to marry. In hindsight this was probably a blessing in disguise, given the hostility and abuse expressed against him. Ezekiel's wife died during his ministry. He was not allowed to mourn for her publicly as a sign to the rebellious house of Israel. In our own day of the "prosperity gospel" and "cheap grace," we need to listen afresh to this message of the cross, already lived out by these prophets who lived before the cross.

4. Finally, and most importantly, both prophets proclaim an astounding "gospel"—*there will be a new and better covenant between the Lord and Israel!* This New Covenant will be not just with the house of Judah, but

with a regathered and regenerated twelve tribes of Israel. The prophecy is so crucial we quote Jeremiah extensively:

> The time is coming, declares the LORD, when I will make a new covenant with the house of Israel and with the house of Judah. It will not be like the covenant I made with their forefathers when I took them by the hand to lead them out of Egypt, because they broke my covenant, though I was a husband to them, declares the LORD. This is the covenant I will make with the house of Israel after that time, declares the LORD. I will put my law in their minds and write it on their hearts. I will be their God, and they will be my people. No longer will a man teach his neighbor, or a man his brother, saying, know the LORD, because they will all know me, from the least of them to the greatest, declares the LORD. For I will forgive their wickedness and will remember their sins no more (Jer 31:31–34).

Ezekiel proclaims a similar promise, though in differing terminology. In his preaching, the New Covenant is styled as "an everlasting covenant," and "a covenant of peace" (Eze 16:60; 34:25; 36; 37:26).

This prophecy of the new covenant is foundational for the NT message. In fact, it is central to Jesus' own understanding of his mission. On the night of the Last Supper, the Synoptic Gospels indicate that Jesus ate a Passover meal with his disciples. At this meal he makes explicit reference to the new covenant prophecy of Jeremiah and Ezekiel. We quote Luke's account of this momentous event:

> I have eagerly desired to eat this Passover with you before I suffer. For I tell you, I will not eat it again until it finds fulfillment in the kingdom of God . . . This cup is the new covenant in my blood, which is poured out for you" (Lu 22:15–16, 20).

Jesus establishes a new covenant with Israel by his death. Just as the old covenant at Mount Sinai is established by blood (cf. Ex 24:6–8), so the new covenant. But the blood of the new covenant is of the only begotten Son of God and thus the basis of a once-for-all sacrifice for sins. The book of Hebrews in the NT contains a sustained exposition of this point.

We conclude, then, that Jeremiah's prophecy of a new covenant looks forward to the death, resurrection and ascension of Jesus, with the subsequent bestowal of the Holy Spirit. The descent of the Spirit on the Day of Pentecost marks the birthday of the Church, the new people of God. A surprise for the first followers of Jesus, who were all Jews, was the inclusion of Gentiles into this new people of God. The book of Acts narrates this new development in redemptive history (cf. Ac 10:44–48; 11:18).

But why was there need of a new covenant? Notice that Jeremiah does not find fault with the Lord when he speaks of the failure under the old covenant—the fault lies in the repeated disobedience of Israel. "They broke my covenant, though I was a husband to them, declares the LORD" (Jer 31:32). Jeremiah locates the great advantage and superiority of the new covenant in the new dynamic enabling fulfillment. The NT elaborates on this inner dynamic and identifies it with the indwelling Spirit (cf. Ro 8:1–4). *The prophecy of the New Covenant by Jeremiah and Ezekiel represents one of the great mountain peaks of the OT revelation.*

Life in Exile: A Misplaced Emphasis

Refugees in a Foreign Land: Putting Life Back Together Again

The fall of Jerusalem. The last picture we have of a Davidic king is tragic indeed. 2 Kings 25:1–25 narrates the end. After an ill-advised revolt against Nebuchadnezzar, Zedekiah endured a two and a half year siege against Jerusalem. At the end of this time, famine and disease took such a toll on the defenders that, when the final assault came, "the city wall was broken through" (2Ki 25:4). Zedekiah and his army tried to escape to Transjordan by way of the Jordan Valley. The attempt failed and the king was captured. He was forced to witness the execution of his sons. Then, with that awful image in his mind, his captors put out his eyes and led him off as a prisoner to Babylon. No Davidic king has reigned over Jerusalem and Judah since that day. It was the end of an era, which began so optimistically at Mount Sinai about a millennium earlier. The people of Israel, who had said, "We will do everything the LORD has said; we will obey," experienced the ultimate curse of the covenant—expulsion from the land of promise and dispersion among the nations of the world (cf. Lev 26:32–33).

The aftermath. But that is not the end of the story. Incredibly, this people did not fade into oblivion. Unlike their conquerors, who left behind only monuments, they survived and live on today. Their survival is not just a tribute to their tenacity or ingenuity—it is a testimony to the covenant-keeping God of Israel.

The book of Lamentations allows us to experience vicariously the anguish occasioned by Jerusalem's destruction. It reflects on the catastrophe that befell Judah. In stark contrast to an idealized past, Jerusalem now lies deserted and forsaken. With deep poignancy the poet describes the downtrodden condition of Zion, here personified as a desolate widow. The mental state of the survivors is best summed up in the words of the poet: "she is in bitter anguish" (La 1:4; cf. vv. 1–9).

How did exiled Judah cope with the trauma of beginning life over again in a strange land? Listen to this powerful affirmation of faith in the living God:

> I remember my affliction and my wandering, the bitterness and the gall. I well remember them, and my soul is downcast within me. Yet this I call to mind and therefore I have hope: Because of the LORD's great love we are not consumed, for his compassions never fail. They are new every morning; *great is your faithfulness*" (La 3:19–23).

We have italicized the last four words because they are the basis for the well-known hymn, "Great Is Thy Faithfulness." The next time you sing it, consciously recall the original setting for the words. When it seemed that God had abandoned Israel to her fate, faith swelled up once again in the God who had promised Joshua, "Do not be afraid or terrified because of them, for the LORD your God goes with you; he will never leave you nor forsake you" (Dt 31:6). Then, right at the end of Lamentations, occurs the fundamental affirmation that sustained Israel through the long, dark night of exile and beyond. In 5:19 we read these triumphant words: "You, O LORD, reign forever; your throne endures from generation to generation." We began our survey of Israel's national history with a similar affirmation: "The LORD will reign for ever and ever" (Ex 15:18). These two affirmations of the kingdom of God frame Israel's history and they account for Israel's continuation as a people.

Sociological and Theological Changes for the Old Covenant People

The exilic and post-exilic periods were not times of intellectual and spiritual stagnation for the Jewish people. On the contrary, it was a time of new vigor and creativity. The prophets challenge Israel to be a "light to the Gentiles" (Isa 42:6; 43:10–12; 44:86). During this time, the people of Israel undergo a number of transformations. We examine several of these for the light they throw on the development of the kingdom of God.

A new name. The first change is perhaps least important in the total picture, but it helps us avoid confusion. This has to do with the new name of this people. Henceforth they are generally known as *Jews*. This term first comes into use just before the exilic period (cf. Jer 32:12; 40:11). Earlier they were called *Hebrews*, children/people/men of Israel; *Israelites*, people/men of Judah; or *Judeans*. The word *Jew* is a shortened form of Judah.

A new way of life. A second, more significant, change involved a gradual shift from an essentially rural to an urban way of life. With this came a move from an agrarian to a commercial and craft based economy. Whereas before the exile most Jews lived in small towns and villages, thereafter they reside primarily in the cities of the various countries of the world.[23] This observation is true even today. In the United States, the great majority of Jewish people dwell in the largest cities, such as New York, Los Angeles, and Chicago. A number of factors are responsible for this situation, and it is beyond our scope to go into this in detail. We should, however, at least mention that, throughout the Middle Ages, Jews were not allowed to own property and often were confined to specific sections of the cities called *ghettos*. (See ch. 9 for further discussion.)

New languages. Hebrew, a member of the Semitic languages, was not widely spoken by the surrounding nations. Dispersed Jews, therefore, necessarily learned new languages.[24] Flourishing in areas of commerce and finance, Jews encountered a number of languages and dialects. Throughout the Persian period (ca. 586–330 B.C.) Aramaic became the lingua franca of the Mediterranean, and thus the primary language of most Jews. Hebrew still maintained its place as the language of worship and scholarship, but fell out of use for most Jews. In fact, Jewish scholars paraphrased the Hebrew Bible into Aramaic, called the Targum, to facilitate understanding of the sacred Scripture. Because of their dispersion among the nations, Jews typically became conversant in more than one language. Today, in the modern State of Israel, Hebrew is the official language. Still, one encounters many of the modern European languages with English and Arabic widely spoken and understood.

Cultic changes. The cult of Israel underwent significant development. With the destruction of the first temple and the dispersion of most Jews, a new center of worship was imperative. To be sure, a rebuilt temple arose in the days of Ezra and the prophet Haggai (completed in 516 B.C.). In fact this temple stood until the first century A.D. Still, most Jews could afford to make but one pilgrimage to Jerusalem in their lifetime.[25] What then was to be done in the various regions where Jews lived? The answer was the synagogue. In Hebrew the expression *bêt k^e^neset* means literally "a house of gathering." The Greek word behind synagogue means "a coming together."

The synagogue became the focal point for Jewish life. Although there is considerable scholarly debate about the origins of this institution, there are good reasons for holding that the synagogue arose as early as the Babylonian period.[26] The felt need to meet together and worship must have led to a spontaneous development of synagogue worship. Be that as it may, by the time of the 1st century B.C., the synagogue was a fixture of Jewish life. The synagogue served not only as a place of worship, but also as a social center for Jewish life. Here the rites of passage unfolded: boys were circumcised, children attended school, couples were married, decisions affecting family status were adjudicated—even a market was held during the week! Of course the Sabbath services took pride of place. The reading and exposition of Scripture conferred upon the synagogue the epithet "house of instruction." Prayers and praises were also offered up to the God of Israel. It was thus a "house of prayer." *The essential features of a synagogue service left an enduring influence upon the worship of*

Christians, since the early church was born in the cradle of Judaism. The glimpses of worship in the NT reveal an unmistakably strong Jewish influence (see further ch. 10).

Intellectual changes. The exilic and post-exilic periods were times of intellectual and spiritual creativity. Inspiration had ceased—prophecy came to an end about the time of Malachi (ca. 400 B.C.). But Jews did not stop reflecting on the ways of God. In fact, a considerable body of literature emerged during this period, which Christians designate as the intertestamental period (ca. 400 B.C.—ca. A.D. 100). Included here would be such diverse collections as the Apocrypha, Pseudepigrapha, Dead Sea Scrolls, as well as the writings of such Jewish figures as Josephus and Philo of Alexandria. Scripture itself underwent a process of final editing, with the latest books recognized as canonical joining the canon toward the early part of the exilic period.

Theological changes. Finally, we note the theological changes that develop in the Judaism of the exilic and post-exilic periods. As one reads the literature mentioned above, differences in emphasis and orientation from the canonical scriptures stand out.

Since the majority of Jews were not able to participate regularly in the cultic activity of the second temple, almsgiving and charity substituted for animal sacrifice. Observing the *mitzvot* (commandments) took on an atoning function. This is reflected, for example, in Tobit, an apocryphal work, dating to the third or second century B.C. (cf. Tobit 4:11; 12:8–9).

One also discerns in this literature a new understanding of how one pleases God and obtains his favor. The inevitable question of the exilic community was: Why did God punish us in this way? The answer was not hard to come by. Israel violated the Sinai Covenant and the Lord requited her for disloyalty (cf. Ne 1:5–11; Da 9:4–19). On the basis of this recognition, the exilic religious leaders set about rectifying the situation. If Israel were ever to experience God's favor nationally again, there must be a concerted effort to keep all the covenant stipulations. This raised a serious problem. Many of the stipulations were addressed to a people living a pastoral-agrarian lifestyle in the land of Canaan. How could Jews keep these laws living in cities all across the known world?

This problem generated one of the most remarkable responses in the history of religion. Jewish scholars set about adapting and amplifying the 613 commandments, negative and positive, found in the Pentateuch. Since the aim was to achieve as much compliance as was humanly possible, these scholars sought to make it difficult to break a *mitzvah* (commandment). This they did by gradually devising other *mitzvot* (commandments) to surround and protect the original ones. This is called "hedging the Law." Obviously, the 613 grew rapidly into an ever-increasing number of regulations. These new rulings were not written down, but taught orally. Hence they became known as the "Oral Torah" or the "tradition of the elders (fathers)" (cf. Mt 15:2; Ga 1:14).

In the process of time, the Oral Torah acquired legitimacy by being ascribed to Moses himself. The tradition arose that on Mount Sinai two Torahs were delivered to Moses: the *Tôrāh kātûv* and the *Tôrāh bᵉ{āl peh* (the Written Torah and the Oral Torah). *Both were equally authoritative.* Eventually this great mass of legal material was written down in what is called the Mishnah (ca. A.D. 200). This body of literature was commented on and expanded over several centuries and eventually codified in the Talmud (ca. A.D. 600).[27] This is the authoritative exposition of the Jewish faith for Orthodox Jews today.

What we see in this long process is a shift in emphasis with regard to salvation. While it would be unfair and inaccurate to label post-biblical Judaism as a religion of works and not of grace, a tendency toward legalism does appear.[28] The stress falls heavily upon performance of deeds and ritual. Jesus' critique of Pharisaism shows us how far afield this process had gone by the first century A.D.:

> Woe to you, teachers of the law and Pharisees, you hypocrites! You give a tenth of your spices—mint, dill and cummin. But you have neglected the more important matters of the law—justice, mercy and faithfulness. You should have practiced the latter, without neglecting the former. You blind guides! You strain out a gnat but swallow a camel (Mt 23:23–24).

The NT insists that salvation is by grace through faith in Christ, with good works demonstrating the genuineness of saving faith (cf. Eph 2:8–10).

The Kingdom of God Dawns

Revival of Kingdom Hopes with John the Baptist

The urgent preaching of John the Baptist broke the silence of heaven. His message reverberated across the Jordan Valley like thunder: "Repent, for the kingdom of heaven is near" (Mt 3:2). Crowds flocked down to the Jordan to see and hear this strange preacher, who seemed like Elijah returned from the dead. John's preaching about the imminent arrival of the kingdom of heaven (the substitution of the word "heaven" for "God" was a common practice among Jews at that time), presupposed the message of a coming king and kingdom by the prophets of canonical scripture. The surprise and shock was that John addressed his remarks to *all Jews*—even those who supposed that their righteousness was already acceptable to God (Mt 3:7–10).

We will not pursue this theme further. That would take us into a consideration of NT literature. We do, however, want to emphasize that the NT message grows out of the unfolding development of the kingdom of God as depicted in the OT. Indeed, the NT proclaims that, in a very real sense, the kingdom of God has arrived and yet has a future consummation. This "now but not yet" character of the NT is crucial for a proper perspective on its writings.

Retrospective View of the Kingdom of God

As we conclude this chapter on the kingdom of God, we provide an overall vantage point from which to view this amazing story. As we mentioned earlier, the Bible has a linear view of history. There is a clear progression toward a goal. The goal is the consummation of the kingdom of God, in which human beings glorify God by exercising rule over this planet in his name and by serving and enjoying him forever. The glory of God is the highest of all ends and purposes.

The biblical account of the unfolding kingdom of God is in the form of a special kind of history—redemptive history. The building blocks of redemptive history consist of two kinds of materials. We have first certain events transpiring in time and space. These "deeds" form a sequential chain like beads on a string. The events may be celebrated in poetic versions such as songs, liturgy, or even wisdom sayings, but this does not diminish their "eventness." The Bible does not, however, consist of mere deeds. It also consists of inspired interpretations of these deeds. *We may characterize biblical history as consisting of a series of deed/word complexes*. These complexes are placed in an overarching framework, the unfolding kingdom of God. Thus God acts in history through his mighty deeds and he speaks in history by means of inspired prophets. As the chain of deeds and interpretations unfolds sequentially, we have *the progressive revelation of redemptive history*. (See ch. 1, p. 17 for a diagram illustrating this feature.) Consequently, the further one stands along the time line, the better one's understanding of God's overall plan and purpose. Believers living after the cross and resurrection see "the big picture" more clearly than OT believers.

Finally, we visualize schematically the unfolding kingdom of God. Note how the cross stands at the midpoint of redemptive history. The OT phase

THE UNFOLDING KINGDOM OF GOD

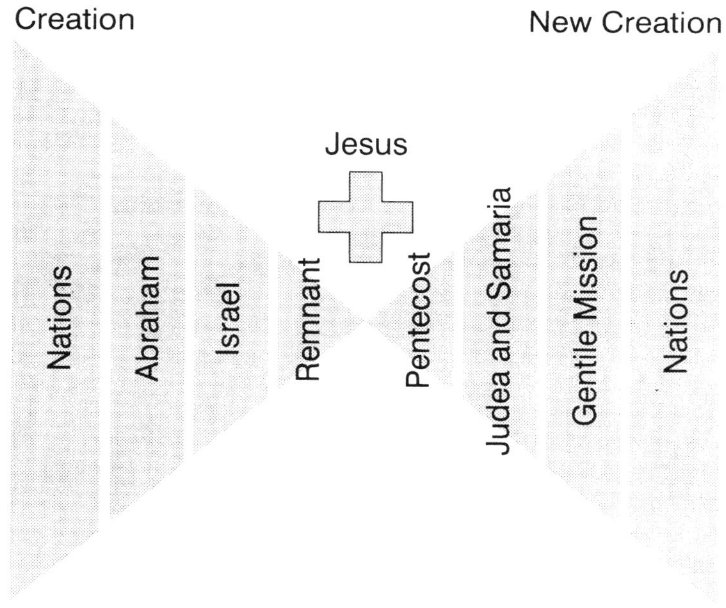

of the kingdom program is preparatory and anticipatory. Beginning with creation and the original mandate for the human race, we can trace the progress of the kingdom. The fall of Adam necessitated redemptive history. We have seen in previous chapters how God's kingdom purposes have been realized in each phase of OT history. But with the coming of Christ the OT phase reaches its crucial moment (the word crucial is carefully chosen here since it is derived from a root meaning "cross"). The incarnation and death of Jesus did not, however, fulfill all that the OT prophesied. There still remains unfinished business. That discussion will occupy our attention in chapter nine.

Relationship of Theme to Core Concepts

The Unity of God's Plan of Salvation: The Davidic Covenant with its promise of a Son of David reigning over an everlasting kingdom unites both testaments. The NT writers, notably Matthew and John, highlight the fulfillment of this great promise in the person of Jesus of Nazareth. Jesus' genealogy and ascension frame Matthew's Gospel. The genealogy stresses that Jesus fulfills the Abrahamic and Davidic covenants, whereas the ascension features a declaration of complete sovereignty ("all authority on heaven and earth") and a promise of abiding presence ("I will be with you to the end of the age"). God's plan of salvation climaxes with a great king exercising cosmic kingship:

> And he made known to us the mystery of his will according to his good pleasure, which he purposed in Christ, to be put into effect when the times will have reached their fulfillment—to bring all things in heaven and on earth together under one head, even Christ (Eph 1:9–10).

Faith and Politics: This chapter has stressed, above all else, the relationship and tension between faith and politics. More questions and concerns have been raised than answers. That is because "pat" answers are misleading, and it is extremely difficult to provide "right" answers. The student should realize that no area of life is more subject to debate and disagreement among Christians. The challenge is to hammer out one's understanding of the relationship on the basis of biblical principles involving justice, righteousness, compassion and mercy.

Several fundamental issues surfaced in our discussion. These are issues with which every political system must struggle. For example, who will exercise power and authority? Will it be an elite, an aristocracy, or will it be more widely shared by the general population? A very important question concerns how power is transferred. Where will this power be exercised? Is it centralized or dispersed? What type of infrastructure exists for carrying out political decisions? These two chapters have especially emphasized the bugaboo of all political systems—the abuse of power. We have also raised the thorny issue of religion and politics. What role should religion play in the political arena? The value of the biblical narration of Israel's political experiment lies in our ability to analyze how Israel dealt with these issues and to compare our own North American response. *With caution we may discern some underlying principles that assist us in responding to the particular form of those issues in our culture and time.*

Finally, we end on a note of encouragement and hope. Though the human attempt to govern this planet has a rather dreary and unsatisfactory history, we must never give up struggling for the biblical ideals of justice, righteousness, and mercy. The coming kingdom of God will at long last bring the peace and harmony visionaries have only dreamed about.

> He will judge between the nations and will settle disputes for many peoples. They will beat their swords into plowshares and their spears into pruning hooks. Nation will not take up sword against nation nor will they train for war anymore (Isa 2:4).

Faith and Ethics: In our examination of the various kings and leaders of Israel, we have had occasion to evaluate their struggles to integrate their faith commitments with the business of living out life on this planet. We have also heard the prophets explode in oracles of judgment upon a generation that failed to see the connection between faith and ethics. Certainly our own generation needs to be warned of the folly of thinking that lifestyle and behavior are separate issues from our religious beliefs. We must be a people who are deeply committed. To the many warnings of the prophets we add that of the Apostle Paul: "Do not be deceived: God cannot be mocked. A man reaps what he sows. The one who sows to please his sinful nature, from that nature will reap destruction. . . . Let us not become weary in doing good . . ." (Gal 6:7–9).

Faith and the Future. This chapter offers us a larger glimpse into the shape of God's future for his people. God deigns to share his authority and rule with his people. Through the promised descendant of the house of David, Christians will rule the nations, indeed, the entire planet. Paul rebukes his mainly Gentile Christian readers at Corinth: "Do you not know that the saints will judge the world?" (1Co 6:2). How does one prepare for such a large task? The pattern is clear: "and whoever wants to be first must be your slave—just as the Son of Man did not come to be served, but to serve, and to give his life as a ransom for many" (Mt 20:27).

For Further Discussion:

What evidences of "sickness" in our society do you see?

Why have these come about?

What changes have taken place in our national life that have permitted these "sicknesses"?

What elements of our national policies (foreign or domestic) should cause Christians to speak out for definite and even drastic changes?

How should Christians express their dissatisfaction or opposition?

When, if ever, is the statement, "My country, right or wrong" a valid one?

Can a Christian make that statement?

To what extent should a Christian practice patriotism?

Is patriotism a Christian virtue? If so, how should it be expressed?

For Further Reading:

For a historical overview:

Bright, John. *A History of Israel.* 2d ed., pp. 179–339. Philadelphia: Westminster, 1972.
Kaiser Jr., Walter C. *A History of Israel: From the Bronze Age Through the Jewish Wars.* Nashville: Broadman & Holman, 1998.

Books discussing the kingdom of God and the messianic hope from a salvation history perspective:

Bright, John. *The Kingdom of God.* Nashville: Abingdon, 1953.
Fuller, Daniel. *The Unity of the Bible*, pp. 387–402. Grand Rapids: Zondervan, 1992.
Goldsworthy, G. "Kingdom of God," *New Dictionary of Biblical Theology*, pp. 615-620. Downers Grove: InterVarsity, 2000.
Kaiser, Jr., Walter C. *Toward an Old Testament Theology*, pp. 122–164. Grand Rapids: Zondervan, 1978.
Satterthwaite, Philip E., Hess, Richard S. and Wenham, Gordon J., eds. *The Lord's Anointed: Interpretation of Old Testament Messianic Texts.* Grand Rapids: Baker, 1995.
Van Groningen, Gerard. "Messiah," Pages 523-524 in *Evangelical Dictionary of Biblical Theology.* Edited by Walter Elwell. Grand Rapids: Baker, 1996.
Wright, Christopher J. *Knowing Jesus Through the Old Testament.* Downers Grove: InterVarsity, 1992.

Works dealing with the topic of faith and politics:

Barron, Bruce. *Politics for the People.* Downers Grove: InterVarsity, 1996.
Boxx, T. William. *Public Morality, Civic Virtue, and the Problem of Modern Liberalism.* Grand Rapids: Eerdmans, 2000.
Colson, Charles. *Kingdoms in Conflict.* Grand Rapids: William Morrow and Zondervan, 1987.
Eberly, Don, ed. *Building a Healthy Culture: Strategies for an American Renaissance.* Grand Rapids: Eerdmans, 2000.
Ellul, Jacques. *The Politics of God and the Politics of Man.* Grand Rapids: Eerdmans, 1972.
Gushee, David P., ed. *Christians and Politics beyond the Culture.* Grand Rapids: Baker, 2000.

Hatfield, Mark. *Between a Rock and a Hard Place*. Waco: Word, 1976.
Haugen, Gary A. *Good News About Injustice*. Downers Grove: InterVarsity, 1999.
Hunter, J. C. "Where Does the Bible Say to Be Involved in Politics?" *Charisma 13*, April 1988, pp. 63–68.
Marshall, Paul. *Thine Is the Kingdom*. Grand Rapids: Eerdmans, 1984.
Mouw, Richard J. *Uncommon Decency: Christian Civility in an Uncivil World.* Downers Grove: InterVarsity, 1992.
Neuhaus, Richard John. *The Naked Public Square: Religion and Democracy in America*. Grand Rapids: Eerdmans, 1988.
Payne, David F. *Kingdoms of the Lord.* Grand Rapids: Eerdmans, 1981.
Schaeffer, Francis. *A Christian Manifesto*. Westchester, IL: Crossway, 1981.
Sider, Ronald J. *Rich Christians in an Age of Hunger: Moving from Affluence to Generosity*. Nashville: Word, 1997.
Smidt, Corwin E., ed. *In God We Trust?* Grand Rapids: Baker, 2001.
Webber, Robert E. *The Secular Saint: A Case for Evangelical Social Responsibility*. Grand Rapids: Zondervan, 1979.

Endnotes

---

1. See Samuel J. Schultz, *The Old Testament Speaks* (New York: Harper, 1960), pp. 105–107.

2. See William Sanford LaSor, "Philistines," *ISBE*, 3:841–846 and bibliog.

3.For the texts, see *ANET*, pp. 262–263.

4. In 2001, archaeologists discovered an iron foundry at Beth Shemesh (See *USA Today*, Thursday, June 20, 2002 6D). In the days of Saul and David this was an Israelite town very close to the border with Philistia. Perhaps it was the first center for the fledgling iron industry in the early days of David's monarchy.

5. See James K. Hoffmeier, "Weapons of War," *ISBE*, 4:1040.

6. See Yohanan Aharoni, *The Land of the Bible: A Historical Geography*, rev. ed., trans. A. F. Rainey (Philadelphia: Westminster, 1979), pp. 277–280.

7. See further Christian E. Hauer, Jr., "David's Army," *Concordia Journal* 4 (March 1978): 68–72.

8. Likewise, the modern State of Israel is a major player in the international arms industry.

9. This observation does not bode well for the current controversy between Israel and the PA with regard to the future status of Jerusalem.

10. See Mendel Kaplan and Yigal Shiloh, "Digging in the City of David," *BAR* V: 4 (July/August 1979): 36 and Shiloh, "Jerusalem's Water Supply During Siege—The Rediscovery of Warren's Shaft," *BAR* VII: 4 (July/August 1981): 24.

11. See Christian E. Hauer, Jr., "The Economics of National Security in Solomonic Israel," *JSOT* 18 (1980): 63–73.

12. See "Survey of Consumer Finances—1983."

13. See *Wall Street Journal*, 5 October 1993 for indication of deepening poverty in America.

14. For an alarming assessment of racial relations, see William Pannell, *The Coming Race Wars?* (Grand Rapids: Zondervan, 1993).

15. For a thought-provoking critique of our economic system from a biblical perspective, see Walter L. Owensby, *Economics for Prophets* (Grand Rapids: Eerdmans, 1988).

16. See John Day, "Asherah," *ABD* 1:483-486. On the complicated relationship between the goddesses Asherah and Ashtoreth, see K. G. Kung (A. H. Sayce), "Asherah," and "Ashtoreth," *ISBE*, 1:317–320.

17. See the essays in *One God, One Lord in a World of Religious Pluralism*, eds. Andrew D. Clarke and Bruce W. Winter (Cambridge: Tyndale House, 1991).

18. See, e.g., illustration 101 in James B. Pritchard, ed., *The Ancient Near East: An Anthology of Texts and Pictures* (Princeton: Princeton University, 1958) for a relief of Sennacherib's siege of Lachish. Note the impaled figures near bottom of relief. See also David Ussishkin, "Answers at Lachish," *BAR* (November/December 1979): 16–39 and esp., Erika Bleibtreu, "Grisly Assyrian Record of Torture and Death," *BAR* (January/February 1991): 52–61.

19. See Bright, *History*, pp. 277–278.

20. See *ANET*, pp. 287–288 for a description of the text and an English translation.

21. Bright, *History*, pp. 323–324.

22. See R. C. Ridall, "Chebar," *ZPEB*, 1:784–785.

23. The exception, of course, was Palestine itself, where the majority of Jews were small farmers. Jews living in the ancestral homeland, however, were always a minority of the total population of Jews after the exile.

24. The *NIVSB* remarks on the surprising fact that, in the days of Hezekiah, the Assyrian field commander could speak Hebrew (p. 560, note on v. 26).

25. See E. P. Sanders, *Judaism: Practice and Belief 63* BCE–*66* CE (London/Philadelphia: SCM and Trinity Press International, 1992), p. 130.

26. See W. White, Jr., "Synagogue," *ZPEB*, 5:555; W. S. LaSor and T. C. Eskenazi, "Synagogue," *ISBE*, 4:677–678; and Sanders, *Judaism*, pp. 198–200.

27. This oversimplifies the situation in that there are actually two Talmuds: *Talmud Yerushalmi* (ca. A.D. 400) and *Talmud Babli*. The latter, the Babylonian Talmud, is considered the more authoritative and is the one usually intended. See Jacob Neusner, "Talmud," *ISBE*, 4:717–724 for more details.

28. This is a highly charged and debated issue. Christian scholars have too easily dismissed Judaism as a religion of works without paying attention to the notion of God's grace. See E. P. Sanders, *Paul and Palestinian Judaism: A Comparison of Patterns of Religions* (Philadelphia: Fortress, 1977) for a critique of past scholarship. On the other hand, legalism does appear in post-biblical Jewish literature. See Donald A. Hagner, "Paul and Judaism: The Jewish Matrix of Early Christianity: Issues in the Current Debate," *Bulletin for Biblical Research* 3 (1993): 117–119 for evidence and arguments. See also Thomas R. Schreiner, *The Law and Its Fulfillment: A Pauline Theology of Law* (Grand Rapids: Baker, 1993), pp. 114–121.

chapter **8**

The Word and the Spirit: Prophecy in Israel

(Scripture readings: 1 Chronicles 29:29; Amos; Hosea; Jonah; Isaiah 1–12; Jeremiah 1–9; 11–13:11; 18–20; 23:9–40; 27–28; Ezekiel 1–14)

Leading Questions

What does it mean to be a prophet?
What are the major terms and titles given to these individuals?
How did one become a prophet?
How did prophets fit into Hebrew society?
What relationship is there between pagan and Hebrew prophets?
What distinguishes Hebrew prophets from their pagan counterparts?
What were the seven stages of Hebrew prophecy?
Why was there a silence of about 400 years in the prophetic activity?
How was this silence broken?
What context should be recognized when studying the prophets?
How did the call to be a prophet change that person?
What were the chief modes of reception and delivery of messages?
How can one discern false from true prophets?
What themes constitute the essential message of the prophets?

Introduction

"Thus says the Lord!" punctuates the prophetic writings of the Hebrew Bible. Prophecy is an aspect of revelation. God spoke in many ways in the past (cf. Heb 1:1), but one of the most important ways was through human spokespersons. As the Spirit of God actualized the creative word in the beginning (Ge 1:2), so the Spirit of God energized human agents who became the proclaimers of the prophetic word in salvation history. This chapter will focus on those proclaimers of the Word who made up the prophetic movement in Israel.[1]

Definition of a Prophet

Key Terms

We first seek to establish the meaning of the concept "prophet." This will require examination of several different terms in Hebrew and their translational equivalents in English. First Chronicles 29:29 contains three such terms:

> As for the events of King David's reign, from beginning to end, they are written in the records of Samuel the seer, the records of Nathan the prophet and the records of Gad the seer, together with the details of his reign and power, and the circumstances that surrounded him and Israel and the kingdoms of all the other lands.

The NIV gives us two different English words, although there are in fact three different Hebrew words behind the English translation.[2] The three terms are:

NIV	HEBREW
seer	*rō'eh*
prophet	*nāvî'*
seer	*ḥōzeh*

The first term comes from a common verb meaning "to see" and refers most often to physical sight; however, in some contexts, the sight connoted by the verb refers to mental perception. Prophets received visions and spoke of things they "saw" as recipients of the Word of the Lord (cf. Am 1:1). The second term is by far the most frequent, occurring some 300 times in the Hebrew Bible. Although there is disagreement over the root meaning of the word *nāvî'*, its usage in the Hebrew Bible refers to one who is an authorized spokesperson. The call to proclaim what God has spoken is the essence of the prophetic office. The third term intensifies the visionary aspect of prophecy. It means, "to gaze intently." Trances and visionary experiences were not uncommon in the prophetic movement.

Important Titles

In addition to the above terms, three titles should be added, each of which throws more light on the office of prophet.

1. The title "man of God" is found some 76 times, most often in the narratives about Elijah and Elisha. This title is never used by the prophet of himself—it is always used by others to refer to the prophet. For example, the widow of Shunem summoned Elisha by calling him the "man of God" (cf. 2Ki 4:9, 16, 22). The title expresses the special relationship that others sensed between the prophet and the Lord God of Israel.

2. The most honorable title was "servant of the Lord." This title stresses the close and holy relationship between God and his faithful messengers. No higher commendation could be given than to be called a servant of the Lord. The prophets collectively were called servants in Jeremiah 7:25: "From the time your forefathers left Egypt until now, day after day, again and again I sent you my servants the prophets."

3. Finally, we note the title "messenger of the Lord." This title defines the prophet in functional terms. Recall that in our discussion of the Sinai Covenant in chapter five, an aspect of the suzerainty treaty was the provision of a special delegate dispatched by the great overlord to a rebellious vassal warning of disloyalty and violations. The Hebrew prophets should be seen in just that role. Douglas Stuart styles the prophets as "covenant enforcement mediators."[3] Thus their task was to call Israel back to their promised obedience to the Sinai Covenant and to warn of the consequences of further disobedience (cf. Hos 4:1–6; Am 3:1–2; Isa 1:2–20; 2Ch 36:15–16). We will discuss this in more detail later under the prophetic activity section.

An Operational Definition

Three passages of scripture assist us in understanding what it means to be a prophet.

1. In Exodus 6:28–7:2 the Lord instructs Moses: "Tell Pharaoh king of Egypt everything I tell you." Hearing and telling the Word of God defines a prophet operationally.

2. Amos 3:7–8 conveys the sense of urgency experienced by a prophet. Amos likens his call to prophesy to the inevitable fear one feels when a lion roars. "The Sovereign LORD has spoken—who can but prophesy?"

3. Jeremiah 1:1–10 provides three insights into the meaning of being a prophet. In the first place, the call to the prophetic office was initiated by the sovereign Lord (v. 4). Secondly, the prophet was incorporated into a plan and purpose originating in the council of Yahweh. Thirdly, the prophet was supremely a spokesperson for the sovereign Lord. We have what is nearly a formal definition in 1:7: "You must go to everyone I send you to and say whatever I command you."

The term "mouthpiece" conveys a notion that is too passive. As is abundantly clear from Jeremiah's own ministry, prophets remain individuals while carrying out their commission. Their own distinctive personalities shape the message. Consequently, we may better employ the term *spokesperson*. What must be insisted upon, however, is that the prophets do not originate their own messages (cf. 2Pe 1:20–21). As the Lord said to Jeremiah: "Now, I have put my words in your mouth" (v. 9). Thus the Word of God comes through Jeremiah in the latter's style and diction.[4]

The Position of the Prophet in Hebrew Society

Where did the prophets fit in the overall framework of Hebrew life and culture? One gets the impression that prophets were never a numerous company. Jeremiah complained about the number of false prophets in his day, and lamented that few prophets truly "stood in the council of the LORD" (Jer 23:9–40). But from what segments of Hebrew society did this select group come?

Not Hereditary

In the first place, we note that the office of prophet is not hereditary. In contrast to the influential and powerful offices of king and priest, the prophet may be called from any tribe and family of Hebrew society. In Judah one must be of the house of David before serious ambitions of royalty be entertained. Likewise, with the priesthood, only those of the tribe of Levi and house of Aaron qualify. (Jeroboam I broke with this tradition in the North as we saw earlier in chapter seven.) Not only are tribal and family considerations unimportant, but occupation and wealth do not figure in Yahweh's qualifications. What we actually find is a rather broad cross-section of Hebrew society as the background for this illustrious company. It includes the shepherd/sycamore fig tree dresser Amos as well as the urbane and cultured Isaiah.[5]

In contrast to pagan religions, which fostered a spiritual elitism, the OT displays an egalitarian bestowal of spiritual privilege. To be sure, this equality is much more evident in the NT, but it is certainly not absent in the OT (cf. Joel 2:28–29; Isa 56:3–8; Gal 3:26–29).

Not Elective

The office of prophet is not elective; nowhere do we read of individuals who actively seek it. Invariably, we find that when individuals are called by God, they feel unqualified and overwhelmed at the prospect. Several offer excuses and seek to evade the heavy responsibility. Moses throws up a series of excuses, the last being that he simply did not want to go (Ex 3:11–4:17); Jeremiah thinks he is too young (Jer 1:6); Isaiah's sin causes him to despair (Isa 6:5). The most celebrated reluctant prophet, of course, is Jonah. His problem is that he is afraid the Ninevites *will repent* and thus be saved from destruction; a misdirected patriotism stifles a merciful spirit (Jnh 4:2–3).

Not Confined to Men

It is especially worth noting that the office of prophet is not confined to men. Several women serve in this capacity with distinction. The Hebrew word *nāvî'* has a feminine form *nᵉvî'â*, which means "prophetess." In this regard we mention Deborah, who not only exercised the office of prophet, but also served as a judge of all Israel (Jdg 4:4–6). Another well-known prophetess, Huldah, was held in such high regard that one of the gates to the temple was named after her (2Ki 22:14–20). A certain Noadiah is also mentioned as a prophetess in the days of the return from exile (Ne 6:14). The NT continues the tradition of women prophets (cf. Ac 21:9; 1Co 11:5).

Determined by a Divine Call

To state the matter positively, what constitutes a prophet is a special relationship with the Lord. All other details are incidental to this all-important fact: *the Lord calls his prophets*. The call from Yahweh is the equivalent of a diploma or certificate so valued by our own culture. This call cannot be enhanced or decreased by human agency; for the prophet, it is decisive. In times of discouragement (and there were plenty of those!) the prophet fell back on that moment when the sovereign Lord summoned him/her into service. Each of the call experiences recorded in scripture merits careful study.

Isaiah's call is typical; in fact, the prophetic call narratives tend to fall into a pattern with certain identifiable features (cf. Ex 3:1–4:16; 1Sa 3:1–21; Jer 1:4–19; Ez 2:1–3:15; Am 7:14–16). 1) They are, for the most part, autobiographical (Moses and Samuel are exceptions since their calls occur in historical narratives) and feature 2) a dialogue between the Lord and prophet. Usually there is evidence of 3) a *visionary experience* as part of the call. In Isaiah's case, he glimpses the throne chariot of Yahweh surrounded by angelic beings. 4) The *initiative* for the experience clearly *comes from the Lord*—it is not the result of Isaiah's quest for a deeper life or a yearning to be a spokesperson for Yahweh. 5) Invariably, the actual or visionary encounter with the Lord's holiness and majesty overwhelms the prophet; a strong sense of *sinfulness and unworthiness* grips the prophet. Isaiah cried out: "Woe to me! I am ruined! For I am a man of unclean lips, and I live among a people of unclean lips. . . ." 6) In every case, however, the weakness of the prophet is matched by a *strong affirmation of acceptance by the Lord.* Sometimes, as in the case of Isaiah, acceptance is symbolic in nature: a live coal placed on his lips conveys the fact that his guilt has been taken away. Thus the enabling power and grace of God are absolutely essential for the performance of the prophetic gift. 7) Isaiah's call, like that of his colleagues, *shapes his theology and preaching thereafter;* the holiness and glory of God are major motifs running through the entire collection of sermons in the book of Isaiah.

Served as a Check on the Power of Kings

With regard to the political structures, the prophet functioned as a check on the power of the kings as we have previously discussed in chapter six. When David violated the unconditional obligations of the Sinai Covenant (in the matter of Bathsheba), Nathan the prophet confronted him (2Sa 12). Likewise, Elijah confronted Ahab in his ruthlessly acquired vineyard (1Ki 21). The prophet was not above the stipulations of the covenant; the duties and obligations of citizenship were incumbent upon him as well. Nonetheless, he was an auditor of the king's performance. Little wonder that later kings surrounded themselves with fawning yes-men and squelched any criticism from true prophets of Yahweh (cf. 2Ch 24:20–21). Jeremiah had to contend with weak-willed and spiritually dwarfed leaders who regularly listened to but ignored his counsel.

International Scope to Ministry

Finally, the messages of the Hebrew prophets were not limited to the land of Israel. Several prophets indicated an international concern in their messages. This flowed out of the theology of Israel. Unlike her pagan neighbors, Israel subscribed to a faith that affirmed one, true and living God who created all things. Hence all humankind was accountable to this one God. Crimes against humanity would certainly elicit Yahweh's stern punishment. Amos (chs. 1–2) declares that the Lord will judge all peoples for their transgressions. On the other hand, the book of Jonah demonstrates that the same God has compassion and concern for all peoples—even the barbarous Assyrians. The entire book of Obadiah revolves around a message of judgment against the country of Edom. Nahum is a judgment oracle against Nineveh, the capital of Assyria. In Isaiah 13–21, 23; Jeremiah 46–50; and Ezekiel 25–32, we have a series of messages against the nations. All of this demonstrates the universality of the message of the Hebrew prophets.

The Relationship of Hebrew Prophets to Pagan Prophets

There are a number of similarities between Hebrew prophecy and the larger phenomenon of prophecy in the ancient Near East. Indeed, prophecy appears at least 500 years before the birth of Abraham.[6] Intermediaries, whether male or female, delivered messages from the various deities to the reigning kings. Furthermore, stereotyped expressions and phrases like "Thus says the god . . . ," "Hear this word of the god . . . ," "Fear not, for the god . . . is with you," parallel similar messenger formulas in the Bible (cf. Am 2:1; 3:1; 4:1; Hos 4:1; Isa 41:10, 13; 43:1). Pagan prophets cautiously chided kings for laxness in the performance of cultic duties and warned them of continued negligence. Even the ecstatic behavior and trances of paganism had counterparts in the record of prophecy found in the Hebrew Bible (cf. e.g. 1Sa 10:5–7, 9–13; 19:23–24).

As, however, in the case of the creation myths, the flood stories, and the law codes of the ancient Near East, there are significant differences. We draw attention to five distinctive aspects of Hebrew prophecy.

The Initiative

The initiative in the revelatory process contrasts sharply between the two phenomena. In paganism prophets or priests initiated the process of revelation. They inquired and probed for a word from the god/gods. In the OT the direction was from Yahweh to his messengers, the prophets. Numbers 12:6 highlights this fact: "When a prophet of the LORD is among you, I reveal myself to him in visions, I speak to him in dreams." At least one passage may seem at first glance to contradict this assertion. In 2 Kings 3:9–19, Jehoshaphat asked for a prophet of the Lord to discern the outcome of a military crisis. Elisha was summoned and after a harpist played music for him, he received a word from the Lord. However, in the larger context of the story, we should understand that Elisha was there in the first place at the leading of the Spirit of God.[7] What is clear in the OT is that Yahweh is not an answering service or genie in a bottle at the beck and call of those who have the secret password. He reveals himself only to those whom he chooses.

Techniques of Divination

This brings us to another important difference. Pagans devised certain techniques called divination in order to pry information out of their gods/goddesses. What were these techniques? They fall into two categories: observation of nature and manipulatory techniques. Given the presupposition of paganism in the ancient world, namely, polytheism, one can understand the rationale. Since nature is controlled by the various deities, one should be able to discern their intent by close attention to what is happening in the environment. Or, one ought to be able to induce the gods to "tip their hand" through certain actions involving the natural order.

1. Observation of nature would include the movements of heavenly bodies, and solar and lunar eclipses. Animal behavior, especially of an unusual nature, was highly regarded by the ancients, as were violent weather and dreams. Handbooks and manuals were written in each of

these areas and closely guarded by the prophets and priests specializing in this lore.

2. A large body of literature has been discovered through archaeology dealing with various manipulatory techniques for discerning the future.[8] We list some of these by their technical names:

1) rhabdomancy: throwing sticks or arrows and observing the pattern in which they fell or lay
2) hydromancy: observing oil droplets on the surface of water
3) chiromancy: reading of palms
4) hepatoscopy: observing and interpreting the folds and creases of livers
5) necromancy: communicating with the dead

The Joseph stories allude to the practice of hydromancy (Ge 44:1–5). The cup Joseph accused his brothers of stealing is called a divining cup (44:5). Actually Joseph discerned the future by means of the interpretation of dreams—a gift bestowed by the Spirit of God. The biblical story demonstrates what we know from their own literature, that Egyptians typically used such divining cups. Joseph used it to incriminate his brothers. Necromancy, of course, features in the famous story of the witch of Endor (1Sa 28).

Ezekiel 21:18–23 provides a classic example of how a pagan general utilized divination in making military decisions. Here Nebuchadnezzar is portrayed as marching toward the west. When he comes to a fork in the road, he has to make a decision about which city to attack first, Jerusalem or Rabbah of the Ammonites (modern Amman, Jordan). Nebuchadnezzar made his choice as a modern general might by calling in his intelligence corps. In Nebuchadnezzar's case that would be his priests and prophets—they were the possessors of such knowledge. This procedure involved three techniques—he wanted to be sure! "For the king of Babylon will stop at the fork in the road, at the junction of the two roads, to seek an omen: He will cast lots with arrows, he will consult his idols, he will examine the liver" (v. 21). Notice that he used rhabdomancy and hepatoscopy as well as an oracle from a prophet. The oracle was probably delivered in the name of Nabu, Nebuchadnezzar's god. At any rate, the three techniques apparently all pointed to Jerusalem as the unfortunate first victim.

None of the above techniques of divination were permitted in Israel. Divination merited capital punishment (cf. Ex 22:18; Lev 19:26; Dt 18:10–12). Unfortunately, the biblical record indicates that divination was in fact practiced by Israel at various times and was a leading factor in the exile (cf. 2Ki 21:6).

Nature of the Literature Produced

A third difference between Hebrew and pagan prophecy has to do with the literature produced by the respective movements. Paganism evidences nothing like the powerful sermons warning of the Lord's judgment for covenant unfaithfulness (cf. e.g., Isa 1; 5; et al.). Nor do we find the urgent exhortations to repent and seek the Lord while he may be found (cf. Jer 29:13). Nowhere do we discover, in extant pagan literature, parallels to the glowing promises of the Lord's intentions for his restored people (cf. Am 9:11–15; Eze 40–48). What we do find in the recovered literature of paganism are manuals on the interpretation of dreams, omens, and rituals of divination. Archaeologists who excavated the great library of Ashurbanipal, one of the great Assyrian kings, found that fully one-quarter of the recovered documents consisted of omens and incantations. Pagan prophets apparently specialized in casting curses upon one's enemies and warding off the same![9]

The OT prophetic books are marked by unity and cohesion. Running through them are the threads of redemptive history, which we have seen already in our study. The covenant of Mount Sinai forms the foundation of the sermons; the election of Abraham and his seed is a presupposition for the kind of relationship that exists between Israel and Yahweh; the promise of the coming kingdom of God constitutes the hope of prophetic faith. The pattern so clearly set out in Deuteronomy concerning blessing for obedience and punishment for disobedience emerges in the prophetic critique of wayward Israel.[10]

In contrast, pagan literature, which has some parallels to Hebrew prophecy, lacks any discernible unity—it is characterized by disunity and diversity. One becomes aware of the dread and anxiety that gripped pagan society. There is a pervading sense of foreboding and resignation to inevitable fate so characteristic of paganism. There is also a preoccupation with an attempt to secure and maintain the favor of the capricious gods and goddesses of the pagan pantheon. Rare indeed are expressions of delight and joy in a personal relationship with the deity.

To date, nothing like the collection of prophetic books found in the OT canon has surfaced.

The Respective Theologies

The above comments are indicative of a more fundamental difference—the respective theologies. Hebrew prophecy, once again, stands out sharply from its pagan counterparts because it has a radically different view of God and the world. The Hebrew prophets champion ethical monotheism, as we have discussed earlier in the chapter on creation. It is this difference that accounts for all the others. The worldviews of ethical monotheism and polytheism are "worlds apart."

Validation of Predictive Prophecy

We mention one more distinction. A remarkable fact about the Hebrew prophets is their amazingly accurate predictions. Most Hebrew prophecy is proclamation, not prediction, but occasionally the prophets included predictions to validate the prophetic word as having its origin in the council of Yahweh and not the imagination of the prophet (cf. Jer 23:18, 22).[11] The OT prophetic books (which include the former prophets like Samuel and Kings) contain a number of predictions, some of which historical research has confirmed.[12] For Christians, this is most significant as it touches on prophecies having to do with the coming of the great descendant of David, the Messiah. Nowhere in pagan prophecy do we discover such an amazing correlation between prediction and fulfillment.

In our own day, so-called prophets and prophetesses do not have a particularly outstanding track record in this regard. Well-publicized prognosticators of the future, like Jean Dixon for example, barely rise above the level of mere chance in their predictions. Of course one does not usually hear this because they only talk about their successes, not their failures! Over against such hits and misses, one must marvel at the reliability of the Hebrew prophets. For their part, the Hebrew prophets never attributed their success to their own ingenuity, techniques or spirituality. They were merely spokespersons for the One who said: "So is my word that goes out from my mouth: It will not return to me empty, but will accomplish what I desire and achieve the purpose for which I sent it" (Isa 55:11).

The Development of Hebrew Prophecy in the Old Testament

Primeval Period

Prophecy in Israel may be divided into seven stages. The first stage appears already in the primeval history (Ge 1–11). The first person who exercises the gift of prophecy is Noah, a preacher of righteousness and judgment (cf. 2Pe 2:5). We also considered in chapter three his prophetic curse upon Canaan (Ge 9:25) and his prophetic blessing upon Shem (Ge 9:26).

Patriarchal Period

The patriarchal era likewise manifests the prophetic gift. Abraham is the first individual in the Bible explicitly called a prophet (*nāvîʾ*). In the episode when Abimelech took Sarah as his wife, we read the Lord's warning: "Now return the man's wife, for he is a prophet, and he will pray for you and you will live" (Ge 20:7). Intercessory prayer is a hallmark of the office of prophet (cf. Ge 18:16–33). Abraham also receives the revelation that Israel will be in bondage four hundred years, but come back to Canaan (Ge 15:13–16). In chapter four, we suggested that on Mount Moriah Abraham catches a glimpse of God's redemptive plan through the near sacrifice of Isaac (Ge 22; cf. Jn 8:56). Jacob has revelatory experiences with the Lord such as at Bethel and Peniel (Ge 28:10–22; 32:22–32). Joseph receives guidance concerning the Lord's plans and purposes by means of dreams (Ge 37:5–11; 40–41).

Mosaic Period

Prophecy really comes into its own during the Mosaic era. Moses is the prototypical prophet. His call experience, involvement in national politics, intercessory prayer, and preaching (see the book of Deuteronomy) establish a pattern for his successors: "The LORD your God will raise up for you a prophet like me from among your own brothers. You must listen to him" (Dt 18:15; cf. 34:10–12). The central significance of Moses, however, is his *mediatorship of the Sinai Covenant*. This constitution of Israel allows for and regulates the practice of prophecy. The office of prophet, as we have seen in our discussion of kingship, is an essential feature in preventing the abuse of power. We examine later in this chapter the criteria for discerning false prophets as contained in the Law of Moses.

Samuel and the School of the Prophets

The next great period of Israelite prophecy occurs in the transition from tribal federation to monarchy in the days of Samuel. He is the next towering figure who exercises the office of prophet. There are many similarities between him and Moses, particularly in the matters of involvement in national politics. Samuel anointed the first two kings of Israel and practiced intercessory prayer (1Sa 12:19, 23; 15:11). When Samuel was called to be a prophet as a youngster, "the word of the LORD was rare; there were not many visions" (1Sa 3:1). That changed with Samuel. He instituted a vigorous reform movement and enlisted young men who studied under his tutelage. They shared his vision and zeal (1Sa 10:5; 19:20).

Elijah and Elisha: Champions of the Covenant

Two figures mark the next great moment in the prophetic movement—Elijah and his successor Elisha. These men appear at a critical juncture in the life of Israel and Judah. As we saw in the discussion of the kingdom of God, Ahab and Jezebel threatened to turn the ancient faith of Israel into a Canaanite fertility cult. As champions of the Sinai Covenant, Elijah and Elisha challenge the syncretism of their day. Elijah's career and ministry has many remarkable parallels to that of Moses. We see this in their common roots as shepherds, association with Mount Sinai, challenge of the false gods, miracles involving nature and in the unique circumstances of their departure from this life in the vicinity of Mount Nebo. One may also note their appearance together on the mount of transfiguration during Jesus' ministry (Mt 17:3; Mk 9:4; Lk 9:30).

Rise of the Classical Prophets

Shortly after the death of Elisha, we come to the sixth era of the so-called classical prophets. The term "classical" simply designates the writing prophets as opposed to the prophets who preceded them and left behind no literary collections of prophetic material. The basic message did not change, only the method. Whereas the earlier prophets focused more upon individuals, the classical prophets address primarily the nation (cf. Da 9:6). The first of these classical prophets seems to have been Amos in about 760 B.C.[13] The writing prophets appear in a steady succession thereafter until about 400 B.C. Malachi was probably the last of the canonical prophets of the OT. This era is well documented by the portion of scripture called the Latter Prophets in the Hebrew Bible. These books, edited anthologies of sermons and messages originally preached orally, are a rich source of information about the period that covers the collapse and exile of the two kingdoms. The theological message of the prophets continues to speak to our own day.

Several reasons may be suggested for the rise of the classical prophets. On the one hand, *growth in the population* required a means of reaching a larger audience. Preservation of the messages in written form assisted in that regard. Secondly, the *nearness of judgment* necessitated a wider circulation of the warnings found in the prophetic oracles. Thirdly, we can assume a *higher literacy rate* during the era of the monarchy than had been the case earlier in the days of the tribal federation.

Cessation of Prophecy

With the end of Malachi's ministry, prophecy in Israel ceases (ca. 400 B.C.). During the intertestamental period, the Jewish people are painfully aware that prophecy has ceased. In 1 Maccabees 4:46 (written in the 2nd century B.C.) we read that at the rededication of the sanctuary by Judas Maccabeus, there was uncertainty about what to do with the stones of the old defiled altar because there was no prophet "to tell what to do with them."

Why did prophecy cease for some 400 years? We speculate and offer the following suggestions. Viewed from the perspective of the entire Bible, one may see a setting of the stage, *a period of preparation for the ultimate revelation of God's purpose and design*. During these so-called "silent years," the Lord plans for the invasion of planet earth by his son Jesus of Nazareth. The Jewish people are scattered widely across the Roman Empire and with them goes the Torah and the message of the one, true and living God who reveals his will to all humankind. The synagogue attracts a number of pagans, dissatisfied with the emptiness of the old religions and unpersuaded by the claims of the many new ones springing up. This network of synagogues is used to great effect by missionaries like the Apostle Paul. Besides this, the Roman Empire speaks a common language, Koine Greek, which facilitates the spread of the Gospel. Furthermore the empire provides a time of peace and relative security in which evangelization may be carried out. Add to this the fine system of Roman roads and the sea routes and you have near optimum conditions for the emerging Church. In short, we may say that God sets the stage and acts at the "right time" (cf. Gal 4:4).

A second reason may be proffered. The lapse of some 400 years between the latest prophecy about the coming Messiah and its fulfillment in Jesus of Nazareth (some went back another 300 years) *validated the prophetic word* as more than mere "words of men." Only an omniscient, omnipotent God can guide events in such a way. The odds against the various prophecies about Messiah's coming being fulfilled by chance in the person of Jesus of Nazareth are astronomical.[14] The delay in fulfillment demonstrates beyond all doubt that God's hand is in this whole process.

Revival of Prophecy with John the Baptist

In about A.D. 26–27, John the Baptist and his cousin, Jesus of Nazareth, shatter the prophetic silence. The long tradition of prophecy revives once again in the community of believers, first called "followers of the Way" and later "Christians" (cf. Ac 9:2; 11:26; 24:14; 26:28). From the standpoint of the entire Bible, the revival of prophecy surrounding the ministry of Christ culminates the entire prophetic tradition. The keynote of the NT is fulfillment—fulfillment climaxing in the return of Jesus Christ as "KING OF KINGS AND LORD OF LORDS" (cf. Heb 9:28; Rev 19:16).

The following chart summarizes the leading figures of the prophetic movement in the Bible:

Prophet/s	Approximate Dates	Distinctive Role in Redemptive History
Noah	?	Mediator of Noahic Covenant
Patriarchs	ca. 2000-1800 B.C.	Mediators of the Abrahamic Covenant
Moses	ca. 1400-1200 B.C.	Mediator of the Sinai Covenant
Samuel	ca. 1040 B.C.	Reformer of the Sinai Covenant
Elijah/Elisha	ca. 850-800 B.C.	Champions of the Sinai Covenant
"Classical Prophets"	ca. 760-400 B.C.	Enforcers of the Sinai Covenant
John the Baptist	ca. A.D. 26	Forerunner of the New Covenant
Jesus of Nazareth	ca. A.D. 26-30	Mediator of the New Covenant
Christian Prophets	ca. A.D. 30-?	Preachers of the New Covenant

The Prophetic Activity

We turn now to a consideration of how the prophet actually performs his or her task as a spokesperson of Yahweh. This activity falls logically into two steps: receiving a message and delivering it. Before we take this up, however, there are two prior questions requiring discussion: the context in which prophetic activity occurred and the self-consciousness of the prophet regarding this activity.

The Prophetic Context

Hebrew prophecy, from the time of Moses onward, functions in the context of the Sinai Covenant.[15] That is, the prophets view themselves as *delegates of Yahweh*, the great overlord and suzerain of Israel (recall our discussion of the Sinai Covenant/Treaty in chapter five). Contrary to much earlier scholarly opinion, the Hebrew prophets are not innovators of a new religious outlook—ethical monotheism, for example. They are, rather, heirs of a long-standing tradition, embodying the revelation at Mount Sinai. Their messages assume, as a point of shared information with the audience, the understanding of covenant stipulations as binding upon all Israel.

One of the keys, therefore, to understanding the prophetic messages is to view them as strongly worded protests of disloyalty by the overlord. *The prophets served as prosecuting attorneys bringing a series of indictments against rebellious Israel.* This framework is clearly seen in several passages, most notably, Amos 3:1–4:13; Hosea 4:1–3; Isaiah 1:2–3; 3:13–15; and Micah 6:1–5. Hosea 4:1–6 illustrates this so well, we quote it in full:

> Hear the word of the LORD, you Israelites, because the LORD has a charge to bring against you who live in the land; "There is no faithfulness, no love, no acknowledgment of God in the land. There is only cursing, lying and murder, stealing and adultery; they break all bounds, and bloodshed follows bloodshed. Because of this the land mourns, and all who live in it waste away; the beasts of the field and the birds of the air and the fish of the sea are dying. But let no man bring a charge, let no man accuse another, for your people are like those who bring charges against a priest. You stumble day and night, and the prophets stumble with you. So I will destroy your mother—my people are destroyed from lack of knowledge. Because you have rejected knowledge, I also reject you as my priests; because you have ignored the law of your God, I also will ignore your children."

Note that the above indictment includes six of the Ten Commandments, which form the basic stipulations of the Sinai Covenant. The first two accusations actually amount to a charge of disloyalty—the equivalent of "You shall have no other gods before me" (Ex 20:3). No surprise either that the prophetic judgment speeches include threats and announcements of curses that correspond to the treaty curses (cf. Am 3:11; 4:6–11; 5:16–17; 6:7; 7:1–9; Isa 1:5–9).

Of course, we should not leave this topic without also mentioning that the delegates of Yahweh always leave the door open for heartfelt repentance. If Israel turns away from her disloyalty and seeks the Lord, she will find forgiveness and favor—the blessings of the covenant will flow from the throne of the great overlord (cf. Isa 4:2–6; 12:1–6; Hos 6:1–3; 14:1–9; Am 5:4–6, 14–15; 9:8–10).

The Prophetic Consciousness

How did the call and commission affect the prophet? Did this experience alter one's personality and character? Did the prophet permanently acquire new capabilities? Was there a great increase in spirituality, such that one now gained complete victory over sin?[16]

The answer, based upon the scriptural evidence, is that prophets remained human beings facing the problems, pitfalls and failures of all human beings, even those deeply committed to the Lord. They did not suddenly become all-wise, all-holy "supersaints," who were above the problems of life. James, in the NT, sums it up nicely when he says, "Elijah was a man just like us" (Jas 5:17).

Several examples illustrate the point. Prophets can be mistaken apart from the inspiration of the Holy Spirit. Nathan, (2Sa 7:3), in response to David's desire to build a temple for the Lord, thinks it a great idea, and encourages him in this endeavor. That night, however, the Lord revealed to Nathan that David was *not* the one to build the temple (7:4–7). When Samuel enters the house of Jesse to anoint a new king of Israel, his first response to Eliab, the firstborn of Jesse, is: "Surely the LORD's anointed stands here before the LORD" (1Sa 16:6). The Lord's response is worth quoting: "Do not consider his appearance or his height, for I have rejected him. The LORD does not look at the things man looks at. Man looks at the outward appearance, but the LORD looks at the heart" (16:7). Samuel makes his judgment the only way a human can—by using human standards. This, of course, falls short of the infallible standards of God. No prophet possessed a complete knowledge of God's plans and purposes; prophetic knowledge always remained partial. As Paul says in the NT: "For we know in part and we prophesy in part . . ." (1Co 13:9).

Furthermore, prophets exhibit the very human traits of discouragement, despair, anger, bitterness, vindictiveness, and vengeance. Instructive here are the "complaints of Jeremiah," where he even has the audacity to accuse the Lord of being unfair in his dealings with him. (Jer 12:1–4; 20:7–10, 14–18). Elijah displays self-pity and depression at one low point in his career (1Ki 19:9–18). Jonah hardly commends himself as an example of compassion in his stubborn wish to see Nineveh destroyed (Jnh 4:1–10). These and many other examples testify to the fact that a call to the office of prophet does not elevate the individual to a new level of existence unaffected by the struggles of humanity. But it is also clear from scripture that when the Holy Spirit speaks through a prophet, the message so conveyed is trustworthy. This is the work of inspiration discussed earlier in chapter one.

The Reception of Messages from the Lord

What then were the means of receiving a message from the Lord? We find at least five different modes of reception.

The external voice. There are several instances when apparently the Lord spoke in an audible voice using the language of the listener. Our first instance is the story of young Samuel's call (1Sa 3). The text makes clear that an actual voice was heard. "The LORD came and stood there, calling as at the other times, 'Samuel! Samuel!'" Then Samuel said, "Speak, for your servant is listening" (v. 10). Most likely Elijah, too, heard an audible voice on Mount Sinai when the Lord asked him, "What are you doing here, Elijah?" (1Ki 19:9). There can be no doubt that the Lord spoke audibly to Moses. Numbers 12:8 states: "With him I speak face to face, clearly and not in riddles. . . ." Thus these three great pre-classical prophets all received messages by means of an audible voice. My impression is, however, that this mode was rare, and not the experience of most prophets.

The internal voice. Probably the most common mode of reception involved the internal voice. This was an interior experience. In his heart and mind the prophet "heard" what the Lord was saying. Although it was an inner phenomenon, it was not thereby any less certain. The prophet possessed an unshakable conviction that the Lord had spoken (Am 3:8). Regularly the classical prophets introduce their books or oracles with a phrase that highlights the origin of the message. We use Hosea as an example: "The word of the LORD that came to Hosea . . ." (Hos 1:1).

The perception of spiritual realities. On occasion the prophet was enabled to catch a glimpse of the spiritual realm, surrounding us on all sides, but not visible to our physical eyes. We distinguish this from a theophany in which the Lord reveals himself in tangible, bodily form. We consider Genesis 18, when Abraham hosted the three travelers, to be an instance of theophany. Likewise Jacob's wrestling with the angel at Peniel was a theophany. In contrast to this are instances when a prophet, or someone associated with a prophet, was enabled to discern spiritual beings normally invisible.

Take, for example, an episode from the life of Elisha. In 2 Kings 6 we read of a period of warfare between Aram (modern Syria) and Israel. During the hostilities, the prophet Elisha informed the king of Israel of the movements of the Aramean armies. Every time the Syrians plan an ambush, the king of Israel knows the exact location, thanks to Elisha. Of course the king of Aram suspects someone in his officers corps is a spy. When he makes his accusation, they protest their innocence and inform him that the Israelites have a secret weapon—namely, Elisha the prophet who "tells the king of Israel the very words you speak in your bedroom" (v. 12). Upon hearing this, the king of Aram decides to capture Elisha and employ him against the Israelites! A powerful Syrian army surrounds Dothan where Elisha is staying. Elisha's servant arises the next morning and spots the army lying in wait. Terrified, he reports to Elisha their predicament. Elisha calmly encourages the servant with these words: "Don't be afraid. . . . Those who are with us are more than those who are with them" (v. 16). One can imagine the servant looking about in disbelief! Where are the troops on their side? "And Elisha prayed, 'O LORD, open his eyes so he may see.' Then the LORD opened the servant's eyes, and he looked and saw the hills full of horses and chariots of fire all around Elisha" (v. 17). What the servant now sees is an angelic army surrounding the Aramean army. They have been there all along—the servant just could not see them until enabled to do so. Elisha had the divinely given capability to perceive the presence of the angelic army. Prophets on occasion received revelation through such means.

The vision or imaginary picture. Within the category of visions we distinguish between two possibilities: 1) an experience involving what is actual, and 2) an experience involving what is potential or symbolic. The first kind is akin to clairvoyance, that is, the power to perceive things that are beyond the normal range of the senses. We can illustrate both of these visionary experiences from the ministry of Ezekiel.

On one occasion, Ezekiel, while in the presence of a group of elders in his house, suddenly goes into a trance (Eze 8:1). In the realm of the spirit, he is transported to Jerusalem (v. 3). In the spirit, Ezekiel observes what is actually happening in the temple at Jerusalem with startling clarity. In this trance-like state all his senses are involved—he even digs through the wall of the courtyard (v. 8)! He sees the graffiti and idols inside a closet of the temple. Activities thought safely hidden from view are closely scrutinized during this spiritual journey. (vv. 10–12). What Ezekiel sees corresponds to actual practices going on in secret.

In contrast to the above, chapter 37 presents a different kind of visionary experience. The vision of the valley of dry bones does not correspond to something actually happening in space and time—it transpires solely within Ezekiel's mind or spirit. In a striking metaphor of physical resurrection, he prophesies the future rebirth of the nation of Israel by means of vivid symbolism.

In both of the visionary experiences mentioned above, the recipient remains conscious. He is not aware of or responding to external stimuli, but neither is he asleep or unconscious.

The dream. On occasion the Lord revealed himself to a prophet through a dream. The difference between the dream and the vision is that in the former the subject is in an inactive, unconscious state. Dreams can be bizarre and grotesque, or very realistic, as most of us can testify by personal experience! The patriarchal era contains well-known examples in the lives of Jacob and his son Joseph (Ge 28:12–15; 37:5–10). But the prophet best known for receiving messages through dreams is Daniel (cf. Da 7:1). In Daniel's case, the dreams are connected to a visionary experience.

Diversity. We conclude this section by noting the great diversity in modes of reception. There is no standardized or uniform method whereby the Lord speaks to his prophets. Numbers 12:6–8 reminds us of several ways the Lord spoke—visions, dreams and face to face. Hebrews 1:1 succinctly summarizes the topic: "In the past God spoke to our forefathers through the prophets at many times and *in various ways* . . ."

The Delivery of Prophetic Messages

Once a prophet received a message from the Lord how did he or she communicate it to the intended audience? As with the reception of messages, there might be several modes.

Brief Oral Statements and Rejoinders

In the historical books the prophets most often convey their messages in brief oral statements. These can be of several kinds. For example, the message may consist of specific orders or directions. One thinks of Deborah's messages to Barak during the Canaanite crisis (Jdg 4:1–24). She directs troop movements during the confrontation with the Canaanites under Sisera. "Go, take with you ten thousand men of Naphtali and Zebulun and lead the way to Mount Tabor. . . . Go! This is the day the LORD has given Sisera into your hands. Has not the LORD gone ahead of you?" (Jdg 4:6, 14).

The message might be one of rebuke—often the case when prophets sought to curb the abuse of power by kings. A classic example is the confrontation between Elijah and Ahab in Naboth's vineyard. "Have you not murdered a man and seized his property?" (1Ki 21:19). One also recalls Nathan's rebuke of David: "You are the man! . . . Why did you despise the word of the LORD by doing what is evil in his eyes?" (2Sa 12:7, 9).

Of course a prophet might also encourage a king to continue to pursue a course of action or to maintain covenant faithfulness. In the days of Asa king of Judah, Azariah son of Oded encourages King Asa with these words: "The LORD is with you when you are with him. If you seek him, he will be found by you, but if you forsake him, he will forsake you. . . . But as for you, be strong and do not give up, for your work will be rewarded" (2Ch 15:2, 7).

It should be noted that the above encouragement included a warning as well. Another example of a clear warning occurs in 2 Kings 16:1–4, where the prophet Jehu son of Hanani minces no words: "So I am about to consume Baasha and his house, and I will make your house like that of Jeroboam son of Nebat. Dogs will eat those belonging to Baasha who die in the city, and the birds of the air will feed on those who die in the country." All the above messages share these characteristics: they are short, to the point and delivered orally.

Longer Oral Messages or Sermons

In the books written by or named after the classical prophets, we have essentially anthologies of sermons, originally preached orally. We do have a few instances of longer written messages that appear not to have been preached at all (Jer 29:1–32). These sermons have undoubtedly been edited since they are considerably shorter than most sermons preached today! Nonetheless, they still convey the power and urgency of the prophetic word. A classic example of a sermon, including the audience response, occurs in Jeremiah 7 and 26. Comparing these two passages, one can follow the main points of the message in chapter 7 and the angry reaction of the religious leaders in chapter 26. The distinguishing feature of Jeremiah's message, as well as the messages of all the classical prophets, is the strong sense of "thus says the Lord." When challenged by a hostile crowd, Jeremiah responds with this defense: "The LORD sent me to prophesy against this house and this city all the things you have heard" (v. 12). The preaching of all the classical prophets was marked by this note of authority. The actual style, however, varied according to the individual prophet—each one left a personal signature on the message.

Description of Visions

Visionary experiences are typical of prophets. Not surprisingly, a frequent mode of delivery involves a description of the vision. This mode may be illustrated in both the historical books and in the collection of writings from the classical prophets.

In the former section we select the story of Micaiah (1Ki 22:1–28). Micaiah was summoned to a high-level meeting between the kings of Israel and Judah to determine the feasibility of attacking Syria in order to recover lost territory. Four hundred false prophets of Ahab unanimously approve the king's objective. Only at the insistence of the godly king Jehoshaphat has Micaiah even been summoned at all. In the face of this potentially life-threatening situation, Micaiah bravely describes what he has seen in a vision from the Lord: "I saw all Israel scattered on the hills like sheep without a shepherd, and the LORD said, 'These people have no master. Let each one go home in peace'" (v. 17). The vision meant that the king of Israel would be killed and the army of Israel defeated. The sequel to the story validates this vision as coming from the Lord: So the king died and was brought to Samaria . . ." (v. 37).

The entire second half of the book of Daniel (chs. 7–13) consists of visions with their interpretation. Ezekiel and Zechariah also contain lengthy sections falling into this category.

Symbolic Actions

The most dramatic mode of delivery is the symbolic action. This is basically an acted parable—an action that, in itself, conveys the message. Thus a symbolic action is a kind of object lesson, which may or may not be accompanied by explanation. The symbolic action effectively communicates because human beings are attuned to movement and action. For example, suppose you are in a church worship service, and in the middle of the pastor's sermon, someone walks right to the front aisle and sits down. What happens? Nearly everyone attending turns to look—a typical human reaction. Symbolic actions gain the attention of onlookers; even of those opposed to the message of the action. It is for this very reason that prophets engage in symbolic actions. Those who do so are usually confronting a hostile, unreceptive audience. In spite of the hostility, the symbolic action "gets the message across."

Two main types. Symbolic actions may be divided into two main categories for purposes of analysis: spontaneous and arranged.

1. In the former, the practitioner does not consciously plan on a certain course of action; rather, something unexpected happens, which provides a "teachable moment," and the action becomes the message. An example is found in 1 Samuel 15:10–35. The Lord reveals to Samuel that Saul has disobeyed his instructions about destroying the Amalekites and all their possessions. Samuel confronts Saul and pronounces a devastating word of rejection: "Because you have rejected the word of the LORD, he has rejected you as king" (v. 23). Then, as Samuel turns to leave, Saul reaches out and seizes the edge of Samuel's garment, which tears. Samuel immediately senses in that action a message: "The LORD has torn the kingdom of Israel from you today and has given it to one of your neighbors—to one better than you" (v. 27). Obviously Samuel had not planned to do that—but it left an unforgettable impression on Saul, and doubtlessly plagued his mind thereafter.

2. As an example of an arranged or premeditated symbolic action we turn to 1 Kings 11:29–39. Here the prophet Ahijah of Shiloh, wearing a new cloak, meets Jeroboam as he is leaving Jerusalem. As the two of

them are traveling together, Ahijah suddenly stops and begins tearing his new cloak into twelve pieces. That certainly got Jeroboam's attention! He then proceeds to hand ten pieces to Jeroboam. The action is accompanied by a word of explanation: "Take ten pieces for yourself, for this is what the LORD, the God of Israel, says: 'See, I am going to tear the kingdom out of Solomon's hand and give you ten tribes . . .'" (v. 31). The impact upon Jeroboam was enormous. Not long afterward, emboldened, he plotted against Solomon. As we saw in chapter seven, he did in fact become the first king of the breakaway kingdom of Israel.

Classic practitioners. When it comes to symbolic actions, however, the classic practitioners are Jeremiah and Ezekiel. The frequency of symbolic actions in their ministries is probably owing to the resistance each faced to his message.

1. For example, after Jeremiah's initial sermon in the temple courtyard (see chs. 7, 26), he frequently resorts to symbolic actions to convey a message, which he knows will not be favorably received. Chapter 13 narrates his first recorded symbolic action. In short, he purchases a new linen belt, a luxury item, and wears it about Jerusalem. Some time later the Lord tells him to hide the belt at the Perath. The latter place name is unknown. It might be either a local stream, not far from Jeremiah's village of Anathoth, or the distant river Euphrates in modern Iraq. In any case, he buries the belt in a very moist environment. After some time passes, the Lord instructs Jeremiah to retrieve the belt and prominently display it around Jerusalem. By now, of course, the belt is mildewy and rotten. In this instance, an explanation accompanies the action. The belt represents Judah and Jerusalem. Whereas the Lord had bound himself in covenant to Judah and Jerusalem, they have been unfaithful and have broken the covenant. Consequently, they are spiritually ruined. The condition of the grungy belt typifies the coming ruin of Judah and Jerusalem.

On another occasion (ch. 19), Jeremiah becomes even more dramatic. He purchases a clay jar (perhaps a flask used for liquids) and takes some of the prominent leaders with him to the cliffs overlooking the Hinnom Valley. Holding the clay jar aloft, he lets it plummet to the bottom of the valley. Like the proverbial Humpty Dumpty, "all the kings' horses and all the kings' men could not put [the jar] back together again." The point is fairly transparent, but Jeremiah leaves nothing to ambiguity: "This is what the LORD Almighty says: I will smash this nation and this city just as this potter's jar is smashed and cannot be repaired" (v. 11).

We consider one more of Jeremiah's symbolic actions—his finest effort. In chapter 27 the Lord instructs Jeremiah to make a yoke and wear it around his neck. A yoke was a rather large wooden collar, fastened around the neck of an ox in order to pull a plow or cart. Jeremiah wears such a device for some time. Imagine the effect upon the citizens of Jerusalem. Each day he jostles through the narrow, crowded streets of Jerusalem with the overhanging yoke, no doubt, forcing many good citizens to move out of the way! Once the meaning of the yoke is explained, the impact is reinforced daily as people encounter Jeremiah in the streets and squares. The yoke symbolizes the coming subjugation of Jerusalem and Judah by Nebuchadnezzar. Though the message of Jeremiah is bitterly rejected by most onlookers, they cannot help but be continually reminded of it.

2. We turn to the prophet who wins the Oscar for best symbolic action. Ezekiel's portrayal of the siege of Jerusalem for over a year outside his house in a refugee camp almost defies imagination. In Ezekiel 3:24–5:6 we read of a series of actions, each one speaking louder than words. Outside his home he draws a map of the city of Jerusalem on a clay tile and pretends to lay siege to it. The sight of a grown man reverting to his childhood and playing toy soldiers certainly got people's attention! This siege is accompanied by even more bizarre behavior. For 390 days he lies on his left side as he enacts the siege. He turns on his right side for another 40 days—the days representing years of disobedience by Israel and Judah respectively. Incredibly, he eats and drinks just enough each day to keep himself alive (cf. *NIVSB* n. at 4:10–11). Recalling that he did this for over a year, one may imagine the gaunt and emaciated appearance Ezekiel begins to exhibit. He is portraying the actual, physical condition of the inhabitants of Jerusalem during the impending siege by Nebuchadnezzar. In addition to all this, he shaves off all his hair and separates it into three piles. One pile he strikes with a sword, another he burns with fire, and a third he throws to the winds. This represents the fate of the defenders and inhabitants of the doomed city of Jerusalem.

What a grim symbolic action, requiring so much physical pain and mental anguish! This gruesome message, however, did have one glimmer of hope. Ezekiel was instructed to hide a few strands of hair in the folds of his garment. This represented the survival of a small remnant, a theme we have seen earlier in Amos and Isaiah. Ezekiel engaged in other symbolic actions throughout his ministry, but we have seen enough to gain an appreciation for the dramatic effect that they undoubtedly had upon the intended audience.

Symbolic actions and the NT. Symbolic actions were an important delivery system for prophetic messages. It should not surprise us to discover that they continue in the New Covenant era. In the ministry of Jesus, there are several examples of his using symbolic actions (cf. Mk 11:12–25). Probably the most meaningful to Christians is the Lord's Supper with its simple, but profound, acted message (Lk 22:14–22). The book of Acts records the symbolic action of the prophet Agabus who bound himself with Paul's belt to symbolize the latter's destiny, if he should proceed to Jerusalem (Ac 21:10–11). Well-conceived symbolic actions are still powerful techniques for the presentation of the Gospel in our own time.

The Discernment of True and False Prophets

The last topic we take up in this chapter is the problem of discerning false prophets. This became a vexing issue for the people of God, especially as the end of the state of Judah approached. During this era many individuals proclaimed themselves to be spokespersons of Yahweh.

A Case Study

Let us turn to a passage constituting a case study for the problem of discerning who is a true and who is a false prophet. Jeremiah 28 narrates a confrontation between two prophets: Hananiah and Jeremiah. Each one proclaims a message in the name of Yahweh. So which one truly speaks for the Lord and upon what basis can one decide? Remember that Jeremiah had been wearing a yoke on his neck as a symbolic action indicating the fate of the city—Nebuchadnezzar would subjugate the city under a yoke of bondage. This greatly angers Hananiah. Consequently, during a convocation at the temple, Hananiah takes the opportunity to challenge Jeremiah. He proclaims: "This is what the LORD Almighty, the God of Israel, says: 'I will break the yoke of the king of Babylon. Within two years I will bring back to this place all the articles of the LORD's house . . . for I will break the yoke of the king of Babylon'" (vv. 2–4).

Jeremiah responds by expressing his desire that Hananiah's prophecy may be fulfilled, but, at the same time, casts doubt upon its actual fulfillment. Hananiah's prophecy, says Jeremiah, is not in keeping with the general tenor of the prophecies that have preceded them. Suddenly, Hananiah resorts to a symbolic action of his own. He tears the yoke off Jeremiah's neck and repeats his prophecy of deliverance (vv. 10–11). At this moment of high drama, we next read "the prophet Jeremiah went on his way."

Seemingly, Hananiah discredited Jeremiah. Jeremiah's lack of response and withdrawal from the confrontation gave the impression that Hananiah was right. If a vote had been taken at that moment, Hananiah would surely have won hands down. Clearly, the message of Hananiah was the one that the majority wanted to believe. But how could the people of God have known which prophet to believe? Was truth to be determined by the outcome of a debate? That is what we seek to discover.

Inadequate Criteria for Distinguishing False Prophets

Modern scholars studying prophecy have suggested certain criteria by which false prophets might be discerned. In some cases, however, these suggested criteria are inadequate to account for all the data.

Ecstasy as a mark of false prophets. Some scholars have posited ecstatic behavior as a sign of false prophecy.[17] Ecstasy, defined as an emotional state so intense that rational thought and self-control are obliterated, introduces a non-cognitive element into the revelatory process, which, it is argued, may result in distortion and error. Sometimes a distinction was made between the earlier "spirit prophets" and the later "word prophets." Along evolutionary lines, the earlier prophecy, modeled after the pattern of pagan prophecy, developed into a more rational cognitive phenomenon. Elements of the earlier ecstatic stage of Hebrew prophecy are said to be discernible in the historical books like 1 and 2 Samuel.

Such a sharp distinction is not supportable from the biblical evidence. What we can say is that some of the genuine Hebrew prophets were occasionally subject to ecstasy. One thinks particularly of Ezekiel (cf. Eze 1:1–3; 3:12–15, 22–24; 8:14). His ecstatic experiences were not, however, such that no rational or verbal content could be given them.

The ecstatic trance was a spiritual experience in which the Lord revealed his plan and purpose to the prophet, a revelation capable of verbal expression.

Cultic prophets as false prophets. Another criterion sometimes singled out by scholars is whether the prophet is attached to a cultic center. Cultic prophets are presumed to be false, because the pressure to deliver prophecies sustaining the livelihood of the cultic officials would have been great. Prophets tended to curry the favor of their congregants and uttered words filling the people with false hopes such as: "You will have peace" and "No harm will come to you" (Jer 23:16–17).

While it must be admitted that this is always a temptation for those who presume to speak in God's name, several outstanding prophets were associated with a cultic center—Samuel being noteworthy in this regard. By itself, this criterion is inadequate.

Professionalism as a criterion. Much like the criterion of cultic prophets, the criterion of professionalism assumes that prophets would succumb to the economic necessities of life and tailor their messages in such a way as to ensure an adequate income. Instead of messages critical of society and individuals within that society, the prophets would speak appealing and encouraging words with, at best, muted criticism. In short the self-interest of the prophet would identify him with the status quo.

No doubt many a false prophet became such through the practice of accepting monetary gifts or gifts in kind. The story of Gehazi, servant of Elisha, shows that such temptation was a real possibility, but it also shows that true prophecy condemned a mercenary approach to being a bearer of the word of God (2Ki 5:15–27). On the other hand, Samuel appears to have been, in some sense, a professional prophet who accepted gifts for services rendered (cf. 1Sa 9:1–9). Professionalism per se did not render one a false prophet.

The above criteria, while sometimes ferreting out false prophets, are simply inadequate to deal with the phenomenon as a whole. We turn to the scriptures themselves for criteria identifying false prophets.

Biblical Criteria for Discerning False Prophets

The scriptures indicate at least four tests that might be employed.

The empirical test (Dt 18:14–22). If the message of a prophet included a prediction about the future, it could be subjected to the empirical test. The empirical test involves an appeal to the outcome of a particular prophecy; that is, whether it is fulfilled or not. Fulfillment is subject to verification (objective evidence may be appealed to in making the determination). This test or criterion first occurs in Deuteronomy 18:14–22 where Moses anticipates the problem of discerning true and false prophecy. In this passage he warns the people about practicing divination (see pages 258–259) and assures them that the Lord will raise up prophets who convey the word of the Lord to Israel. Verses 21 and 22 highlight the issue at hand:

> You may say to yourselves, "How can we know when a message has not been spoken by the LORD?" If what a prophet proclaims in the name of the LORD does not take place or come true, that is a message the LORD has not spoken. That prophet has spoken presumptuously. Do not be afraid of him.

Notice that this test is a *negative test*, that is, it specifies who was *not* a true prophet in cases where a prediction has been made in the name of the Lord. It does not necessarily follow, however, that if a certain prophecy is fulfilled, this guarantees the prophet's genuineness. The test operates on the principle of failure not success. In chemistry, students are sometimes required to determine the identity of an unknown substance. Some tests are run which, if positive, simply eliminate a certain class of compounds or substances. In like manner, the empirical test for prophecy eliminates self-proclaimed prophets from being genuine by virtue of failure to live up to an essential characteristic of God's word—reliability. What God says, he will do (cf. Isa 55:11).

There is, however, one qualification to this test: sometimes the Lord utters a conditional prophecy. That is, the fulfillment of the prophecy is contingent upon some action or attitude on the part of the recipients. If this condition is met, then the prophecy will be fulfilled; otherwise, it will not. An example comes from the book of Jonah, where we have an implied condition attached to the prophecy that in forty more days

Nineveh would be destroyed. The condition was repentance on the part of the inhabitants. This condition was met and, much to the distress of Jonah, the city was spared. We should note, however, that *the fulfillment of a so-called prophecy, or even the performance of a miraculous sign, is not in itself a sign of a true prophet.*

The theological test (Dt 13:1–5). A second test focuses on the content of the alleged prophecy and inquires into its conformity with previous revelation known to be genuine and authoritative. In practice, the touchstone for determining authenticity was the Law of Moses which, as we have seen, was functionally the constitution of Israel. If a prophecy (and remember that most OT prophecy consisted of preaching, not prediction) contradicts the Law of Moses, or is hostile to it, there is no need for further inquiry—that person is a false prophet deserving of death. Note that even if signs or wonders accompany the prophecy, this does not override the decisive criterion of the Lord's clear revelation of his will and purpose in the law.

This test is also negative in that it can only eliminate certain individuals from the ranks of the genuine. Thus, it may be possible for an individual to slip through this test, at least for a while, by simply avoiding any public proclamation that contradicts the Law of Moses. The real allegiance and heart attitude of the individual may remain temporarily unknown.

The ethical test (Jeremiah 23; Ezekiel 13). The third test focuses upon the individual in terms of lifestyle and behavior. Does the prophet live in accordance with the demands of the Sinai Covenant? Does the prophet preach a message that upholds and preserves the standard of behavior required by the Law of Moses?

Both Jeremiah and Ezekiel faced intense opposition from false prophets. Their writings include a description of self-styled prophets, and we can see a defection from the revealed standards of Sinai. Listen to some of the indictments of Jeremiah: "The prophets follow an evil course and use their power unjustly. . . . They prophesied by Baal and led my people astray. . . . They commit adultery and live a lie. They strengthen the hands of evildoers, so that no one turns from his wickedness . . . from the prophets of Jerusalem ungodliness has spread throughout the land" (23:10, 13–15). Ezekiel adds this charge: "You have not gone up to the breaks in the wall to repair it for the house of Israel so that it will stand firm in the battle on the day of the LORD" (13:5). ". . . when a flimsy wall is built, they cover it with whitewash" (13:10).

In short, false prophets were not a bulwark against immorality and godlessness; they actually contributed to the spiritual and moral decline of the nation. This test assumes that one cannot separate the individual from his message—there should be an inseparable link between what is proclaimed and what is practiced on a daily basis. True prophets should "walk the talk."

The witness of the Holy Spirit. We now return to our case study of Hananiah and Jeremiah (Jer 28). Do these three tests mentioned above enable us to identify Hananiah as a false prophet? The problem with the empirical test is that one must wait two years before saying confidently that Hananiah is a false prophet (28:3). The problem with the theological test is that, while it was certainly a minority report, one cannot find anything directly contradicting the Lord's previous revelation in the Law of Moses. Indeed, Hananiah could appeal to the numerous instances where the Lord came to the rescue of his oppressed people. The problem with the ethical test for many of the original listeners and, certainly for a later reader, is simply lack of information about Hananiah. It may well be that if we had known more about him, we would have discerned behavior and attitudes that belied his claim of having stood in the council of Yahweh. Lacking that, however, we would be hard-pressed to make a judgment. Are we then forced to admit that in spite of the three tests mentioned above, our particular test case leaves us in a quandary? How would genuine believers who heard Hananiah have been able to discern who was true and who was false? No doubt a majority of the original audience voted with their hearts; they believed the favorable message concerning the fate of Jerusalem.

There is an important resource believers possess, assisting them to detect false prophecy—the inner witness of the Holy Spirit. The problem here, of course, is the objection that the Holy Spirit did not function in this way for believers until after the Cross. Certainly the NT indicates that the Holy Spirit alerts believers to false teaching (see, e.g. 1Th 5:21; 1Co 14:29; 1Jn 2:20, 27; 4:1; 5:10). If one looks at Isaiah 63:7–13, however, we have a description of the guiding and protecting ministry of the Spirit comparable to that of the NT. Did God leave his people without such a resource? We suggest that he did not, and thus, those who truly sought God's will sensed that Hananiah was not proclaiming God's word.[18]

Outcome of the test case. At any rate, the issue is finally resolved through the more visible and tangible test—the empirical test. As Paul Harvey is fond of saying: "And now, the rest of the story." After Jeremiah has seemingly been discredited, the word of the Lord comes to him, and he reappears and confronts Hananiah. Jeremiah proclaims that the Lord will replace the wooden yoke with a yoke of iron, which symbolizes the complete subjugation of Judah to Nebuchadnezzar. Furthermore, and here the empirical test becomes of utmost importance, Hananiah will die *within the year*. The account ends with this historical note: "In the seventh month of that same year, Hananiah the prophet died" (v. 17). For those loyal to the Sinai Covenant, the issue was settled.

False Prophets and the NT

The problem of false prophecy and false teaching also surfaces in the NT. Recall that Jesus warned his disciples of false prophets in the Sermon on the Mount (Mt 7:15–20). We mentioned earlier several Pauline passages addressing the issue. The Apostle John encountered false prophets and teachers in Asia Minor and gave appropriate instruction on discerning and dealing with such individuals (cf. 1Jn 2:18–23; 4:1–3; 2Jn 7–11; Rev 2–3), as did the Apostles Peter and Jude (2Pe 2; Jude).

Our own time is marked by numerous cults and sects, many of which are headed up by "prophets." The criteria for discerning false prophecy are still relevant and essential for preserving the spiritual health of the church. These tests are still reliable and, when joined with the ministry of the Holy Spirit, serve as a bulwark against error. "But you have an anointing from the Holy One, and all of you know the truth" (1Jn 2:20). But the Church must not relax its guard! Paul's admonition is still timely: "Test everything. Hold on to the good" (1Th 5:21). "Two or three prophets should speak, and the others should weigh carefully what is said" (1Co 14:29).

Conclusion

From our discussion of the prophetic movement, it is evident that the prophets were first and foremost preachers to their own times. The burden of their messages centered upon a crisis: Israel had broken their covenant obligations to their great overlord and was liable to the curses of the covenant. The curses consisted of specific penalties for disobedience. The ultimate covenant curse was expulsion from the land. Beginning with Amos and continuing through Jeremiah, the prophets announced this sanction as imminent.

When it was finally carried out in 722 and 586 B.C., the prophets, amazingly, proclaimed the certainty of a new act of God; he would make a new covenant with the house of Israel and Judah, and restore the nation to its inheritance. This new redemptive act of God was cast in language transcending the historical realities of the time. We suddenly read passages that speak of the "latter days," "the Day of the Lord," and other expressions referring to the end of human history. The prophets foretold days of blessing and salvation. It is to this great block of material that we turn in the next chapter, in order to discern what the OT has to say, through the prophets, about the consummation of human history and the glorious appearance of the kingdom of God.

Relationship of Theme to Core Concepts

Faith and the Unity of Salvation: This chapter has emphasized a point made in chapter seven, namely, the role of the prophets in the ongoing history of redemption. There is an inner unity to this history because the same Spirit was revealing and guiding these inspired spokespersons. Stepping back for a moment, we may say that virtually the entire Bible manifests the spirit of prophecy. The selfsame Spirit who came upon Moses and his successors also quickened John the Baptist in the womb and empowered him throughout his preparatory ministry. Jesus of Nazareth, in the power of the Spirit, brought this history to a climax by fulfilling all that the prophets had foretold (cf. Lk 4:21; 16:16; 24:25–27, 44–47; Ac 1:16; 2:17–39; 3:18–26; 13:26–41; et al.) and by sending forth his apostles, in the power of the Spirit, to witness to this final word of redemption (cf. Ac 1:8, 21–22; 2:32; 3:15; 5:32; 9:15–17, 20–22; 11:19–24; 13:30–41; et al.). What was said to John on the isle of Patmos sums up the prophetic dimension of scripture: "These words are trustworthy and true. The Lord, the God of the spirits of the prophets, sent his angel to show his servants the things that must soon take place" (Rev 22:6).

Faith and Ethics: Chapter seven stressed the crisis in Israel and Judah resulting from a dichotomy between faith and ethics. This dichotomy was worsened by false prophets who sought to promote their own interests rather than those of the kingdom of God. The prophets, too, were obliged to "practice what they preached." Satan has sought consistently to undermine the kingdom of God, and one of his most successful approaches has been to employ false spokespersons. The tests for false prophets are vitally important for our own day as tragedies like those in Waco, Texas (David Koresh) and Rancho La Mesa, California (Marshall Applewhite) so tragically illustrate. In short, the genuine prophetic movement in both Old and New Testaments calls upon the people of God to live in light of the covenant obligations. These are summarized in the two cardinal commandments: Love God and love one's neighbor.

Faith and Politics: As we saw in this chapter, the prophets took an active role in the political life of Israel. This serves as a reminder that believers must not live in a vacuum; the truths of revelation must be integrated with the hard political decisions of this world. The prophets remain a valuable resource for us today as we grapple with problems of crime, racial injustice, environmental degradation, and a whole host of social and political problems. We must return time and again to the ever-relevant pleas of spokespersons like Amos who urge us: "But let justice roll on like a river, righteousness like a never-failing stream!" (Am 5:24).

Faith and the Future: As discussed in this chapter, most prophecy is simply inspired preaching designed to convict of sin, to produce repentance and faith, and to encourage and comfort. Occasionally, however, the prophets made predictions about the future. These predictions and promises usually concerned some aspect of the Day of the Lord. This phase of redemptive history will be our special focus in chapter nine, and so we will reserve any further comments on this core concept until then.

For Further Discussion:

Why is a study of OT prophets important for modern Christians?

Why is it so important to establish the uniqueness of the Hebrew prophets vis-à-vis their pagan counterparts?

Does prophecy continue in our day? If so, are there any differences from the OT prophets?

How should modern Christians seek guidance from the Lord?

Why is it so important today to know the tests for false prophets?

What spiritual lessons have you learned from the messages of the OT prophets?

For Further Reading:

Barton, John. "Prophecy (Postexilic Hebrew Prophecy)," in vol. 5 of *The Anchor Bible Dictionary*, pp. 489-495. Edited by David Noel Freedman. 6 vols. New York: Doubleday, 1992. Standard survey written from a historical-critical perspective.

Blenkinsopp, Joseph. *A History of Prophecy in Israel.*, rev. and enl. ed. Louisville, KY: Westminster John Knox, 1996. Written from a historical-critical perspective, but containing helpful background and observations.

Brueggemann, Walter. "The Prophet as Mediator," in *Theology of the Old Testament*, pp. 622-649. Minneapolis: Fortress, 1997. Stimulating work by a leading OT scholar in the confessional tradition.

Bullock, C. Hassell. *An Introduction to the Old Testament Prophetic Books,* pp. 9-36. Chicago: Moody, 1986. A fine survey of the literature from an evangelical perspective.

Fee, Gordon D., and Douglas Stuart. *How to Read the Bible for All Its Worth,* 2d ed., pp. 165-186. Grand Rapids: Zondervan, 1993. Helpful guidelines for interpreting and applying the prophetic literature.

Freeman, Hobart E. *An Introduction to the Old Testament Prophets*, pp. 11-132. Chicago: Moody, 1968. This is a fine overview of Hebrew prophecy. Tragically, the author himself became a false prophet in his later years of ministry near Fort Wayne, Indiana, and was responsible for the deaths of several members of his congregation when he forbade them to consult medical doctors.

Grudem, W. A. "Prophecy, Prophets," in *New Dictionary of Biblical Theology*, pp. 701-710. Edited by T. Desmond Alexander and Brian S. Rosner. Downers Grove: InterVarsity, 2000.

Heschel, Abraham. *The Prophets*. 2 vols. New York: Harper, 1962. Insightful book written by an outstanding Jewish scholar.

Huffmon, H. B. "Prophecy (Ancient Near Eastern)," in vol. 5 of *The Anchor Bible Dictionary*, pp. 477-482. Edited by David Noel Freedman. 6 vols. New York: Doubleday, 1992. Helpful on the background of prophecy in the ANE.

Kaiser, Jr., Walter C. *Toward an Old Testament Theology*. Chs. 11-15. Grand Rapids: Zondervan, 1978.

MacRae, A. A. "Prophets and Prophecy," in vol. 4 of *The Zondervan Pictorial Encyclopedia of the Bible*, pp. 875-903. Edited by Merrill C. Tenney. 5 vols. Grand Rapids: Zondervan, 1975, 1976. Very helpful overview of the entire topic.

Martens, Elmer A. *God's Design: A Focus on Old Testament Theology*, pp. 148–156, 171–174, 186–189, 197–223. Grand Rapids: Baker, 1981.

Matthews, Victor H. *Social World of the Hebrew Prophets*. Peabody, Mass.: Hendrickson, 2001. Helpful for locating the prophets within their cultural milieu.

Schmitt, John J. "Prophecy (Preexilic Hebrew Prophecy)," in vol. 5 of *The Anchor Bible Dictionary*, pp. 482-488. Edited by David Noel Freedman. 6 vols. New York: Doubleday, 1992. Treats the material from a historical-critical perspective.

Smith, Gary V. "Prophet," in vol. 3 of *The International Standard Bible Encyclopedia*, pp. 986-1004. Edited by Geoffrey W. Bromiley. 4 vols. Grand Rapids: Eerdmans, 1979. Perhaps the single best introduction to the subject. Written by an evangelical scholar.

Smith, Gary V. *The Prophets as Preachers*. Nashville: Broadman & Holman, 2000.

Von Rad, Gerhard. *The Message of the Prophets*. New York: Harper & Row, 1962, 1965. Classic work employing a tradition-history methodology.

Westermann, Claus. *Basic Forms of Prophetic Speech*. Translated by Hugh Clayton White. Philadelphia: Westminster, 1967. Classic work on the rhetorical and literary aspects of prophecy.

Wood, Leon J. *The Prophets of Israel*, pp. 13–131. Grand Rapids: Baker, 1979. Now available in paperback (1998).

Endnotes

1. I am greatly indebted to these scholars for the following discussion: J. A. Motyer, "Prophecy, Prophets," *NBD* (1963), pp. 1036–1044; A. A. MacRae, "Prophets and Prophecy," *ZPED*, 4:875–903; Hobart E. Freeman, *An Introduction to the Old Testament Prophets* (Chicago: Moody, 1968), pp. 11–132; Gary V. Smith, "Prophet; Prophecy," *ISBE* 3:986-1004; Leon J. Wood, *The Prophets of Israel* (Grand Rapids: Baker, 1979), pp. 13–131; F. B. Huey, Jr., *Yesterday's Prophets for Today's World* (Nashville: Broadman, 1980); C. Hassell Bullock, *An Introduction to the Old Testament Prophetic Books* (Chicago: Moody, 1986), pp. 9–36.

2. The following discussion relies on Robert D. Culver, "*Nāvî*," *TWOT*, 2:823–824; "*Hōzeh*," *TWOT*, 1:275; "*Rō'eh*," *TWOT*, 2:823–824 and Karl Heinrich Rengstorf, "*Prophētēs*," *Theological Dictionary of the New Testament*, trans. Geoffrey W. Bromiley (Grand Rapids: Eerdmans, 1964–1976), 6:796–812.

3. *How to Read*, pp. 167–170.

4. Abraham J. Heschel expresses it this way:

> The prophet is a person, not a microphone. He is endowed with a mission, with the power of a word not his own that accounts for his greatness—but also with temperament, concern, character, and individuality. As there was no resisting the impact of divine inspiration, so at times there was no resisting the vortex of his own temperament. The word of God reverberated in the voice of man (*The Prophets*, 2 vols. [New York: Harper, 1962], 1:x).

5. See Joseph Blenkinsopp, *A History of Prophecy in Israel* (Philadelphia: Westminster, 1983), pp. 38–46, especially p. 42 where he observes: "It appears, then, that little importance was attached to the life, activity, and station prior to the commissioning. . . ."

6. See on this G. Pettinato, "The Royal Archives of Tell Mardikh-Ebla," *BA* 39/2 (May 1976): 44–52.

7. As C. F. Keil points out:

> Elisha may perhaps have come to the neighbourhood of the army at the instigation of the Spirit of God, because the distress of the kings was to be one means in the hand of the

Lord, not only of distinguishing the prophet in the eyes of Joram, but also of pointing Joram to the Lord as the only true God ("The Books of the Kings," in *Biblical Commentary on the Old Testament*, 25 vols. [Grand Rapids: Eerdmans, repr. 1950], 6:303–304).

8. See further D. E. Anne, "Divination," *ISBE*, 1:971–974.

9. For examples of rituals, incantations, oracular prophecies, and omens see *ANET*, pp. 325–358, 441–451, 497, 604–606.

10. As an example of the kind of unity one finds in the books of the prophets see Paul R. House, *The Unity of the Twelve* (Sheffield: Almond Press, 1990).

11. See further Stuart, *How to Read*, pp. 165–167.

12. See further the discussion of Bernard Ramm, *Protestant Christian Evidences* (Chicago: Moody, 1953), pp. 81–124. Ramm's approach is interesting because he accepts, for the sake of argument, the dating of liberal critics for the various predictive prophecies he selects. Even with this stricture he makes an impressive case.

13. See Blenkinsopp, *History of Prophecy*, pp. 86–87.

14. See Josh McDowell, *Evidence that Demands a Verdict*, rev. ed. (San Bernardino, CA: Here's Life Publishers, 1979), pp. 166–167.

15. For a defense of this way of viewing the prophets, see E. C. Lucas, "Covenant, Treaty, and Prophecy," *Themelios* 8/1 (September 1982): 19–25. Earlier studies arguing the same point are by J. A. Thompson, *The Ancient Near Eastern Treaties and the Old Testament* (London: Tyndale, 1964), pp. 29–31; Kenneth A. Kitchen, *Ancient Orient and Old Testament* (Chicago: InterVarsity, 1966), pp. 90–102; id., *The Bible in Its World: The Bible and Archaeology Today* (Downers Grove: InterVarsity 1977), pp. 79–85; Elmer A. Martens, *God's Design: A Focus on Old Testament Theology* (Grand Rapids: Baker, 1981), pp. 148–156.

16. For an excellent treatment of this issue, see Douglas Stuart, "The Old Testament Prophets' Self Understanding of Their Prophecy," *Themelios* 6/1 (September 1980): 9–14.

17. Gary V. Smith has a helpful discussion of this issue in "Prophet; Prophecy," *ISBE*, 3:995–996.

18. See further on this Wood, *Prophets of Israel*, pp. 102–104.

chapter 9

Eschatology of the Old Testament

(Scripture reading: Joel 2:1–11, 28–3:21; Amos 5:18–20; 9:11–15; Isaiah 2; 11; 13; 24–25; 32:1–8; 34–35; 42:1–9; 49:1–7; 50:4–11; 52:13–53:12; 61:1–11; Jeremiah 23:5–8; 25:30–38; 30–31; 33; Ezekiel 20:30–44; 36–40:4; 43:1–5; 47:1–12; Daniel 7; 12; Hosea 13:14; Micah 5:1–5; Zechariah 12–14; Malachi 4:1–3)

Leading Questions:

Why is a study of the eschatology of the OT important for us today?

What are the two broad categories of OT eschatology?

What time expression in the OT is a primary vehicle for studying eschatology?

What do we mean by the dual aspects of the Day of the Lord?

Who are the three eschatological figures in the OT and how are they treated in the NT?

What are the four basic approaches to the prophecies of the return and restoration of Israel?

What are the arguments for taking these prophecies literally?

According to the OT what are the basic components of a human being?

What is death and why does it occur?

What was the earlier view of the OT writers about the place and condition of the dead?

How and why did this change?

Why is a study of life after death so vital today?

Introduction

This chapter deals with a topic of vital interest to every human being: What does the future hold for the cosmos and for the individual? The theological term used for this subject is eschatology. Eschatology means literally "a study of last things" (from *eschatos*, "last," and *logos* referring to a rational study of something), and is the branch of theology that is concerned with the ultimate or last things, such as death, judgment, heaven and hell. Thus we turn our attention to the final consummation of God's kingdom program. We get a glimpse of the fulfillment of the petition Jesus taught his disciples to pray: "Your kingdom come, your will be done on earth as it is in heaven" (Mt 6:10).

This subject holds great importance for human beings because it influences the way we live. As Paul Jewett has said: "Life without faith is empty, and faith without hope is impossible."[1] Humans find reasons to be hopeful; many of these are not well-founded, but the human psyche is such that something, be it ever so fragile, must be held onto to justify existence. It may be something quite mundane, like Annie who consoled herself with the thought that the sun would come up tomorrow; it may be something more personal, like a profound religious experience, leading to a conviction of a God who cares for and guides one's life. Whereas the object of hope varies widely, the vast majority of people find some reason to be hopeful, in spite of the inevitable struggles of life. Only when hope ebbs away do we have a sufficient condition for suicide. Suicide is extremely rare in the OT. Only those individuals who lose all hope commit, or even contemplate, suicide. The reason is that biblical faith engenders hope. In contrast to the biblical culture, however, suicide is the third leading cause of death for young people between the ages of 15-24 in the United States. This shocking statistic should awaken the church to the importance of anchoring young people in a biblical view of life and death (cf. Job 13:15).[2]

The importance of eschatology becomes even more urgent in our day, when it is remembered that modern naturalism and secular humanism project a definite eschatology. This eschatology is hardly one of hope; on the contrary, it projects a bleak and empty future—death for the cosmos and death for the individual. Various scenarios are sketched for the future of the solar system: we may anticipate that, in the very remote future, the sun, at last, totally consumes its vast supply of fuel—the result is a frozen earth with no life-forms surviving—or, the earth may be bombarded by an errant asteroid and blown to bits! As for the individual, secularism offers no hope of life after death; when you are dead, you are dead—you simply cease to exist. Naturalism assumes that the universe is a chance happening. As such there is no premeditated meaning in the process and, obviously, no ultimate meaning in the outcome. If consciously adopted as a worldview, it is no surprise that behavior follows a pattern of self-centeredness. After all, "you only go around once, so go for the gusto!"

Over against such pessimism or hedonism, the Bible radiates with hope for the future; indeed, the Bible declares repeatedly that earth's best days are ahead. There will be a new earth enduring forever—a veritable return to paradise. This is the picture of God's tomorrow for his people and planet that we now examine.

Eschatology in the OT falls into three broad categories: cosmic, national, and individual.[3] National eschatology, of course, focuses on the future of God's people, Israel. But there are also indications that Gentiles who trust in the Lord experience the grace and blessings of the kingdom. Indeed, some passages even depict blessing upon the entire created order in the days to come. We may thus speak of a *cosmic eschatology* in the message of the prophets. In addition, there are a few passages indicating the outcome for individuals, addressing the persistent question of whether there is life after death.

The Fundamentals of Eschatology

The bulk of eschatological passages in the OT focus on the destiny of God's people. This destiny becomes the hope of Israel. The basis of the hope rests squarely on the covenant made with Abraham and his seed (Ge 12:1–7, cf. ch. four). The following point is fundamental for understanding the eschatology of the Bible: *the Abrahamic Covenant forms the outline of God's redemptive plan.* The Lord's promise of an heir, an inheritance, and a heritage constitutes the essence of God's future for his people. In a real sense, the rest of the Bible, after Genesis 12, simply elaborates God's great, covenantal promise to the patriarchs (see ch. four). In the following discussion we demonstrate how this is so.

It is important to stress another truth about God's eschatological blessing. In no sense may the people of God congratulate themselves on their achievement. Enjoyment of God's favor and blessing does not depend upon human resources, ingenuity, merit or spirituality—everything is dependent upon God's undeserved grace and mercy (see Dt 7:7–8; 9:6; 31:27). As we saw in chapter five, only as God himself intervenes in a powerful display of his might are people redeemed. Left to themselves, human beings are helpless and without hope. No wonder that, at the consummation of all things, the redeemed never tire of praising their gracious God (see Rev 5:9–10; 7:10; 19:1)!

The eschatology of the people of God may be likened to a drama with several acts. As we have already tried to make clear in chapters six and seven, the unfolding kingdom of God provides the story line for the great redemptive drama. What we wish to do now is isolate three key components of the drama that enable us to appreciate more fully what God has in store for his people. First, we look at the focal point of the eschatological drama. This is a temporal expression incorporating some of the leading actions of the end times. The expression is "the Day of the Lord." Secondly, we briefly examine three characters in the cast who play leading roles in the eschatological drama. We will discover a surprising fact about these three "stars" of the play. Thirdly, we direct attention to one of the climactic moments in the eschatological drama, namely, the return and restoration of the people of Israel to their national homeland.

The Focal Point of the Eschatological Drama: The Day of the Lord

Background

The expression, "Day of the Lord," refers to an extended period of time (not a mere 24 hours) during which the redemptive purposes of God are fully achieved.[4] The term, or its equivalent, is found throughout the prophetic books. The biblical writers may simply say "in that day" (Am 9:11; Joel 1:15) or "the days are coming" (Am 9:13). However it is phrased, the notion that the God of Israel finally intervenes and judges the wicked and rewards the righteous is a major doctrine in the faith of Israel.

Scholars are not agreed on the origins and background of the expression.[5] Some see it as stemming from the creation account in six days with a day of rest culminating the sequence. The Day of the Lord would correspond to a sort of new creation capped off with a perpetual

Sabbath rest. Others look at the practice of holy war and draw a parallel. Just as Israel under Joshua was charged with exterminating the wicked Canaanites, so, in the Day of the Lord, the angelic army will finally eliminate all evildoers from the glorious kingdom of God.[6]

More important, however, than determining possible backgrounds for the expression is its actual usage in Scripture. It would appear that Amos is the first biblical writer to use the expression (ca. 760 B.C.). In Amos 5:18–20, he warns his audience about the consequences of the Day of the Lord: "Woe to you who long for the day of the LORD! Why do you long for the day of the LORD? That day will be darkness, not light." Evidently Amos corrects a misunderstanding on the part of his listeners about what the day entails. From this we may infer that the expression and concept were already known before the preaching of Amos. Just how much earlier the idea was current in Israel is impossible to say given the evidence we have. Following on the heels of Amos, prophets like Hosea, Isaiah and Micah, all from the eighth century, likewise employ the expression and flesh out more details concerning the events connected with it.

We return for a moment to Amos and his preaching. The misunderstanding Amos attacks concerns the doctrine of election. The majority of Israelites apparently assume that Israel's election at Mount Sinai guarantees future blessing in the Day of the Lord, regardless of one's morality. This is the dichotomy between faith and ethics we discussed in chapters six and seven. Amos attacks such presumption straight on and in memorable language. In stark contrast to their rosy expectations, Amos warns of darkness and gloom. Instead of security and prosperity, there will be terror and total loss for covenant violators.[7]

To make his point, Amos uses an extended word picture drawn from his experience as a shepherd. He depicts a person who manages to escape the clutches of both a lion and a bear, only to fall prey to the deadly bite of a middle eastern viper living in the cracks of the mud-plastered wall (5:19). Just when he thinks himself safe, disaster falls. Amos roundly warns his listeners: you are living an illusion; the Lord is about to bring judgment upon those who think they are secure from all harm. In short, Amos tries to shake Israel out of a delusion. The Day of the Lord will be a day of blessing and joy only for those who are walking in a covenant relationship—who live out their faith, not pretend about or presume upon their supposed faith.

About a generation after Amos, Isaiah of Jerusalem adds to the landscape of the Day of the Lord, by sketching a scene of cosmic judgment. In graphic and horrifying language, Isaiah says:

> Men will flee to caves in the rocks and to holes in the ground from dread of the LORD and the splendor of his majesty, when he rises to shake the earth. In that day men will throw away to the rodents and bats their idols of silver and idols of gold, which they made to worship. They will flee to caverns in the rocks and to the overhanging crags from dread of the LORD and the splendor of his majesty, when he rises to shake the earth (Isa 2:19–21).

Another passage from Isaiah graphically illustrates the universal scope of this Day of the Lord:

> See, the day of the LORD is coming—a cruel day, with wrath and fierce anger—to make the land desolate and destroy the sinners within it. The stars of heaven and their constellations will not show their light. The rising sun will be darkened and the moon will not give its light. I will punish the world for its evil, the wicked for their sins. I will put an end to the arrogance of the haughty and will humble the pride of the ruthless. I will make man scarcer than pure gold, more rare than the gold of Ophir. Therefore I will make the heavens tremble; and the earth will shake from its place at the wrath of the LORD Almighty, in the day of his burning anger (Isa 13:9–13).

Other prophets like Joel (Joel 3:2) and Zephaniah (Zep 3:8) make clear that all nations of the earth will fall under the judgment of the Lord Almighty on that great day. Indeed, as Isaiah 24:21 states: "In that day the LORD will punish the powers in the heavens above and the kings on the earth below." We are thus justified in using the term cosmic to describe the extent of the activity of this time period.

What we observe, then, is a steady development of the notion of the Day of the Lord. Beginning with Amos in the mid-eighth century and continuing down to the end of the fifth century (see Mal 4:1–6), the various prophets add details and perspectives on this climactic period in the history of redemption.

The Dual Character of the Day of the Lord

1. One of the interesting features of this time period is its *dual nature*. The Day of the Lord, like a coin, has two sides. This may be seen first in reference to the quality of life experienced at the time. As we noted above, Amos rudely awakens his audience from their misplaced security and complacency; he warns them that the day will be darkness and misery for the wicked—and the Israelites qualify as the wicked! Yet when we get to Amos 9:11–15, we read a glowing description of paradise on earth. Clearly, those who experience this aspect of the Day of the Lord are the righteous—those putting their complete trust and confidence in the God of Israel, and who comply with the covenant stipulations of Mount Sinai (cf. 5:4–6, 14–15, 24). In short, the side of the coin one experiences during this epic period is a function of one's relationship to the sovereign Lord. The righteous have nothing to fear and everything to gain; the wicked have everything to fear and nothing to gain.

2. There is another aspect to the dual nature of the Day of the Lord. This has to do with whether or not the description of that day includes a *messianic figure* as the key actor. That is, some passages feature a descendant of the house of David as the primary agent who accomplishes the purposes of God during that time. In contrast, other passages simply ascribe the activity to the God of Israel, with no mention of a messianic figure.

We can illustrate this difference by comparing several passages. In Isaiah 2:1–5 we have a magnificent vision of Jerusalem as the center of a peaceful world, where all nations come to worship the God of Jacob. It is this God of Jacob who transforms the world into a safe and secure place ("He will teach us. . . . He will judge between the nations and will settle disputes for many people . . ."). On the other hand, Isaiah 11:1–16, which seemingly describes the same general time period, features a "shoot . . . from the stump of Jesse . . . the Root of Jesse" who will accomplish the transformation of nature and restore Israel to her land. This Spirit-endowed Root of Jesse is clearly the Messiah. Other passages could be cited which likewise display this dual character.

The resolution to this duality does not occur until the NT. Only with the new revelation concerning the person of Jesus Christ do we understand how these two kinds of passages relate to each other: Jesus Christ, the son of David, *is* the Lord!

Features of the Day of the Lord

The following are selected features of this climactic phase of the kingdom of God.

1. Obviously, the Day of the Lord cannot be a 24-hour period. When all the passages dealing with this "day" are examined, we realize that it covers an extended period of time. Our discussion of the days of Genesis 1 already mentioned the fact that the Hebrew word *yôm* does have, in certain contexts, an extended meaning of "time," or "era."[8] The Day of the Lord, then, is an extended period of time in which God concludes human history and ushers in the final form of the kingdom. Most passages describing the Day of the Lord focus upon the upheavals and judgments preceding the triumphant appearance of the New Jerusalem. In NT language, this time period is called the "great tribulation" (cf. Rev 7:14). We quote Isaiah's vision of this terrifying prospect:

> See, the LORD is going to lay waste the earth and devastate it: he will ruin its face and scatter its inhabitants. . . . The earth is broken up, the earth is split asunder, the earth is thoroughly shaken. The earth reels like a drunkard, it sways like a hut in the wind; so heavy upon it is the guilt of its rebellion that it falls—never to rise again (Isa 24:1, 19–20).

Events or episodes connected to this period include an invasion of Jerusalem followed by the establishment of a worldwide kingdom centered in Jerusalem (Joel 3:9–17; Zep 3:8–13; Zec 12–14 et al.), the national restoration of the nation Israel (Am 9:11–15; Zep 3:14–20; Eze 37), the invasion of Gog and Magog (Eze 38–39), the building of a new temple and re-institution of the priestly and Levitical ministry (Eze 40–44), and the creation of a new heaven and new earth (Isa 65:17–25), to mention but a few. Whether all these should be taken literally is a matter of much dispute, but our purpose here is to show that the agenda for this period is full and seemingly requires more than 24 hours to accomplish.

2. Another feature to be reckoned with involves *prophetic foreshortening*. What we mean is that the prophet views the future as one unified picture. Since everything is future to him or her, the view or perspective

lacks depth; that is, events are combined into one picture, which in fact are widely separated in time. When looking through binoculars into the distance, objects in the foreground appear close to objects in the distance. It is an optical illusion, however, since depth of field is lacking with magnification. To take another example, a great mountain range appears from a distance as a single peak, although in reality it comprises many foothills and intervening valleys with considerable distances between. Similarly, we encounter prophetic passages in which widely-separated events are presented as if they occurred simultaneously.

Two illustrations may suffice. In Joel 1 the prophet describes an imminent invasion of locusts. Locust plagues were the scourge of the ancient Near East resulting in many deaths due to starvation. The reason is that locusts literally devour edible plants. They sometimes came in such numbers that no vegetation to speak of survived their infestation. In the words of Joel, "Surely the joy of mankind is withered away" (Joel 1:12).[9]

What is fascinating about Joel's prophecy, however, is that this swarm of locusts suddenly becomes the army of the Lord rendering judgment upon a disobedient land. "What a dreadful day! For the day of the LORD is near; it will come like destruction from the Almighty" (1:15). In short, the historic locust plague is a harbinger of the final judgments of the Day of the Lord. Joel even prophesies the outpouring of the Holy Spirit on the day of Pentecost "before the coming of the great and dreadful day of the LORD" (2:31). Thus historical events sometimes prefigure the end times, but are presented in such a way that they seem contemporaneous with the end. This is why care must be taken in the interpretation of OT prophecy.

One other example demonstrates prophetic foreshortening. In Isaiah 61: 1–3, the servant of the Lord (see below), proclaims the nature of his ministry. In verse 1 we read of a ministry to the poor and oppressed. This thought continues in the first part of verse 2, but then shifts from deliverance to judgment: "and the day of vengeance of our God. . . ." Now it is precisely this text that Jesus quoted at his hometown synagogue in Nazareth (Lk 4:16–21). What is instructive is the fact that Jesus stopped reading right in the middle of a verse (Isa 61:2). He did not read the phrase referring to vengeance, but instead, sat down and stunned the congregation by announcing, "Today this scripture is fulfilled in your hearing" (Lk 4:21). Jesus' preaching fulfilled the ancient prophecy! His role as judge, however, remains yet future—indeed, we have not yet witnessed it. Again, we see a unified picture in the prophetic witness, where, in fact, there is a sequence of events widely separated in time. A key to sound interpretation lies in a careful and patient reading of the Old and New Testaments as part of one unfolding redemptive history.

3. The third feature of passages dealing with the Day of the Lord relates to the notion of *imminence*. Imminence refers to something about to occur, an event that is impending. The prophets who speak of the Day of the Lord do so with a sense of urgency, because the events of that time are about to unfold. In fact, it is a characteristic of both Testaments that God's decisive acts during the Day of the Lord loom very near. We lift out a few passages to illustrate: "Prepare to meet your God, O Israel. . . . Seek the LORD and live. . . . The time is ripe for my people Israel; I will spare them no longer . . ." (Amos). Joel adds his siren call: "For the day of the LORD is near. . . . Let all who live in the land tremble, for the day of the LORD is coming. It is close at hand. . . ." Of course, many passages in the NT could also be cited manifesting the same sense of imminence for the Day of the Lord Jesus Christ (cf. e.g., Mk 13:32–37; 1Th 5:1–6; Ro 13:12–14; Jas 5:9; Rev 22:7, 20).

This urgent message of imminence challenges each generation: one must be ready to face the divine judgment seat. Complacency is an enemy to spiritual readiness. For modern readers, this involves a tension between the truthfulness of God's Word and historical reality. After all, it has not happened yet! The believer must hold on to both, however. To abandon the authority of Scripture leaves us adrift in a morass of "isms." To close our eyes to historical reality condemns us to subjectivism. Grasping the near and far aspects of the Day of the Lord may assist us in this regard. If judgments in history are harbingers of eschatological judgment, then the imminent appearing of the Judge confronts each and every generation. Furthermore, from God's vantage point, the time span involved is very short indeed. As Peter reminds his readers, "But do not forget this one thing, dear friends: With the Lord a day is like a thousand years, and a thousand years are like a day" (2Pe 3:8).

4. This leads to our fourth observation: both prophet and apostle stress that this day is *certain*. There is no appeal to myth or legend as a means of manipulating behavior. For them the moment of truth breaks upon humanity with the same surety as death and taxes. And when it does, there are two things one can count on: *impartial justice* and *unbounded mercy*. In the words of Amos, "prepare to meet your God . . ." (Am 4:12). Joel

announces the imminent judgment in these words: "for there I will sit to judge all the nations on every side" (Joel 3:12). And, of course, Daniel presents an unforgettable scene:

> As I looked, thrones were set in place, and the Ancient of Days took his seat. . . . His throne was flaming with fire and its wheels were all ablaze. . . . Thousands upon thousands attended him: ten thousand times ten thousand stood before him. The court was seated, and the books were opened" (Dan 7:9–10).

For those who have not repented and cast themselves on the mercy of the Lord, the verdict is just and impartial: "Woe to the wicked! Disaster is upon them! They will be paid back for what their hands have done" (Isa 3:11). "According to what they have done, so will he repay wrath to his enemies and retribution to his foes; he will repay the islands their due" (Isa 59:18). "Your eyes are open to all the ways of men; you reward everyone according to his conduct and as his deeds deserve" (Jer 32:19). But for those who sense their deep need and cry out for forgiveness and pardon the outcome is radically different: "Tell the righteous it will be well with them, for they will enjoy the fruit of their deeds" (Isa 3:10). The righteous are those who despair of their own efforts to gain God's favor; they cast themselves on the living God and seek to conform to the covenant. They are those who, like Abraham, simply believe the Lord and are thus credited with righteousness (cf. Ge 15:6). In the words of the prophet Habakkuk, "the righteous will live by his faith" (Hab 2:4), a text of great importance for the doctrine of justification by faith alone (cf. Ro 1:17; Gal 3:11). The doctrine of final rewards and punishment will be taken up later in the chapter when we discuss individual eschatology.

5. Finally, we must say something about the truly cosmic nature of the Day of the Lord. What are Yahweh's intentions for planet earth? Has he no enduring interest in this blue planet that abounds with the miracle of life? The answer according to the OT is that he has great plans for the planet! Beyond the horrifying judgments of the Day of the Lord, we glimpse a return to paradise. In the imagery of ancient myth, we catch vistas of unparalleled fertility, prosperity, peace, and above all, righteousness. The holiness of God descends upon the cosmos and envelopes it like a bridal veil. The operative word is "new." Isaiah

announces Yahweh's intentions: "Behold, I will create new heavens and a new earth. The former things will not be remembered, nor will they come to mind" (Isa 65:17; cf. 66: 22).

This leads to an important theological consideration. What should be our view toward the present earth? Are we to adopt a consumer attitude since its resources will be renewed in the eschaton? Or, should we rather read the end of Scripture in light of the beginning and vice versa? If we do, only one answer seems consistent with the witness of the OT. We were originally created to be stewards and caretakers of planet earth. We botched it; we have plundered and raped our environment. Surely our Creator Redeemer offers kingdom citizens an opportunity in the history of redemption to start working now on a better alternative. Should we not attempt seriously to carry out the original creation mandate? This would involve protecting and preserving our natural resources and plant and animal life. If the Creator deemed it "good" when he made the incredible variety of living things, how arrogant and presumptuous of us to destroy them. To be sure, this stance may seem pointless at times, and it certainly runs against the grain of our prevailing culture. But is not a part of Christian discipleship being part of a global ecosystem? Evangelicals have typically narrowed the sphere of discipleship to the realm of the personal with unfortunate results. In my opinion, every Christian should be an environmentalist!

Three Figures Who Play a Role in the Eschatological Drama

The Son of David

The first figure we consider is already familiar to us from the chapter on kingship. The promised ideal king from the line of David is a major theme in prophetic literature. Beginning in the promise to David (2Sa 7), we may trace an emerging portrait through prophet and poet. We will not spend much time on this figure, but rather call attention to the treatment in chapters six and seven.[10]

We do, however, wish to point out the background of the term "messiah." In the Hebrew Bible, the verb *māshaḥ* means "to rub with oil," or "to pour oil upon." A derived noun, *māshîaḥ* means "something/ someone anointed." In Hebrew culture, persons and objects set apart for sacred purposes were anointed. The offices of prophet, priest, and king involved installation by means of anointing. In the book of Samuel "the anointed of the Lord" is synonymous with "king" (cf. 1Sa 2:10; 2Sa 22:51). The term *māshîaḥ* is always translated in the NIV as "anointed." In the Greek OT (LXX), *māshîaḥ* is regularly translated by the Greek term *christos*, which, in the Greek NT, the NIV renders as "Christ." It is this latter term that is applied to Jesus of Nazareth by NT writers and which becomes virtually a proper name. In two instances, the Greek NT employs a transliteration of the Hebrew *māshîaḥ*, namely, *messias*, which the NIV translates as "messiah" (Jn 1:41; 4:25). Both of the latter passages also contain an explanatory gloss, *christos*, for readers not understanding the meaning of *messias*.

Even though the English term "messiah" does not occur even once in the NIV of the OT, the notion of an anointed one is of central importance. As we already mentioned, the messianic idea really blossoms in Yahweh's dynastic promise to David (2Sa 7:14), but the primeval history also seems to contain a messianic hope. Thus, in the story of the fall, we read this enigmatic declaration: "And I will put enmity between you and the woman and between your offspring and hers, he will crush your head, and you will strike his heel"(Ge 3:15). Traditional scholarship generally infers from this the future victory of Jesus Christ over Satan at the Cross. Although Satan strikes Jesus' heel (a non-fatal wound), Jesus crushes the head of the serpent (a fatal wound). Many see in this cryptic announcement the "Gospel in a Nutshell." The outcome of this cosmic combat issues in complete victory through the offspring of Eve—Jesus Christ and his people.[11] Believers in Jesus assist in this struggle as they faithfully proclaim the gospel and, as a result, sinners (offspring of the devil) change their allegiance by an act of faith and become children of God. The Apostle Paul depicts the church participating in this epic struggle, as witnessed in the Letter to the Romans: "The God of peace will soon crush Satan under your feet" (Ro 16:20).

Two other passages in the Pentateuch deserve consideration in this regard. In the patriarchal blessing of Jacob (Ge 49), the blessing upon Judah is especially intriguing. "The scepter will not depart from Judah, nor the ruler's staff from between his feet, until he comes to whom it belongs and the obedience of the nations is his" (Ge 49:10). As the *NIVSB* indicates, "Though difficult to translate . . . the verse has been traditionally understood as Messianic. It was initially fulfilled in David, and ultimately in Christ."[12] The other pentateuchal passage, which may have messianic overtones, occurs in the fourth of Balaam's oracles: "I see him, but not now; I behold him, but not near. A star will come out of Jacob; a scepter will rise out of Israel" (Nu 24:17). Again, the *NIVSB* suggests that this prophecy was "perhaps fulfilled initially in David, but ultimately in the coming Messianic ruler. Israel's future Deliverer will be like a star (cf. Rev 22:16) and scepter in his royalty and will bring victory over the enemies of his people."[13]

We conclude this section by noting that one of the key actors in the drama of redemption is the Son of David. Through him the Lord has determined to wrest control of planet earth away from the unlawful usurper, Satan. King David was privileged to be one of the great ancestors and types of this King of kings and Lord of lords.

The Servant of the Lord

Another key actor appears in five passages in Isaiah. This person is styled "the Servant of the Lord." Who is this person? Perhaps the best way to proceed is to draw up a profile based upon these passages.

The five passages we will briefly examine are sometimes called "the Servant Songs" because of their highly lyrical quality and the fact that each one seems to be an independent composition. To complicate matters, throughout Isaiah 40-55, the nation of Israel is styled as Yahweh's servant (Isa 41:8-9; 43:10; 44:1-2, 21; 45:4) and Cyrus the Persian is called Yahweh's shepherd and anointed (Isa 44:23; 45:1). In five passages, however (42:1–9; 49:1–13; 50:4–11; 52:13–53:12; 61:1–4), a seemingly solitary figure plays a leading role in the eschatological drama.[14]

Here are some of the characteristics and accomplishments of this servant:

1) He is elected by the Lord, anointed by the Spirit, and promised success in his endeavor (42:1, 4).
2) Justice is a prime concern of his ministry (42:1, 4).
3) His ministry has an international scope (42:1, 6).
4) God predestined him to his calling (49:1).
5) He is a gifted teacher (49:2).
6) He experiences discouragement in his ministry (49:4).
7) His ministry extends to the Gentiles (49:6).

8) The servant encounters strong opposition and resistance to his teaching, even of a physically violent nature (49:5–6).
9) He is determined to finish what God called him to do (49:7).
10) The servant has very humble origins with little outward prospects for success (53:1–2).
11) He experiences suffering and affliction (53:3).
12) The servant accepts vicarious and substitutionary suffering on behalf of his people (53:4–6, 12).
13) He is put to death after being condemned (53:7–9).
14) Incredibly, he comes back to life and is exalted above all rulers (53:11–12; 52:15).

Of course, when Christians read this résumé, they do so from within a well-established tradition; there can be little doubt that the earliest Christians confessed and contended that the servant was Jesus of Nazareth (cf. Ac 8:26–38). Can this view stand up under close scrutiny? Several rival views put forward competing claims:

1. The autobiographical view. Some scholars insist that the prophet himself is the servant. That is, prophets were part of that noble company known as "my servants the prophets (Jer 7:25; 25:4; 26:5; 35:15; 44:4)." Of course, this view is generally held by scholars who also maintain that this section of Isaiah was written by an unknown, exilic prophet, so-called Deutero-Isaiah, well after the eighth century Isaiah of Jerusalem.[15] At any rate, "Servant of the Lord" was unquestionably one of the titles bestowed upon Yahweh's spokespersons (see ch. 8).

The problem with this view (already broached by the Ethiopian eunuch, Ac 8:34) lies in the disparity between what is said of the servant and what was historically true of any prophet of Yahweh. How can a prophet suffer on behalf of the sins of the entire people, much less his own sins? Though martyrdom was not unknown to the prophetic company (cf. 1Ki 18:4, 13; 2Ch 24:21–22), the death of the Servant of the Lord in Isaiah 53 functions in a uniquely redemptive manner. Furthermore, the passage in Isaiah 53 seems to point to a remarkable return to life and exaltation above all powers and rulers. The gap between what is proclaimed and what actually happened to Deutero-Isaiah stretches credulity!

2. The biographical or historical view. This position is similar to the above, except that some other individual is designated as the servant—

such as Uzziah, Hezekiah, Josiah (godly kings of Judah), or Zerrubabel of the exilic era. The same objection holds for this alternative, namely, the distance between prophecy and fulfillment. Can one be content with saying that we have an example of hyperbole, that is, deliberate exaggeration to make a point? This does not seem consistent with either the intent of the passage or the character of the prophetic witness in general.

3. The collective or corporate view. Probably the majority view among liberal biblical scholars, and certainly Jewish scholars, is the notion that Israel as an entity, or a righteous remnant within Israel, is the servant. This is often connected to the idea of corporate solidarity whereby an individual sums up and represents a larger group. In this case Israel is pictured as an individual who suffers on behalf of others and these sufferings have a redemptive or cleansing effect, not only for the nation Israel, but, in some sense, for Gentiles as well.

While there is a certain plausibility in this identification, severe problems arise: How can Israel have a ministry of restoring itself as required by 49:6? How can one speak meaningfully of death and restoration to life (resurrection?) as applied to Israel in the context of atonement? Later we will argue for the national restoration of Israel, and, as we have already seen, Ezekiel portrays that as a bodily resurrection; but that is a far cry from a resurrection resulting in the justification of sins.

4. The messianic or Christological view. In our opinion, the view that best fits the evidence is the messianic identification of the servant. Interestingly, a Jewish Rabbi of the 1st century A.D., Jonathan ben Uzziel, held that Isaiah 42 and 53 referred to the Messiah. Certainly, the early Christians identified this servant with Jesus (cf. Mt 3:17; 8:17; 12:15–21; 26:24, 63, 67; 27:38; Lk 9:51; et al.). A careful study of the Gospels indicates that they followed Jesus in this identification; that is, he viewed himself and his ministry in terms of the Servant of the Lord. This is especially evident when one compares Luke 4:16–21 with Isaiah 61:1–2. The historic position of the Christian Church has been uniform on this point until the rise of theological liberalism: Jesus is the servant about whom Isaiah prophesied. In the final analysis, the Spirit of Christ witnesses with our spirits that Jesus is the one about whom the prophet spoke in these matchless pen portraits.[16]

Note, however, that this servant is never explicitly called the Son of David, although there are a few royal features mentioned (cf. 42:4; 52:13). The servant of the Lord suddenly appears on the scene of redemptive history, seemingly unrelated to any other figure in the preceding history. For those living during the time of the old covenant, there would be few clues that this servant should be identified with the great royal figure of the house of David. This puzzling feature deepens when we consider our third leading actor.

The Son of Man

Over 90 times in the book of Ezekiel, the prophet is called "son of man." The expression "son of man" is a curious one in Hebrew. Being somewhat deficient in adjectives, the Hebrew language compensates by employing two nouns together (called a construct state) in order to convey the notions of nature, quality, character, or condition. The second noun in this construction is in the genitive case and modifies the first noun adjectivally. In Exodus 4:10, Moses says "I have never been eloquent." The adjective "eloquent" is a combination of the Hebrew nouns "man" and "words," literally, "a man of words." This construct relation is best rendered into English with an adjective such as eloquent, or with an adjective-noun combination such as "ready speaker," or "good speaker." In our example, the Hebrew construct phrase (*bĕn-'ādām*) "son of man," conveys the notion of humanness or humanity. The *Good News Bible* renders it "mortal man," the *New English Bible* as "Man," whereas the *NIV* prefers to stick with a more literal rendering "son of man." To a native speaker, the expression would serve to identify the referent, in this case, Ezekiel, with a larger class, namely, human beings. The phrase draws attention to the mortality, frailty, and limitations that go with being human.

The question that engages our attention is why this expression should be used almost exclusively of Ezekiel and no other. In the context of the book of Ezekiel, one discerns three major roles in which the son of man plays a part: (1) passages in which Ezekiel symbolically bears the punishment of Israel and Judah (4:4–8; cf. chapter eight on symbolic actions); (2) passages in which Ezekiel performs the role of a judge (20:4; 22:2; 23:36); (3) passages in which Ezekiel performs both functions of prophet and priest (passim). As Hassell Bullock points out, these three roles are precisely the ones that Jesus of Nazareth actually performs.[17] It is as if Ezekiel, in his ministry, anticipates the one who consistently refers to himself as "Son of Man." Further points of comparison are impressive: zeal for a purified temple, emphasis on the Holy Spirit, teaching concerning the resurrection, use of parables and allegories. Perhaps Ezekiel was especially called as a prophet to be a harbinger of that one who was a priest after the order of Melchizedek and the prophet who was the final word of God to sinful humanity. Whether, however, anyone would have made this connection is doubtful. The NT itself does not make any explicit mention of Ezekiel in this regard. The correspondences are fascinating just the same.

There is one passage in the OT, however, in which the phrase "son of man" assumes major importance for determining its meaning on the lips of Jesus. This is the celebrated Daniel 7:13–14:

> In my vision at night I looked, and there before me was one like a son of man, coming with the clouds of heaven. He approached the Ancient of Days and was led into his presence. He was given authority, glory and sovereign power; all peoples, nations and men of every language worshiped him. His dominion is an everlasting dominion that will not pass away, and his kingdom is one that will never be destroyed.

In the context of Daniel 7, this scene occurs in connection with the destruction of the world empires and the final judgment. This appears to be the consummation of the kingdom of God. The sovereign God entrusts all authority to this "one like a son of man."

The description of this son of man in vv. 13–14 deserves further discussion. We note several salient features of the scene:

1. Arrival at the scene. The son of man comes on the "clouds of heaven." The description hardly applies to a mere mortal. Only angelic beings or a divine being could be so depicted. Thus we have a human-like figure who possesses a divine-like capability.

2. Access to the throne. Admission to the throne of an ancient oriental king was strictly regulated and restricted. No one simply presented herself or himself and approached for an audience unless a strict protocol had been followed. One may recall the story of Queen Esther and King Xerxes (Est 5). She risked her life even appearing unbidden at the entrance to the throne room. The amazing thing about this throne room scene in Daniel 7 is the easy and uncontested access this individual has to the throne—he is admitted right into God's presence. There can be only one explanation: he possesses equal standing and dignity with the great king himself. The son of man is a divine being.

3. *Ascription of worship*. Even more compelling is the fact that worship is directed toward this son of man right in the presence of God, and there is no protest; indeed, there is every indication that God approves! Only if this individual were himself God could such a procedure be possible, since the first commandment clearly forbids the worship of any other god, save the God of Israel.

4. *Acceptance of universal sovereignty*. The son of man exercises the kind of sovereignty that only God possesses. The whole world is his kingdom.

5. *Attribute of eternity*. The kingdom ruled over by the son of man partakes of the attribute of eternity—something only God possesses. It can be inferred from this that he too is eternal. From all the above, one can only conclude that the son of man, though appearing in form as a human being, also possesses divine attributes. There is no attempt to resolve this seeming contradiction. Only the NT revelation of Jesus Christ will eventually provide a way of reconciling this puzzle: *the Son of Man is also the Son of God.*

In light of the above analysis, it is of great interest to observe that one time in his earthly ministry Jesus referred to this passage and virtually identified himself as the Son of Man. The occasion was his trial before the high priest, Caiaphas. According to Mark's account (Mk 14:53–65), there were unsuccessful attempts to condemn Jesus on the basis of false witnesses. When these witnesses were clearly seen to be inconsistent, the case against Jesus was in danger of collapsing. To prevent this, the high priest, in opposition to later Jewish law, personally intervened in the questioning procedure. He asked Jesus if he was the Messiah (v. 61). Jesus responded that he was and then dropped a bombshell on the courtroom. He proceeded to tell the high priest that he would "see the Son of Man sitting at the right hand of the Mighty One and coming on the clouds of heaven." (v. 62). The high priest tore his robes as a sign that blasphemy had been committed and the Sanhedrin passed a verdict of "worthy of death." (vv. 63–64). The high priest and Sanhedrin understood

Jesus to be claiming the majesty and authority that belong to God alone.[18] The irony is that they were quite correct—Jesus was and is God incarnate.

There is one more observation that should be made about Daniel 7. The angel interpreted the great statue vision for Daniel and concluded by indicating that the saints of the Most High would receive the kingdom (vv. 18, 22). This truth is taught by the NT in several passages (see 1Co 6:2–3; Mt 5:5; 19:28; Ro 8:17; Rev 1:6; 2:26; 3:21; 5:10; 11:15; 17:14; 19:14–16; 20:4–6). As we have seen earlier, the Lord shares his sovereignty with his people who rule in his name. Thus we have in Daniel 7 the twin notions of the vindication of the saints and their sharing in his glory.

Conclusion

As we survey these three figures who appear in the drama of redemption, we suddenly realize a startling fact—nowhere in the OT is a connection made between them. If we had only the OT, it is not likely that we would identify them as one and the same person. But that is exactly what the NT does! In the NT there is an amazing congruence in which the three, seemingly independent figures, merge into a composite portrait of one superlative figure—Jesus of Nazareth. Thus Jesus is the promised Son of David, the mysterious Servant of the Lord, and the majestic Son of Man. All three titles and pen portraits appear in the NT and unerringly point to Jesus as their ultimate fulfillment.[19]

The Restoration of Israel

We come now to a very controversial issue. Christians disagree rather strongly over the question of a future restoration for the nation of Israel in her ancestral homeland. We will outline the alternative positions and then defend an affirmative answer. We set out our argument in four theses.

Thesis One: The Scriptures that predict a national regathering and restoration of Israel will be literally fulfilled.

The restoration passages. At the outset of our discussion, we establish some common ground. All parties in the debate agree that the OT contains a number of passages describing a future regathering and restoration. The precise number varies according to the sentiments of the investigator, but at the very least they number in the dozens.[20]

Rather than give an exhaustive listing, we provide a chronological cross-section from the prophetic writings in order to demonstrate that, from the beginning of the "classical prophets" to the end, each one contributed something to this theme. Thus we offer this sampling:

Amos 9:14–15 (ca. 760 B.C.)

Isaiah 11:10–16 (ca. 730 B.C.)

Zephaniah 3:20 (ca. 640 B.C.)

Jeremiah 32:37–41 (ca. 587 B.C.)

Ezekiel 36:24–25; 39:25–28; (ca. 585 B.C.)

Zechariah 8:1–23; 14:1–20 (ca. 520 B.C.)

For nearly 250 years, there is a steady stream of prophetic teaching to the effect that God would restore Israel in her ancient homeland. Remember that we have only lifted out a mere handful of the total.

The problem of interpretation, however, makes this more than merely a question of citing texts. The question becomes: What do these passages *mean*, especially in light of the fuller revelation of the NT? At least four different responses have been given to the question. The first three are not mutually exclusive answers, and may occur in some combination, whereas the last one considered, the literal fulfillment view, excludes the first three as *inadequate* explanations.

1. Historical fulfillment. These prophecies were all fulfilled in the return of the Jews under Sheshbazzar, Zerubbabel, Ezra, Nehemiah and subsequent decades (cf. Ezr 1–2; 7–8; Ne 2; 7). This position acknowledges the many restoration passages and notes that God did indeed fulfill them historically. These passages demonstrate the validity of predictive prophecy and serve today as examples of the trustworthy nature of Scripture. Since the prophecies are now behind us historically, they should not be taken to refer to some future restoration of Israel, whether the modern State of Israel or some other future manifestation of Jewish nationalism.

To this we offer the following objections. First, a major problem with the above view is that it *minimizes* the language used to describe the return of the exiles. That is, several passages depict a return from "the four quarters of the earth" (Isa 11:12). They assume a *world-wide dispersion* from which Jews would return to their homeland. Clearly this was not the case with the return in the days of Ezra and his contemporaries. That return was from the area known today as Iraq and Kuwait. Even the Pentateuch predicts that Israel will be dispersed to the farthest reaches of the earth. We cite several passages to buttress our point:

> Then the LORD your God will restore your fortunes and have compassion on you and gather you again from all the nations where he scattered you. Even if you have been banished to the most distant land under the heavens, from there the LORD your God will gather you and bring you back. He will bring you to the land that belonged to your fathers, and you will take possession of it. He will make you more prosperous and numerous than your fathers (Dt 30:3).
>
> He will raise a banner for the nations and gather the exiles of Israel; he will assemble the scattered people of Judah from the four quarters of the earth (Isa 11:12).
>
> Lift up your eyes and look about you: All assemble and come to you; your sons come from afar, and your daughters are carried on the arm (Isa 60:4).
>
> Surely the islands look to me; in the lead are the ships of Tarshish, bringing your sons from afar, with their silver and gold, to the honor of the LORD your God, the Holy One of Israel, for he has endowed you with splendor (Isa 60:9).
>
> Therefore say: This is what the Sovereign LORD says: I will gather you from the nations and bring you back from the countries where you have been scattered, and I will give you back the land of Israel again" (Eze 11:17).

The language employed is simply incompatible with a return from a highly localized area.

A second major objection is that, in the restoration passages, there are indications that this return, when it takes place, will be a *permanent* one. The historical returns in the days of Ezra and Nehemiah obviously were not permanent. Jews living in Israel were dispersed in great numbers by the Romans in the period 63 B.C. to A.D. 135. To this very day, more Jews live in Diaspora than in Eretz Israel (the land of Israel), though this may change in the new millennium.[21] We will discuss this further below. We cite in support the following:

> I will plant Israel in their own land, never again to be uprooted from the land I have given them, says the LORD your God (Am 9:15).

> Judah will be inhabited forever and Jerusalem through all generations (Joel 3:20).

2. Rejection view. This view holds that Israel, because of her rejection of Jesus of Nazareth as her Messiah, has *forfeited all the promises of restoration*. In effect, God has discontinued his covenant relationship with Israel and thus is no longer obligated to fulfill her national hopes; *ethnic Israel has been rejected as the people of God.* In support of this, NT passages such as the following have been advanced:

> I say to you that many will come from the east and the west, and will take their places at the feast with Abraham, Isaac and Jacob in the kingdom of heaven. But the subjects of the kingdom will be thrown outside, into the darkness, where there will be weeping and gnashing of teeth (Mt 8:11–12).

> Therefore I tell you that the kingdom of God will be taken away from you and given to a people who will produce its fruit (Mt 21:43).

> Then Paul and Barnabas answered them boldly: "We had to speak the word of God to you first. Since you reject it and do not consider yourselves worthy of eternal life, we now turn to the Gentiles" (Ac 13:46).

But to this we reply: *Israel's apostasy and disobedience were foreseen by the very prophets who spoke of her future repentance and restoration.* In this regard Moses himself outlines the sad course of Israel's history in Deuteronomy 29–32. But as already seen above, this very passage holds out the sure promise of forgiveness and restoration, consequent upon sincere repentance (Dt 30:3–10).

Of even greater significance are the repeated affirmations by God himself that *he would never totally reject his people Israel.* Here we cite both OT and NT texts:

> This is what the LORD says, he who appoints the sun to shine by day, who decrees the moon and stars to shine by night, who stirs up the sea so that its waves roar—the LORD Almighty is his name: "Only if these decrees vanish from my sight," declares the LORD, "will the descendants of Israel ever cease to be a nation before me." This is what the LORD says: "Only if the heavens above can be measured and the foundations of the earth below be searched out will I reject all the descendants of Israel because of all they have done," declares the LORD (Jer 31:35–37).
>
> I ask then: Did God reject his people? By no means! I am an Israelite myself, a descendant of Abraham, from the tribe of Benjamin. . . . Again I ask: Did they stumble so as to fall beyond recovery? Not at all! Rather, because of their transgression, salvation has come to the Gentiles to make Israel envious. . . . I do not want you to be ignorant of this mystery, brothers, so that you may not be conceited: Israel has experienced a hardening in part until the full number of the Gentiles has come in. And so all Israel will be saved, as it is written: "The deliverer will come from Zion; he will turn godlessness away from Jacob. And this is my covenant with them when I take away their sins." . . . for God's gifts and his call are irrevocable (Ro 11:1, 11, 25–27, 29).

The last text, in particular, should give anyone pause before assuming that God is through with his people Israel. While it is true that salvation is available only through Christ, and the Apostle Paul acknowledges that unbelieving Jews are *not* included in the new people of God (Ro 10:2), this does not preclude their future inclusion (Ro 11:26) into the body of Christ, nor their national restoration in their ancient homeland in fulfillment of God's covenant promise to Abraham (Ge 12:7; 13:15, 17; 15:18; 17:8; 23:18; 24:7). In other words, it is not a question of one or the other—spiritual restoration versus national restoration—but of both! *No convincing argument can be brought from the NT demonstrating an incompatibility between these two notions coexisting for the people of Israel.* Israel will be a Christian nation one day![22]

Furthermore, the OT Scriptures indicate that Gentiles will flow to Mount Zion in worship and homage (Isa 2:2–3; 11:10; Zec. 14:16). Does not this presage the influx of Gentiles into the covenant family? *The future land of Israel will belong not only to Jews, but also to Gentile Christians who have been grafted into the new people of God* (cf. Ro 11:17–24). Territorialism has no place in the future phase of the kingdom of God. But it appears that God intends for his ancient covenant people Israel, under the greatly superior conditions and blessings of the new covenant, to be the specially designated caretakers of that historic piece of real estate, the Promised Land.

Is this favoritism? We think not. After all, the history of redemption is characterized throughout by election. God chooses a few to reach the many. His choice eliminates some from crucial roles or benefits. All, in the end, have opportunity to experience God's grace and blessings forever in a new earth (Ro 11:32; cf. Isa 65:17; Rev 21:1–8). Surely, we who are Gentile Christians would not begrudge this people, the natural branches of the olive tree (Ro 11:13–24), the special privilege of being stewards in the Holy Land—the land destined to be the center from which God's glory covers the entire planet (cf. Hab 2:14)!

3. The replacement theory. This view, also called supersecessionism, picks up on the foregoing notion that God rejected Israel because of her unbelief, and asserts that *the Church is the New Israel* and now fulfills, in a spiritual sense, those ancient promises of restoration. The same texts as cited above for the rejection view are enlisted, as well as many other NT texts indicating that in Christ there is a new creation, a new humanity, a new temple, a new people of God (Gal 3:26–29; Ro 4:16; 2Co 5:17; Eph 2:11–22). Passages where a NT writer applies an OT text to the church are marshaled to show that Israel has been displaced by the church (cf. 1Pe 2:9–10). The new Israel is a multi-ethnic, multi-national, spiritual fellowship with no claims to specific territory now, but anticipating an inheritance of the new heavens and new earth after Christ returns.[23]

Objections: This approach must adopt a way of reading the restoration passages that ignores their literal meaning and imports a "spiritual" meaning—sometimes called "spiritualizing." Thus one understands by "Israel," in these restoration passages, the new Israel, the church. This is justified by appealing to the practice of the early church, both in the NT and in the post-apostolic period. Because of Israel's rejection of Christ, and because there has been a *redefinition of Israel,* we should now see these fulfilled in the church.

This way of interpreting the OT passages about restoration poses a serious problem. All other passages are handled in a literal way—taking into account, of course, the fact that authors employ a wide variety of literary devices and that figurative meanings are often intended. None of this, however, is analogous to transposing a known, historical entity into quite another and then saying that the latter takes the place of the former!

Such an approach leads to confusion and misunderstanding. Passages that speak of Israel being regathered and restored to their land can be related to the church only with great ingenuity and imagination. How do we understand the church as the disobedient people of God, who must be regathered from dispersion and then restored both nationally and spiritually? *As Gentile Christians, we have no pre-history as the people of God* (cf. Eph 2:11–12)! A telling criticism of this approach is that passages in the Pentateuch and the Prophets foretelling the covenant curses to befall disobedient Israel are invariably taken as *literal* by the proponents of this approach! How do we justify this inconsistency? How convenient it all seems to assert, on the one hand, that the church inherits all the blessings, and, on the other, the Jews experience all the curses! Jewish scholars may be forgiven if they sniff some anti-Semitic sentiments in all this.

4. Literal fulfillment. It seems to us that a consistently *literal* approach to the OT is the better course. All parties in the debate agree that a strictly literal reading of the prophets leads inevitably to the understanding that Israel will be restored both spiritually and nationally. This position, however, is not free from objections.

Objection: The NT says nothing *explicit* about a restoration of Israel to the land. In this regard we cite a quotation from Paul Jewett expressing this reservation:

> If the final meaning of the OT is revealed in the new, what shall be made of the fact that the NT says nothing of the

> restoration of Israel to the land? Paul, the only NT writer to discuss Israel's future in detail (Ro 9–11), deals only with the spiritual aspect of the promises made to the fathers. For Paul, the salvation of Israel is that they shall be grafted back into the olive tree into which the Gentiles have been grafted, through faith in Christ (Ro 11:13, 36). It seems best, therefore, to take the many prophecies of restoration to the land as having their literal fulfillment in the return under Ezra and Nehemiah, when the Temple and city of Jerusalem were restored; and to construe their final fulfillment in terms of those blessings of a heavenly land, secured to all God's people in Jesus Christ. The present-day return of Israel to Pal. [Palestine] should indeed give one pause, yet it is difficult to see in this interesting development a clear fulfillment of prophecy, as long as the Israeli remain a nation in unbelief and their prosperity in the land is more a tribute to their technological ingenuity than to any divine, supernatural act of eschatological redemption.[24]

To this we reply: it is true there are no explicit statements in the NT about the national restoration of Israel. But, we argue, *the NT does imply restoration.* This assertion requires validation.

We should not be surprised that the NT does not explicitly refer to restoration. After all, one of the agreed upon principles of NT study is that the epistolary literature is highly circumstantial in nature, that is, dependent on a particular situation.[25] Paul's letters, for example, were written to respond to specific needs and problems. Since the letters were sent to primarily Gentile Christian congregations, we would expect, and this is the case, that they reflect issues of concern to them. The national restoration of Israel is hardly a topic one would expect to be of much interest to Gentiles. There are passages where it is clear that problems arose when Jewish and Gentile Christians worshiped together, but these were invariably matters of tradition, ritual, and custom (Gal 4:8-11; Ro 14:1-15:13; Col 2:16-23).

On the other hand, one can surmise that, sooner or later, tensions might arise over Jewish Christian claims that Messiah Jesus would restore the kingdom to Israel. Gentiles might well wonder if this was favoritism. Given the relative brevity of the canon, however, we are not surprised that this issue does not surface in a direct way. As for the Gospels and Acts, by their very nature, they are ill-suited to address the question. They are the foundational documents narrating the saving events of Jesus Christ and the birth of the church. The issue of Israel's restoration can only be inferred from these documents.

That brings us to our second point. There are, in fact, in the Gospels, Acts, and the Letters of Paul *hints of a future national restoration for Israel*. We do not have the space for an in-depth treatment of this issue here, but we can provide an outline response. In this regard, it is fascinating that our "star witness" is none other than a Gentile Christian! It is in the writings of Dr. Luke, author of the gospel bearing his name and the book of Acts, that we detect hints of Israel's restoration.[26] In Luke's gospel, chapters 1–2, *the narratives convey an atmosphere of restorationism*. Elizabeth, Zechariah, Mary, the aged Simeon and Anna all express hopes of national restoration (cf. Lk 1:54–55, 68–74; 2:25, 38). The language and concepts pick up on the prophetic hope of the OT.

The crucial question is whether Jesus corrects or dashes this hope. Nowhere is there convincing evidence that he does the latter; indeed, he promises his disciples that: "You are those who have stood by me in my trials. And I confer on you a kingdom, just as my Father conferred one on me, so that you may eat and drink at my table in my kingdom and sit on thrones, judging the twelve tribes of Israel" (Lk 22:28–30; cf. Mat 19:28).

But, one may object, does not Jesus redefine Israel, so that this prophecy now finds its fulfillment in the Church? The conclusion of the Gospel of Luke and the beginning of Acts are definitive for this question. The two disciples on the way to Emmaus express their disappointment by saying: "but we had hoped that he was the one who was going to redeem Israel (Lk 24:21). Jesus' response is emphatic: "How foolish you are, and how slow of heart to believe *all that the prophets have spoken!* Did not the Christ have to suffer these things and then enter his glory?" (v. 25). [Italics mine.] The "all" must have included national restoration, because the very last question the disciples asked Jesus before his ascension to heaven is recorded in Acts 1:6: "Lord, are you *at this time* going to restore the kingdom to Israel?" [Italics mine.] His response is crucial to this entire debate. Whereas views one through three above generally interpret Jesus' response as a mild rebuke, it seems difficult to deny that Jesus simply redirects their attention to the immediate program of world evangelization:

> It is not for you to know the times or dates the Father has set by his own authority. But you will receive power when the

> Holy Spirit comes on you; and you will be my witnesses in Jerusalem, and in all Judea and Samaria, and to the ends of the earth (v. 7).

This hardly reads like a denial of a cherished dream—simply a postponement until the appointed time in God's kingdom program.

Furthermore, after the descent of the Holy Spirit on the Day of Pentecost, the disciples do not alter their views on this subject. Peter urges his audience in Acts 3:19:

> Repent, then, and turn to God, so that your sins may be wiped out, that the times of refreshing may come from the Lord, and that he may send the Christ, who has been appointed for you—even Jesus. He must remain in heaven until the time comes for God *to restore everything as he promised long ago through his holy prophets.* [Italics mine.]

Luke's views on the restoration of Israel, in all likelihood, were not original to him. His theological mentor seems to have been none other than the Apostle Paul. As we mentioned above, Paul's letters do not directly address the issue of Israel's national restoration. Paul does, however, speak of Israel's future, spiritual restoration in Romans 11:25–27. Whereas there is considerable debate on the precise meaning of the phrase "And so all Israel will be saved," it seems to us that the most probable meaning is that the majority of Jews living at the time of the second coming of Christ will turn in faith to him.[27] They will accept him as Messiah and Savior. What is fascinating is that the very passages of Scripture Paul cites to buttress his assertion are found in contexts describing a national restoration (see Isa 59:20–21; 27:9; Jer 31:33–34).

We think the NT at least implies a future restoration for Israel. Add to this the evidence that first century Pharisaism, the Apostle Paul's background, embraced the hope of national restoration, and one has a presumptive case.[28] Nothing in the NT militates against a literal fulfillment of the restoration prophecies, even when the NT applies OT passages to the new people of God. Typological and analogical use of the OT by the NT hardly justifies evacuating the promises of Israel's restoration of their literal meaning. Thus the redefinition of Israel and the "spiritualizing" of OT prophecies seem to us to be unjustified.[29]

This leads into our third argument. Among evangelical scholars, there is no disagreement that the OT contains prophecies about the Advent of Christ. One thinks here of the birth narratives indicating the place and family of the Messiah (cf. Mic 5:2; Isa 7:14; 9:6–7). The prophecies about his ministry, betrayal, death and resurrection are well-known (cf., e.g., the Servant Songs). Since these passages were literally fulfilled, we think consistency requires treating prophecies relating to the Second Advent in like manner. Pressing this one step further, should we not also interpret those passages speaking of a national restoration literally?

Our fourth argument is simply an appeal to the early church fathers of the post-apostolic period. Whenever they speak about end time events, they invariably include in the agenda the restoration of Israel. This is quite remarkable given the pronounced anti-Judaism so evident in some of these fathers. The fact that they did not abandon this teaching must surely be attributed to its secure place in apostolic tradition.[30] This historical argument supports the more important exegetical arguments above.

Thesis Two: The rise of modern Israel may be the prelude to this final regathering.

Note that this thesis is not stated as a position beyond all doubt. We admit to some uncertainty here. Still, there are some compelling pieces of evidence that cause us to view this remarkable, historical event as a part of redemptive history. We marshall the evidence below.

The uniqueness of the Jewish people and their history. This part of the evidence is so extensive that we can only give the barest outline. We refer the reader to works that examine this in some detail.[31] What is so impressive about the establishment of the State of Israel in 1948 is that one can find *no other parallel in history*. No other people has been exiled from their ancestral homeland for nearly 2,000 years and then returned and reconstituted an autonomous government. Not only that, but no other people has ever revived their ancestral language so that it is the official and daily language of its citizens. This kind of unparalleled phenomenon requires some explanation.[32]

The sheer survival of the Jew over nearly two millennia, against almost overwhelming pressure and persecution, surely says something. Where are the ancient Egyptians, Canaanites, Philistines, Assyrians, Babylonians,

Edomites, Ammonites and Moabites? Their DNA may, of course, exist in the mixed population of the Arab-speaking peoples of the Middle East, but their ancient identities are forever gone. But there are Jews, speaking their ancient tongue and rebuilding their ancient homeland. This is remarkable.

Anti-Semitism. Anti-Semitism refers to hostile attitudes and actions toward Jews simply because they are Jews. The term was coined in 1879 by Wilhelm Marr in Germany. For him anti-Semitism was praiseworthy, since he had an irrational hatred of Jews. Sadly, anti-Semitism existed long before this term was coined. Already in the book of Esther we read of a murderous plot by Haman, the vizier of Persia, to exterminate all Jews. Throughout Jewish history from the fifth century B.C. until the present, anti-Semitism has reared its ugly head. Once again we are unable to go into this area in any detail; instead we refer the student to several helpful sources.[33]

Anti-Semitism appeared in its most virulent form during the Nazi occupation of Europe in World War II. Six million Jews were exterminated in Nazi death camps. This horrifying episode in Jewish history galvanized Jews in their efforts to secure their ancient homeland where they would no longer be a persecuted minority in someone else's country. It also smote the conscience of Western powers and was a major factor in the final push for independence.

Zionism and Arab nationalism. Zionism is the Jewish nationalistic movement. Nurtured by the undying religious hope of a return to Zion, this political movement was born out of the conviction that Jews would never be secure in Diaspora (Jews living outside the land of Israel). Zionism took shape in Czarist Russia where Jews were periodically persecuted and even killed.[34] After an especially bloody persecution in 1882, Leo Pinsker published a book entitled *Auto-Emancipation*, in which he argued for a Jewish State.[35] Theodor Herzl, an Austrian journalist, took it a step further. While covering a trial in France, in which a Jew in the French army, Alfred Dreyfus, was unjustly accused of treason, he, too, came to the conclusion that Gentiles would never let Jews truly assimilate into their various cultures.[36] Herzl convened the first World Zionist Congress at Basle, Switzerland in 1897. At this congress the representatives outlined their plans for a Jewish State. After considerable debate on the preferred location for this Jewish State, the delegates decided on Palestine.

This ambitious plan was a long way from reality. Palestine was part of the decaying Ottoman Empire. The Sultan refused to sell Palestine to the Jews. Some Jews did migrate to Israel, especially from Eastern Europe. The first wave of immigration was during 1882–1902. They bought any land they could from landlords and sought to scratch a living from a badly neglected and eroded landscape. Under Turkish (Ottoman) rule Palestine had become a wasteland. For some idea of how it looked in 1869, read Mark Twain's delightful book *The Innocents Abroad*.[37] Those who returned to the Holy Land faced a bleak prospect and many hardships. As more Jews nonetheless returned, and as some strides were made in reclaiming the land, another nationalistic movement arose—Arab nationalism. These two movements had the same aspirations for, unfortunately, the same piece of real estate. They were on a collision course.

The British Government entered the picture with an important declaration called the Balfour Declaration. In the government were some individuals who were sympathetic to the Zionist cause. Lord Balfour, the prime minister, drafted this declaration in 1917. It began as follows:

> His Majesty's Government will view with favour the establishment in Palestine of a national home for the Jewish people, and will use their best endeavors to facilitate the achievement of this object, it being clearly understood that nothing shall be done which may prejudice the civil and religious right of the existing non-Jewish communities in Palestine, or the rights and political status enjoyed by Jews in any other country.[38]

1917 was also during the First World War. The Ottoman Empire had entered the war allied with Germany. The British and French saw an opportunity to break the control of the Turks over the Middle East. Jews saw a golden opportunity to realize their dream of an independent state, assuming British support. A careful reading of the Balfour Declaration, however, raises a problem: how would Great Britain be able to satisfy both Jews and Arabs? The answer became clear: she could not. British policy in Palestine veered in favor of Arab nationalism. Tensions rose and violence flared between Jews and Arabs in the 1920s and 1930s.

Then World War II engulfed Europe. As the "Final Solution" (the death camps employing gas chambers and ovens) became known to the Jewish communities in the West, there was an extreme urgency to fulfill the objective of Zionism and provide a safe haven for Jews. Unfortunately, the British did not see this as being in their national interest anymore. The oil reserves lying in Arab lands were a major factor in the equation. They blockaded the coast of Palestine and forbade any more Jews from immigrating.

After World War II, small splinter groups of Jews engaged in terrorist activity against the British in an attempt to secure more immigration. As violence escalated, the British thrust the problem into the lap of the fledgling United Nations. A commission was appointed the task of studying the Palestine question. In 1947, the commission recommended that Palestine be partitioned into two separate states, Jewish and Arab. This plan was adopted by the UN, but flatly rejected by the surrounding Arab states. Finally, in May of 1948, the British, in effect, threw up their hands and decided to withdraw their forces. The Israelis declared their independence immediately thereafter. When the British withdrew, they fully expected that the Arab states would crush the new Israeli state. To the surprise of many, the Israelis not only threw back the invading armies, they actually gained more ground.

In 1949, an armistice, sponsored by the UN, froze the borders between the new State of Israel and her Arab neighbors (the so-called "Green Line"). Israel was a reality, but surrounded by hostile neighbors. Since then, Israel has fought four major wars (1956, 1967, 1973, 1982) and engaged in numerous military operations against her enemies. There have been a few positive steps, such as a formal peace treaty with Egypt and Jordan, but Arab (and Islamic) animosity against Israel continues to seeth. The current intifada featuring suicide bombers has plunged the nation into one of its darkest eras. The future of the entire region remains uncertain.

What is our point in narrating this history? So many times the hope of a Jewish state seemed but a pipe dream. The circumstances and forces against such a proposal were so overwhelming. And yet, against all odds, a state emerged for the first time since the Maccabees in 142–63 B.C., a span of over 2,000 years! Can such an occurrence be a mere coincidence?

Furthermore, can such an unprecedented, historical happening be dismissed when it is placed alongside the many OT prophecies about the restoration of Israel? I share with many Christians the conviction that the rise of modern Israel is not without significance for God's final act in the drama of redemption, the second coming of Jesus Christ.[39] In short, there is a convergence between prophecy and history that is compelling.

Objection to thesis two: How can the modern State of Israel be a part of redemptive history when it is essentially a secular state, and those who are religious are, for the most part, not Christians? This objection, succinctly stated by Jewett in his article, overlooks the fact that the restoration takes place in phases. There are clear indications that *the regathering phase must unfold before the regeneration of the nation.* Our key witness to this is the prophet Ezekiel. Chapters 36 and 37 of his book depict a return to the land and a spiritual cleansing. But notice that it is in precisely that sequence—first a return and then the regeneration. We quote at length from 36:24–28:

> For I will take you out of the nations; I will gather you from all the countries and bring you back into your own land. I will sprinkle clean water on you, and you will be clean; I will cleanse you from all your impurities and from all your idols. I will give you a new heart and put a new spirit in you; I will remove from you your heart of stone and give you a heart of flesh. And I will put my Spirit in you and move you to follow my decrees and be careful to keep my laws. You will live in the land I gave your forefathers; you will be my people, and I will be your God.

In the famous vision of the valley of dry bones, the same sequence unfolds. The bones are clearly identified as the house of Israel (v. 11):

> Then he said to me, "Prophesy to these bones and say to them, 'Dry bones, hear the word of the LORD! This is what the Sovereign LORD says to these bones: I will make breath enter you, and you will come to life. I will attach tendons to you and make flesh come upon you and cover you with skin; I will put breath in you, and you will come to life. Then you will know that I am the LORD.'" So I prophesied as I was commanded. And as I was prophesying, there was a noise, a

> rattling sound, and the bones came together, bone to bone. I looked, and tendons and flesh appeared on them and skin covered them, but there was no breath in them. Then he said to me, "Prophesy to the breath; prophesy, son of man, and say to it, 'This is what the Sovereign LORD says: Come from the four winds, O breath, and breathe into these slain, that they may live.'" So I prophesied as he commanded me, and breath entered them; they came to life and stood up on their feet—a vast army (Eze 37:4–10).

In both passages there is a process that unfolds, not a simultaneous action. We could multiply passages that speak of the final drama of redemption centered in the land of Israel. The land is an important aspect of God's dealings with Israel; it is there that the last act is played out.

Thesis Three: A siege of Jerusalem precedes the Second Coming of Jesus Christ and precipitates the conversion of the nation.

The vision of Zechariah (chs. 12–14). This section is composed using the "sandwich" technique. That is, it falls into a pattern of A–B–A. The two A portions, 12:1–9 and 14:1–21 frame the central B section, 12:10–13:9. In this case, the A portions relate, in some detail, an international siege of Jerusalem. The B portion describes a remarkable conversion scene. The portion 14:6–21 also constitutes a final concluding section and caps off the entire book.

Our interest first centers on the meaning of the invasion sections. Note that Zechariah 12:1–9 describes a siege of Jerusalem having the following characteristics:

1. It is international in scope. "All the nations of the earth" participate.
2. The Lord takes an active role in bringing about this siege ("I am going to make . . .").
3. The Jewish defenders fight ferociously for their city ("like a firepot in a woodpile, like a flaming torch among sheaves . . . the feeblest among them will be like David").

4. The invaders pay a heavy price—many casualties will be suffered.

The second A section, 14:1–5, adds the following details to the scenario:

1. The international siege is finally successful ("the city will be taken").
2. Half the population is forcibly deported.
3. The Lord himself enters the conflict and destroys the invading armies (v. 12).
4. The Lord establishes Jerusalem as the capital of a worldwide kingdom.

Several questions cry out for answers: When will this siege take place? Has it occurred in history? Is it merely symbolic with no literal fulfillment? The symbolic view has little to commend it—the passage has so many details relating to the topography of Jerusalem and its environs, all placed in such a graphic and realistic depiction of warfare, that one seems compelled to take a literal interpretation. In fact, no siege of Jerusalem, among its many sieges, fits the description here.[40] Lastly, and most importantly, the siege is positioned right before the coming of the Lord in glory (14:3–4). Thus we must place this siege in the future, just before the Second Coming of Jesus Christ. This prophecy of a siege of Jerusalem, during the Day of the Lord, is not unique to Zechariah 12–14. Isaiah 63:1–6; Ezekiel 38–39; Joel 3:11–14; Micah 4:11–13 and 5:7–15 depict a similar event, as does Revelation 16:12–15 in the NT.

The B section is fascinating. The entire mood changes. Instead of a siege, we read of a time of national repentance and cleansing from sin. Especially intriguing is 12:10: "And I will pour out on the house of David and the inhabitants of Jerusalem a spirit of grace and supplication. They will look on me, the one they have pierced, and they will mourn for him as one mourns for an only child, and grieve bitterly for him as one grieves for a firstborn son." Since the Lord is the speaker, who is this "one they have pierced"? This individual must be the Lord himself, who just prior to that says: "They will look on me." Christians will immediately recall that John's Gospel cites this very passage in reference to Jesus' crucifixion (cf. Jn 19:37). Thus it must be that Jesus is the Lord whom the embattled Jews of Zechariah 12–14 finally recognize as their Messiah! What follows is a moving description of national penitence and regeneration. At long last Israel acknowledges her Messiah. This passage is undoubtedly one that inspired Paul's confidence that his kinsmen according to the flesh would at last believe in Jesus of Nazareth:

> I do not want you to be ignorant of this mystery, brothers, so that you may not be conceited: Israel has experienced a hardening in part until the full number of the Gentiles has come in. And so all Israel will be saved, as it is written: "The deliverer will come from Zion; he will turn godlessness away from Jacob. And this is my covenant with them when I take away their sins" (Ro 11:25–27).

The conversion of Israel apparently takes place against the backdrop of an international invasion and siege of Jerusalem.

The final A section provides information on the outcome of the international siege. In spite of valiant resistance, the Jewish defenders of Jerusalem are overwhelmed by sheer numbers and the city falls. The inevitable atrocities of war occur (14:2). Just when all hope seems gone for the Jewish people, a supernatural intervention occurs—one exceeding even the magnitude of the exodus from Egypt or the conquest of Canaan. Even Joshua's long day and Elijah's fire from heaven pale before this demonstration of divine power. We have an event of the same magnitude as the resurrection of Jesus—the Lord himself descends from heaven and personally takes charge of operations! (cf. Zec 14:3–4). The location of his descent should not surprise us—the angel on the Mount of Olives told the disciples that Jesus' return would be "in the same way you have seen him go into heaven." (Ac 1:11). It is to this very spot that the Lord descends. In Jerusalem he sets up his capital and from there he reigns over the entire earth (Zec 14:3–21).

The current international scene. We make a few observations about the current world scene. This prophecy of an international invasion of Israel would not have been possible before 1967, because Israel did not control the entire city of Jerusalem prior to then. From the days of the last Maccabean monarch (63 B.C.), Jerusalem had been under Gentile domination. Since 1967 there have been numerous initiatives to internationalize Jerusalem. To these, Israel has replied: "Over our dead bodies!" It will be extremely difficult for an Israeli government to relinquish control over the Holy City. The Jerusalem question may one day lead to the scene described in Zechariah 12–14. For whatever reason, it does appear that before Jesus returns, there will be a multinational invasion of Israel and a siege of Jerusalem. Though it pains us to envision such suffering, it does seem that there will be one more terrible travail for this city. Yet out of this travail, faith in Jesus will be born!

We remain convinced that the land of Israel will be the focal point of earth's final days before the coming of Jesus. We also believe that events preceding that coming will result in the conversion of a majority of Jews living at that time. They will become part of the body of Christ and reign with him during his millennial reign in Jerusalem, along with a great host of Gentiles, who likewise make up the number of the redeemed (cf. Rev 7).

Thesis Four: The State of Israel has a right to exist as an independent Jewish state. This right, however, should not be at the expense of the Palestinians' right to their own state.

1. This is the most controversial of the four theses. In support of this thesis, we first offer a theological and biblical basis in the promise to the patriarchs. The argument here proceeds along the same lines as our discussion of the restoration promises. (See also our discussion of the Abrahamic covenant in chapter four.) The promise to Abraham and his descendants, to the effect that they would inherit the land of Canaan as an everlasting possession, should be understood literally, not spiritually. In spite of disobedience, the promise still holds (Ro 11:29). As we saw in thesis three, there will be a national turning to Messiah Jesus at the end of the age, giving rise to a complete fulfillment of the patriarchal promises during the millennial reign of Christ. The present State of Israel is not the fulfillment of the patriarchal promises; it is, however, in my opinion, an important prelude to the final chapter of Israel's history. We may be living closer to the last chapter of redemptive history than we realize!

2. Thesis Four also has a legal basis in various international agreements. Our argument proceeds as follows: the legality of the State of Israel has been secured through a number of internationally recognized and sanctioned declarations, beginning with the Balfour Declaration in 1917. Most importantly, the UN vote on partition in November 1947 and the recognition and acceptance of the State of Israel by the United Nations in May 1948 has guaranteed her membership in the world of nations. Since

then Israel has had to fight a series of wars against her Arab neighbors, bent upon annihilating the fledgling state (1956, 1967, 1973, 1984). Currently, the prospects for a comprehensive peace settlement are uncertain at best. As always, the Middle East remains a rough neighborhood, and there are many thorny issues to be resolved. A feature of Islam has made it more difficult to achieve a comprehensive settlement in the region. This is the dogma that Palestine lies within Dar-al-Islam, that is, the realm where Islam should always reign supreme. With a resurgence of Fundamentalist Islam, particularly in the Middle East, this does not bode well for future peace.

We emphasize, however, that until the Lord Jesus Christ returns, who will render impartial justice and decide the allotment of nations under his reign, the goal should still be the implementation of the UN Partition Plan of 1947, a Palestinian state alongside a Jewish state. Palestinians should not to be displaced from nor oppressed in their ancestral homeland. They, too, deserve security and self determination. The Oslo Declaration of Principles (September 13, 1993) provides a framework for a solution to the problem. In this document, both sides recognized the rights of the other to exist as a people within the borders of Palestine/Israel, and committed themselves to negotiating a permanent settlement and to improving relations between the two peoples. The two states, living side by side in mutual peace and respect, cooperating economically, would be a boon not only to the region, but the whole world. This, in my opinion, should be the ultimate objective of American foreign policy in the region.

3. We also argue on humanitarian grounds. The tragedy of the Holocaust (the murder of six million Jews by the Nazis) and the general failure of the West to respond to the plight of the Jews under Hitler demands compensation. No doubt a major factor in the successful establishment of the Jewish State of Israel was the smitten conscience of the western allies.[41] A little known fact of the Holocaust is that the truth of what was happening in occupied Europe was verified by late November 1942. By then 1,500,000 Jews had already been exterminated. Tragically, our government did nothing substantial to help and "as late as December 1944 a Roper poll indicated that the majority of Americans still did not believe reports of a mass murder of European Jewry."[42]

The Jewish catastrophe was viewed from a purely military and political point of view. Deciding that resources should not be diverted away from the objective of defeating the Nazi war machine in the field, the Allies bombed the ball-bearing factories of Dresden into rubble, leaving intact the many railroads leading to the death camps (located strategically all across eastern Europe, as well as in Germany). Nor did we attempt any rescue efforts to liberate these infernos of hell.[43] When the western world saw the end result of these camps, the shock and horror led to a belated sympathy for the Jewish people. A question that must not be allowed to remain unverbalized is this: If it had been Anglo-Saxons or Scandinavians being exterminated in the death camps, would our governments have made the same decision? The answer seems clear and the resulting guilt has, in my opinion, been a major factor in the rise of the modern State of Israel. Accordingly, it is my position that we owe it to the Jewish people to make sure that they survive in the family of nations, and that they possess at least a portion of their ancestral homeland as the location of their re-born state.

Christians need to pray unceasingly for the "peace of Jerusalem" (Ps 122:6). There is a desparate need for a just and lasting peace in the region. God cares about both the Arabs and Jews, and desires that they come to a saving knowledge of Jesus Christ. May it be our united prayer that both Arab and Jew be reconciled by the grace of our Lord Jesus Christ.

Israel's Restoration and the Millennial Kingdom

We briefly mention one last issue with regard to national eschatology, also a highly debated one. Will there be a millennial reign, during which the Lord Jesus Christ will visibly rule over the earth with his capital at Jerusalem? As the above discussion has already implied, I think a good case can be made in favor of such a view. This reign connects with the above issue of Israel's restoration, in that the old covenant people of God would be brought under the blessings of the new covenant and restored to their ancient homeland as a part of that millennial era. In other words, the complete fulfillment of Israel's restoration promises transpires during the Millennium. Though not without some lingering problems, we think this scenario best corresponds with the many prophecies of a coming age of peace and security (see e.g., Isa 2). The student is referred to several works that discuss and debate the various alternatives with regard to the millennial question.[44]

Individual Eschatology

Whereas the bulk of the teaching in the OT on eschatology focuses on the destiny of Israel, there are, especially toward the end of the OT, passages that throw some light on the destiny of the individual, whether believer or unbeliever. This becomes our focus in this section.

Introduction

We inquire first into the significance of this study. Why, after all, should Christians be interested in what the OT may have to say about life after death and the hope of resurrection? We mention two reasons:

1. This doctrine demonstrates the concept of progressive revelation in a very clear and convincing manner. What we mean is that God has not seen fit to reveal his plan and purpose for humankind all at once (see ch. 1). Rather, he has gradually unveiled the future state of the redeemed. Various spokespersons added pieces to the puzzle resulting in an ever clearer picture of the future. Thus the patriarchal period provides little information on the state and condition of the dead. But, by the time of Daniel, the prospect of a bodily resurrection and a glorious, everlasting life emerges from the pages of holy writ. Carrying this forward into the NT, we see the doctrine of life after death illuminated in the resurrection of Jesus: "but it has now been revealed through the appearing of our Savior, Christ Jesus, who has destroyed death and has brought life and immortality to light through the gospel" (2Ti 1:10).

This notion of progressive revelation, as we have already seen, characterizes God's revelation to us in Scripture, and distinguishes Christianity from all other religions, except, of course, the parent faith of Judaism. Both Judaism and Christianity embody the concept of revelation in time and space, a revelation that unfolds progressively.

The big difference between Judaism and Christianity, with regard to this issue, is that the promises of full redemption in the OT still remain a vague, unfulfilled hope for Judaism. Christians see the fulfillment of the progressive revelation in the OT as culminating in Jesus Christ. Of course, even Christians are awaiting the last chapter of redemptive history, the redemption of our bodies (Ro 8:23).

The doctrines of bodily resurrection and everlasting life are like anchors, securing us in the storms of life to the solid rock. To John the Apostle, imprisoned on the rocky island of Patmos, comes this word of the risen Christ: "I am the First and the Last. I am the Living One; I was dead, and behold I am alive for ever and ever! And I hold the keys of death and Hades" (Rev 1:17b, 18).

2. This doctrine provides a good counterbalance for much current speculation about life after death. Our age has been thoroughly captivated with the notion of life after death. Numerous books, movies, talk shows and personal testimonies have explored the topic, often featuring the experiences of those who have "died" and returned, or of those who have visited the "other side" and glimpsed what awaits us all.[45] Because there are so many conflicting and bizarre ideas in circulation, it behooves the Christian student to test these notions against Scripture. In the words of Peter: "And we have the word of the prophets made more certain, and you will do well to pay attention to it, as to a light shining in a dark place, until the day dawns and the morning star rises in your hearts" (2Pe 1:19).

Especially disquieting are the many testimonials of those who have "died," in which they claim that there is no judgment on the other side. We are led to believe that what one has done in this life really matters very little because all are accepted into the realms of light and beauty. What becomes even more suspicious is that these experiences are reported by members of many different faiths, and often they mention seeing figures like Mohammed, Buddha, or some other reputed holy person. If one were to take at face value these testimonies, it seemingly makes no difference what faith you believe—all are admitted. This may be in line with our pluralistic, postmodern, and "politically correct" culture, but is it true? One wonders whether these experiences are simply projections of wishful thinking rather than sober reality. Certainly, the unambiguous statements of Scripture affirming the reality of judgment calls into question such testimonials (Heb 9:27; 2Co 5:10).[46]

We conclude, then, that sufficient grounds exist to explore in more detail what the OT has to say on this all-important question of life after death. We think you will be surprised by joy at the end of our investigation!

The Essence of Humanity and Life: An Analysis of Genesis 2

Before we analyze the notion of death in the Hebrew Bible, we must first review the meaning of life.[47] Here we return to the creation account in Genesis 2. Note that in this highly anthropomorphic description of Yahweh's creative activity (he is described as a potter forming a body out of clay), we discover the two fundamental components comprising a human being: dust and the breath of life.

Dust of the ground *('āpār)*. Chemical analysis of a decayed human body reveals most of the trace elements and constituents of dirt. It is not a particularly ennobling idea, but it is a salutary reminder of our lowly estate! Theologically, the importance of this text is in its insistence that human beings share with the created order the essential building materials that surround us all the time. We are a part of God's creation. When God had finished his creative activity in Genesis 1:31, he declared that it was very good. Our bodies are fearfully and wonderfully made (Ps 139:14). They are perfectly adapted to life on planet earth. But they are not indestructible, and, without the following component, they quickly decompose into a rather smelly corpse!

Breath of life (*nᵉshāmâ* or *rûah*). The second fundamental component is more difficult, if not impossible, to describe. God's breath is the animating principle of life. It is that which energizes the body and gives it vitality. We speak of our spirit as the essential person—the "real me." Thus it seems that we recognize the core of our personality to reside in this mysterious component, although there is a feeling that "we" are in every part of our body—we claim ownership of it all. Sometimes, to be sure, we would like very much to dispossess certain features of our bodies! But, for the most part, Paul is quite right when he says in another context, "no one ever hated his own body, but he feeds and cares for it . . ." (Eph 5:29).

Conclusion (*nepesh*). The infusion of breath (the vital life force) into a body results in what the Hebrew Bible calls a *nepesh*, a "life," "soul," "creature," or "person." We usually speak of having a soul, but the Bible says we *are* a soul. Note that even an animal is said to be a *nepesh*. That which distinguishes and elevates us above the animals is that we alone are created in the image of God. This most likely consists of that complex of attributes and capabilities we call "personality." Human beings are thus thinking, willing, feeling persons capable of objectifying themselves over against others (self-consciousness) and of relating to God (cf. ch. 2).

The OT account of humankind's creation makes abundantly clear that *life is a gift from God.* Our proper response is one of gratitude and thanksgiving to the Creator who made our life possible and who sustains it in remarkable ways. But life is limited. That raises the question of death.

The Essence of Death

What, according to the OT, is death? Why is such a phenomenon part of a creation that God said was very good? Can anything be done about this grim reaper? Can one survive this terrifying prospect? These and other questions crowd our minds as we ponder this inevitable event.

The withdrawal of the life principle. Once again the Genesis narrative provides our primary information. We recall that God warned the man about the consequences of eating of the tree of the knowledge of good and evil: "for when you eat of it you will surely die" (Ge 2:17). In fact, Adam did not physically die immediately after his disobedience, since the text clearly affirms that he lived to the age of 930 years. However, as we have already seen in chapter three, Adam and Eve both died spiritually, immediately after their act of disobedience. The ensuing narrative demonstrates the tragic loss of fellowship with God experienced by the first human pair (cf. ch. 3). Death must be seen in its close connection with the first act of disobedience. As the Apostle Paul makes clear in Romans 5:12–21, Adam's act of disobedience resulted in a death sentence for the entire human race.

What we can say, then, is that death is both spiritual and physical, with both resulting in a separation: spiritual death leads to separation from God, and physical death leads to a separation of the body from the life force, the breath of life. In short, the Hebrew Bible portrays death as a *withdrawal of the life force*. As a direct consequence of Adam's sin, a limitation is placed on the length of human life; the body decays and returns to dust (Ge 3:19) and the spirit returns to God who gave it. The despair of the teacher in Ecclesiastes is poignant: "Man's fate is like that of the animals; the same fate awaits them both: As one dies, so dies the other. All have the same breath; man has no advantage over the animal. Everything is meaningless" (Ecc 3:19). It is his question that follows, however, that prompts our further inquiry: "Who knows if the spirit of man rises upward and if the spirit of the animal goes down into the earth" (Ecc 3:21)?

An unwelcome intruder. Before we pursue the answer to the above question, we need to make one further point. In the OT, death is consistently portrayed as *an unwelcome intruder*. We find many prayers for a long or prolonged life, but none for a speedy death! Death was to be postponed as long as possible.

This leads to a consideration of suicide. Only two instances of suicide are recorded in the OT. The first is the account of Saul, during his last desperate hours on Mount Gilboa. One account has him fall on his own sword. Of course, the picture is obscured somewhat by the Amalekite's version of Saul's death in which the Amalekite administered the coup de grâce at Saul's request (cf. 1Sa 31 with 2Sa 1). Putting aside these conflicting versions, the point we make is that, if, in fact, Saul did commit suicide himself or had the Amalekite kill him (assisted suicide, so controversial these days!), the option was one of sheer desperation to avoid torture and humiliation by the Philistines.

The other instance is Ahithophel, the advisor of David who betrayed him and sided with Absalom. When Ahithophel saw that young Absalom had blundered by rejecting his advice and delayed pursuit of David, he went home and hanged himself (cf 2Sa 17). He knew full well what would happen; he would be arrested and tried for treason. Rather than suffer that humiliation, he chose to kill himself. Only one other individual contemplates suicide, and that is Job. He does not, however, seriously entertain the option (Job 2:9-10).

The consistent picture we get in the OT is that, apart from grievous circumstances (cf. Job 3:20–21), death is not welcomed, but rather, avoided for as long as possible. It is an unwelcome intruder, disrupting the relationships of life and ending worship and praise of the Creator.

The Hebrew View of Death

We are now ready to survey the OT and determine more precisely how the Hebrews viewed death. This necessitates a closer look at a key term in the Hebrew Bible. The Hebrews used the term Sheol [Heb. *shᵉôl*] to refer to the place to which one departed at death. Its basic meaning seems to be "underworld."[48] The best way to describe Sheol is to turn to two passages that we might call "guided tours of Sheol."

A guided tour of Sheol. In Isaiah 14:3–20 we reexamine (cf. ch. 5) this "taunt song" composed to celebrate the death of a Babylonian king, a tyrant and oppressor. Now he gets his just desert. He descends into Sheol, pictured as somewhere below the earth. We note that his arrival is greeted by those who preceded him—called "spirits of the departed." Thus there is conscious existence of some sort. These spirits are not only aware of a newcomer, they talk to him and almost taunt him with the new realities he must face. Foremost among these realities is the fact that he has "become weak," just like them. This expression must mean something like lacking animation or the dynamism of human life. One gets the impression that life in Sheol is like suspended animation or a slow-motion movie in black and white. All that gives life zest, color, interest and meaning is absent.

The body of the deceased king is described in verse 11: "maggots are spread out beneath you and worms cover you." Also verses 18–20 describe the desecration of his tomb whereby his body is cast out of his stately sepulchre into a mass grave and covered with the corpses of soldiers killed in battle. But the spirit of the king appears to survive in a sort of shadowy existence.

This description of Sheol, which is similar to that found in Ezekiel 32:11–31 in reference to one of the Pharaohs of Egypt, is very close to that of the place of the dead among other peoples in the Mediterranean, from Mesopotamia to Greece. One thinks of Ishtar's descent to the underworld in Babylonian literature and Odysseus' visit to Hades in *The Odyssey*.

Descriptions of Sheol. We now collate a number of passages from the OT in which we have some description of Sheol. Taken together they provide a better glimpse of this unwelcome end to human life.

1. It is a place to which one descends and from which there can be no return. "In mourning will I go down to the grave (*$sh^e\hat{o}l$*) to my son" (Ge 37:35b). "Can I bring him back again: I will go to him, but he will not return to me" (2Sa 12:23). In a poetic passage in Job 26:5–6 it is said to be under the waters (of the seas).

2. It is a place where the dead know nothing of what happens on earth. "If his sons are honored, he does not know it: if they are brought low, he does not see it" (Job 14:21). "For the living know that they will die, but the dead know nothing; they have no further reward, and even the memory of them is forgotten" (Ecc 9:5). "Where you are going, there is neither working nor planning nor knowledge nor wisdom" (Ecc 9:10).

3. It is a place of deep darkness. "Turn away from me so I can have a moment's joy before I go to the place of no return, to the land of gloom and deep shadow, to the land of deepest night, and of deep shadow and disorder, where even the light is like darkness" (Job 10:20b–22).

4. It is a place of complete silence and isolation from God. "It is not the dead who praise the Lord, those who go down to silence" (Ps 115:17). "Do you show your wonders to the dead? Do those who are dead rise up and praise you? Is your love declared in the grave, your faithfulness in destruction? Are your wonders known in the place of darkness, or your righteous deeds in the land of oblivion?" (Ps 88:10–12). "I would soon have dwelt in the silence of death" (Ps 94:17).

5. It is a place of continual existence rather than annihilation, and it does not lie beyond the reach of God. "The grave (*$sh^e\hat{o}l$*) below is all astir to meet you at your coming: it rouses the spirits of the departed to greet you . . . they will all respond . . ." (Isa 14:9–10). ". . . if I make my bed in the depths (*$sh^e\hat{o}l$*), you are there" (Ps 139:8b). "Death (*$sh^e\hat{o}l$*) is naked before God; destruction lies uncovered" (Job 20:6).

6. It is a place characterized by lack of vitality and animation. "They will say to you, 'You also have become weak, as we are: you have become like us . . .'" (Isa 14:10).

The theological problem of Sheol. The student may, at this point, be puzzled by the above descriptions of Sheol. It does not tally with the intimations of life after death, for the righteous at least, discovered in the NT. For example, the Apostle Paul speaks of being with the Lord, which is better by far (Php 1:22–24), a state he would much prefer over continuing on in the physical body (2Co 5:8). Does the NT contradict the OT on this teaching?

Three different approaches to handling this issue deserve consideration:

1. The first is the so-called "two compartment view." This view, already found among the early church fathers, holds that Sheol was divided into two levels or compartments, the upper being reserved for the righteous and the lower for the wicked.

There is some plausibility to this notion in that some OT passages suggest that the wicked were cast into the deepest part of Sheol, perhaps to be equated with "the pit" (cf. Pr 9:18; 15:11; Ps 88:4). On this understanding, Christ, after his resurrection, rescued the righteous from their confinement to Sheol and transferred them to Paradise, a heavenly location. Recall that on the cross Jesus promised the repentant thief: "I tell you the truth, today you will be with me in paradise" (Lk 23:43). Earlier Jesus had told the story of Lazarus and the rich man where Lazarus at death is in Abraham's bosom (equivalent in this view to the compartment of the righteous) and the rich man wound up in Hades (the place for the wicked). (See Lk 16: 19–31.) 1 Peter 3:19 and Ephesians 4:9–10 are said to describe this transfer of the righteous to paradise by the victorious Christ.[49] It should be noted, however, that this interpretation of the latter two NT passages is problematical.

2. A second approach is to identify Sheol, not with a shadowy underworld, akin to the widespread similar notion all across the ancient Near East, but rather, with the grave. That is, the descriptions of a dark, gloomy place, where worms and maggots mingle with musty bones, appropriately suits a Palestinian tomb of a cave variety so common in the biblical era.[50] This view satisfies the requirement that all, righteous and unrighteous, experience Sheol, that is entombment, without causing a seeming contradiction with the NT teaching. In short, Sheol says nothing about the fate of the spirit of individuals, just their bodies. The problem with this view is that several passages suggest a more than somatic experience in Sheol for its victims (see esp. Isa 14 and Eze 32).

3. A third approach is to admit that the Hebrews, in keeping with all their neighbors, held to the notion of an underworld; but in the progress of revelation, the Lord revealed glimmers of hope that the ultimate destiny of the righteous was a bodily resurrection to a vastly better world.[51] This view would then hold that, whereas the early Hebrews held a view not unlike their pagan neighbors, the Scriptures did not teach such a view as a

normative belief. What, in the progress of revelation, becomes a normative belief is the hope of bodily resurrection, clearly the view of the later NT. Though not without its difficulties, we think this latter view has the most to commend it.[52]

Early Hebrew Views about the Afterlife

The primeval period. The earliest phase of redemptive history contains tantalizing hints that something better than a dreary existence in Sheol might be possible.

1. The tree of life. We recall the setting for the kingdom of God on earth in the Garden of Eden. After Adam and Eve's transgression, the Lord God banished them from the garden with these words: "He must not be allowed to reach out his hand and take also from the tree of life and eat, and live forever" (Ge 3:22b). On the east side of the garden stood cherubim and a flaming sword, guarding the entrance (3:24). Even though the tree of life functions symbolically in the story, the reality behind the symbol is the possibility that the Lord God might relent and allow at least some to experience immortality.[53] Note that in the symbolism of the book of Revelation, the tree of life reappears in the paradise of God (Rev. 2:7; 22:2, 14, 19) when the history of redemption is complete.
2. The litany of death and the translation of Enoch (Ge 5:21–24). The account of the rapture of Enoch preserves a tradition about a man who escaped death. This remarkable event, like the motif of the tree of life, engendered hope that perhaps an exceptionally pious individual might escape death entirely. In the period of the monarchy, Elijah likewise was raptured into heaven (2Ki 2:1–18), undoubtedly strengthening this hope.
3. All of Israel's neighbors had rather elaborate burial practices, anticipating some sort of life after death. The Egyptians, of course, had the most developed and persistent doctrine of afterlife among the peoples of the ancient Near East. Though the Hebrew's funerary practices were not as elaborate, they do, nonetheless, presuppose a similar belief in afterlife.[54]

The patriarchal period. Some scholars have denied that there was any belief in the afterlife in the earlier periods of Israel's history—only in the exilic era did such a notion arise, primarily under the influence of the

Persians, and then later, the Greeks.[55] The above discussion calls this assertion into question, and a closer look at the patriarchal narratives would likewise speak against such a denial.

1. "Gathered to one's fathers." There are in Genesis several occurrences of this phrase (Ge 25:8, 17; 35:29; 49:29, 33) used in connection with the deaths of Abraham, Ishmael, Isaac and Jacob. Scholars in the liberal tradition have generally assumed that the expression is a euphemism for being placed in the family tomb. In the second millennium in Canaan, the typical burial site was a natural or artificially enlarged cave in which shelves were carved out of the soft limestone on which to lay the bodies of the deceased. After the bodies had decomposed, the bones were gathered into a pit within the cave (an example of secondary burial). Hence the expression "gathered to one's fathers" is said to refer to this bone pile!

This explanation for the expression in Genesis is inadequate. Neither Abraham nor Jacob was buried in the family tomb (Abraham's family was hundreds of miles away in Ur and Jacob was buried in Egypt). Furthermore, Jacob thought that he would "go down to the grave" (*shᵉôl*) to his son Joseph, presumed to have been devoured by a wild beast (Ge 37:35). Thus the phrase must refer to more than a depository for the bones of the family.[56] We conclude, therefore, that the Hebrews, like the pagan neighbors around them, held to some concept of afterlife.

2. To this evidence we add another important testimony. According to the writer to the Hebrews in the NT, "Abraham reasoned that God could raise the dead" (Heb 11:19). While this text does not say that Abraham believed that all the righteous are raised, it does point to the possibility of resurrection (see ch. 4). To be sure, it does not appear that a firm belief in the bodily resurrection of the righteous was held in the patriarchal period. On the other hand, there was a notion of life after death and that Yahweh held the power of life and death (cf. Ge 18:23-33; 19:23-29; 20:3; 38:7, 10).

3. Finally, we recall God's word to Moses at the burning bush: "Then he said, 'I am the God of your father, the God of Abraham, the God of Isaac and the God of Jacob'" (Ex 3:6). Jesus' rebuttal of the Sadducees, who did not believe in bodily resurrection, turned on the use of the present tense ("I am"). According to Jesus, God is the God of the living; therefore, the ancestors must also be living in his presence, as surely as Moses stood before the living God at the burning bush (Mk 12:26 and par.).[57]

Factors Leading to a Clearer Hope of Life After Death

Given that the patriarchs did have some notion of life after death, we next inquire into the obvious development that takes place in the OT canon. By the end of the OT, we have unambiguous statements pointing to a hope in bodily resurrection. Our interest here is to trace out, as best we can, the factors that may have contributed to the growth of this most important doctrine.

The covenant bond. We begin with a fundamental concept of OT thought, namely, the covenant. We have seen earlier how God was pleased to enter into a covenant with various individuals and with the nation of Israel (chs. 4–5). Foundational to the covenant idea is the faithfulness of God. His promise is inviolable. We have seen this truth repeatedly in our study of the OT. Because of the Lord's great faithfulness, believers exulted in the sense of security now possible. Surely this relationship with the eternal covenant-keeping God could not be severed by death. Yahweh was supreme master over life and death. If then he had promised that his great lovingkindness would be upon an individual and his descendants forever, then death could not change this established fact. This inference, based upon the nature and character of God, surfaces in some of the psalms, especially those traditionally assigned to David.

We turn first to Psalm 16. As to type, this psalm can be categorized as a song of trust. It opens with a plea for safety and a confession of trust in God (v. 1). Then it moves to an affirmation of loyalty by the vassal (vv. 2–4) and a recital of covenant blessings, celebrating God's goodness and gifts to the psalmist (vv. 5–8). At this point the psalmist contemplates the future (vv. 9–11). It too, like the present, is bounded by the lovingkindness of the overlord. The psalmist is confident that the Lord will not abandon him to Sheol (note the *NIV* footnote). Then, amazingly, we hear the confident expectation of eternal life at the right hand of God himself.

Christians familiar with the NT will recall that the Apostle Peter, on the Day of Pentecost, applied this psalm to Jesus' resurrection (Ac 2:25–28), and Paul did likewise in the synagogue at Antioch (Ac 13:35). Here is another of those instances in the OT in which the meaning reaches beyond the historic David and speaks of David's greater Son, Jesus Christ. What we should not overlook, however, is the fact that David himself is promised an eternal existence in the presence of God. He could not conceive of death ending a covenant relationship with God.

One more psalm deserves special mention, perhaps the most well-known and beloved portion of Scripture, Psalm 23. This psalm, like Psalm 16, is a song of trust. It opens with an affirmation of faith in the Lord under the figure of a shepherd (v. 1). This affirmation is then followed, in two distinct sections, by a recital of covenant blessings. The two sections are recognized by the metaphors employed to narrate the Lord's covenant blessings. In verses 2–4, Yahweh is the good shepherd, in verse 5, he is the gracious host. Both metaphors are rich and need to be carefully explored to gain new insights into the meanings conveyed. The psalm comes to a climactic outpouring of sheer exultation in verse 6 (the "surely" is an exclamation). Once again, the psalmist expresses an expectation of an eternal relationship with the Lord: "I will dwell in the house of the LORD forever." What should not be overlooked from both psalms is the implication that the eternal pleasures are experienced in a body.

The need for vindication. Another possible factor in the emerging belief in a glorious afterlife for the righteous grew out of a longstanding religious problem—the problem of the prosperity of the wicked. We recall in our study of the Sinai Covenant that disobedience to the covenant stipulations rendered Israel liable to various curses or punishments (see ch. 5 and cf. Lev 26:14–45; Dt 28: 15–68). Furthermore, in the wisdom tradition of Israel (see ch. 10), it was nearly an axiom that obedience led to blessing, but disobedience to certain punishment and disgrace (cf. Pr 1:20–9:18). A problem arose, however. What explanation could be given when a wicked person did not experience retribution and affliction? To add to the problem, what if a righteous person experienced great affliction and suffering? This seemed to fly in the face of the accepted traditions and called into question the veracity of Israel's belief system. It is no wonder that such glaring discrepancies led, on occasion, to a crisis of faith.

Two psalms reflect such a crisis, Psalms 49 and 73, both of which are good examples of "wisdom psalms." Let us consider Psalm 73 and the dilemma that lies behind it. This didactic composition opens with an ascription of praise and closes with a pointed admonition and personal testimony, designed to reaffirm Israel's basic conviction—obedience will, ultimately, be rewarded and disobedience, punished (vv. 1, 27–28). But unbelief. Verses 2–3 describe both the seriousness and the source of the crisis: “I nearly lost my foothold . . . when I saw the prosperity of the wicked.” Verses 4–12 depict what seemed to the psalmist a carefree and luxurious existence enjoyed by his faithless neighbor. The psalmist candidly divulges his wavering commitment (vv. 13–16). Pragmatically, faith in Yahweh had not “paid off.” It did not seem to work the way the teachers and sages said it was supposed to. He contemplated voicing his doubts and complaints to others (v. 15), but instead, he wrestled within himself for some kind of solution (v. 16).

No answer came until, in a moment of revelation, at the sanctuary, the resolution to the dilemma came with a sense of unshakable confidence. What he now realized was that the wicked will be punished—if not in this life, then certainly in the life hereafter. And the life hereafter was of unending duration! The fate of the wicked was so awful as to make the brief time spent in this life seem inconsequential. The destinies of the righteous and wicked are set in stark contrast: the wicked have only sudden terror, ruin, destruction awaiting them; the righteous anticipate a reception into the realms of glory. Note how clearly the text intimates what lies beyond: “afterward you will take me into glory” (v. 24). The psalmist now looks back on his flirtation with unbelief and realizes how foolish he had been (vv. 21–22). His experience is shared with the community of Israel in order to reassure others struggling with the same issue that faithfulness, in spite of suffering or whatever, will be rewarded. The righteous will be vindicated: “it is good to be near God” (v. 28). Thus, the need for vindication became the occasion for more focus upon the ultimate destinies of the “two ways” (cf. Ps 1).

The drama of national restoration. In our discussion of the national restoration of Israel, we had occasion to look briefly at Ezekiel 37, the famous vision of the dry bones. We recall that, in this visionary experience, Ezekiel is told to prophesy to the dry bones, which represent the people of Israel. Incredibly, as he prophesied, the bones came together as a skeleton. As he continued to prophesy, the Spirit of the Lord caused the skeletons to become corpses, and then, in a final, climactic sequence, living people!

The context of the vision requires that we understand the prophecy as predicting a future, national regathering and restoration. But the depiction

The context of the vision requires that we understand the prophecy as predicting a future, national regathering and restoration. But the depiction of this restoration was that of the bodily resurrection of an individual. We are but one step removed from the notion of a personal, bodily resurrection for the righteous at some point beyond death. We are, of course, in the exilic era when Ezekiel receives this amazing vision.

The appearance of the concept of personal resurrection. Finally, we call attention to three passages that seem to affirm a bodily resurrection for the righteous. The three passages are: Isaiah 25:6–8; Job 19:23–27 and, most clearly and indisputably, Daniel 12:1–3.

The Isaiah passage involves a remarkable use of metaphor and symbol. Isaiah portrays a luxurious banquet table spread out by the Lord himself for his people—a people made up of many different people groups. This passage becomes the basis for the common expectation in second temple Judaism (ca. 516 B.C.–A.D. 70) of a messianic banquet enjoyed by the righteous in "the age to come" (cf. Mt 8:11; Rev 19:9). The next verse employs the metaphor of a burial shroud being whisked away like a magician waving his cape. Implied in the image is the coming to life of those who had previously been covered in death, since God will banish death itself. Though not explicitly stated, resurrection to life seems to be implied. One thinks here of the book of Revelation with its announcement that "death and Hades were thrown into the lake of fire" (Rev 20:14) and the Apostle Paul's citation of this very Isaiah passage in 1 Corinthians 15:54 as confirming his teaching on the bodily resurrection of the righteous.

The dating of the Isaiah text involves some dispute. Mainline or liberal scholars generally assign chapters 24–27 to the early sixth century B.C., assuming that the section was inserted into Isaianic material of the eighth century B.C.[58] Conservative scholars, on the other hand, generally see no compelling reason for denying this section to Isaiah of Jerusalem in the latter part of the eighth century and the first part of the seventh century B.C.[59] On either reckoning, we are still near the latter stages of the OT. If we assign a date around 700 B.C., this might be the earliest passage in the OT that anticipates a bodily resurrection. To this passage we should compare Isaiah 53:10–11, where the prophet predicts the return to life of the Servant of the Lord (see above). Isaiah the "evangelical prophet" may have been the first divine spokesperson who clearly grasped what God's ultimate intentions were for the human body.

The dating of Job is notoriously difficult, and the best one can do is offer a range of dates. The *NIVSB* (p. 731) suggests anytime between Solomon (ca. 1000 B.C.) and the exile. The *HarperCollins Study Bible* (p. 750) prefers some time in the late sixth or fifth century B.C. Most likely the composition is toward the end of the OT era. If so, it fits well with the assumption of a gradually emerging notion of bodily resurrection, and would be close in time to the Ezekiel 37 passage.

The passage in Job is set in a context in which Job anticipates ultimate vindication before God at the judgment. He goes beyond this, however, and expresses his hope in what seems to be a resurrection. The note in the *NIVSB* says: "He is absolutely certain, however, that death is not the end of existence and that someday he will stand in the presence of his Redeemer and see him with his own eyes."[60]

With Daniel 12:1–3, we have an unequivocal affirmation of the doctrine of bodily resurrection. "Multitudes who sleep in the dust of the earth will awake: some to everlasting life, others to shame and everlasting contempt. Those who are wise will shine like the brightness of the heavens, and those who lead many to righteousness, like the stars for ever and ever" (Daniel 12:2-3). Here again we run into the problem of dating and a rather clear divide between mainline and conservative scholarship. Conservative scholars generally, though not always, date Daniel in the sixth century B.C. Mainline scholars place the book in the second century B.C. It is not our purpose here to argue for one or the other, since in either case we have a document that falls into the latter stages of OT redemptive history.

Development in the Intertestamental Period

The Daniel passage brings together several themes that will be elaborated by the Jewish literature of the intertestamental era, as well as by NT literature: the role of archangels (in this case, Michael), the Great Tribulation, the book of life, the bodily resurrection and glorification of the saints ("shine like the brightness of the heavens") and the "shame and everlasting contempt" of unbelievers.[61] In addition to these we call attention to two concepts that are especially important for NT thought.

The doctrine of the "two ages." During the intertestamental era, Jewish thought about God's plan of redemption envisioned two ages, "this age" and "the age to come." This age began at creation and was marked by the great epochs such as the patriarchs, the exodus and the Sinai Covenant, the conquest, the Davidic kingdom, the classical prophets and the exile. This latter, tragic reality would be brought to an end by the glorious appearance of the Messiah, who would regather and restore Israel. This ushered in the age to come, a time of resurrection and of eternal bliss for the faithful.

Jesus and his apostles accepted this basic framework, with an important modification. Following the lead of Jesus, the NT writers believed that, with the coming of Jesus, the age to come had already, in a preliminary, mysterious way, broken into the present age. Believers are thus living "between the ages," enjoying a foretaste of the coming age of resurrection, but not the full inheritance. The operative phrase that describes such a situation is *"now, but not yet."* Already believers in Christ experience the forgiveness of sins, the gifts and graces of the Holy Spirit, the fellowship of the saints (cf. Heb 6:4–5), but they know that these things are but a "down payment" on the full possession of salvation (Ro 8:23; Eph 1:14). The consummation of "this age" is the coming of Christ in glory when believers will be resurrected and transformed into his image (Ro 8:29; Php 3:20). At that time the "age to come" completely replaces "this age" and there follows an unbroken reign with Christ in a new Jerusalem on a new earth forever (Rev 20–21). This concept of the "two ages" is fundamental to a grasp of the NT message.

The doctrine of an "intermediate state." Another important NT doctrine that takes up a development of intertestamental Judaism is the notion of an intermediate state. This expression refers to the state or condition of an individual after death, but before the resurrection of the body, when Christ returns and takes his place as judge of all humankind (cf. Mt 25:2). This is what is referred to when people say that such and such a person "died and went to heaven." Intertestamental Judaism conceived of the OT Sheol as having either two different compartments or at least two different conditions. The wicked are in torment in flames or in nether regions of gloom and darkness. This portion of Sheol is designated as either Hades or Gehenna (cf. Mt 5:22, 29–30; 10:28; 18:9). The righteous are in a blissful state in "Abraham's bosom," "paradise" or "the third heaven." This understanding seems presupposed by Jesus and his apostles (cf. Lk 16:19–31; 23:43; 2Co 12:2–5; 2Pe 2:4; Jude 6).

Climax in the Resurrection of Jesus Christ

The resurrection of Jesus Christ transforms the entire concept of life after death. The NT, most notably the apostle Paul, anchors the salvation of believers to the certainty of the resurrection of Jesus, a resurrection guaranteeing their own (1Co 15:12–28). Christ is styled as "the firstborn among many brothers" (Ro 8:29); "the firstfruits of those who have fallen asleep" (1Co 15:20); "the firstborn from among the dead" (Col 1:18 and Rev 1:5); the one who, by his death, freed those held in slavery by their fear of death (Heb 2:14–15); the one who has "given us new birth into a living hope through [his] resurrection . . . from the dead" (1Pe 1:3); and as the one who told John on the isle of Patmos: "Do not be afraid. I am the First and the Last. I am the Living One; I was dead, and behold I am alive for ever and ever! And I hold the keys of death and Hades" (Rev 1:17b–18). Now, when a believer dies, she or he has the prospect of being "at home with the Lord" (2Co 5:8), which, according to Paul, "is better by far" than living in the body (Php 1:23).

This condition of conscious bliss in the presence of Christ is not, however, permanent. It is, in theological terms, an intermediate state. This condition gives way, at the second coming of Christ, to the ultimate experience of salvation—life in a spiritual body adapted perfectly for life on a new earth (cf. 2Co 5:1–10; Php 3:20; 1Th 4:13–18; Rev 6:9–11; 19:11–20:6). No wonder that Paul, reflecting upon God's great plan of salvation could say: "This grace was given us in Christ Jesus before the beginning of time, but it has now been revealed through the appearing of our Savior, Christ Jesus, who has destroyed death and has brought life and immortality to light through the gospel" (2Ti 1:9b–10).

Relationship of Theme to Core Concepts

Faith and the Unity of Salvation: This chapter has again drawn attention to the progressive nature of God's revelation to us in Holy Scripture. He was not pleased to reveal clearly and completely his plan for our redemption in the initial phases of salvation history. Rather, there was a gradual unfolding of the specifics of his saving intentions. But one plan there is and this discussion has underlined that fact. Because of the witness of Christ to the authority of Scripture, we have assumed in this study that there is a fundamental coherence between earlier and later revelation.

Thus we have argued that, even though in the earliest times all believers went to be with the Lord at death, this fact was not plainly grasped by believers nor revealed by the Lord. At first, the Hebrews assumed that all alike went to a subterranean, gloomy, netherworld existence, similar to that of their pagan neighbors. Later, based upon confidence in the covenant-keeping God, there emerged a belief, rooted in God's revelation to inspired spokespersons, that the fate of the righteous was not the same as that of the wicked. Several Psalms, notably 49 and 73, point to a glorious future for the righteous and a terrifying prospect of judgment for the wicked. The righteous will be vindicated in the next life. Towards the end of the OT era, several inspired spokespersons received explicit revelation in this matter. They communicated to their peers a new prospect—God would raise up these mortal bodies that decay into dust. Isaiah, Job, and Daniel anticipate the full revelation of life after death, brought to light in the resurrection of Jesus Christ. He now offers this freely to all who believe in him.

This offer of everlasting life is predicated, however, upon the efficacy of the atoning work of the Suffering Servant, depicted in Isaiah 52:13–53:12. As we have seen in this chapter, the outlines of Jesus' ministry, death, and resurrection are marvelously portrayed centuries before the actual events themselves. We thus conclude that God's plan of salvation has been determined from before the creation of the world, just as Peter says: "He was chosen before the creation of the world, but was revealed in these last times for your sake" (1Pe 1:20). The revelation of "such a great salvation" (Heb 2:3) has been progressive and according to his good pleasure (Heb 1:1–2). It is, however, unchanging in its essential nature (cf. Heb 13:8).

Faith and Ethics: Our study of eschatology has uncovered a primary motivation for the ethical life. There is, on the one hand, the incentive to live a life pleasing to God in order to enjoy forever his presence and the pleasures of being at his right hand. On the other hand, there is the fear of failing to trust in God and thus to experience that ultimate death—the second death—separation from his presence forever (cf. Heb 2:3; 3:12; 4:1–3; 6:4–6; 10:26; 12:25). Ends do matter, especially when the ends are so disproportionate to the beginnings! The 90th Psalm, traditionally assigned to Moses, puts things into perspective:

> You turn men back to dust, saying, "Return to dust, O sons of men." For a thousand years in your sight are like a day that has just gone by, or like a watch in the night. You sweep men away in the sleep of death; they are like the new grass of the morning—though in the morning it springs up new, by evening it is dry and withered. We are consumed by your anger and terrified by your indignation. You have set our iniquities before you, our secret sins in the light of your presence. All our days pass away under your wrath; we finish our years with a moan. The length of our days is seventy years—or eighty, if we have the strength; yet their span is but trouble and sorrow, for they quickly pass, and we fly away. Who knows the power of your anger? For your wrath is as great as the fear that is due you. Teach us to number our days aright, that we may gain a heart of wisdom (Ps 90:3–12).

The ethical life is one in which the end is clearly perceived and exercises a powerful influence upon present behavior.

Faith and Politics: How does politics relate to eschatology? God's ultimate intentions for human beings do not involve some celestial picnic! God intends for us to finish the job assigned the first human couple in Eden—to be stewards of planet earth and rule over it in his name. That is precisely what we shall do when the kingdom of God comes in all its fullness.

Inasmuch as politics, rightly understood, deals with policy and the exercise of authority, it will never be passé. The OT consistently pictures the future of God's kingdom in very this-worldly terms. In Isaiah 2 we have mention of nations coming to Jerusalem, the hub of the world. Amos 9:11–15; Jeremiah 31–33 and Ezekiel 40–48, to name but a few, are all very concrete and specific about the future age—it is here on planet earth.

Though many Christians are quite unaware of this fact, the NT picture of the climax of the kingdom of God agrees with the OT. One need only read Matthew 5:5; 1 Corinthians 6:2 and Revelation 21:1–8 to see this.

The final vision of the kingdom of God on earth is depicted in terms of a very political kind of entity—a huge city, the capital of a worldwide kingdom. God dwells in the New Jerusalem with believers on a new earth forever (Rev 21:3). According to the Bible, the final form of human government—a blasphemous, demonic dictatorship—suffers total destruction at the hands of God (Da 7:26; Rev 18), and the ultimate form of human government—a theocracy—endures forever (Da 7:27; Rev 11:15). Jesus Christ is Lord of lords and King of kings (Rev 19:16)! There are intimations in the NT that believers who have been faithful in the exercise of their gifts will be assigned positions of authority in the age to come ("I will put you in charge of many things" Mt 25:21 et al). What a joy it will be, however, when politics are no longer sabotaged by a sin nature, the fallen world, and the devil! Politics will be a sheer delight in such a setting.

Faith and the Future: Inasmuch as this entire chapter has focused on the future, we simply summarize our discussion. God has a future for Israel, a future that includes Gentiles (Am 9:11–12; Isa 2:1–5; cf. Ro 1:5). In order to realize this future, he must intervene in a radical and supernatural way, at the time called the Day of the Lord. This Day of the Lord includes fearful judgments upon the earth (Isa 2:6–25; cf. Mt 24:15–25 and parallels; Rev 6:12–17). The righteous and the wicked are separated at that time (Isa 10:20–23; cf. Mt 13:24–30, 36–43, 47–50; 25:31–45). Finally, God's future for his redeemed people includes a renewed earth (Isa 65:17–25; 66:22; cf. Rev 21:1–8).

The individual believer who dies before this grand event goes to be with the Lord in conscious bliss awaiting the day of resurrection (Da 12:13; cf. 2Co 5:8). This truth of a bodily resurrection unto a glorious existence was progressively revealed throughout the OT. This revelation was further developed by intertestamental Judaism, taken up and elaborated by NT writers, who founded their faith on the resurrection of Jesus Christ.

Salvation of the individual rests upon the Servant of the Lord, whose career is sketched out in the Servant Songs of Isaiah. In one of the most profound passages in the Bible, the servant gives his life as a substitutionary atonement for the sins of his people (Isa 52:13–53:12). The NT identifies the servant-redeemer as none other than Jesus of Nazareth.[62]

For Further Discussion:

What depictions of life after death in the popular media are in accordance with the Scriptures? Which are in contradiction?

What influence does one's view of the millennium have on the issue of the restoration of Israel?

Is Christian Zionism (view that the creation of the State of Israel in 1948 was part of God's plan and that Jews should have a state of their own in their ancestral homeland) a biblical view? Why or why not?

What attitude should Christians have toward the Arab peoples?

How seriously do modern people take the many OT passages warning of God's final judgment at the end of the age?

How do we account for the observation that some NT teachings are developments of the intertestamental era and do not come directly from the OT?

Why have so many Christians failed to realize that God's future for his people is centered on a new earth?

For Further Reading:

Baker, David W., ed. *Looking into the Future: Evangelical Studies in Eschatology.* Grand Rapids: Baker, 2001. Essays discussing different aspects of eschatology.

Bright, John. *The Kingdom of God*, pp. 156–186. Nashville: Abingdon, 1953.

Brower, Kent E. and Mark W. Elliot, eds. *Eschatology in Bible and Theology: Evangelical Essays at the Dawn of a New Millennium.* Downers Grove: InterVarsity, 1999. Essays written for the most part from a non-dispensational, amillennial viewpoint.

Bruce, F. F. *The New Testament Development of Old Testament Themes*, pp. 83–99. Grand Rapids: Eerdmans, 1968.

Dyer, Charles, ed. *Storm Clouds on the Horizon: Bible Prophecy and the Current Middle East Crisis*. Chicago: Moody, 2001. Essays written from a dispensational perspective.

Dyrness, William. *Themes in Old Testament Theology*, pp. 227–242. Downers Grove: InterVarsity, 1979.

Erickson, Millard J. *A Basic Guide to Eschatology: Making Sense of the Millennium*. Grand Rapids: Baker, 1999. Good overview of the millennial options.

Eichrodt, Walter. *Theology of the Old Testament*, pp. 472-511. Translated by J. A. Baker. 2 vols.; London: SCM; Philadelphia: Westminster, 1961-1967. A classic work written by a moderately critical, confessional scholar.

Fuller, Daniel P. *The Unity of the Bible*, pp. 405–457. Grand Rapids: Zondervan, 1992.

House, H. Wayne, ed. *Israel: The Land and the People: An Evangelical Affirmation of God's Promises*. Grand Rapids: Kregel, 1998. Essays defending the position adopted by the author of this textbook on the question of Israel's restoration.

Jewett, Paul. "Eschatology," *ZPEB*, 2:342–358.

Johnston, Philip S. and Peter Walker, eds. *The Land of Promise: Biblical, Theological and Contemporary Perspectives*. Downers Grove: InterVarsity, 2000. Essays for the most part taking a different stance on the restoration of Israel than that argued in this chapter.

Kaiser, Jr., Walter C. *Toward an Old Testament Theology*, pp. 192–196, 201–219, 228–261. Grand Rapids: Zondervan, 1978.

Ladd, George Eldon. "Eschatology," *ISBE*, 2:130–133.

Payne, J. Barton. *The Theology of the Older Testament*, pp. 443–463, 527–529. Grand Rapids: Zondervan, 1962.

Sauer, Erich. *The Dawn of World Redemption*, pp. 156–186. Grand Rapids: Eerdmans, 1961.

Schwarz, Hans. *Eschatology*. Grand Rapids: Eerdmans, 2000. Summary of what the Bible teaches on both cosmic and personal eschatology. Interacts with modern thought on the topic.

Vriezen, Th. C. *An Outline of Old Testament Theology*, pp. 350-372. Oxford: Basil Blackwell, 1966. Written from a moderately critical point of view.

Walker, P. W. L, ed. *Jerusalem Past and Present in the Purposes of God*. Cambridge: Tyndale House, 1992. This is a collection of essays reflecting diverse opinions about the rise of modern Israel and God's plan of redemption.

Endnotes

1. "Eschatology," *ZPEB*, 2:342.

2. See "Some Things You Should Know about Preventing Teen Suicide," *American Academy of Pediatrics* (2002). Online: http://www.aap.org/advocacy/childhealthmonth/prevteensuicide.htm

3. I am greatly indebted to Paul Jewett, "Eschatology," *ZPEB*, 2:342–347 and Robert L. Saucy, "The Eschatology of the Bible," *EBC*, 1:103–128 for this discussion of eschatology.

4. The following discussion is based on Colin Brown's, "Day of the Lord (Yahweh)," *ZPEB*, 2:46–47.

5. For further discussion see Elmer A. Martens, *God's Design: A Focus on Old Testament Theology* (Grand Rapids: Baker, 1981), pp. 125–130.

6. See von Rad, *Old Testament Theology*, 2:119-125.

7. See Eichrodt, *Theology of the Old Testament*, 1:479-481.

8. L. J. Coppes, "*Yôm*," *TWOT*, 1:370–371.

9. For a visual impression of the devastation of such a plague, consult *The National Geographic Magazine* (vol. 28:6 [December 1915], pp. 511–550), which shows a before and after photographic sequence of an actual locust plague in the Jerusalem area.

10. See also Bruce, *Development*, pp. 68–82.

11. See Martens, *God's Design*, p. 131.

12. P. 79, n. on 49:10.

13. See n. on 24:17, p. 226 and cf. Martens, *God's Design*, pp. 131–132.

14. See further F. Duane Lindsey, "The Call of the Servant in Isaiah 42:1–9, Part I of Isaiah's Songs of the Servant," *BSac* 139 (January–March 1982): 12–31; "The Commission of the Servant in Isaiah 49:1–13, Part 2," ibid. (April–June 1982): 129–145; "The Commitment of the Servant in Isaiah 50:4–11, Part

3," ibid. (July–September 1982):216–229; "The Career of the Servant in Isaiah 52:13–53:12, Part 4," ibid. (October–December 1982): 312–329.

15. For discussion of issues see R. T. France, "Servant of the Lord," *ZPEB*, 5:359–362 and R. K. Harrison, "Servant of the Lord," *ISBE*, 3d ed., 4:422.

16. See also Ringgren, *Messiah*, pp. 54–67.

17. See his article, "Ezekiel, Bridge between the Testaments," *JETS* 25:1 (March 1982): 23–32 for a full discussion of this point.

18. For a detailed, exegetical study of this saying, see Ben Witherington III, *The Christology of Jesus* (Minneapolis: Fortress, 1990), pp. 256–262.

19. See further George E. Ladd, "Eschatology," *ISBE*, 2:133.

20. Arthur W. Kac, *The Rebirth of the State of Israel* (Chicago: Moody, 1958), p. 30 lists about 86 passages involving the national and spiritual aspects of restoration. See also Walter C. Kaiser, Jr., "The Land of Israel and the Future Return (Zechariah 10:6-12)," in *Israel: The Land and the People: An Affirmation of God's Promises,* ed. H. Wayne House (Grand Rapids: Kregel, 1998), pp. 209-227.

21. According to the *Statistical Abstract of Israel*, no. 52, 2001, the population of Israel in 2000 was 6,289,200, representing 37% of world Jewry.

22. For further argumentation in defense of this point, see Robert L. Saucy, "The Church as the Mystery of God," in *Dispensationalism, Israel and the Church: The Search for Definition*, eds. Craig A. Blaising and Darrell L. Bock (Grand Rapids: Zondervan, 1992), pp. 127–155.

23. For more on this view see Colin Chapman, *Whose Promised Land?* (Tring: Lion, 1983); Joel B. Green, *How to Read Prophecy* (Downers Grove: InterVarsity, 1984), pp. 109–121; Tom Wright, "Jerusalem in the New Testament," in *Jerusalem Past and Present in the Purposes of God*, ed. P. W. L. Walker (Cambridge: Tyndale House, 1992), pp. 53–77; and Bruce K. Waltke, "A Response," in *Dispensationalism, Israel and the Church*, pp. 347–359.

24. "Eschatology," *ZPEB*, 2:345.

25. See Fee and Stuart, *How to Read*, p. 48.

26. For further discussion, see Larry R. Helyer, "Luke and the Restoration of Israel," *JETS* 36/3 (September 1993): 317–329 and Darrell L. Bock, "The Reign of the Lord Christ," in *Dispensationalism, Israel and the Church* (Grand Rapids: Zondervan, 1992), pp. 37-67.

27. See further, J. M. Scott, "Restoration of Israel," in *Dictionary of Paul and His Letters,* eds. Gerald H. Hawthorne, Ralph P. Martin, Daniel G. Reid (Downers Grove: InterVarsity, 1993), pp. 796-805 and idem, "And then all Israel will be saved (Ro 11:26)," (paper presented at the annual meeting of the Evangelical Theological Society, Colorado Springs, CO, 16 November 2001), pp. 1-38.

28. See further Larry R. Helyer, "Was Paul a Restorationist?" Unpublished paper read at the annual meeting of the Evangelical Theological Society, Washington, D. C., 1993. We have also discussed this in *Exploring Jewish Literature*, pp. 56, 59-61, 119.

29. We are aware how inadequate this discussion is since there are significant theological and hermeneutical issues at stake. For those in the Reformed tradition, Paul's letter to the Ephesians and the book of Hebrews point decisively to the church as the culmination of redemptive history. Taken in isolation, these two documents would belie any claims for a future, national restoration of Israel. But therein lies an important hermeneutical question. Can one simply take these portions in isolation from the rest of the canon of Scripture, or, more pointedly, can they serve as a privileged "canon within the canon?" A few in the Reformed tradition, and those who identify with Dispensationalism in its various forms, think that there is a larger scope to redemptive history than the church, glorious as it is. Within a larger scheme of things, the future restoration of Israel takes its place, however untidy it may seem. For further discussion of these issues, see especially the essays by Robert L. Saucy, The Church as the Mystery of God," pp. 127-155 and W. Edward Glenny, "The Israelite Imagery in 1 Peter 2," pp. 156-187 in Craig A. Blaising and Darrell L. Bock, eds., *Dispensationalism, Israel and the Church* (Grand Rapids: Zondervan, 1992).

30. The church historian, Philip Schaff, puts it this way:

> The most striking point in the eschatology of the ante-Nicene age is the prominent chiliasm, or millenarianism, that is the belief of a visible reign of Christ in glory on earth with the risen saints for a thousand years, before the general resurrection and judgment. It was indeed not the doctrine of the church embodied in any creed or form of devotion, but a widely current opinion of distinguished teachers (*History of the Christian Church*, 4 vols., rev. ed. [New York: Scribner's Sons, 1887], 2:614).

31. See Max I. Dimont, *Jews, God and History* (New York: Penguin, 1962) and Charles E. Silberman, *A Certain People: American Jews and Their Lives Today* (New York: Simon and Schuster, 1985).

32. Ronald B. Allen nicely captures the significance of Israel's rebirth as a nation:

> There is likely nothing in history that can compare to the restoration of the Hebrew people to their ancient land. What other people of any time, any continent, any lineage can claim what the people of modern Israel can claim? No people group has ever been removed from its land, dispersed among the nations, survived with a sense of self-awareness and identity, and–many hundreds of years later–been regathered to one place, their old place, and has become a nation and state once again. This is simply without parallel ("The Land of Israel," in *Israel: The Land and the People*, p. 26).

Allen mentions hearing the noted historian Arnold Toynbee speak about the "historically unparalleled phenomenon of the formation of the State of Israel" (n. 34, p. 33).

33. See Richard E. Gade, *A Historical Survey of Anti-Semitism* (Grand Rapids: Baker, 1981); David A. Rausch, *A Legacy of Hatred* (Chicago: Moody, 1984); Marvin Wilson, *Our Father Abraham* (Grand Rapids: Eerdmans, 1989).

34. For more details, see Louis Goldberg, "Historical and Political Factors in the Twentieth Century Affecting the Identity of Israel," in *Israel: The Land and the People*, pp. 113-141.

35. See Leo Pinsker, *Auto-Emancipation*, ed. A. S. Eban (London: Federation of Zionist Youth, 1932).

36. This was the infamous "Dreyfus Affair," named after the Jewish officer who was convicted (1894), and later exonerated (1906), of passing French military secrets to the Germans. See Max I. Dimont, *Jews, God and History* (New York: Penguin, 1962), pp. 324–328 for a brief overview. An in-depth analysis of the eposide may be found in Leslie Derfler, ed., *The Dreyfus Affair: Tragedy of Errors?* (Boston: D. C. Heath, 1963).

37. See Mark Twain, *The Innocents Abroad* (Hartford, CT: American Publishing, 1870), esp. chs. 18–30.

38. For the text and commentary see L. J. S, "Balfour Declaration," *Encyclopedia Judaica*, 16 vols. (Jerusalem: Macmillan, 1971), 4:131–135.

39. See further Kac, *Rebirth*, pp. 47–56. Lawrence J. Epstein documents the contribution of Christian Zionists in *Zion's Call: Christian Contributions to the Origins and Development of Israel* (Lanham, MD: University Press of America, 1984). See also Timothy P. Weber's account in *Living in the Shadow of the Second Coming*, enlarged ed. (Grand Rapids: Zondervan, 1983); K. Crombie, *For the Love of Zion: Christian Witness and the Restoration of Israel* (London: Hodder and Stoughton, 1991) and the essays in House, *Israel: The Land and the People*.

40. Charles Lee Feinberg makes these observations:

> Strangely enough, this passage has been explained as recording the invasion of Palestine by Nebuchadnezzar in the days before the Babylonian captivity. This is impossible for a number of reasons, particularly because the results of the conflicts were not at all the same. Another student of the text refers verses 1–9 to the Maccabean conquests. . . . The fact is, no such coalition of nations (not even in the Roman war of the first century) against Israel has ever occurred in the past (*The Minor Prophets* [Chicago: Moody, 1951], p. 330).

41. We reject as utterly unfounded the widespread Arab denial of the Holocaust as a "Zionist lie" and the equation of Israeli occupation and reprissals against terrorism as Nazism. The denial of a historical fact and blatant anti-Semitic slander for propaganda purposes only exacerbates an already supercharged situation.

42. Peter Grose, *Israel in the Mind of America* (New York: Alfred Knopf, 1983), p. 127. See the entire chapter for further details. See also *Lest We Forget: A History of the Holocaust on CD-ROM*. Logos Research Systems Version 2.0, 1995.

43. See Berl Wein, *Triumph of Survival on CD-ROM*. Disk 2. Davka Corporation. 1996; Michael J. Neufeld and Michael Berenbaum, eds., *The Bombing of Auschwitz: Should the Allies Have Attempted It* (New York: St. Martins Press, 2000); Walter Laqueur, ed., *The Holocaust Encyclopedia* (New Haven: Yale University Press, 2001).

44. See Robert Clouse, *Four Views of the Millennium* (Grand Rapids: Zondervan, 1977) and Millard J. Erickson, *Contemporary Options in Eschatology* (Grand Rapids: Baker, 1977) for further treatment of this issue.

45. The writing of Raymond Moody sparked a renewal of this topic. See his *Life After Death: The Investigation of a Phenomenon—Survival of Bodily Death* (New York: Bantam Books, 1975).

46. For a biblical critique of these phenomena, see Stephen Board, "Light at the End of the Tunnel," *Eternity* (July 1977): 13–17, 30.

47. Once again we are greatly indebted to Dr. David Allan Hubbard's lecture notes in the class "Themes in Old Testament Theology."

48. See *BDB*, pp. 982–983. For a different interpretation of the meaning and referent of Sheol, see R. Laird Harris, "*shᵉôl*," *TWOT*, 2:892–893.

49. See the *New Scofield Reference Bible*, p. 1106 (notes 1–3) for further elaboration of this view.

50. See R. Laird Harris, "*shᵉôl*," *TWOT*, 2:892–893 and idem, "The Meaning of the Word Sheol as Shown by Parallels in Poetic Passages," *JETS*, 4:129–135 for a defense of this view.

51. For a comparative study of pagan notions of life after death in the ancient Near East, one may read the following: *ANET*, pp. 32–36 (Egyptian views); pp. 52–56, "Inanna's Descent to the Nether World," (Sumerian); pp. 106–110, "Descent of Ishtar to the Nether World," and "A Vision of the Nether World" (Akkadian); and *The Odyssey*, pp. 172–188 in the Penguin Classics series (Greek).

52. For further discussion of this difficult topic see: H. Buis, "Sheol," *ZPEB*, 5:395; Douglas K. Stuart, "Sheol," *ISBE*, 4:472 and H. Bietenhard, "Hell," *The New International Dictionary of New Testament Theology*, ed. Colin Brown (Grand Rapids: Zondervan, 1975), 2:206–209.

53. See Elmer Smick, "Tree of Knowledge; Tree of Life," *ISBE*, 3d ed., 4:901–903, for an extended discussion of this matter.

54. See the full treatment by J. B. Payne, "Burial," *ISBE*, 3d ed., 1:556–561.

55. See, e. g., Norman H. Snaith, *The Distinctive Ideas of the Old Testament* (New York: Schocken, 1964), p. 89.

56. See further J. Barton Payne, *The Theology of the Older Testament* (Grand Rapids: Zondervan, 1962), pp. 445–446 and id., "Burial," 1:556–561.

57. See further on this Kaiser, *Toward an Old Testament Theology*, p. 99.

58. See, e.g., *HarperCollins Study Bible*, pp. 1011–1013.

59. See *NIVSB*, pp. 1014–1016.

60. *NIVSB*, p. 755, n. on 19:26.

61. See further G. E. Ladd, "Eschatology," *ISBE*, 2:133–134.

62. *The Greek New Testament*, 4th rev. ed. (Stuttgart: Deutsche Bibelgesellschaft/United Bible Societies, 1993). Lists 34 NT allusions to Isaiah 52:13–53:12.

chapter **10**

The Way of Wisdom and Worship

(Scripture reading: Song of Songs; Psalms 1; 4; 6; 24; 98; 122; Proverbs 1; 3; 7; 10; 31; Ecclesiastes 1–3; 12; Job 1–7; 38–42)

Leading Questions:

What types of literature make up the wisdom writings?
What is distinctive about the wisdom tradition?
Upon what issues do the wisdom books reflect?
What is wisdom and how does one acquire it?
Why is the wisdom tradition important for understanding the NT?
How should we view the book of Psalms?
How does the Psalter help us understand the worship experiences of Israelites?
How does the book of Psalms continue to speak to us?

Introduction

The books we will study in this chapter "contain some of the most potent literature of human history, and the ideas they treat are among the most cogent that the human heart has entertained." So states Hassell Bullock in his introductory text on the wisdom and poetic books of the OT.[1] He is right; they engage the timeless questions of human existence. But they also convey an eternal perspective on these questions that we ignore only to our detriment.

To this point, our study of the OT has stressed the prophetic dimension of God's revelation to his people. That is, the word of God has been transmitted through the medium of the prophet(s). We have characterized redemptive history as a deed-word complex. God's redemptive acts receive their explanation by means of a prophetic word. This chain of deed-word complexes constitutes the bulk of the OT Scriptures (see chs. one, seven and eight).

But this is not the only way God revealed himself to Israel. Being made in God's image involves the capacity to perceive his handiwork imbedded in the created order. The sages of Israel, led by the Spirit, discerned this divine order in the nature of things. They distilled their observations and passed them on for posterity. In this chapter, we will sit at the feet of the sages and listen to their observations and admonitions. Their most important observation and admonition is this: "Wisdom is supreme; therefore get wisdom. Though it cost all you have, get understanding" (Pr 4:7).

WISDOM AND PROPHECY

God-Source of Wisdom
Wise man/woman
Indirect revelation

God-Source of Revelation
Prophet
Direct revelation

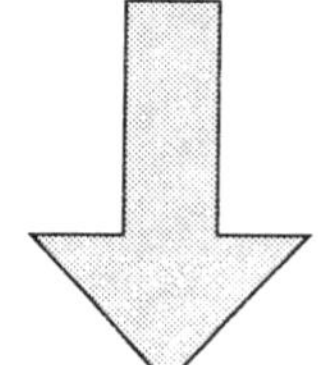

"Thus says the Lord"

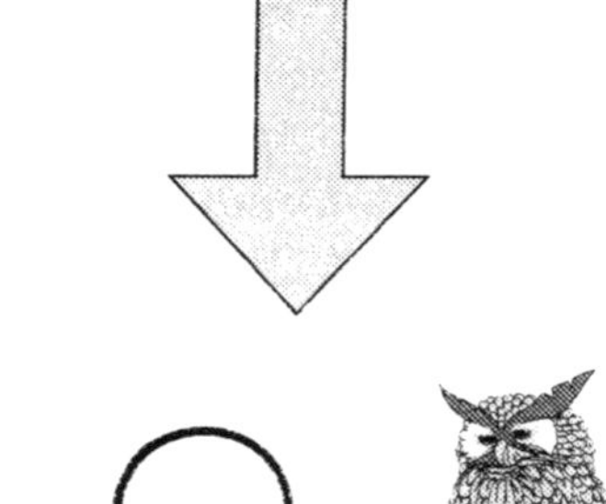

Observation of the details of life and meditation

Inspiration and proclamation

We will also take time in this chapter to "know that the LORD is God. It is he who made us and we are his; we are his people, the sheep of his pasture. Enter his gates with thanksgiving and his courts with praise" (Ps 100:3-4). Thus we enter imaginatively the worship experiences of Israel and seek to inform our own worship of God by their praises and prayers. The rituals and liturgies of Israel have a time-transcending quality. They continue to beckon us away from the preoccupations of the temporal in order to catch a glimpse of the eternal.

The Way of Wisdom

Classification of Old Testament Wisdom Books

So what are the books that scholars classify as belonging to the wisdom tradition of Israel, and precisely what are we talking about when we use the expression "wisdom tradition"? Let us take up the first question.

The Hebrew canon is divided into three sections: the Pentateuch (Genesis-Deuteronomy); the Prophets, consisting of the former prophets (Joshua-2 Kings) and the latter prophets (Isaiah-Malachi); and the Writings.[2] The expression "Writings" comes from the Greek translation of the Hebrew OT, designated by the abbreviation LXX.[3] In the LXX, the term Hagiographa, literally, "holy writings," was used for this third division of the canon.[4] The wisdom books are in this section, along with the book of Psalms. They are as follows: Job, Proverbs, Ecclesiastes and Song of Songs. However, some of the psalms should be included as well, since they too partake of the characteristics of wisdom. Among the psalms included are 1; 10; 14; 37; 49; 73; 90 and 112. In addition, the "Prayer of Habakkuk" (Hab 3) displays wisdom features. Even this listing, however, is misleading, since the wisdom tradition has left its distinctive mark in the Pentateuch and Prophets as well. We will draw attention to several instances.

Wisdom literature does not end with the OT. In the interval between the Old and New Testaments, several fine examples of wisdom writings emerged. In the Apocrypha we have Ecclesiasticus (not to be confused with canonical Ecclesiastes), or, as it was known in the rabbinic tradition, The Book (or instruction) of Ben Sira, written about 180 B.C. Also in the Apocrypha is a wisdom passage from Baruch (3:9–4:4). Another work, not part of the Apocrypha, but coming from the intertestamental era, is 4 Maccabees. Of course, in the NT, we have a splendid example of wisdom teaching in the epistle of James. Furthermore, in the teaching of Jesus, as recorded in the Gospels, we have sayings that resemble wisdom literature.[5]

The Song of Songs requires separate mention. In terms of its formal characteristics, this piece is a collection of lyrical songs, having as their principal theme romantic love. The atmosphere of the songs is highly emotional and joyous. The lovers are enthralled with each other and the beauty of nature. This work is an invitation to enjoy God's good gifts.

Classification of Types of Wisdom

What distinguishes wisdom from other kinds of literature? And what, after all, is wisdom according to the biblical writers? We begin with a definition. The most important term is the word (*ḥokmâ*). The root meaning is probably "firm" or "well-grounded." At any rate, "the usages of *ḥokmâ* in the Hebrew Bible cover the whole gamut of human experience."[6] The NIV uses such translations as "wisdom" (131 times), "skill" or "skilled" (3 times), "learning" (2 times), "ability" (1 time), and "wise" or "wise advice" (2 times).[7] Drawing together related terms found in the Hebrew Bible, we can flesh out this definition even further. Words belonging to the same semantic field as *ḥokmâ*, or wisdom, include understanding, insight, discernment, good sense, and intelligence. We may summarize as follows: *Wisdom refers to the practical art of being skillful and successful in life*. William Dyrness puts it this way: "If cult is the form of worship in the temple or tabernacle, wisdom is the life of worship extended to the home and marketplace. Wisdom is religion outside of church."[8]

Wisdom literature, like other kinds of literature in the OT that we have already studied, was not a Hebrew innovation. On the contrary, Wisdom literature in the ancient Near East goes back well before the time of Abraham (see below). That which distinguishes wisdom in the Hebrew Bible from its counterpart among Israel's neighbors relates to its ultimate source and purpose. Biblical wisdom is a divine gift and is fundamentally moral and spiritual. Ancient Near Eastern wisdom stems from a polytheistic worldview and is essentially secular in orientation. Solomon's prayer, at the beginning of his reign, highlights the moral dimension of Hebrew wisdom: "So give your servant a discerning heart to govern your people and to distinguish between right and wrong" (1Ki 3:9a). In other words, the seat of wisdom is the heart, the center of moral discernment and decision. Wisdom is essentially a divine gift of discernment. The opening of the book of Proverbs, where the purpose and theme of the work are stated, makes this point:

> The proverbs of Solomon son of David, king of Israel: for attaining wisdom and discipline; for understanding words of insight; for acquiring a disciplined and prudent life, doing what is right and just and fair; for giving prudence to the simple, knowledge and discretion to the young—let the wise listen and add to their learning, and let the discerning get guidance—for understanding proverbs and parables, the sayings and riddles of the wise. The fear of the LORD is the beginning of knowledge, but fools despise wisdom and discipline (Pr 1:1-7).

From this, it would appear that wisdom involves having a proper perspective on all of life. That perspective is defined in the Wisdom literature as "the fear of the Lord." In operational terms, we might say that *wisdom means seeing life from God's point of view* (cf. Pr 2:6).

The above quotation from Proverbs designates several different "forms" in which wisdom might be transmitted: proverbs and parables, sayings and riddles. Each of these deserves scrutiny.

Proverbs. First, what is a proverb and how is it different from a parable? Underlying both terms is one Hebrew word, *māshāl*. *Māshāl* has a rather wide range of meanings as reflected by the various English translations: proverb, parable, allegory, byword, taunt, or discourse.[9] A proverb is a short, pithy saying that draws attention to a widely recognized observation or principle. But an observation or principle can also be underscored by drawing an extended comparison from the realm of nature or human experience. This is in the form of a short narrative framework. We illustrate the difference with several biblical examples of proverbs:

> Lazy hands make a man poor,
> but diligent hands bring wealth (Pr 10:4).
> Hatred stirs up dissension,
> but love covers over all wrongs (10:12).
> When words are many, sin is not absent,
> but he who holds his tongue is wise (10:19).

Note that each of the above examples consists of two parallel, antithetical lines, which we call a couplet. The first line makes an observation of a causal nature, in the above cases, a negative relationship: laziness, hatred and talkativeness all result in unpleasant or harmful outcomes. The second line states attitudes or actions that result in positive outcomes. We could also find examples of proverbs in which the first line sets out a positive attitude or relationship and the second a negative. Scholars classify both kinds of proverbs as antithetical parallelism in that the second line states the opposite of the first. These may easily be spotted in the NIV, because the second line usually begins with the conjunction "but" (see, however, Pr 11:24).

Now consider the following proverbs:

> He who winks maliciously causes grief,
> and a chattering fool comes to ruin (10:10).
> He who conceals his hatred has lying lips,
> and whoever spreads slander is a fool (10:18).
> As vinegar to the teeth and smoke to the eyes,
> so is a sluggard to those who send him (10:26).

In each of the above examples we have the typical couplet; however, the second line is not an antithesis of the first, but rather, a similar idea or reinforcement of the first—synonymous parallelism. Each of the above examples states an undesirable or harmful course of action. One may, however, find examples of positive or useful behavior set forth as a model or paradigm. Note that the second line usually begins with the conjunction "and." This is not always the case, however, as the following proverb demonstrates:

> Like a gold ring in a pig's snout
> is a beautiful woman who shows no discretion (11:22).

The connective word "like" (or "as") draws attention to a similarity, and a rather attention-arresting one at that! "Better . . . than" and "not . . . nor" may also be employed (cf. 12:9 and 19:2).

There are, in fact, even more developed forms of proverbs than antithetic and synonymous parallelism. Sometimes extra lines are added to develop the comparison even further. This is called a synthetic parallelism (cf. 22:22; 23:4-5). Another form is the so-called numerical proverb:[10]

> There are six things the LORD hates, seven that are detestable to him: haughty eyes, a lying tongue, hands that shed innocent blood, a heart that devises wicked schemes, feet that are quick to rush into evil, a false witness who pours out lies and a man who stirs up dissension among brothers (6:16-17).

Parable. The parable is a relatively simple, short, realistic story. It is designed to convey a single point, in most instances, and to do so in a memorable way. The point is usually moral or spiritual in nature. Perhaps the best way to begin illustrating parables is to go back to one we have already read in the historical books. In 2 Samuel 12, Nathan the prophet received a very difficult and potentially dangerous mission: he is to confront King David and announce his punishment for adultery and murder. The approach Nathan adopted is a classic. He purports to bring an appeal to the supreme court of Israel (a function of the king) from a peasant who has a claim against a rich neighbor. The rich man stole and ate the poor man's pet ewe lamb. Although it is credible enough for David to react to it as a real incident, the case is fictitious.

By means of this parable, Nathan forces David, unwittingly, to pass sentence on himself. The verdict that David renders is based upon the Mosaic Law: if one had stolen a sheep from another, he must repay fourfold (Ex 22:1). In his anger, David asserts that the offender really deserves to die, owing to the outrageous character of the theft. In this David condemns himself: he too is guilty of crimes meriting death. The Lord graciously passes a lesser sentence, though in retrospect, David would no doubt have preferred his own death than to witness the disasters that befell his family. In this connection it is interesting to note that, according to 2 Samuel 13–1 Kings 2, four family members of David suffer disgrace and death: Tamar, Amnon, Absalom and Adonijah—the four sheep that he must repay! It was a price far too expensive in human terms. Sexual immorality is always too expensive in human terms to be worth it. Get wisdom!

Another illustration of an extended parable is found in 2 Samuel 14:1-17. In this case the creator of the parable is "a wise woman" from the town of Tekoa, the hometown of Amos the prophet. Again, the parable is designed to change King David's mind and policy—in this case, concerning his exiled son Absalom. In the guise of a real case, the woman is able to elicit from the king a ruling that has direct bearing on his own situation.

Related to a parable is the fable, "a concise narrative making an edifying or cautionary point and often employing as characters animals that speak and act like human beings."[11] The classic example of this in the OT is Jotham's fable of the olive, fig and vine (Jdg 9:8-15). The warning was directed to the inhabitants of Shechem, who had foolishly selected Abimelech as their king. F. F. Bruce explains how the fable "works" in its setting:

> The point is that trees, which have useful work to do, are too busy to accept the offer of kingship; the only tree to accept the offer is the useless briar, which, far from providing food or shelter, catches fire and burns the other trees down. In the actual situation the moral is plain, and does not require to be spelled out, although Jotham draws his hearers' attention to the lesson of his tale.[12]

Riddle. The riddle is a hidden saying, a conundrum, that is, a fanciful question to which the answer is a pun, or a problem having no known solution. The primary point of a riddle is its aim, which is to puzzle the reader. The clearest example in the OT is Samson's riddle for the Philistines (Jdg 14:14): "Out of the eater, something to eat; out of the strong, something sweet." Only by knowing the unique circumstances involving Samson's slaying of a lion and the subsequent beehive in its carcass, could anyone hope to provide an answer. Of course, the Philistines acquired the answer through extortion. In the account of the Queen of Sheba's visit to Solomon, it says "she came to test him with hard questions" (1Ki 10:1). These "hard questions" were riddles. The riddles were questions that seemed insoluble to the Queen of Sheba. The biblical historian, perhaps with some pride, narrates the outcome of her examination of Solomon: "Solomon answered all her questions; nothing was too hard for the king to explain to her" (1Ki 10:3).

Reflective discourses on problem areas. The Books of Job and Ecclesiastes, while having examples of proverbs, are better known for their discursive passages. A discourse is defined as a passage displaying coherence, unity and completeness. In the context of the Wisdom literature, we discover that the discourses center on problem areas—areas in which the received faith of Israel seemed inadequate or questionable. Several psalms also feature problematical issues and deserve to be included in this category (e.g., 49; 73). The problem areas are usually a variation on the universal question: Why do bad things happen to good people? In short, the problem of evil spawned a number of reflective discourses by the sages of Israel. In this regard, they had plenty of company, inasmuch as the other peoples of the ancient Near East likewise grappled with this vexing problem (see below).

Comparison of Hebrew and Ancient Near East Wisdom

As in the case of virtually all the genres we have encountered during our survey of the OT, none of them were unique to or invented by Israel. The uniqueness of OT literature resides not in its various forms, but in its message. And, of course, the uniqueness of the message goes back to the uniqueness of the God of Israel.

Clearly, the cultural currents flowing across the Middle East left an impression on Israel. Human experience has common denominators, and peoples in the same region of the world very often share common approaches to life. The Lord was pleased to accommodate his revelation to Israel in modes and forms indigenous to that time and part of the world. Thus we find that the dialogue or monologue form already existed in Mesopotamia and Egypt, long before the Books of Job or Ecclesiastes. Likewise, the genre of instructions, admonitions and proverbial sayings, represented in the Bible primarily by Proverbs and Ecclesiastes, has earlier exemplars in Mesopotamia and Egypt. The *Sayings of Amenemope* from Egypt are especially close to Proverbs 22:17–24:22. Fables and contest literature, occurring in Judges 9:7-15; 14:13-14 and 1 Kings 10:1-3 have predecessors in ancient Mesopotamia, and the same may be said for lyrical love songs.[13]

Did the Israelites simply copy the wisdom writings of their neighbors? John Walton carefully analyzes the cognate materials from Mesopotamia and Egypt. Since it is generally recognized that the closest parallels stem from the Egyptian wisdom writings, we cite his judicious summary with regard to the *Sayings of Amenemope*:

> In the end, it cannot be denied that Israelite wisdom shares much with the wisdom of Egypt, and there is no reason to doubt or deny that the Israelites were aware of and influenced by Egyptian literature. Whatever the amount of this general indebtedness, it has not yet been demonstrated that any specific Israelite work was merely an adaptation of any specific Egyptian work.[14]

We give but one example of the superiority of the Hebrew wisdom tradition. The book of Job justly takes its place as one of the great literary masterpieces of all time. Job wrestles with the classic problem of faith: How do you justify God's fairness when bad things happen to good people? We cannot delve into all the twists and turns of the various arguments advanced by Job's three friends. What is important is the conclusion. God appears to Job. He asks him the critical question: "Would you discredit my justice? Would you condemn me to justify yourself?" (40:8). Job's experience of God's presence revolutionizes his attitude. He does not receive an intellectual solution to the problem of evil; he does not receive an explanation at all! But it no longer matters. Job knows that God cares about him, and that is sufficient. "Surely I spoke of things I did not understand, things too wonderful for me to know. . . . My ears had heard of you but now my eyes have seen you. Therefore I despise myself and repent in dust and ashes." (42:3b, 5-6). Nothing compares to this among the neighboring cultures.

Listen in on the "advice" given by a friend to a sufferer in Mesopotamian literature, "The Babylonian Theodicy":[15]

> Respected friend, what you say is sad.
> Dear friend, you have let your mind dwell on evil.
> You have made your good sense like that of an incompetent person;
> You have changed your beaming face to scowls.
> Our fathers do indeed give up and go the way of death.
> He who looks to his god has a protective spirit;
>
> Ever seek the [correct standards] of justice.
> Your . . . , the mighty one, will show kindness,
> [. . .] will grant mercy.
>
> The arrow will turn to the gorer who trampled down the fields.
> The opulent prominent person who heaps up goods
> Will be burned to death by the king before his time.
> Would you wish to go the way these have gone?
> Rather seek the lasting reward of (your) god!
>
> My just, knowledgeable friend, your thoughts are perverse.
> You have now forsaken justice and blaspheme against your god's plans.
>
> Follow in the way of the god, observe his rites,
>
> Unless you seek the will of the god, what success can you have?
> He that bears his god's yoke never lacks food, even though it be sparse.
> Seek the favorable breath of the god,
> What you have lost in a year you will make up in a moment.
>
> The mind of the god, like the center of the heavens, is remote;
> Knowledge of it is very difficult; people cannot know it.

> Though it is possible to find out what the will of the god is, people do not know how to do it.

Notice the assumption that something has angered the god/goddess (thus the basic similarity to Job's friends). Furthermore, the sufferer should just "shape up" and have a better mental attitude (an early example of positive thinking!). The problem for the sufferer is to discover what his offense is and then take the appropriate steps *ritually* to regain the favor of the deity. The offense, of course, is understood to be societal or ritual in nature—not one of personal sin against a holy God. But alas, there is nowhere the confident trust of Job at the end of his quest. The poor Babylonian sufferer could only cry out: "Can a life of happiness be assured? I wish I knew how!" Examples could be multiplied to demonstrate the more satisfying and optimistic viewpoint of the Hebrew wisdom tradition.[16] God's will and way were not past finding out.

> If you call out for insight and cry aloud for understanding, and if you look for it as for silver and search for it as for hidden treasure, then you will understand the fear of the LORD and find the knowledge of God. For the LORD gives wisdom, and from his mouth come knowledge and understanding (Pr 2:3-6).

Channels of OT Wisdom

Where did wise men and women fit in the larger context of Hebrew society? Was there a recognized caste or office of sages? If so, how and where did they function? We begin with a text in Jeremiah 18:18: "for the teaching of the law by the priest will not be lost, nor will counsel from the wise, nor the word from the prophets. . . ." At least by the end of the first commonwealth (beginning of the sixth century B.C.), there appears to be a recognizable class whose function was to provide counsel to kings and governmental leaders.

But there is evidence that sages operated much earlier, even in the early monarchy. One recalls Joab's employment of a wise woman of Tekoa in order to effect reconciliation between David and his exiled son Absalom (2Sa 14:1-20). The story of Ahithophel requires consideration since he is explicitly called "David's counselor" (2Sa 15:12). The sacred historian comments on his standing by noting "in those days the advice Ahithophel gave was like that of one who inquires of God. That was how both David and Absalom regarded all of Ahithophel's advice" (2Sa 16:23). Both of the above instances depict sages serving in the royal court. Does this mean that the wisdom movement in Israel was essentially a product of the ruling class?

More likely, the roots of wisdom spring from village and family life. In 2 Samuel 20 we read of a rebellion by Sheba son of Bichri. When he flees to Abel Beth Maacah in northern Galilee, Joab besieges the city. In the course of the siege, "a wise woman called from the city, 'Listen! Listen! . . . Long ago they used to say, "Get your answer at Abel," and that settled it'" (20:16, 18). She is able to persuade the city to turn over Sheba and thus spare the city. What is interesting is the reference to a long tradition of wise sages at this northern city. Tekoa in Judah, the home of Amos the prophet, likewise had such a reputation. In this regard, scholars have long noted the presence of sayings typical of the wisdom tradition in Amos' oracles.[17] We think a good case can be made for the assumption that parents and village elders constituted the taproot of Hebrew wisdom. They were the primary channels through which the wisdom of Israel was passed on to a new generation.[18]

On the other hand, there can be little doubt that the united monarchy, under the impetus of Solomon's reputation as the wise man par excellence, ushered the Israelite wisdom tradition into a new era. Israelite wisdom competed with and was augmented by the wisdom of the ancient Near East. Note the obvious pride of the sacred historian when he describes the wisdom of Solomon:

> God gave Solomon wisdom and very great insight, and a breadth of understanding as measureless as the sand on the seashore. Solomon's wisdom was greater than the wisdom of all the men of the East, and greater than all the wisdom of Egypt. He was wiser than any other man, including Ethan the Ezrahite—wiser than Heman, Calcol and Darda, the sons of Mahol. And his fame spread to all the surrounding nations. He spoke three thousand proverbs and his songs numbered a thousand and five. He described plant life, from the cedar of Lebanon to the hyssop that grows out of walls. He also taught about animals and birds, reptiles and fish. Men of all nations came to listen to Solomon's wisdom, sent by all the kings of the world, who had heard of his wisdom (1Ki 4:29-34).

Just as Moses would be definitively associated with the Torah (the Pentateuch), "so Solomon became linked with a set of 'wisdom books': Proverbs, Ecclesiastes, and Canticles [Song of Songs]."[19]

It may be that in the Solomonic era, and thereafter, official schools for scribes and sages arose. We must be cautious on this point, however, since the biblical text itself does not explicitly refer to such, nor has their existence been confirmed by extra-biblical evidence. What we can say is that by the time of Jesus Son of Sirach in the second century B.C. we do have an official school devoted to imparting wisdom (cf. Sir 51:23). Prior to Jesus Son of Sirach, if there were "wisdom schools," they were probably more informal than official.[20]

Contribution of Wisdom

What are some leading themes in the wisdom tradition of Israel, and how do they speak to our world today? We select four motifs: Learning to be wise, listening to the created order, living with limitations and loving wisely. Each one deserves extended discussion, but we must be content with a few observations.

Learning to be wise. The book of Proverbs is a collection of sayings and observations designed to train young leaders in the fine art of diplomacy and leadership.[21] We think, however, that it incorporates the rich legacy of Hebrew sages going back into the earliest periods of Israelite history. One thinks of young Joseph, "a discerning and wise man" whom the Spirit of God "gave success in whatever he did" (Ge 39–41). In the days of the exodus we read of Bezalel whom the Spirit of God filled "with skill, ability and knowledge in all kinds of crafts" (Ex 31:3). The latter instance highlights a very practical dimension of wisdom. In other words, wisdom has a broader audience than merely administrators and aristocrats—it casts its net around the working classes as well.[22]

The wisdom teaching enshrined in Proverbs passionately appeals to young people to make a choice—a choice to live wisely. In framing this choice, the book utilizes a common wisdom motif: the two ways. Just as Psalm 1 begins with a didactic or wisdom psalm, inviting the reader/listener to pursue the way of the righteous rather than the way of the wicked, so Proverbs holds out the same two options. The difference, however, is that the way of the wicked in Proverbs is generally characterized as folly or foolishness. We thus have the polar opposites, wisdom and folly. The options of wisdom and folly are even personified as two women who stand at the street corners and public squares soliciting customers (cf. 2:20-33; 5:3-23; 7:6-27; 8:1-21). It is a bold metaphor, but highly effective. Will the young person succumb to the shameless enticements of Dame Folly, or turn instead to the invitation of Dame

Wisdom, who offers that which is sweeter than honey and more precious than gold? Each reader must decide.

We sketch the portrait of a fool first. In so doing we synthesize many sayings scattered throughout the book. The result is a composite sketch—a portrait that we might call "the perfect fool"! In that regard it is somewhat artificial, but nonetheless, highly instructive.

1. The characteristics of a fool. Who is a fool? The various Hebrew words rendered as "fool," "foolish," "simple," "wicked," "base," and "lawless," do not refer to one who is intellectually deficient. IQ, SAT or ACT scores do not determine who is a "fool"; on the contrary, the fool may be very bright and clever. For the wise men and women of Israel, religious and moral issues define the class known as fools. The fool is one who denies the claims of God upon his or her life.[23] The fool is a practical atheist in that he/she lives as if God does not really have anything to do with day-to-day living.

The makings of a fool apparently begin with an attitude of complacency ("the complacency of fools will destroy them" [1:32]). Life is not taken with a moral seriousness. Before one becomes a fool, there is a certain "openness" to the various options available. (The notion of being open seems to be the root idea of one Hebrew word used here for the simple).[24] With this openness is the willingness to experiment, the inclination to try out the intriguing alternatives. Others readily influence this frame of mind. The enticements of sinners, who seem to be enjoying life, find a warm reception in the heart of the simple (1:10-16, 22-24). Not surprisingly, this fascination with the rebellious is often coupled with rejection of parental advice and discipline. "A fool spurns his father's discipline . . . a foolish man despises his mother" (15:5, 20). Complacency is a form of passive rebellion; it rarely ends there, however.

"A fool finds pleasure in evil conduct" (10:23). There is a certain excitement in doing what cuts against the grain of societal norms and community standards. "For they cannot sleep till they do evil" (Pr 4:16). But what is worse, to the fool, these standards are not anchored in the moral nature of the Creator. According to the fool, morality consists of rules devised by some killjoy rather than an essential component of the created order. This fundamental miscalculation is costly: "fools die for lack of judgment" (10:21).

The behavior of the fool must be justified. This he/she does. "The way of a fool seems right to him" (12:15). The fool can always find arguments to support his actions or lack thereof. There is a decided resistance toward receiving advice. Very often the need to justify sinful behavior leads to a denial of basic truths about God and his creation. This alternative worldview, of course, puts the fool on a collision course with the accepted views of the larger community. In the inevitable arguments and debates that ensue, the fool displays contempt for accepted authority and cherishes an exalted view of his/her own understanding of things: "A fool shows his annoyance at once" (12:16). "Stay away from a foolish man, for you will not find knowledge on his lips" (14:7); "a fool is hot-headed and reckless" (14:16); "A fool finds no pleasure in understanding but delights in airing his own opinions" (18:2); "A fool's lips bring him strife, and his mouth invites a beating. A fool's mouth is his undoing, and his lips are a snare to his soul" (18:6-7); "every fool is quick to quarrel" (20:3).

Does this conflict with accepted morality lead to repentance? Alas, the usual pattern is just the opposite. The fool persists, to his/her own hurt, in sinful behavior and its justification. "As a dog returns to its vomit, so a fool repeats his folly" (26:11). "Though you grind a fool in a mortar, grinding him like grain with a pestle, you will not remove his folly from him" (27:22). "A rebuke impresses a man of discernment more than a hundred lashes a fool" (17:10).

Not surprisingly, this kind of behavior eventually alienates and destroys the fool. The following warning highlights the outcome of a fool's life—it is not a pretty picture:

> How long will you simple ones love your simple ways? How long will mockers delight in mockery and fools hate knowledge? If you had responded to my rebuke, I would have poured out my heart to you and made my thoughts known to you. But since you rejected me when I called and no one gave heed when I stretched out my hand, since you ignored all my advice and would not accept my rebuke, I in turn will laugh at your disaster; I will mock when calamity overtakes you—when calamity overtakes you like a storm, when disaster sweeps over you like a whirlwind, when distress and trouble overwhelm you. Then they will call to me but I will not answer; they will look for me but will not find me. Since they hated knowledge and did not choose to fear the LORD, since they would not accept my advice and spurned my rebuke, they will eat the fruit of their ways and be filled with the fruit of their schemes. For the waywardness of the simple will kill them, and the complacency of fools will destroy them (Pr 1:22-32).

> At the end of your life you will groan, when your flesh and body are spent. You will say, "How I hated discipline! How my heart spurned correction! I would not obey my teachers or listen to my instructors. I

> have come to the brink of utter ruin in the midst of the whole assembly" (Pr 5:11-14).

2. The characteristics of the wise. Who then are the wise? The winsome portrait of the wise markedly contrasts to the waywardness of fools. Surprisingly, the wise are a diverse lot. What they hold in common is an agreed-upon foundation: they build their lives upon the "fear of the Lord." Because they seek the knowledge of God, they discover the gift of wisdom. As Proverbs explains:

> For the LORD gives wisdom, and from his mouth come knowledge and understanding. He holds victory in store for the upright, he is a shield to those whose walk is blameless, for he guards the course of the just and protects the way of his faithful ones. Then you will understand what is right and just and fair—every good path. For wisdom will enter your heart, and knowledge will be pleasant to your soul. Discretion will protect you, and understanding will guard you (Pr 2:6-11).

The wise invite God into their lives and depend upon him for guidance: "Trust in the LORD with all your heart and lean not on your own understanding; in all your ways acknowledge him, and he will make your paths straight" (Pr 3:5-6).

One of the distinguishing features of the wise is their reaction to difficulties and trials. The wise, in contrast to the foolish, see these times as opportunities for growth rather than hindrances to personal plans and ambitions. They are indications of divine discipline, not the whims of a jealous, selfish deity. "Do not despise the LORD'S discipline and do not resent his rebuke, because the LORD disciplines those he loves, as a father the son he delights in" (Pr 3:11-12). Fools rail against God and all whom they imagine are conspiring to thwart their aims and objectives; the wise patiently endure suffering and difficulty, confident in their Father's beneficence.

The wise never assume they have all the answers. They are always open to the counsel and advice of others who seek the Lord. In other words, wisdom is not a commodity to be traded on the market and turned into personal profit and fortune. It is an attitude of humility and trust, an attitude always in need of cultivation and refinement. "Do not be wise in your own eyes" (Pr 3:7). "Do not forsake wisdom (Pr 4:6). "Hold on to instruction, do not let it go; guard it well, for it is your life" (Pr 4:13). "Pay attention to what I say" (Pr 4:20). "Above all else, guard your heart, for it is the wellspring of life" (Pr 4:23).

Especially noteworthy in the profile of the wise is the careful monitoring of their speech. Words are such potent instruments in life—with potential for good or evil. "Reckless words pierce like a sword, but the tongue of the wise brings healing" (Pr 12:18). The wise are not perfect in speech, but careful in speech. "When words are many, sin is not absent, but he who holds his tongue is wise" (Pr 10:19). Neither garrulous nor mute, they have mastered the fine art of saying what is appropriate: "The lips of the righteous know what is fitting, but the mouth of the wicked only what is perverse" (Pr 10:32). "The lips of the righteous nourish many" (Pr 10:21). "Pleasant words are a honeycomb, sweet to the soul and healing to the bones" (Pr 16:24). "A man finds joy in giving an apt reply—and how good is a timely word!" (Pr 15:23). Above all, the wise person has learned control in the face of provocation. "Better a patient man than a warrior, a man who controls his temper than one who takes a city" (Pr 16:32).

The wise person is a faithful and loyal friend. The wise guard information told in confidence. "A gossip betrays a confidence, but a trustworthy man keeps a secret" (Pr 11:13). The wise are there for others when even family members may prove undependable or hostile. "A friend loves at all times . . . there is a friend who sticks closer than a brother" (Pr 17:17; 18:24). In short, the wise are the kind of people who make wonderful neighbors. William Dyrness captures the essence of the wise in this description:

> It should be clear by now that wisdom is a matter of character rather than intellect. It is the pattern of a life that is "tuned up" and harmonious. A person is considered to be wise only when the whole of life is shaped by the insights of wisdom. From one point of view the wise person is nothing extraordinary; he or she is simply someone you would like to live beside, or with, or meet on the street or the market.[25]

Listening to the created order. Another major contribution of Proverbs lies in its insistence that there is an order built into the world. Here we think back to our discussion of creation. Genesis 1 reflects the incredibly intelligent mind of a Creator who creates with purpose, design and order (cf. ch. 2). According to the sages of Israel, the wise person listens to and learns from this built-in order.

Here a cultural difference becomes highly visible. Our North American culture generally has a stance towards creation that insists upon mastering it. For example, when rivers flood, we demand that engineers control it; when earthquakes rumble, we devise earthquake-proof housing, and so on. We are problem solvers. Now this approach has some real benefits. North Americans live in a culture that has, to an unparalleled extent, modified forces operating on this planet. However, we have also created problems of immense magnitude in the process! (One thinks here of a fundamental law of physics: for every action, there is an equal and opposite reaction). On the other hand, the culture of the Bible, for the most part, adopts a stance of living in harmony with nature.[26]

Because the Bible was written in a culture adopting the live-in-harmony approach, should we revert to that perspective? We probably should not view the question as an either/or proposition. Rather, by dialoguing with the sages of Israel, we discover insights toward establishing a sensible balance between living in harmony with nature and ruling over it. Because we live in a fallen world, we must seek to alleviate the consequences of the fall, so far as we are able. But because we are also fallen, we must be vigilant lest our efforts to remedy cause even greater harm. The wisdom tradition provides help at just this point. *We rule best by discerning divine order in the cosmos and by living in harmony with that order.*

The kind of order we are talking about is supremely a *moral order*. Relationships, whether of neighbor, family, community, business or government, are conditioned by moral issues. The glue of any healthy society is integrity. We must be able to trust each other. Surveys show that most Americans say they tell the truth all the time. Clearly, this is not so, but the perception of respondents is that they do! It would appear, however, that most Americans do tell the truth *most* of the time. If it were not so, our nation would collapse into chaos. Proverbs insists that basic honesty is essential for the well being of the individual. By implication, the same holds true for larger societal groupings. "The LORD detests lying lips, but he delights in men who are truthful" (Pr 12:22; cf. 24:26). We all know the feeling of being lied to; and if we are honest, we all remember times when we lied or were less than honest. Why do we feel either injured or guilty? The sages of Israel say: because the world we live in is constructed so that violation of God's moral standards interferes with the order of the universe and causes disorder, confusion, evil and injury. Not to put it too dramatically, moral wrong introduces a cosmic disturbance into the universe; one has no way of knowing how extensive the disturbance will be, but it will certainly have undesirable consequences (cf. ch. 3).

Fools scoff at such an idea. "The fool says in his heart, 'There is no God'" (Ps 14:1). Modern secularists ground morality in evolutionary and developmental theories of social conditioning; there are no moral absolutes.

The sages of Israel knew better and so do those who accept biblical authority. We think C. S. Lewis' classic book *Mere Christianity* argues the case brilliantly.[27] There is a moral order built into the universe and the explanation for this fact is that a moral Creator designed it that way. Notice how the following quotations from Proverbs draw attention to this reality:

> "The eyes of the LORD are everywhere,
> keeping watch on the wicked and the good." (Pr 15:3)
> "Death and Destruction lie open before the LORD—
> how much more the hearts of men!" (Pr 15:11)
> "All a man's ways seem innocent to him,
> but motives are weighed by the LORD." (Pr 16:2)

These verses assume a moral government. This government operates, not by "the force," but by a personal moral governor. The sages of Israel exhorted their listeners/readers to acknowledge this moral governor and to discern his moral order, living in harmony with it. As Gerhard von Rad observes:

> According to the convictions of the wise men, Yahweh obviously delegated to creation so much truth, indeed he was present in it in such a way that man reaches ethical *terra firma* [firm ground] when he learns to read these orders and adjust his behaviour to the experiences gained.[28]

One of the valuable contributions of the sages of Israel, therefore, is sustained observation and reflection upon the created order and the human experience of living within such a system. Fathers and mothers, husbands and wives, teachers and students, rulers and servants, buyers and sellers, farmers and laborers, merchants and craftsmen—all may profit from the collaborative insight contained in the pithy sentences of proverbial wisdom.

This order is not confined to the sphere of human relationships and interactions. According to 1 Kings 4:33, Solomon "described plant life, from the cedar of Lebanon to the hyssop that grows out of walls. He also taught about animals and birds, reptiles and fish." One aspect of wisdom is the realm we refer to today as the natural sciences. Of course, we must not read into the experience of Israel the modern scientific method or the vast reservoir of current knowledge; but we are dealing with knowledge obtained by study and practice, as well as a body of systematized knowledge. This knowledge was not an end in itself, however. Here, too, the notion of morality is not absent.

That is, the sages believed that an intimate knowledge of the natural order speaks volumes to the wise about how to live life in this world.

The behavior of the ant speaks to the sluggard: "Consider its ways and be wise!" (Pr 6:6). Metallurgy provides instructive insight into politics: "Remove the dross from the silver, and out comes material for the silversmith: remove the wicked from the king's presence, and his throne will be established through righteousness" (Pr 25:4-5). Agur son of Jakeh found the animal kingdom alive with "lessons." Industrious coneys, locusts, lizards, roaring lions, strutting roosters, he-goats, soaring eagles and slithering snakes all demonstrate characteristics that ought to be imitated—or avoided! (Pr 30). To this the book of Job adds:

> But ask the animals, and they will teach you, or the birds of the air, and they will tell you; or speak to the earth, and it will teach you, or let the fish of the sea inform you. Which of all these does not know that the hand of the LORD has done this? (Job 12:7-9)

The prophets, too, in their sermons occasionally draw on the insights of the sages in order to impel their audiences to action. One thinks of Jeremiah's comparison of Israel's insatiable desire for idolatry to camels and wild donkeys in heat! (Jer 2:23-25). He also likened the plight of besieged Judah to that of a speckled bird of prey attacked by its own kind (Jer 12:9; an interesting example from nature of the human tendency to reject those who are different from ourselves—the "stranger syndrome"). Of course, Job 38–42 takes pride of place in this regard. Here we have an Israelite short course in natural history. The purpose of this section is to underscore the wisdom and power of the Lord. The mysteries and marvels of the created order eloquently witness to the incomparable God: "The heavens declare the glory of God; the skies proclaim the work of his hands" (Ps 19:1).

This brings us to perhaps the most profound insight of the wisdom tradition. There is an order in the universe, and that order reflects God's wisdom. In a remarkable passage, Proverbs 8, God's wisdom is personified—as if Wisdom were a separate person—distinct from but intimately associated with God. The role and function of Wisdom in Proverbs 8 is nothing short of cosmic. Indeed, according to the text, Wisdom, antedating creation, was the master craftsman who undertook the actual work of creating (v. 30). Here we have, in a short compass, a pre-existent builder, who assists the Lord in the awesome task of setting the universe in order. Not only so, but Wisdom must be personally accepted by human beings in order for them to experience real life (vv. 33-36). Recall our discussion of this in the chapter on creation (pp. 53-54).

This personified Wisdom theme becomes a vehicle for conveying truth concerning Jesus Christ. The process, however, is not a direct one from Old Testament to New.[29] During the intertestamental period (ca. 400 B.C. to A.D. 30), the motif of personified Wisdom underwent considerable development. For example, in the apocryphal work, Sirach, we read a lovely poem in chapter 24, obviously patterned after Proverbs 8, celebrating Wisdom.[30] Like Proverbs 8, Wisdom in Sirach is pre-existent: "I came forth from the mouth of the Most High, and covered the earth like a mist" (v. 3). "Before the ages, in the beginning, he created me, and for all the ages I shall not cease to be" (v. 9). Unlike Proverbs 8, however, Sirach explicitly identifies Wisdom with the Torah: "I took root in an honored people, in the portion of the Lord, his heritage" (v. 12). "All this is the book of the covenant of the Most High God, the law that Moses commanded us . . ." (v. 23). In another apocryphal work, The Wisdom of Solomon, written near the end of the first century B.C., this theme is taken further. In chapter seven Wisdom is again personified and described:

> . . . for wisdom, **the fashioner of all things**, taught me. For in her there is a spirit that is intelligent, **holy, unique**, manifold, subtle, mobile, clear, **unpolluted**, distinct, invulnerable, **loving the good**, keen, irresistible, beneficent, humane, **steadfast, sure**, free from anxiety, **all-powerful, overseeing all, and penetrating through all spirits** that are intelligent and pure and most subtle. For wisdom is more mobile than any motion; **because of her pureness she pervades and penetrates all things**. For she is **a breath of the power of God**, and **a pure emanation of the glory of the Almighty**; therefore nothing defiled gains entrance into her. For **she is a reflection of eternal light, a spotless mirror of the working of God, and an image of his goodness**. Though she is but one, she can do all things, and while remaining in herself, **she renews all things; in every generation she passes into holy souls and makes them friends of God**, and prophets . . . (Wis 7:22-27; RSV).

I have set several words and phrases in boldface because they are so similar to the wording and phrasing of several NT authors as they describe Jesus Christ. Consider the following quotations:

In the beginning was the Word, and the Word was with God, and the Word was God. He was with God in the beginning. Through him all things were made: without him nothing was made that has been made. In him was life, and that life was the light of men . . . the world was made through him. . . . We have seen his glory, the glory of the One and Only, who came from the Father, full of grace and truth . . . (Jn 1:1-3, 10, 14).

It is because of him that you are in Christ Jesus, who has become for us wisdom from God—that is, our righteousness, holiness and redemption (1Co 1:30).

There is but one Lord, Jesus Christ, through whom all things came and through whom we live (1Co 8:6).

The light of the gospel of the glory of Christ, who is the image of God (2Co 4:4).

Who, being in very nature God, did not consider equality with God something to be grasped, but made himself nothing . . . that at the name of Jesus . . . every tongue [should] confess that Jesus Christ is Lord, to the glory of God the Father (Php 2:6, 10-11).

He is the image of the invisible God, the firstborn over all creation. For by him all things were created: things in heaven and on earth, visible and invisible, whether thrones or powers or rulers or authorities; all things were created by him and for him. He is before all things, and in him all things hold together. And he is the head of the body, the church; he is the beginning and the firstborn from among the dead, so that in everything he might have the supremacy. For God was pleased to have all his fullness dwell in him, and through him to reconcile to himself all things, whether things on earth or things in heaven, by making peace through his blood, shed on the cross (Col 1:15-20).

In the past God spoke to our forefathers through the prophets at many times and in various ways, but in these last days he has spoken to us by his Son, whom he appointed heir of all things, and through whom he made the universe. The Son is the radiance of God's glory and the exact representation of his being, sustaining all things by his powerful word. After he had provided purification for sins, he sat down at the right hand of the Majesty in heaven (Heb 1:1-3).

> Such a high priest meets our need—one who is holy, blameless, pure, set apart from sinners, exalted above the heavens (Heb 7:26).

> For you know that it was not with perishable things such as silver or gold that you were redeemed . . . but with the precious blood of Christ, a lamb without blemish or defect. He was chosen before the creation of the world . . . (1Pe 1:19).

The similarity is readily apparent. Our point is that during the intertestamental era, although special revelation ceased for the time, reflection about God and his ways continued. *Some* aspects of this reflection are taken up in the revelation that comes to us in the NT. As Dr. Hubbard, my mentor at Fuller Theological Seminary was fond of saying, the train of revelation enters a tunnel during the intertestamental period; but clearly it picks up some baggage and freight as it emerges from the tunnel into the light of NT revelation.

What we see then is a trajectory in which the OT personification of Wisdom, an attribute of God, undergoes development during the intertestamental era.[31] That trajectory reaches its climactic point in the NT. There we have not a mere personification, but the mystery of incarnation. Jesus Christ is God of very God and, at the same time, the seed of David, a real human being. The pre-existent and eternal Word of God is also the Wisdom of God, the mediator of all creation. As the NT writers testify, he is the continuing Lord over all the creation. Thus, if we can view wisdom as seeing life from God's point of view, then ultimate wisdom is found in Christ, the creator, sustainer and savior of all things (Col 1:15-20; 2:3).

There is an important way in which the thought of Jesus Son of Sirach was *not* carried forward. Wisdom in the NT is *not* identified with the Torah, as Judaism continues to hold, but rather, with the person of Jesus Christ. He is the one who fulfills the Law and the Prophets and sets his people free from its curse (Mt 5:17; Jn 1:17; Gal 3:10, 13; 6:2; Ro 7:4-6; 13:9-10).[32]

We conclude this section with a word of gratitude to the wisdom teachers of Israel. Their reflections upon the order in the universe, an order having its basis in the divine nature itself, assisted the NT apostles in setting forth the doctrine of the person and work of Christ. The wisdom tradition played a vital role in the portrait of Jesus Christ now found in the NT.

Living with limitations. One might get the impression, reading Proverbs for example, that the sages of Israel had an answer for every question. This is not really the case. In fact, a major contribution of the Wisdom tradition, when viewed as a whole, is its recognition that wisdom is not an end in itself, nor is it a self-contained, totally sufficient approach to life. As Dyrness indicates, Proverbs 25:2 already hints that wisdom has limitations: "It is the glory of God to conceal a matter; to search out a matter is the glory of kings."[33] Furthermore, uncertainty surfaces in at least one saying: "Do not boast about tomorrow, for you do not know what a day may bring forth" (27:1). Hiddenness and uncertainty—nagging aspects of the human experience; yet the sayings of Agur contain an even more agnostic refrain:

> I am the most ignorant of men; I do not have a man's understanding. I have not learned wisdom, nor have I knowledge of the Holy One. Who has gone up to heaven and come down? Who has gathered up the wind in the hollow of his hands? Who has wrapped up the waters in his cloak? Who has established all the ends of the earth? What is his name, and the name of his son? Tell me if you know! (Pr 30:2-4)

These brief admissions of limitations are taken up and explored in some detail in Job and Ecclesiastes.

The book of Job is a classic by virtually any standard one uses for great literature. The traditional reading of this epic drama,[34] a work cast in superb Hebrew, regards it as a treatment of the age-old problem of evil. Why do bad things happen to good people? The reader, unlike the narrative figure Job, is not left in the dark by the author. A prose prologue (1–2) and epilogue (42:7-17) encase the poetical central section (cf. the A-B-A pattern in Zec 12–14, p. 325). Here we learn that the afflictions of Job unfold within the setting of a larger cosmic confrontation of good and evil, and that in the end Job is restored to his position of blessing and prosperity.

The central section, however, unfolding in three cycles of dialogues with Job's comforters, prosecutes a single aim: to convince and convict Job of some secret sin in his life. Only this can explain his unparalleled suffering, say his would-be consolers, the spokespersons for tradition. To this is added the contribution of Elihu, "an angry, young, presumptuous man."[35] He only develops further an argument already advanced, namely, that suffering is an aspect of divine discipline. Of course, the climactic speech occurs in chapters 38–41, when God speaks to Job.

The book of Job raises an acute challenge to a given in the wisdom tradition, one we just considered above: the notion that there is a moral order to the universe. Job voices an anguished query, at one point even a defiant denial of received tradition:

> It is all the same; that is why I say, "He destroys both the blameless and the wicked." When a scourge brings sudden death, he mocks the despair of the innocent. When a land falls into the hands of the wicked, he blindfolds its judges. If it is not he, then who is it? (Job 9:22-24)

The New Oxford Annotated Bible (NRSV) is correct in saying that "the book of Job does not explain the mystery of suffering or 'justify the ways of God' with human beings, but it does probe the depths of faith in the midst of suffering."[36] It is a remarkable fact that the book of Job does not provide an "orthodox answer" to the problem of unmerited suffering. Job "gets his day in court" (Job 9:32-35), as it were. God does speak to him. But what does God say? He does not even tell Job what the narrator tells the reader! The author of the work wants the reader to be content with this: behind the stage set of the visible, material work are larger, cosmic, spiritual issues. The struggle between good and evil cannot be comprehended in its concrete manifestations on planet earth. But evil has limits—just as wisdom has limits in understanding![37] Satan must have permission (1:12; 2:6). Can we accept that? Only if we can be sure that God has our ultimate good in mind. And that is what Job is convinced of *after God speaks to him*.

> Then Job replied to the LORD: "I know that you can do all things; no plan of yours can be thwarted. [You asked,] 'Who is this that obscures my counsel without knowledge?' Surely I spoke of things I did not understand, things too wonderful for me to know. [You said,] 'Listen now, and I will speak; I will question you, and you shall answer me.' My ears had heard of you but now my eyes have seen you. Therefore I despise myself and repent in dust and ashes." (Job 42:1-6)

This passage anticipates Romans 8:37-39. Faith in a loving, heavenly Father, who has demonstrated his unquestionable love for us in the cross, (Ro 5:1-8; 8:18, 31-32) must ever and again take up its stance alongside of Job: "I know that my Redeemer lives" (Job 19:25).

The author of Qoheleth, the Hebrew title of Ecclesiastes, provides the greatest challenge to the mainstream wisdom tradition. Expositors have struggled with this work like no other. Some have wondered if it really deserves a place in the canon of sacred scripture. We think that a careful understanding of the purpose of Qoheleth enables us to affirm the valuable contribution of this work to the Church.

This book forces us to face up to reality: nothing in the created order ("under the sun") can provide assured and lasting happiness. "'Meaningless! Meaningless!' says the Teacher, 'Utterly meaningless! Everything is meaningless!'" (Ecc 1:2). But people of faith may protest such a verdict. How can Christians, having the full light of revelation in Christ, share such a view? How does one reconcile the Teacher's verdict with 2 Corinthians 5:17: "Therefore, if anyone is in Christ, he is a new creation; the old has gone, the new has come!" But does not this latter text clearly point to the difference in perspective? The Teacher, living well before the gospel dispensation, is only making explicit what Jesus and the Apostles also taught, namely, that *this world can never be our place of refuge or hope*—it is fallen and passing away. The spiritual realm must totally transform the created order, as it now exists under the baneful curse of original sin. As we saw in chapter three, "The Fall and the Flood," human beings now live "east of Eden," amongst the thistles and thorns. Listen to these NT passages, all of which make the point that the present created order is not our real home or destiny as believers in Christ:

> Do not store up for yourselves treasures on earth, where moth and rust destroy, and where thieves break in and steal. But store up for yourselves treasures in heaven, where moth and rust do not destroy, and where thieves do not break in and steal. For where your treasure is, there your heart will be also (Mt 6:19-21).
>
> What good will it be for a man if he gains the whole world, yet forfeits his soul? Or what can a man give in exchange for his soul? (Mt 16:26).
>
> If you belonged to the world, it would love you as its own. As it is, you do not belong to the world, but I have chosen you out of the world. That is why the world hates you (Jn 15:19).
>
> Do not conform any longer to the pattern of this world, but be transformed by the renewing of your mind. Then you will be able to test and approve what God's will is—his good, pleasing and perfect will (Ro 12:2).
>
> . . . those who use the things of the world, as if not engrossed in them. For this world in its present form is passing away (1Co 7:31).

> Set your minds on things above, not on earthly things (Col 3:2).
>
> Though you have not seen him, you love him; and even though you do not see him now, you believe in him and are filled with an inexpressible and glorious joy, for you are receiving the goal of your faith, the salvation of your soul (1Pe 1:8-9).
>
> Dear friends, I urge you, as aliens and strangers in the world, to abstain from sinful desires, which war against your soul (1Pe 2:11).
>
> Do not love the world or anything in the world. If anyone loves the world, the love of the Father is not in him (1Jn 2:15).
>
> Then I saw a new heaven and a new earth, for the first heaven and the first earth had passed away, and there was no longer any sea (Rev 21:1).

The Teacher is a demolition expert. He marshalls devastating arguments against the possibility of finding lasting happiness and fulfillment "under the sun." Does he really hold this pessimistic view? Scholars differ in their response. We think Doug Stuart is correct in his assessment:

> Why, then, you ask, is it [Ecclesiastes] in the Bible at all? The answer is that it is there as a foil, i.e., as a contrast to what the rest of the Bible teaches. . . . The bulk of the book, everything but these two final verses, represents a brilliant, artful argument for the way one would look at life—*if* God did *not* play a direct, intervening role in life and *if* there were no life after death. . . . The view presented ought to leave you unsatisfied, for it is hardly the truth. It is the secular, fatalistic wisdom that a practical (not theoretical) atheism produces.[38]

In order to convince his students, the Teacher draws upon his long experience with life under the sun. He had engaged in a quest during his youthful days. This quest was for happiness and fulfillment.

First, he threw himself into the relentless search for wisdom and knowledge. Thinking that once he had understood the nature of things, he could enjoy life, the Teacher found this disappointing reality: all the knowledge and wisdom that can possibly be gained cannot alter the flaws and failures of existence on the earth. Wisdom has limitations! "What a heavy burden God has laid on men!" (1:13). "For with much wisdom comes much sorrow; the more knowledge, the more grief" (1:18).

If knowledge proved ultimately so unsatisfying, then perhaps pleasure was "where it was at." More than a few philosophers have thought so. Laughter, wine and folly, however, proved unable to fill the void. Like so many North Americans, the Teacher turned to work as the ultimate pleasure of life. Accomplishment must surely be the secret! He found it otherwise. Furthermore, neither property and possessions, nor wealth and power, nor sexual indulgence and entertainment, nor fame and popularity procured the sought-after joy: "Yet when I surveyed all that my hands had done and what I had toiled to achieve, everything was meaningless, a chasing after the wind; nothing was gained under the sun" (2:11).

To add to his distress, the Teacher realized that everything he did in life was part of a larger cosmic plan, a plan over which he exercised no control. This is the justly famous passage about the "time for everything" (Ecc 3). The Teacher does not celebrate the passages of life; the fact that he has no say or control over them vexes his soul.[39] ("Nothing can be added to it and nothing taken from it" [3:14]). He can only weakly resign himself to the divine determinations that oversee his life and that of all others under the sun.

The Teacher's quest for happiness is not furthered by his observation that life is filled with injustice and oppression (3:16–4:3; 5:8). The poor are at the mercy of the rich, and the rich leave their wealth behind (5:13-15). Those in authority are often totally incompetent, and those who are saviors today become scapegoats tomorrow (4:13-16). That which drives the economy is greed and envy (4:4; 5:10-11). We may not like it, but the Teacher's observations read like today's newspaper and news broadcast. They are a depiction of life as it really is.

Another source of unhappiness stalks everyone. Death is the great leveler and is no respecter of persons. Life is just too short and often filled with too much grief and sadness. Even if one has a relatively good life, in the end, death takes it all away (9:1-6). No one can control the day of his or her death; that remains in God's hands.

Now all of this seems so gloomy and unappealing (when was the last time you heard a thoughtful sermon on Ecclesiastes, by the way?). It hardly fits the modern penchant for positive thinking! Yet, we insist the message of the Teacher is highly relevant for our particular day and age. The realization of how fallen the present world order is creates a yearning within us for the new earth promised in the gospel. The problem facing most North American Christians is that we are feeling quite at home in this world. The book of Ecclesiastes, coupled with the witness of the NT, will greatly assist us in refocusing our hearts and minds. In the words of the gospel song: "This world is not my home, I'm just a passing through."

So what are the limitations of wisdom? Wisdom, defined as the fine art of being successful in life, cannot explain the mysteries of evil, much less formulate a plan for its banishment. Neither can it guarantee our personal happiness. The reason is that wisdom has no control over unwanted events that intrude into our lives. Even if we experience blessing and prosperity, this cannot compensate for the brevity of life. True wisdom can only point to that which is of ultimate value and meaning. The "fear of the Lord" is the key. Once we find our sufficiency in God, we will find true happiness—perhaps not in this life, but most assuredly, in the age to come. Of course the Teacher has virtually nothing to say about the age to come. No wonder his message seems so empty.

In the progress of revelation, Scripture gradually paints a glowing picture of the final estate of the redeemed (cf. Rev 21:1-8). But the Teacher performs a most valuable service. He shows us where true happiness *does not reside*. He testifies to the limitations of traditional Hebrew wisdom. The accumulated wisdom of Israel could not make a flawed world right, nor could it guarantee personal happiness. How glorious that Jesus Christ, the incarnate Wisdom of God, will do precisely that! "But in keeping with his promise we are looking forward to a new heaven and a new earth, the home of righteousness" (2Pe 3:13).

Loving wisely. So, where does the Song of Songs fit in the wisdom tradition? According to Douglas Stuart, "The Song of Songs is a lengthy love song. It is an extended ballad about human romance, written in the style of ancient Near Eastern lyric poetry. We may call it lyric wisdom."[40] John H. Stek, in the *NIVSB* concurs:

> The closest parallels appear to be those found in Proverbs. . . . The description of love in 8:6-7 . . . seems to confirm that the Song belongs to the Biblical wisdom literature and that it is wisdom's description of an amorous relationship. The Bible speaks of both wisdom and love as gifts of God, to be received with gratitude and celebration. . . . [The Song of Songs] is a linked chain of lyrics depicting love in all its spontaneity, beauty, power and exclusiveness—experienced in its varied moments of separation and intimacy, anguish and ecstasy, tension and contentment. The Song shares with the love poetry of

> many cultures its extensive use of highly sensuous and suggestive imagery drawn from nature.[41]

Like Ecclesiastes, Song of Songs has occasioned much perplexity.[42] We will not traverse all the terrain here.[43] For our part, we prefer to read Songs as a lyrical love ballad. We think there are three main characters: a virtuous maiden (Shulammite, 6:13), a Galilean shepherd with whom she is in love, and King Solomon, who attempts to add Shulammite to his harem. Bullock nicely summarizes the plot in this way:

> The Song then may be viewed in its literal sense as a celebration of love between man and woman, but more than that, the elevation of a love so genuine that it cannot be purchased with royal enticements. It is, like divine, given freely and unmeritoriously.[44]

How does this beautifully worded ballad speak to our sex-sated society? In the first place, the Song celebrates what we all know: romantic and physical love is a vital part of our lives. The power and attraction of our sexual natures is frankly presented. This series of songs reaffirms the intention of the Creator in making us sexual beings. Sexuality is not sinful; it is a gift to be enjoyed.

Although Norman Gottwald protests against the notion that the Song teaches a lesson, or should be read as a religious document, he admits "since the Song is in the Christian canon, it is not amiss to see it in total context."[45] We would reply that the total context of the canon means that this work certainly does teach a lesson. At this point the reader of the English Bible needs to know that, in the Hebrew Bible, the Song of Songs follows Ruth.[46] The book of Ruth narrates the story of a virtuous woman who married Boaz, the great grandfather of King David. Also notice that Proverbs precedes Ruth and concludes with the celebrated description of a virtuous wife (ch. 31). In other words, there is a *thematic linking* of Proverbs, Ruth and Song of Songs.[47] The lesson of Songs centers on the theme of conjugal love. The overall context from which one should read Songs is that of covenantal love—the divine institution of marriage. Song of Songs places parameters around sexuality. Love is committed, not casual. "My lover is mine and I am his" (2:16).

Herein lies a problem. The curse of so much "love" today is casual sex. Reports indicate that the percentage of sexually active teens has steadily increased, in spite of spiraling sexually transmitted diseases and AIDS. The popular media show little restraint and responsibility in this regard, but feed a growing appetite for explicit, raw sex. The age of cyberspace has opened a

Pandora's box of online pornography and depravity.[48] We no longer experience sexuality in Eden—like all other aspects of the human condition, sex takes place "east of Eden." In other words, the fall has opened this gift up to distortion and misuse, just like all other divine gifts. We are living in a time when misuse and abuse are not just nightmares; they are tragic realities. Because so many of us are emotionally scarred in this area, we need some divine guidance in finding our way back to the innocence of Eden. The Song of Songs greatly assists in this endeavor: it celebrates the ecstasy of physical intimacy within the confines of marriage.

In this regard, what is noteworthy in the lyrics of the ballad is stress upon pleasing the beloved one. Sexual intimacy, so delighted in, is not exploitative and certainly not painfully inflicted, but gentle and giving. As Paul House aptly points out, "It suggests lovers should enjoy praising one another as a prelude to sexual fulfillment."[49] It is all right to enjoy sex when God's moral boundaries are respected and observed and when it is intended to bring pleasure to one's beloved.

Finally, Song of Songs highlights the power of love. Love produces constancy and devotion.

> Place me like a seal over your heart, like a seal on your arm; for love is as strong as death, its jealousy unyielding as the grave. It burns like blazing fire, like a mighty flame. Many waters cannot quench love; rivers cannot wash it away. If one were to give all the wealth of his house for love, it would be utterly scorned (SS 8:6-7).

But alas, human love can ebb away. So many marriages, beginning with vows of "till death do us part," die early deaths. Love becomes loathing. Though strong, human love can be and often is fickle. But divine love is constant and faithful. This is the key to maintaining a love as strong as death. May we not rightfully say that Song of Songs points to a love greater than all human loves—the love of God in Christ?[50] Human love unaided by divine resources is uncertain at best. But human love, infused by the love of Christ, withstands the tests of life—"many waters cannot quench love: rivers cannot wash it away." Here is the secret to a life-long love:

> For this reason I kneel before the Father, from whom his whole family in heaven and on earth derives its name. I pray that out of his glorious riches he may strengthen you with power through his Spirit in your inner being, so that Christ may dwell in your hearts through faith. And

> I pray that you, being rooted and established in love, may have power, together with all the saints, to grasp how wide and long and high and deep is the love of Christ, and to know this love that surpasses knowledge—that you may be filled to the measure of all the fullness of God (Eph 3:14-19).

The Way of Worship

Introduction

We have earlier given some attention to the cultic practices of ancient Israel, especially in the chapter dealing with the exodus and the Sinai Covenant (ch. 5). There we surveyed the various divine appointments with regard to assembly, sacrifice and ritual. We wish now to return to the cult of Israel from the standpoint of the first and second temple and enter imaginatively into the services that unfolded on that sacred mount.

Our primary source is the hymnbook of ancient Israel, that is, the book of Psalms. We have already referred to various psalms in our study to throw light on certain themes. For example, the Royal Psalms illuminate the theme of kingship and the messianic hope (ch. 6) and Psalm 19, a hymn, contributes to our discussion of creation (ch. 2). This collection of hymns, petitions, thanksgivings, laments, introits, doxologies and other songs serves as a rich repository of the religious experiences and expressions of the faithful from approximately the time of David down to post-exilic times.[51]

A helpful exercise in this regard is to thumb through a modern hymnal and note its contents, organization and categories of sacred songs. These are useful analogies to what we observe in Psalms. Indeed, the Church's hymnal is a direct descendant of the liturgical traditions of ancient Israel. If the church was born with a canon in its hands, then it was also born with a hymnal on its lips—and those songs bear the unmistakable impress of a Hebraic legacy.[52]

Structure and Setting of Psalms

Technical discussion concerning the various types and functions of the songs in the Psalter (an early Christian term for the book of Psalms), as well as interpretive approaches may be pursued in other works.[53] We simply provide here in chart form a brief overview of the various "types" of psalms encountered in the Psalter and suggest how they may have functioned in the temple liturgy.[54]

Psalms Classified by Literary Type

Type	Life-setting	Examples
Individual Song of Thanksgiving	Formal act of worship in order to give thanks for a specific blessing	Ps 8, 29, 33, 104, 111, 113
Individual Lament	Most common in Psalter; reflects personal crises of various kinds (illness, enemies, afflictions)	Ps 6, 13, 31, 39
Communal Lament	Formal act of worship; some external crisis threatening the nation	Ps 12, 44, 74, 79
Royal Psalms	More a functional than a literary designation; aspects of kingship	Ps 2, 20, 21, 45, 72, 110
Hymns	Regular worship or festivals in the temple	Ps 8, 29, 33, 104, 111, 113
Wisdom Psalms	Reflects the wisdom tradition; didactic in character	Ps 1, 37, 49, 73, 119

Significance of the Book of Psalms

Experiencing the holy. We recall our earlier study of the cult of Israel. The tabernacle, by its very structure, was an object lesson for the faithful and a type for the later Church—a foreshadowing of the work of Christ. Israel's meetings with her God were holy meetings. Engraved on the High Priest's forehead were the words "HOLY TO THE LORD" (Ex 28:36). Leviticus, the priestly handbook, contains the refrain that establishes the prerequisite for all of Israel's encounters with her God: "Be holy because I, the LORD your God, am holy" (Lev 19:1). When Israelites came up to the great temple of Solomon and participated in the worship services, they entered into the sphere of holiness, the very presence of the Holy One of Israel (Isa 12:6). The ark of the Covenant was the Lord's footstool. "You who sit enthroned between the cherubim, shine forth before Ephraim, Benjamin and Manasseh" (Ps 80:1; cf.

1Ch 28:2; Ps 99:5). The entire temple mountain partook of this holiness (e.g., Ps 2:6; 3:4; 43:3; 48:1).

Going up to worship the Lord at Mount Zion was not a light matter. Preparation of body and spirit were essential. Both ritual and ethical cleanness were mandatory. We have earlier said something about the ritual dimensions of worship. Here we note two psalms that address the moral and ethical requisites (15, 24). By their structure and content, scholars have labelled these psalms as "entrance liturgies." One may, without too much "reading into the text," imagine the cultic setting of Psalm 15. Pilgrims standing at the gates to the temple compound may have sung the opening line: "LORD, who may dwell in your sanctuary? Who may live on your holy hill?" To this question the Levitical choir (located on the battlements?) or a priest may have chanted this summary of the second table of the moral law:

> He whose walk is blameless and who does what is righteous, who speaks the truth from his heart and has no slander on his tongue, who does his neighbor no wrong and casts no slur on his fellowman, who despises a vile man but honors those who fear the LORD, who keeps his oath even when it hurts, who lends his money without usury and does not accept a bribe against the innocent (Ps 15:2-5a).

These descriptions of the worthy entrant to God's holy mountain simply amplify what it means to "love your neighbor as yourself" (Lev 19:18). Perhaps then, as a grand refrain, both Levitical choir and assembled worshipers sang out the words of acceptance:

> He who does these things will never be shaken (Ps 15:5b).

Psalm 24 is similar. Many scholars describe it as a processional liturgy. At any rate, after an affirmation of the lordship of Yahweh over all creation (v. 1), a solo voice, priestly or Levitical, intones the question of fitness for entry:

> Who may ascend the hill of the LORD? Who may stand in his holy place? (v. 3).

The answer may well have come back by the combined Levitical choir:

> He who has clean hands and a pure heart, who does not lift up his soul to an idol or swear by what is false. He will receive blessing from the

> LORD and vindication from God his Savior. Such is the generation of those who seek him, who seek your face, O God of Jacob. *Selah* (vv. 4-6).

Note how compactly this priestly torah ("teaching") encapsulates the Ten Words of Exodus 20:1-17. Love for God and neighbor is a prerequisite to meet with God on his holy mountain. This re-emphasizes a point we made in chapter five: the divinely prescribed protocol for worship includes the following necessary conditions: redemption and sanctification.

While we cannot be sure, verse seven may be a request for admission:

> Lift up your heads, O you gates; be lifted up, you ancient doors, that the King of glory may come in.

A priest, or the Levitical choir, responds with a counter question, requiring a confession of faith:

> Who is this King of glory?

The worshipers in unison ascribe praise to Yahweh:

> The LORD strong and mighty, the LORD mighty in battle.

This is repeated again for emphasis, with only a small, but significant, change in the final confession of the participants:

> he is the King of glory. *Selah* (v. 10).

Thus we are brought to this fundamental theological truth: genuine worship must always be oriented toward the glory of God. "Glorify the LORD with me; let us exalt his name together" (Ps 34:3; cf. Ro 15:6).

We should not imagine going up to Jerusalem, to the holy mount, as a somber prospect; nor was it an inconvenient drudgery. It was a joyous meeting, anticipated with intense longing. Who can read the Psalter and not sense how keenly the psalmist looked forward to being in the courtyards of the Most High? Listen to these passages:

> One thing I ask of the LORD, this is what I seek: that I may dwell in the house of the LORD all the days of my life, to gaze upon the beauty of the LORD and to seek him in his temple. (Ps 27:4)

> As the deer pants for streams of water, so my soul pants for you, O God. My soul thirsts for God, for the living God. When can I go and meet with God? . . . I used to go with the multitude, leading the procession to the house of God, with shouts of joy and thanksgiving among the festive throng. (Ps 42:1, 4b)

> I rejoiced with those who said to me, "Let us go to the house of the LORD." Our feet are standing in your gates, O Jerusalem. (Ps 122:1-2)

This does not sound like joyless worship! In fact, the psalmist in Psalm 122 seems to be pinching himself to verify that he really is in the city of God. Like an awestruck tourist, like a person in a dream, he surveys the scene drinking in its visual impression. No more eloquent testimony to the attraction and appeal of the temple may be read than in this beautiful prayer:

> How lovely is your dwelling place, O LORD Almighty! My soul yearns, even faints, for the courts of the LORD; my heart and my flesh cry out for the living God. Even the sparrow has found a home, and the swallow a nest for herself, where she may have her young—a place near your altar, O LORD Almighty, my King and my God. Blessed are those who dwell in your house; they are ever praising you. *Selah* (Ps 84:1-4).

So, what does this say to our own time? Is there not a need for recovering the joy of our salvation? Does not so much modern worship exude the atmosphere of dry routine? Do we sense the eager anticipation of being with the people of God and worshiping together? "I love the house where you live, O LORD, the place where your glory dwells" (Ps 26:8). "How good and pleasant it is when brothers live together in unity!" (Ps 133:1). Or, are we elsewhere in our thoughts, planning a quick exit after the service in order to beat the crowd to that favorite restaurant!

Perhaps an even more fundamental problem exists. If entrance liturgies were taken seriously today—and many worship traditions do indeed have a corresponding component—would we have many admissions? In other words, dull and insipid worship may well be a result of moral and ethical laxness. Will a holy God meet with a disobedient people? The NT stands in continuity with the OT on this question. One thinks of the Apostle Paul's censure of the Corinthians for a variety of moral and ethical failures (1Co 1:10; 3:1-3; 5:1, 8, 11; 6:1, 9-10; 8:9; 10:6-10; 11:27-32).

The church, like Israel, is called to a life of holiness. This is a necessity for genuine worship. The pressing need of the hour is for Christians to take with utmost seriousness their baptismal and confirmation vows. Repentance rather than restructuring the worship service offers better prospects for spiritual renewal. Only then will we experience the joy of our salvation.

Exalting the Holy One. We do not want to give the impression, however, that worldliness is the *only* problem involved. There are many other causes for unfulfilling worship. We make a few suggestions based upon the religious experience of worshipers as we read of them in the Psalter. What stands out in bold relief in Psalms is the stress on praise to God. Here is a fundamental ingredient without which worship lacks zest. In fact the Hebrew title for the book of Psalms is *t^ehillîm*, meaning "praises." The Psalter is filled with the praises of God; rarely was this dimension missing from Hebrew worship. Psalm 92 gives a rationale:

> It is good to praise the LORD and make music to your name, O Most High, to proclaim your love in the morning and your faithfulness at night, to the music of the ten-stringed lyre and the melody of the harp. For you make me glad by your deeds, O LORD; I sing for joy at the works of your hands. How great are your works, O LORD, how profound your thoughts! (Ps 92:1-5).

God's character and deeds are the bottom line. It is good to praise God because he is good; it is good to praise God because he is great. "Say to God, 'How awesome are your deeds! So great is your power . . .'" (Ps 66:2). Listen to these psalms.

> Shout for joy to the LORD, all the earth. Worship the LORD with gladness; come before him with joyful songs. Know that the LORD is God. It is he who made us, and we are his; we are his people, the sheep of his pasture (Ps 100:1-3).

> Praise the LORD, O my soul; all my inmost being, praise his holy name. Praise the LORD, O my soul, and forget not all his benefits— who forgives all your sins and heals all your diseases, who redeems your life from the pit and crowns you with love and compassion, who

> satisfies your desires with good things so that your youth is renewed like the eagle's (Ps 103:1-5).

Many other psalms make a similar point.

We sense, in reading these praises, that worship in the temple was exuberant; indeed, one might even say that the services, on occasion, took on a boisterous character. We read of dancing (30:11; 149:3; 150:4), of a variety of musical instruments (trumpet, harp, lyre, tambourine, flute and cymbals [150]), of a ram's horn (81:2), of singing by choirs and worshipers (33:1-3) and even of shouting (33:3; 47:1; 66:1; et al.).

In modern terms, it sounds like a charismatic service! One must remember, however, that a cultural factor is also at work here. The Israelites were part of the ancient Middle East. Even today, communal worship in Middle Eastern settings exhibits a much greater degree of spontaneous, fervent expression of worship and devotion than many are accustomed to in the West. Those who are culturally and temperamentally more reserved feel some uneasiness and embarrassment when free reign is given to emotions in worship. Since, however, the NT gives some indications of a freewheeling worship style in at least some congregations (cf. 1Co 14; Col 3:15-17), we cannot simply write off the portrait in Psalms as part of the Old Covenant having no relevance for the church. More openness to the moving of the Spirit is probably desirable. On the other hand, even a liturgical form of worship can be joyous when the Spirit of God truly touches the participants.

We would urge a more serious commitment to enlarging our worship repertoire. In this connection, we would especially urge the recovery of some of the ancient Jewish festivals as an aspect of Christian worship. Christian congregations can be greatly edified and blessed by re-enacting the Passover, for example. Israel's story is our story, and celebrating the history of salvation should commence with events well before Pentecost!

Unfortunately, the choice of music and introduction of new styles of Christian worship, including drama and sacred dance, continue to create tensions and divisions in the Body of Christ. Into this unsettled atmosphere we hazard an opinion: we think Christian worship can be greatly enriched by the sanctified use of a wide range of artistic expression whether vocal, instrumental, dramatic or visual. In fact, if one takes a broader view of things, and surveys the various worship practices of Christians across the globe, a remarkable diversity already exists. We think God enjoys this montage of praise, arising in his presence like the sweet-smelling incense of the ancient Holy Place (Ps 141:2; cf. Rev 5:8; 8:4).

Expressing the heart to God. The Psalter runs the entire gamut of prayer experiences. We hear praises, doxologies, thanksgivings, petitions—for life, health, healing, forgiveness, guidance, deliverance from enemies, prosperity, vindication, assurance—even desperate cries for help. Are there, however, any common threads in these prayers?

One senses a lively spontaneity in the prayers of Israel. There were, of course, set prayers, such as the lovely priestly benediction of Numbers 6:24-26:

> The LORD bless you and keep you; the LORD make his face shine upon you and be gracious to you; the LORD turn his face toward you and give you peace.

Furthermore, we know that in the second temple priestly prayer accompanied the sacrifices. Isaiah 56:7 even designates the temple as "a house of prayer for all nations." We have already noted how some of the psalms reflect communal worship (i.e., the entrance liturgies of Ps 15 and 24). But what stand out in Psalms are the prayers of individuals. We read of "I" in many of these compositions. While these personal prayers have now been incorporated into the hymnbook of Israel, we get the impression that many of them originated in the real life experiences of individuals.[55] "This poor man called, and the LORD heard him; he saved him out of all his troubles" (Ps 34:6). "Out of the depths I cry to you, O LORD; O Lord hear my voice" (Ps 130:1-2a). In fact, 73 of the psalms are attributed to David, of which nine have, in the title, a brief description of a specific occasion in the life of David. Thus, for example, Psalm 57 states: "When he fled from Saul into the cave."

From the diverse experiences reflected in these prayers, we draw this observation. Prayer in the OT springs from the heart. Our prayer life should do the same. *Any time is prime time for prayer*. God should be included in our lives as an essential and assumed participant. In this regard, does not the prayer life of Jesus, as recorded in the Gospels, reinforce this observation? Luke's Gospel, in particular, stresses Jesus as a man of prayer. On all major occasions, as well as on a regular basis, he communed with his heavenly Father (Lk 5:16). Significantly, the passion narratives portray him reciting the Psalms as he died on the Cross (cf. Mt 27:46 with Ps 22:1 and Lk 23:46 with Ps 31:5). We all need to emulate the psalmist who said: "I am a man of prayer" (Ps 109:4b).

When one scrutinizes the pattern and order of these prayers, no one form or formula demands strict imitation. By no means do we gain the impression that magic or manipulation played any role in genuine prayer. This is not to say, however, that repeating a canonical prayer is of no value, and that every prayer must be ad-lib. The fact is that the prayers of individuals have, in the process of inspiration, become the living prayers of a larger worshiping community. There can be much value in praying the prayers of the Psalter. Our only caveat, however, would be to protect against the notion that by repetition of "sacred words" we can coerce God into pleading our case, an essentially pagan approach. The warning of Jesus is apropos: "And when you pray, do not keep on babbling like pagans, for they think they will be heard because of their many words. Do not be like them, for your Father knows what you need before you ask him" (Mt 6:7-8).

This last quotation from Jesus draws our attention to a fundamental requirement for a rich prayer life. Notice how Jesus referred to God as our Father. Now we ought not read into the OT the later revelation that only fully breaks through in Jesus of Nazareth. The doctrine of God as our personal heavenly Father is uniquely a NT truth. However, the saints of the OT approached God in an attitude of trust and submission, "the fear of the Lord." Notice how closely the psalmist approximates the teaching of Jesus about God our heavenly Father: "As a father has compassion on his children, so the LORD has compassion on those who fear him . . ." (Ps 103:13). If not directly addressed as Father, he was at least *like* a father. We could, in fact, cite numerous passages that underscore the point we are making. Prayer for pious Israelites started with recognition of deep need and great dependence. "To you, O LORD, I lift up my soul; in you I trust, O my God" (Ps 25:1). "I lift up my eyes to the hills—where does my help come from? My help comes from the LORD, the maker of heaven and earth" (Ps 121:1-2).

It is another indication of the unity of Scripture that Jesus likewise taught his disciples to pray by first focusing upon God and his kingdom: "This, then, is how you should pray: 'Our Father in heaven, hallowed be your name, your kingdom come, your will be done on earth as it is in heaven'" (Mt 6:9-10). Just as the first four of the Ten Commandments focus on God and his glory, so the first three petitions of the Lord's Prayer (really the disciples' prayer) direct the mind of the believer to God and his kingdom.

Humble submission to the God of Israel, who is like a father, lies securely anchored to another fundamental idea that we have traced throughout the OT. This is the notion of the covenant. Several psalms are thoroughly covenantal in character. We call attention to the psalms that have been categorized as the "historical psalms" (e.g., 89; 105–107; 114; 126; 132; 135; et al.). The three foundational covenants—Abrahamic, Sinaitic or Mosaic and the Davidic—all reverberate in the songs of Zion. We note especially the following:

> O descendants of Abraham his servant, O sons of Jacob, his chosen ones. He is the LORD our God; his judgments are in all the earth. He remembers his covenant forever, the word he commanded, for a thousand generations, the covenant he made with Abraham, the oath he swore to Isaac. He confirmed it to Jacob as a decree, to Israel as an everlasting covenant: "To you I will give the land of Canaan as the portion you will inherit." For he remembered his holy promise given to his servant Abraham (Ps 105:6-11, 42).

> He made known his ways to Moses, his deeds to the people of Israel: (Ps 103:7).

> I have found David my servant; with my sacred oil I have anointed him. . . . I will maintain my love to him forever, and my covenant with him will never fail. I will establish his line forever, his throne as long as the heavens endure. "If his sons forsake my law and do not follow my statutes, if they violate my decrees and fail to keep my commands, I will punish their sin with the rod, their iniquity with flogging; but I will not take my love from him, nor will I ever betray my faithfulness. I will not violate my covenant or alter what my lips have uttered. Once for all, I have sworn by my holiness—and I will not lie to David—that his line will continue forever and his throne endure before me like the sun; it will be established forever like the moon, the faithful witness in the sky" *Selah* (Ps 89:20, 28-37).

NT believers likewise approach the heavenly Father based on a covenant—the New Covenant. This bond, established by the blood of Jesus, assures us of our access to the audience room of heaven (cf. Ro 5:2; Heb 4:14-16; 6:16-20; 8:3-13).

One does not detect, in the prayers of the Psalter, a sense of passive resignation to the evils of life. We are not moving in the realm of fatalism. On the contrary, the Psalms exhibit a robust sense of human responsibility. One must "put feet" on one's prayers. The believer must offer himself/herself to the Lord, and this involves an energetic cooperation in actualizing his will. We are not suggesting here that human beings contribute to their own salvation—far from it. The Psalms resonate with the doctrine of the sovereignty of God.

> I know that the LORD is great, that our Lord is greater than all gods.
> The LORD does whatever pleases him, in the heavens and on the earth,
> in the seas and all their depths (Ps 135:5-6).

But there is a real sense in which believers actively seek to bring about the good by obeying God's will. The starting point in ethical behavior according to the Psalms is theological: "You are not a God who takes pleasure in evil; with you the wicked cannot dwell" (Ps 5:4). This leads the psalmist to pray: "Lead me, O LORD, in your righteousness because of my enemies—make straight your way before me" (v. 8). This may be no easy matter. "When the foundations are being destroyed, what can the righteous do?" (Ps 11:3). "Everyone lies to his neighbor; their flattering lips speak with deception" (Ps 12:2). In such an environment the believer must be courageous: "Be strong and take heart, all you who hope in the LORD" (Ps 31:24). "The LORD is my light and my salvation—whom shall I fear? The LORD is the stronghold of my life—of whom shall I be afraid?" (Ps 27:1). In the midst of moral decay, the psalmists add a choral refrain to the prophetic word: "Turn from evil and do good; seek peace and pursue it" (Ps 34:13; cf. Am 5:14-15; Mic 6:8).

This leads to an important observation. In spite of passages that, on first sight, urge retribution against evildoers, the primary way one battles against evil is to do what is right, champion the cause of the oppressed (cf. Ps 9:9; 10:17-18; 62:10-12) and entrust oneself to God. Thus, we read many petitions in which the psalmist cries out to God against unnamed enemies (Ps 3:7; 7:6; 9:13; et al.). The so-called imprecatory psalms—psalms invoking a curse upon one's enemies—are not, however, expressions of personal revenge. Rather, they take up the Lord's cause against the impenitent. They reflect the divine verdict against those who persist in defying the Lord's authority and in defaming his honor. In such circumstances, it is legitimate to ask God to restrain, even destroy, the wicked—so long as motives are right before God. It is not legitimate to be the avenging angel![56]

> If only you would slay the wicked, O God! Away from me, you bloodthirsty men! They speak of you with evil intent; your adversaries misuse your name. Do I not hate those who hate you, O LORD, and abhor those who rise up against you? I have nothing but hatred for them; I count them my enemies. Search me, O God, and know my heart; test me and know my anxious thoughts. See if there is any offensive way in me, and lead me in the way everlasting (Ps 139:19-24).

> Be still before the LORD and wait patiently for him; do not fret when men succeed in their ways, when they carry out their wicked schemes. Refrain from anger and turn from wrath; do not fret—it leads only to evil. For evil men will be cut off, but those who hope in the LORD will inherit the land. A little while, and the wicked will be no more; though you look for them, they will not be found. But the meek will inherit the land and enjoy great peace (Ps 37:7-11).

Neither Testament, properly interpreted, grants believers the right to become "God's militiamen." Against the injustices of his day, the psalmist expresses confidence that "the righteous will be glad when they are avenged" (Ps 58:10). The context makes clear, however, that God does the avenging (cf. Mt 5:5, 9, 11, 38-48; 26:52; Lk 22:51; Ro 12:17-21; 13:1-7; 1Pe 4:12-19; Rev 13:9-10; 14:12).

We are not arguing that the Scripture teaches an unqualified pacifism, but we are insisting that *retaliation* for personal or societal wrongs runs counter to the biblical pattern. Whether it is ever right for a Christian to take up arms to redress wrongs on a national or societal level is a difficult issue. That discussion takes us beyond our scope.[57] What is clear, however, is the biblical mandate requiring non-retaliation on the personal level.

Conclusion

We can scarcely summarize the spiritual riches discovered in the hymnbook of Israel and the church. We can only hope our observations lead to further study and reflection. In conclusion, listen to one of the acrostic psalms (a composition in which the initial letters of each line form a word, phrase, or alphabet),[58] celebrating the glories of God's Word:

> The law from your mouth is more precious to me than thousands of pieces of silver and gold. . . . Oh, how I love your law! I meditate on it all day long. I have more insight than all my teachers, for I meditate on your statutes. Your word is a lamp to my feet and a light for my path (Ps 119:72, 97, 99, 105).

Relationship to the Core Concepts

Faith and the Unity of Salvation: Sage observations on life and songs of the heart: they all assume the one, true and living God of Israel, the creator and redeemer. All creation manifests his moral government, all creation sings his mighty power. The faith of Israel, whether displayed in the pathways of life, the palace of kings or the porticoes of the temple, testifies to God's redemptive love. "His love endures forever" (Psalm 136).

In the wise sayings of the wisdom teachers, we are reminded of the Galilean teacher of whom it was exclaimed: "Where did this man get this wisdom?" (Mt 13:54). "No one ever spoke the way this man does" (Jn 7:46). Many of Jesus' sayings reflect the ancient wisdom tradition of Israel (cf. Mt 11:19). As we noted, the personification of wisdom was an important part of God's self-revelation, culminating in the cosmic christology of the NT (Pr 8:22-31; cf. Col 1:15-20; Heb 1:1-3; Jn 1:1-3). There are many passages from the Psalms that NT authors apply to Jesus' ministry and passion. An index of OT passages cited in the NT illuminates this connection. The apostles were not innovating; they were simply reading the OT as Jesus himself taught them. "Everything must be fulfilled that is written about me in the Law of Moses, the Prophets *and the Psalms*" (Lk 24:44).

The Psalms also testify to the truth of justification by faith:

> Blessed is he whose transgressions are forgiven, whose sins are covered. Blessed is the man whose sin the LORD does not count against him and in whose spirit is no deceit (Ps 32:1-2).

The Apostle Paul, in Romans 4:6-8, shows that David, like Abraham, experienced the liberating feeling of being justified by faith alone. There is, again, a reassuring continuity in God's redemptive plan.

Faith and Politics: The proverbial wisdom of Israel provides common sense guidance for successful human relationships, including what we call politics. While the political systems of our own day are quite different from those of ancient Israel, there are some common denominators in the exercise of authority and power. Certainly the admonition "Do not exploit the poor because they are poor and do not crush the needy in court" (Pr 22:22) is still timely. The observation that "by justice a king gives a country stability, but one who is greedy for bribes tears it down" (Pr 29:4) is still relevant for officials in all levels of government (cf. Ps 72:1-4, 12-14; 94:20).

But the primary contribution of the wisdom tradition to the realm of faith and politics has to do with the limitations of politics. Ecclesiastes makes very clear that political solutions are temporary at best. We cannot legislate human happiness. Nonetheless, political involvement by believers is essential, and

Christian activism should not be despised. But the Christian must also be a realist. "What is twisted cannot be straightened; what is lacking cannot be counted" (Ecc 1:15). Until the King of Kings assumes his rightful rule over planet earth, human folly and failure will plague politics.

> If you see the poor oppressed in a district, and justice and rights denied, *do not be surprised at such things;* for one official is eyed by a higher one, and over them both are others higher still. The increase from the land is taken by all; the king himself profits from the fields (Ecc 5:8-9; italics added for emphasis).

Faith and Ethics: The wisdom tradition and the hymnic literature of Israel take their departure from a common commitment: the fear of the Lord. If "the fear [reverence and awe] of the LORD is the beginning of knowledge" (Pr 1:7), then it follows that one should "serve the LORD with fear" (Ps 2:11). And "the fear of the LORD is pure" (Ps 19:9). The Sinai Covenant is the presupposition of both the collective wisdom of the sages and the praises and prayers of the worshiping community. This section of the canon embodies concrete examples of how to love God and neighbor, the two tables of the Law. These writings also prod our consciences with penetrating questions: "Who can discern his errors?" (Ps 19:12a). "Who can say, 'I have kept my heart pure; I am clean and without sin'?" (Pr 20:9).

Faith and the Future: In the hymns and songs of the Psalter we celebrate the anticipated coronation of the Son (Ps 2), the king of glory (Ps 24), the most excellent of men (Ps 45), the Shepherd of Israel (Ps 80; cf. 23). We have already discussed the messianic nature of the Royal Psalms in chapter six. We also saw in chapter nine that the Psalms contain glimmers of glory beyond the grave (Ps 16; 23; 73). Plainly, however, the Psalter's eschatology celebrates God's kingdom rule (e.g., Ps 93; 97–99). In those psalms, sometimes called "enthronement psalms," the whole world bows down before the Lord. Do not those passages anticipate the grand finale of redemptive history? "The kingdom of the world has become the kingdom of our Lord and of his Christ, and he will reign for ever and ever" (Rev 11:15b). And finally, do we not transcend the historical Jerusalem when we read a passage like the following: "There is a river whose streams make glad the city of God, the holy place where the Most High dwells. . . . The LORD Almighty is with us . . ." (Ps 46:4, 7)? We believe so. "Then the angel showed me the river of the water of life, as clear as crystal, flowing from the throne of God and of the Lamb down the middle of the great street of the city" (Rev 22:1).

For Further Discussion:

How does the wisdom tradition relate to the prophetic movement?

What insights do we gain from the wisdom literature that enables us to cope with the problems of suffering?

What guidelines and cautions are necessary in applying proverbial wisdom to the modern world?

How can we incorporate Ecclesiastes into a Christian philosophy of life?

How can we use Song of Songs as a preparation and guide for Christian marriage?

How can the book of Psalms enrich Christian worship?

How can Psalms enrich our prayer life?

For Further Reading:

Berry, Donald K. *Introduction to the Wisdom and Poetry of the Old Testament.* Nashville: Broadman & Holman, 1999. Overview of literature from an evangelical perspective.

Brueggemann, Walter. "Zion: The Jerusalem Offer of Presence," pp. 654-662 and "The Sage as Mediator," pp. 680-694 in *Theology of the Old Testament: Testimony, Dispute, Advocacy.* Minneapolis: Fortress, 1997. Good insights from a non-evangelical scholar in the confessional tradition.

Bullock, C. Hassell. *An Introduction to the Old Testament Poetic Books*. Rev. and enl. ed. Chicago: Moody, 1988. A fine introduction to this literature by an evangelical OT scholar.

Bullock, C. Hassell. *Encountering the Books of Psalms: A Literary and Theological Introduction.* Chicago: Moody, 2001.

Dillard, Raymond B., and Tremper Longman, III. *An Introduction to the Old Testament,* pp. 199-265. Grand Rapids: Zondervan, 1994.

Dyrness, William. *Themes in Old Testament Theology*, pp. 189-200. Downers Grove: InterVarsity, 1979.
Fox, Michael V. *A Time to Tear Down and a Time to Build Up: A Rereading of Ecclesiastes*. Grand Rapids: Eerdmans, 1999.
Gledhill, T. D. "Song of Songs." In *New Dictionary of Biblical Theology*, edited by T. Desmond Alexander, Brian S. Rosner, D. A. Carson, and Graeme Goldsworthy, pp. 215-217. Downers Grove: InterVarsity, 2000.
Hiebert, Robert J. V. "Psalms, Theology of." In *Evangelical Dictionary of Biblical Theology,* edited by Walter E. Elwell, pp. 653-658. Grand Rapids: Baker, 1996.
Hill, Andrew E., and John H. Walton. *A Survey of the Old Testament*, pp. 247-299. Grand Rapids: Zondervan, 1991.
House, Paul R. *Old Testament Survey*, pp. 201-245. Nashville: Broadman, 1992.
LaSor, William Sanford, David Allan Hubbard, and Frederic Wm. Bush. *Old Testament Survey*, pp. 307-318, 507-610. Grand Rapids: Eerdmans, 1982.
Longman III, Tremper. *The Song of Songs*. Grand Rapids: Eerdmans, 2001.
Schnabel, E. J. "Wisdom." In *New Dictionary of Biblical Theology,* pp. 843-848.
Schultz, R. L. "Ecclesiastes." In *New Dictionary of Biblical Theology,* pp. 211-215.
Viberg, A. "Job." In *New Dictionary of Biblical Theology,* pp. 200-203.
Von Rad, Gerhard. "Israel Before Yahweh." In *Old Testament Theology,* Vol. 1, pp. 355-459. New York and Evanston: Harper & Row, 1962. Good insights from a non-evangelical scholar employing a history of traditions approach.
Waltke, Bruce K. "Proverbs, Theology of." In *Evangelical Dictionary of Biblical Theology,* edited by Walter E. Elwell, pp. 648-650. Grand Rapids: Baker, 1996.
Walton, John H. *Ancient Israelite Literature in Its Cultural Context*, pp. 169-197. Grand Rapids: Zondervan, 1989. Helpful on parallels to the ancient Near Eastern wisdom literature.
Westermann, Claus. *Praise and Lament in the Psalms*. Atlanta: John Knox, 1981. Classic work by non-evangelical scholar in the confessional tradition.

Endnotes

1. C. Hassell Bullock, *An Introduction to the Old Testament Poetic Books: The Wisdom and Songs of Israel* (Chicago: Moody, 1979), p. 13.

2. For further discussion of the formation of the OT canon, see William Sanford LaSor, David Allan Hubbard, and Frederic Wm. Bush, *Old Testament Survey* (Grand Rapids: Eerdmans, 1982), pp. 17-25 and Andrew E. Hill and John H. Walton, A *Survey of the Old Testament* (Grand Rapids: Zondervan, 1991), pp. 12-25.

3. See *NIVSB,* pp. 1431 (bottom) and 1432 for more background on the LXX.

4. See Luke 24:44 for evidence that already in Jesus' day the Hebrew canon was composed of these three sections. The earliest witness to a threefold canon occurs in the prologue to Ben Sira (ca. 132 B.C.), well before Jesus' ministry.

5. See further on this G. T. Sheppard, "Wisdom," *ISBE*, 3d ed., 4:1080.

6. Louis Goldberg, "*ḥokmâ* ," *TWOT,* 1:283-284. See also Bullock, *Poetic Books*, p. 21.

7. *The NIV Exhaustive Concordance*, eds. Goodrick and Kohlenberger III (Grand Rapids: Zondervan, 1990), p. 1449.

8. *Themes*, p. 189.

9. See Victor P. Hamilton, "*māshāl,*" *TWOT*, 1:533.

10. *Poetic Books*, pp. 41-48.

11. *The American Heritage Dictionary of the English Language* (New York: American Heritage, 1969), p. 468.

12. "Parable," *ZPEB*, 4:590.

13. These may be read in English translation in *ANET,* 3d ed., pp. 405-440, 589-607.

14. *Ancient Israelite*, pp. 196-197. His discussion of the entire range of wisdom literature parallels is very helpful on pp. 167-197. See also Bullock, *Poetic Books*, pp. 27-41.

15. *ANET*, pp. 601-604.

16. As Walton observes:

> The ancient Near Eastern advice then is "enjoy life," while the Israelite advice is "enjoy life and fear God." The pessimism literature in Israel was not blasphemous or set against religious practice. Religion had a very significant part to play, even if all of the pieces of how the world operates could not be put together. (*Ancient Israelite*, p. 189)

17. See J. M. Ward, "Amos," *IDBS*, pp. 22-23.

18. Although dealing with the tradition behind the Synoptic Gospels, Kenneth E. Bailey describes a process that probably applies to the wisdom tradition in ancient Israel as well. "Informal controlled oral tradition and the Synoptic Gospels," *Themelios* 20/2 (January 1995): 4-11. See also Dyrness, *Themes*, p. 192.

19. Sheppard, "Wisdom," 4:1078.

20. Ibid., p. 1077.

21. See Hill, *Survey*, p. 257.

22. Bullock agrees that there were wisdom schools available to the upper classes from the time of Solomon. However, he also suggests that "wisdom was not limited to the upper class. . . . In view . . . of the emphasis upon marriage, the home, childrearing, and domestic stability and responsibility, it is conceivable that wisdom was popularly employed in the family as a part of the home educational process" (*Poetic Books*, p. 23).

23. See Louis Goldberg, "*'ĕwîl*," *TWOT*, 1:19-20; id., "*kᵉsîl*," 1:449-450; and id., "*nābāl*," 2:547-548, for further discussion.

24. See *TWOT*, 2:742.

25. *Themes*, p. 197.

26. See Pilch and Malina, *Biblical Social Values*, pp. xiii-xxxix for a good overview of this issue.

27. (New York: Macmillan, 1952). A helpful treatment of the reasonableness of the biblical view of reality is in R. Douglas Geivett, "Is Jesus the Only Way?" in *Jesus Under Fire: Modern Scholarship Reinvents the Historical Jesus*, eds. Michael J. Wilkins and J. P. Moreland (Grand Rapids: Zondervan, 1995), pp. 192-195.

28. *Wisdom in Israel* (Nashville and New York: Abingdon, 1972), p. 92.

29. See Larry R. Helyer, *Jewish Literature of the Second Temple Period: A Guide for New Testament Students* (Downers Grove: IVP, 2002), pp. 101-102, 296-300.

30. Sirach, or Ecclesiasticus, was written sometime before 180 B.C. For further background see Donald A. Hagner, "Ecclesiasticus," *ZPEB*, 2:190-197.

31. See further on this Hubbard, *Old Testament*, pp. 550-551 and Bullock, *Poetic Books*, pp. 38-41.

32. The question of the precise relationship of the believer to the Law continues to be debated in evangelicalism. See *The Law, the Gospel, and the Modern Christian: Five Views*, ed. Wayne G. Strickland (Grand Rapids: Zondervan, 1993) for the differing viewpoints. See also Stephen Westerholm, *Israel's Law and the Church's Faith: Paul and His Recent Interpreters* (Grand Rapids: Eerdmans, 1988).

33. *Themes*, p. 198.

34. On the question of genre see Bullock, *Poetic Books*, p. 69.

35. Ibid., pp. 76-77.

36. Eds. Bruce M. Metzger and Roland E. Murphy (New York: Oxford University Press, 1991), p. 625 OT.

37. Lindsay Wilson has a stimulating slant on Job:

> The book does not seek to overturn the mainstream wisdom concept of the "fear of the Lord", but it establishes that it is beside the point in Job's case. It is neither the reason for his suffering, nor the solution to his struggle of faith. The function of the "fear of

God" motif in the book of Job is to insist that the totality of the wise living cannot be subsumed under the "fear of the Lord" concept. While the "fear of the Lord" is the beginning of wisdom, it is not all that there is to wisdom. Wisdom is a wider category than the "fear of the Lord" ("The Book of Job and the Fear of God," *TynBul* 46.1 [May 1995]: 77-78).

38. *How to Read*, p. 214 [italics his].

39. See also ibid., p. 207; *NIVSB*, p. 994, note on 3:1-22; and commentaries for justification of this interpretation.

40. *How to Read*, p. 226.

41. P. 1003.

42. "The book . . . has been pronounced the enigma of the Old Testament, as the Apocalypse is the enigma of the New" (*The Wisdom Literature of the Old Testament* [London: Charles H. Kelley, 1900], p. 272). "No single book of the Old Testament has proved more perplexing for biblical interpreters than the Song of Songs. Centuries of careful study by scholars of various religious traditions and theological persuasions have produced little interpretive consensus" (Hill, *Survey*, p. 301).

43. See Hubbard, *Old Testament*, pp. 606-610; Bullock, *Poetic Books*, pp. 224-237; Hill, ibid., pp. 301-304.

44. *Poetic Books*, p. 237. Agreeing with Bullock is Hill, ibid., p. 303. For the view that Song is simply a series of songs celebrating the love of a man and woman for each other, see Stek, *NIVSB*, p. 1003 and House, *Survey*, pp. 238-241.

45. "Song of Songs," *IDB*, 4:424.

46. See House, *Survey*, pp. 19-21, 201 for further discussion.

47. This is what John H. Sailhammer calls "con-textuality." See his discussion of this in *Introduction to Old Testament Theology: A Canonical Approach* (Grand Rapids: Zondervan, 1995), pp. 213-215.

48. See Philip Elmer-Dewitt, "On Screen Near You: Cyberporn," *Time* (July 3, 1995): 38-45.

49. *Survey*, p. 241.

50. E. J. Young puts it this way: "Not only does it speak of the purity of human love; but, by its very inclusion in the canon, it reminds us of a love that is purer than our own." (*An Introduction to the Old Testament*, rev. ed. [Grand Rapids: Eerdmans, 1958], p. 354.)

51. For a cogent defense of the view that most of the psalms are in fact pre-exilic, see Roger T. Beckwith, "The Early History of the Psalter," *TynBul* 46.1 (May 1995): 1-27.

52. See Ralph P. Martin, *Worship in the Early Church* (London: Marshall, Morgan and Scott, 1964), pp. 18-27 and Robert E. Webber, *Worship*, pp. 23-43.

53. Accessible sources include: LaSor, Hubbard, and Bush, *Old Testament*, pp. 510-532; Stek, *NIVSB*, pp. 781-786; Bullock, *Poetic Books*, pp. 113-153. We are not convinced that John Walton's approach to the canonical shape of Psalms is correct, but it is interesting. He holds that one may trace the history of Israel in Psalms, beginning with David's conflict with Saul and continuing through the exilic and post-exilic eras. (Walton, *Survey*, pp. 278-281) He is followed in this by House, *Survey*, pp. 204-205.

54. Adapted from Peter C. Craigie, "Psalms," *ISBE*, 3:1034-1035.

55. See ibid., 3:1036 for further discussion.

56. On the problem of interpreting the imprecatory psalms, see Hubbard, *Old Testament*, pp. 530-531 and J. B. Payne, "Psalms, Book of," *ZPEB*, 4:938-939.

57. For a discussion probing this question, see Francis A. Schaeffer, *A Christian Manifesto* (Westchester, IL: Crossway Books, 1981), esp. pp. 117-130. For the larger issue of the Christian and war, see Robert G. Clouse, ed., *War: 4 Christian Views* (Downers Grove: InterVarsity, 1981).

58. See *NIVSB* notes on Psalm 119, p. 914.

chapter **11**

Epilogue: The Relationship of the Old and New Testaments

He said to them, "This is what I told you while I was still with you: Everything must be fulfilled that is written about me in the Law of Moses, the Prophets and the Psalms" (Lk 24:44).

For everything that was written in the past was written to teach us, so that through endurance and the encouragement of the Scriptures we might have hope (Ro 15:4).

Introduction

As we conclude our study of major themes in the OT and their relevance for today, we need to take one last look at how the OT relates to the NT. At numerous points in our discussion, we have drawn attention to lines of connection. We observed that there are many points of *continuity*, that is, elements of the OT are taken up and developed in the later NT revelation; the messianic hope is one clear example. However, there are instances of *discontinuity* as well. Some aspects of the OT, for example, the dietary laws of the Mosaic Law, are no longer binding on Christians. We propose a brief synopsis of this rather complex, but highly important, issue of the relationship between the Testaments.[1]

Wrong Solutions

Before we outline the ways in which the OT connects with the NT, we briefly mention a couple of "wrong turns" in church history. Already in the second century A.D., a dangerous option surfaced. A rather prominent leader in the Roman church, Marcion, came under the influence of Hellenistic philosophy, perhaps a form of early Gnosticism.[2] Since in Gnosticism matter is evil, Marcion dissociated the inferior god of the OT (demiurge) from the supreme God Most High, who was unknowable and unapproachable. This being the case, the OT as a whole was jettisoned as unworthy and erroneous. Of course, this presented a problem since many passages of the NT refer favorably to the OT. Marcion went through the NT and deleted all such passages, or nearly so. Only a greatly reduced version of Luke's gospel and a highly edited version of Paul's epistles survived. This became the "bible" of the true faith according to Marcion. More could be said about Marcion's agenda, but for our purposes the important point is that Marcion believed the OT was expendable—the Church would be better off without it. Marcion was declared a heretic and excommunicated.

Unfortunately, the "Marcionite heresy" has occasionally reappeared throughout church history. In much modern, theological liberalism, there are vestiges of Marcionism. Liberalism tends to view the Hebrew Scriptures as documents of a primitive, sub-Christian religion. At best, the OT is gleaned for enduring truths, or, at least, worthy ideas, but much is dismissed as culturally bound and irrelevant.[3] Even in evangelical churches, however, one too often discovers a benign neglect of the OT. Many church members have a nebulous understanding of its content and importance.

Fortunately, the majority of Christians have resisted the false option of dispensing with the OT. Taking their stand with Jesus and his apostles, believers down through the ages have proclaimed that the OT is an essential and enduring part of God's revelation—the written Word of God. All major creeds have confessed it to be a part of the inspired, infallible and authoritative Scripture.

The early church fathers defended the inspiration and authority of the OT. Unfortunately, in their attempts to hold the Testaments together, they tended to fall into an opposite error, namely, identifying the Old and New Testaments. That is, the newer revelation of the NT was read back into the OT, with the result being, in effect, one Testament. Everywhere in the OT, by means of the allegorical method,[4] NT doctrine was discovered—for example, any mention of wood and wine in the OT suggested to the allegorists the cross and the Eucharist! An especially significant figure in this regard was Origen of Alexandria.[5] His employment of allegorical interpretation influenced the interpretation of the Bible for centuries—one may still hear sermons employing the same basic approach today!

The Reformers (Luther, Calvin, Knox, Zwingli and others) led us back to the literal meaning of the text as the meaning intended by the Holy Spirit. The Reformers also laid the foundations for a more clearly articulated view of how the OT relates to the NT. In what follows, we set out the various ways in which one may articulate this relationship. We are greatly indebted to the theological reflection of the Reformers in this endeavor.[6]

Legitimate Lines of Connection

Prooftexts

A good starting point in this discussion is the simple observation that the NT contains hundreds of citations or allusions to the OT. The precise numbers vary according to the investigator, but we may use the United Bible Society's *The Greek New Testament* (4th rev. ed.) as a guide. The index to OT quotations lists some 260 direct quotations.[7] Add to this several thousand allusions, and one begins to sense the organic connection that exists between these two collections.[8] This requires reflection. An examination of the various quotations demonstrates that NT authors cite the OT as proof that the gospel message was already anticipated or promised in the OT (cf. Ro 1:2; 3:21; Gal 3:8; Ac 3:24-25; et al.). Very often an argument is clinched by an appeal to the OT (cf. Ro 4:3). The preaching and pastoral teaching of the early church assumes the full authority of the Hebrew Scriptures.

Perspective

We have repeatedly made the point that both Testaments share the same perspective: there is one, true and living Creator God who directs the unfolding of his kingdom on earth.[9] *Redemptive history is the essence of both Testaments* (cf. chs. 1, 4, 6, 9). The God and Father of our Lord Jesus Christ is the selfsame God of Abraham, Isaac and Jacob. Marcion was terribly wrong here. We are not dealing with a wrathful God of judgment in the OT as opposed to a merciful, heavenly Father in the New. God's justice and mercy are constants in both Testaments. God's character and objectives are the same in both Testaments. God's method of saving sinful human beings is always the same (cf. ch. 5). This should cause no surprise—both Testaments share the same scriptwriter! (ch. 1)

Pattern

Another helpful way to verbalize the relationship between the Testaments is in terms of typology. That is to say, persons, institutions and events in the OT prefigure or anticipate the saving work of Jesus Christ in the NT. One may speak of a foreshadowing in this regard. Here we recall our discussion of the life of Abraham, especially the near sacrifice of Isaac (ch. 4). In this singular event we have a remarkable preview of the sacrifice of Jesus on Golgotha. We spent some time noting how the tabernacle foreshadows Christ's atonement on the cross. The very arrangement of the tabernacle typifies God's way of saving his people and his ultimate intentions for them (cf. ch. 5). In the words of the author of Hebrews, these things were "a shadow of the good things that are coming" (Heb 10:1). At several points the life of David, especially the promises granted him, prefigures the ministry and reign of Jesus Christ (cf. chs. 6 and 9). In these and other instances we see a correspondence and analogy between the Old and New Testaments.

Promise

We have often used the category of promise and fulfillment in our survey of the various themes. Beginning with the fall, the Lord issued a series of promises bespeaking a final and complete deliverance from bondage to sin and the Evil One. The planet will be totally liberated! The *protoevangelium* of Genesis 3:15 directs our hopes to one who can reverse the dire consequences of Adam and Eve's disobedience and defeat the schemes of the devil (cf. chs. 3, 6, 8-9). Building on that initial promise, we can chart the course of redemptive history through a process of gradual elaboration. Of course, central to this is the threefold promise to Abraham (cf. ch. 4). We have highlighted the fact that the Abrahamic covenant, which embodies the threefold promise, is the framework for the rest of redemptive history. The plot of the Bible revolves around an heir (and his fellow-heirs), an inheritance, and a heritage. The book of Revelation culminates the unfolding promise to Abraham and his seed with a spectacular vision of a new heaven and new earth (cf. Gal 3:15-18 and Rev 21–22). However, the promises of God are not confined to Abraham in the history of salvation. There are promises to redeem his people from bondage, dwell in the midst of them, and raise up a descendant of David to rule the world with justice and righteousness. There are promises to restore Israel to her ancient homeland, to make a new covenant with the house of Israel, to include Gentiles in the kingdom blessings, and to raise the bodies of saints, empowering them to reign in everlasting glory. These and other precious promises are taken up in the Gospel message of the NT.[10] It is a remarkable fact how many realities of the OT are said to be fulfilled in the NT.

Preparation

It is a truism to say that one cannot understand adequately the NT without a basic knowledge of the OT. The vocabulary and thought world of the NT are rooted in the OT. Whereas Hellenism has left its mark on NT thought, the determinative factor is clearly the Hebrew Scriptures. It is thus the prerequisite for grasping the message of the NT. The OT prepares us for the revelation of God in Christ. In this regard, we have an instance of sound pedagogy. The OT is a primer, enabling us to receive the later revelation embodied in the NT, of which Paul could say: "Beyond all question, the mystery of godliness is great" (1Ti 3:16a). "Oh, the depth of the riches of the wisdom and knowledge of God" (Ro 11:33). We should also note that the OT, in its rather negative portrayal of human nature, prepares the human heart subjectively to respond to the gracious offer of salvation by grace through faith in Christ. Without overstating the case, we may say that the OT draws attention to failure—failure to obey and trust God fully.[11] It is thus a mirror of the human condition. Against this self-understanding, how good it is to hear the invitation of the Savior:

> Come to me, all you who are weary and burdened, and I will give you rest. Take my yoke upon you and learn from me, for I am gentle and humble in heart, and you will find rest for your souls. For my yoke is easy and my burden is light (Mt 11: 28-29).

Progress

Finally, we again call attention to the fact that there is one basic story line running through Genesis to Revelation. In redemptive history, God reveals himself progressively to sinful, rebellious human beings. He comes to them in a series of gracious and merciful acts, climaxed by the sending of his beloved son, "when the time had fully come" (Gal 4:4). He has plans for this planet and its redeemed people. He has revealed certain aspects of that plan and has done so sequentially through time. Redemptive history is linear; it has movement and is teleological, that is, there is a goal and purpose. The ultimate goal of redemptive history is the full revelation of the glory of God. For the redeemed the goal is to glorify God and to enjoy him forever. The Bible is the story of how this may be actualized. The OT constitutes the initial phases of "such a great salvation."

Parting Word

We began this book by drawing attention to the fact that the OT was the Bible of Jesus and the Apostles. Only toward the end of the first century A.D. did the NT writings begin to take their place as canonical Scripture. This is not to minimize the place and importance of the NT—clearly, God speaks his last word in it! (cf. Heb 1:1-2). Nevertheless, the OT has not been superseded—it continues to witness to the good news. It was the OT Scriptures that Paul had in mind when he said "all Scripture is God-breathed" (2Ti 3:16), and "everything that was written in the past was written to teach us, so that through endurance and the encouragement of the Scriptures we might have hope" (Ro 15:4). In light of that, we conclude with an exhortation. *Make sure the OT Scriptures are a part of your regular reading and meditation.* They continue to be "a lamp to [our] feet and a light for [our] path" (Ps 119:105). We let Jesus have the final word: "These are the Scriptures that testify about me" (Jn 5:39b).

Endnotes

1. We are indebted to a number of studies on this issue. See Pieter Verhoef, "The Relationship Between the Old and New Testaments," in *New Perspectives on the Old Testament*, ed. J. Barton Payne (Waco: Word, 1970), pp. 280-303; D. L. Baker, *Two Testaments, One Bible* (Downers Grove: InterVarsity, 1976); Walter C. Kaiser, Jr., *The Uses of the Old Testament in the New* (Chicago: Moody, 1985); Kenneth L. Barker, "False Dichotomies Between the Testaments," *JETS* 25 (1982): 3-16; idem, "The Scope and Center of Old and New Testament Theology and Hope," in *Dispensationalism, Israel and the Church: The Search for Definition*, eds. Craig A. Blaising and Darrell L. Bock (Grand Rapids: Zondervan, 1992), pp. 293-328.

2. See "Gnosis/Gnostic/Gnosticism," in *A Student's Dictionary for Biblical and Theological Studies*, eds. F. B. Huey and Bruce Corley (Grand Rapids: Zondervan, 1983), pp. 88-89:

> From Greek gnosis, "knowledge." A widespread and highly diverse religious movement with roots in Greek philosophy and folk religion. Its chief emphases are the utter transcendence of God, created matter as fallen and evil, and salvation by esoteric knowledge. The Gnostic heresy or Gnosticism is the developed system that emerged in the second century A.D. and is associated with the names of Marcion, Basilides, and Valentinius. . . .

For a brief background of Gnosticism and Marcion, see *Eerdmans' Handbook of the History of Christianity*, ed. Tim Dowley (Grand Rapids: Eerdmans, 1977), pp. 98-103.

3. This approach is often described by the phrase "a canon within the canon." The result is that within the acknowledged canon of Scripture, only those truths compatible with "modern educated mentality" are accorded any status. The rest is dispensed with as lacking authority and value.

4. A good definition of allegory as it applies to the interpretation of Scripture is the following:

> An interpretation that assumes that a text has a secondary and hidden meaning underlying its primary and obvious meaning: a story that presents its true meaning through figure: it has been called a prolonged metaphor. Allegorical interpretation of the Bible was widespread in the early church . . . (*Student's Dictionary*, pp. 17-18).

5. See *Handbook*, p. 104.

6. For more background see ibid. pp. 360-398.

7. Eds. Barbara Aland, Kurt Aland, Johannes Karavidopoulos, Carlo M. Martini, and Bruce M. Metzger (Stuttgart: Deutsche Bibelgesellshaft/United Bible Societies, 1993), pp. 887-888.

8. For further statistics see Kaiser, *The Uses*, pp. 1-3.

9. Walter Eichrodt puts it this way: “That which binds together indivisibly the two realms of the Old and New Testaments, different in externals though they may be, is the irruption of the Kingship of God into this world and its establishment here.”

Theology of the Old Testament, trans. J. A. Baker, 2 vols. (Philadelphia: Westminster, 1961) 1:26.

10. Walter Zimmerli expresses it well:

> When we survey the entire Old Testament, we find ourselves involved in a great history of movement from promise toward fulfillment. It flows like a large brook—here rushing swiftly, there apparently coming to rest in a quiet backwater, and yet moving forward as a whole toward a distant goal which lies beyond itself ("Promise and Fulfillment," in *Essays on Old Testament Hermeneutics*, trans. James Wharton, eds. Claus Westermann and James Mays [Richmond: John Knox, 1963], pp. 11-12).

11. We think Rudolf Bultmann greatly overstated the case, however, when he argued that the OT could only be used "for pedagogical reasons . . . to make man conscious of standing under God's demand." "The Significance of the Old Testament for the Christian Faith," in *The Old Testament and Christian Faith*, ed. Bernhard W. Anderson (New York: Herder and Herder, 1969), p. 17. See his entire essay pp. 8-35 and further in "Prophecy and Fulfillment," in *Essays on Old Testament Hermeneutics*, ed. Claus Westermann (Richmond: John Knox, 1963), pp. 50-75.

Author Index

Biblical Names Index

Chart Index

Scripture Index

Topic Index